797,885 Books

are available to read at

Forgotten Books

www.ForgottenBooks.com

Forgotten Books' App
Available for mobile, tablet & eReader

ISBN 978-1-330-91031-3
PIBN 10120257

This book is a reproduction of an important historical work. Forgotten Books uses state-of-the-art technology to digitally reconstruct the work, preserving the original format whilst repairing imperfections present in the aged copy. In rare cases, an imperfection in the original, such as a blemish or missing page, may be replicated in our edition. We do, however, repair the vast majority of imperfections successfully; any imperfections that remain are intentionally left to preserve the state of such historical works.

Forgotten Books is a registered trademark of FB &c Ltd.
Copyright © 2015 FB &c Ltd.
FB &c Ltd, Dalton House, 60 Windsor Avenue, London, SW19 2RR.
Company number 08720141. Registered in England and Wales.

For support please visit www.forgottenbooks.com

1 MONTH OF
FREE
READING

at
www.ForgottenBooks.com

By purchasing this book you are eligible for one month membership to ForgottenBooks.com, giving you unlimited access to our entire collection of over 700,000 titles via our web site and mobile apps.

To claim your free month visit:
www.forgottenbooks.com/free120257

* Offer is valid for 45 days from date of purchase. Terms and conditions apply.

English
Français
Deutsche
Italiano
Español
Português

www.forgottenbooks.com

Mythology Photography **Fiction**
Fishing Christianity **Art** Cooking
Essays Buddhism Freemasonry
Medicine **Biology** Music **Ancient
Egypt** Evolution Carpentry Physics
Dance Geology **Mathematics** Fitness
Shakespeare **Folklore** Yoga Marketing
Confidence Immortality Biographies
Poetry **Psychology** Witchcraft
Electronics Chemistry History **Law**
Accounting **Philosophy** Anthropology
Alchemy Drama Quantum Mechanics
Atheism Sexual Health **Ancient History**
Entrepreneurship Languages Sport
Paleontology Needlework Islam
Metaphysics Investment Archaeology
Parenting Statistics Criminology
Motivational

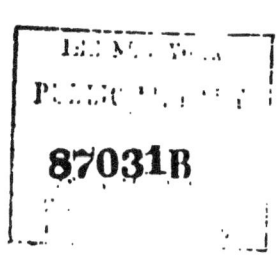

THE SAMOAN EDITION DE LUXE
Limited to One Thousand numbered sets

Copyright, 1906, by
Charles Curtis Bigelow

FAMILIAR STUDIES

A FAMILY OF ENGINEERS

AN ESSAY ON STEVENSON

FAMILIAR STUDIES

EDITORIAL NOTE

THE first edition of FAMILIAR STUDIES OF MEN AND BOOKS was published by Messrs. Chatto and Windus in March, 1882. The essays of which it is composed, were as Stevenson says in his critical preface, collected from periodicals. One, Walt Whitman, appeared in *The New Quarterly Magazine*, another, John Knox and his Relations to Women, in *Macmillan's Magazine* and all the others in *The Cornhill Magazine*. In point of time they cover seven years, the first, Victor Hugo's Romances, appearing in August, 1874, and the last, Samuel Pepys, in July, 1881. The essay on Victor Hugo's Romances deserves careful study, for it marked, in Stevenson's own opinion, the beginning of his command of style. He told Mr. Graham Balfour long afterwards in Samoa that in this paper he had first found himself able to say several things in the way in which he felt they should be said.

CONTENTS

FAMILIAR STUDIES

	PAGE
PREFACE	1
VICTOR HUGO'S ROMANCES	13
SOME ASPECTS OF ROBERT BURNS	36
WALT WHITMAN	68
HENRY DAVID THOREAU	91
YOSHIDA-TORAJIRO	117
FRANCOIS VILLON, STUDENT, POET, AND HOUSEBREAKER	129
CHARLES OF ORLEANS	156
SAMUEL PEPYS	189
JOHN KNOX AND HIS RELATIONS TO WOMEN	212
JOHN KNOX AND HIS RELATIONS TO WOMEN	233

RECORDS OF A FAMILY OF ENGINEERS

I. DOMESTIC ANNALS	267
II. THE SERVICE OF THE NORTHERN LIGHTS	288
III. THE BUILDING OF THE BELL ROCK	315

THREE LETTERS

THREE LETTERS	431
LIFE OF ROBERT LOUIS STEVENSON, BY SIDNEY COLVIN	439
VALEDICTION	461

PREFACE

BY WAY OF CRITICISM

These studies are collected from the monthly press. One appeared in the *New Quarterly*, one in *Macmillan's*, and the rest in the *Cornhill Magazine*. To the *Cornhill* I owe a double debt of thanks; first, that I was received there in the very best society, and under the eye of the very best of editors; and second, that the proprietors have allowed me to republish so considerable an amount of copy.

These nine worthies have been brought together from many different ages and countries. Not the most erudite of men could be perfectly prepared to deal with so many and such various sides of human life and manners. To pass a true judgment upon Knox and Burns implies a grasp upon the very deepest strain of thought in Scotland,—a country far more essentially different from England than many parts of America; for, in a sense, the first of these men re-created Scotland, and the second is its most essentially national production. To treat fitly of Hugo and Villon would involve yet wider knowledge, not only of a country foreign to the author by race, history, and religion, but of the growth and liberties of art. Of the two Americans, Whitman and Thoreau, each is the type of something not so much realized as widely sought after among the late generations, of their countrymen; and to see them clearly in a nice relation to the society that brought them forth, an author would require a large habit of life among modern Americans. As for Yoshida, I have already disclaimed responsibility; it was but my hand that held the pen.

In truth, these are but the readings of a literary vagrant. One book led to another, one study to another. The first was published with trepidation. Since no bones were broken,

PREFACE

the second was launched with greater confidence. So, by insensible degrees, a young man of our generation acquires, in his own eyes, a kind of roving judicial commission through the ages: and, having once escaped the perils of the Freemans and the Furnivalls sets himself up to right the wrongs of universal history and criticism. Now, it is one thing to write with enjoyment on a subject while the story is hot in your mind from recent reading, colored with recent prejudice; and it is quite another business to put these writings coldly forth again in a bound volume. We are most of us attached to our opinions; that is one of the "natural affections" of which we hear so much in youth: but few of us are altogether free from paralyzing doubts and scruples. For my part, I have a small idea of the degree of accuracy possible to man, and I feel sure these studies teem with error. One and all were written with genuine interest in the subject; many, however, have been conceived and finished with imperfect knowledge; and all have lain, from beginning to end, under the disadvantages inherent in this style of writing.

Of these disadvantages a word must here be said. The writer of short studies, having to condense in a few pages the events of a whole lifetime, and the effect on his own mind of many various volumes, is bound, above all things, to make that condensation logical and striking. For the only justification of his writing at all is that he shall present a brief, reasoned, and memorable view. By the necessity of the case, all the more neutral circumstances are omitted from his narrative; and that of itself, by the negative exaggeration of which I have spoken in the text, lends to the matter in hand a certain false and specious glitter. By the necessity of the case, again, he is forced to view his subject throughout in a particular illumination, like a studio artifice. Like Hales with Pepys, he must nearly break his sitter's neck to get the proper shadows on the portrait. It is from one side only that he has time to represent his subject. The side selected will either be the one most striking to himself, or the one most obscured by controversy; and in both cases that

PREFACE

will be the one most liable to strained and sophistical reading. In a biography, this and that is displayed; the hero is seen at home, playing the flute; the different tendencies of his work come, one after another, into notice; and thus something like a true, general impression of the subject may at last be struck. But in the short study, the writer, having seized his "point of view," must keep his eye steadily to that. He seeks, perhaps, rather to differentiate than truly characterize. The proportions of the sitter must be sacrificed to the proportions of the portrait; the lights are heightened, the shadows overcharged; the chosen expression, continually forced, may degenerate at length into a grimace; and we have at best something of a caricature, at worst a calumny. Hence, if they be readable at all, and hang together by their own ends, the peculiar convincing force of these brief representations. They take so little while to read, and yet in that little while the subject is so repeatedly introduced in the same light and with the same expression, that, by sheer force of repetition, that view is imposed upon the reader. The two English masters of the style, Macaulay and Carlyle, largely exemplify its dangers. Carlyle, indeed, had so much more depth and knowledge of the heart, his portraits of mankind are felt and rendered with so much more poetic comprehension, and he, like his favourite Ram Dass, had a fire in his belly so much more hotly burning than the patent reading lamp by which Macaulay studied, that it seems at first sight hardly fair to bracket them together. But the "point of view" was imposed by Carlyle on the men he judged of in his writings with an austerity not only cruel but almost stupid. They are too often broken outright on the Procrustean bed; they are probably always disfigured. The rhetorical artifice of Macaulay is easily spied; it will take longer to appreciate the moral bias of Carlyle. So with all writers who insist on forcing some significance from all that comes before them; and the writer of short studies is bound, by the necessity of the case, to write entirely in that spirit. What he cannot vivify he should omit.

Had it been possible to rewrite some of these papers, I

PREFACE

hope I should have had the courage to attempt it. But it is not possible. Short studies are, or should be, things woven like a carpet, from which it is impossible to detach a strand. What is perverted has its place there forever, as a part of the technical means by which what is right has been presented. It is only possible to write another study, and then, with a new "point of view," would follow new perversions and perhaps a fresh caricature. Hence, it will be, at least, honest to offer a few grains of salt to be taken with the text; and as some words of apology, addition, correction, or amplification fall to be said on almost every study in the volume, it will be most simple to run them over in their order. But this must not be taken as a propitiatory offering to the gods of shipwreck; I trust my cargo unreservedly to the chances of the sea; and do not, by criticising myself, seek to disarm the wrath of other and less partial critics.

Hugo's Romances.—This is an instance of the "point of view." The five romances studied with a different purpose might have given different results, even with a critic so warmly interested in their favor. The great contemporary master of wordmanship, and indeed of all literary arts and technicalities, had not unnaturally dazzled a beginner. But it is best to dwell on merits, for it is these that are most often overlooked.

Burns.—I have left the introductory sentences on Principal Shairp, partly to explain my own paper, which was merely supplemental to his amiable but imperfect book, partly because that book appears to me truly misleading both as to the character and the genius of Burns. This seems ungracious, but Mr. Shairp has himself to blame; so good a Wordsworthian was out of character upon that stage.

This half apology apart, nothing more falls to be said except upon a remark called forth by my study in the columns of a literary Review. The exact terms in which that sheet disposed of Burns I cannot now recall; but they were to this effect—that Burns was a bad man, the impure vehicle of fine verses; and that this was the view to which all

PREFACE

criticism tended. Now I knew, for my own part, that it was with the profoundest pity, but with a growing esteem, that I studied the man's desperate efforts to do right; and the more I reflected, the stranger it appeared to me that any thinking being should feel otherwise. The complete letters shed, indeed, a light on the depths to which Burns had sunk in his character of Don Juan, but they enhance in the same proportion the hopeless nobility of his marrying Jean. That I ought to have stated this more noisily I now see; but that any one should fail to see it for himself, is to me a thing both incomprehensible and worthy of open scorn. If Burns, on the facts dealt with in this study, is to be called a bad man, I question very much whether either I or the writer in the Review have ever encountered what it would be fair to call a good one. All have some fault. The fault of each grinds down the hearts of those about him, and—let us not blink the truth—hurries both him and them into the grave. And when we find a man persevering, indeed, in his fault, as all of us do, and openly overtaken, as not all of us are, by its consequences, to gloss the matter over, with too polite biographers, is to do the work of the wrecker disfiguring beacons on a perilous seaboard; but to call him bad, with a self-righteous chuckle, is to be talking in one's sleep with Heedless and Too-bold in the arbor.

Yet it is undeniable that much anger and distress is raised in many quarters by the least attempt to state plainly, what every one well knows, of Burns's profligacy, and of the fatal consequences of his marriage. And for this there are perhaps two subsidiary reasons. For, first, there is, in our drunken land, a certain privilege extended to drunkenness. In Scotland, in particular, it is almost respectable, above all when compared with any " irregularity between the sexes." The selfishness of the one, so much more gross in essence, is so much less immediately conspicuous in its results that our demiurgeous Mrs. Grundy smiles apologetically on its victims. It is often said—I have heard it with these ears—that drunkenness " may lead to vice." Now I did not think it at all proved that Burns was what is called a drunkard; and

PREFACE

I was obliged to dwell very plainly on the irregularity and the too frequent vanity and meanness of his relations to women. Hence, in the eyes of many, my study was a step toward the demonstration of Burns's radical badness.

But second, there is a certain class, professors of that low morality so greatly more distressing than the better sort of vice, to whom you must never represent an act that was virtuous in itself, as attended by any other consequences than a large family and fortune. To hint that Burns's marriage had an evil influence is, with this class, to deny the moral law. Yet such is the fact. It was bravely done; but he had presumed too far on his strength. One after another the lights of his life went out, and he fell from circle to circle to the dishonored sickbed of the end. And surely for any one that has a thing to call a soul he shines out tenfold more nobly in the failure of that frantic effort to do right, than if he had turned on his heel with Worldly Wiseman, married a congenial spouse, and lived orderly and died reputably an old man. It is his chief title that he refrained from "the wrong that amendeth wrong." But the common, trashy mind of our generation is still aghast, like the Jews of old, at any word of unsuccessful virtue. Job has been written and read; the tower of Siloam fell nineteen hundred years ago; yet we have still to desire a little Christianity, or, failing that, a little even of that rude, old, Norse nobility of soul, which saw virtue and vice alike go unrewarded, and was yet not shaken in its faith.

Walt Whitman.—This is a case of a second difficulty which lies continually before the writer of critical studies: that he has to mediate between the author whom he loves and the public who are certainly indifferent and frequently averse. Many articles had been written on this notable man. One after another had leaned, in my eyes, either to praise or blame unduly. In the last case they helped to blindfold our fastidious public to an inspiring writer; in the other, by an excess of unadulterated praise, they moved the more candid to revolt. I was here on the horns of a dilemma; and between these horns I squeezed myself with perhaps some loss

PREFACE

to the substance of the paper. Seeing so much in Whitman that was merely ridiculous, as well as so much more that was unsurpassed in force and fitness—seeing the true prophet doubled, as I thought, in places with the Bull in a China Shop,—it appeared best to steer a middle course, and to laugh with the scorners when I thought they had any excuse, while I made haste to rejoice with the rejoicers over what is imperishably good, lovely, human, or divine, in his extraordinary poems. That was perhaps the right road; yet I cannot help feeling that in this attempt to trim my sails between an author whom I love and honor and a public too averse to recognize his merit, I have been led into a tone unbecoming from one of my stature to one of Whitman's. But the good and the great man will go on his way not vexed with my little shafts of merriment. He, first of any one, will understand how, in the attempt to explain him credibly to Mrs. Grundy, I have been led into certain airs of the man of the world, which are merely ridiculous in me, and were not intentionally discourteous to himself. But there is a worse side to the question; for in my eagerness to be all things to all men, I am afraid I may have sinned against proportion. It will be enough to say here that Whitman's faults are few and unimportant when they are set beside his surprising merits. I had written another paper full of gratitude for the help that had been given me in my life, full of enthusiasm for the intrinsic merit of the poems, and conceived in the noisiest extreme of youthful eloquence. The present study was a *rifacimento*. From it, with the design already mentioned, and in a fit of horror at my old excess, the big words and emphatic passages were ruthlessly excised. But this sort of prudence is frequently its own punishment; along with the exaggeration, some of the truth is sacrificed; and the result is cold, constrained, and grudging. In short, I might almost everywhere have spoken more strongly than I did.

Thoreau.—Here is an admirable instance of the "point of view" forced throughout, and of too earnest reflection on imperfect facts. Upon me this pure, narrow, sunnily-

PREFACE

ascetic Thoreau had exercised a great charm. I have scarce written ten sentences since I was introduced to him, but his influence might be somewhere detected by a close observer. Still it was as a writer that I had made his acquaintance; I took him on his own explicit terms; and when I learned details of his life, they were, by the nature of the case and my own *parti-pris*, read even with a certain violence in terms of his writings. There could scarce be a perversion more justifiable than that; yet it was still a perversion. The study, indeed, raised so much ire in the breast of Dr. Japp (H A Page), Thoreau's sincere and learned disciple, that had either of us been men, I please myself with thinking, of less temper and justice, the difference might have made us enemies instead of making us friends. To him who knew the man from the inside, many of my statements sounded like inversions made on purpose; and yet when we came to talk of them together, and he had understood how I was looking at the man through the books, while he had long since learned to read the books through the man, I believe he understood the spirit in which I had been led astray.

On two most important points, Dr. Japp added to my knowledge, and with the same blow fairly demolished that part of my criticism. First, if Thoreau were content to dwell by Walden Pond, it was not merely with designs of self-improvement, but to serve mankind in the highest sense. Hither came the fleeing slave; thence was he despatched along the road to freedom. That shanty in the woods was a station in the great Underground Railroad; that adroit and philosophic solitary was an ardent worker, soul and body, in that so much more than honorable movement, which, if atonement were possible for nations, should have gone far to wipe away the guilt of slavery. But in history sin always meets with condign punishment; the generation passes, the offence remains, and the innocent must suffer. No underground railroad could atone for slavery, even as no bills in Parliament can redeem the ancient wrongs of Ireland. But here at least is a new light shed on the Walden episode.

Second, it appears, and the point is capital, that Thoreau

PREFACE

was once fairly and manfully in love, and, with perhaps too much aping of the angel, relinquished the woman to his brother. Even though the brother were like to die of it, we have not yet heard the last opinion of the woman. But be that as it may, we have here the explanation of the " rarefied and freezing air " in which I complained that he had taught himself to breathe. Reading the man through the books, I took his professions in good faith. He made a dupe of me, even as he was seeking to make a dupe of himself, wresting philosophy to the needs of his own sorrow. But in the light of this new fact, those pages, seemingly so cold, are seen to be alive with feeling. What appeared to be a lack of interest in the philosopher turns out to have been a touching insincerity of the man to his own heart; and that fine-spun airy theory of friendship, so devoid, as I complained, of any quality of flesh and blood, a mere anodyne to lull his pains. The most temperate of living critics once marked a passage of my own with a cross and the words, " This seems nonsense." It not only seemed; it was so. It was a private bravado of my own, which I had so often repeated to keep up my spirits, that I had grown at last wholly to believe it, and had ended by setting it down as a contribution to the theory of life. So with the more icy parts of this philosophy of Thoreau's. He was affecting the Spartanism he had not; and the old sentimental wound still bled afresh, while he deceived himself with reasons.

Thoreau's theory, in short, was one thing and himself another: of the first the reader will find what I believe to be a pretty faithful statement and a fairly just criticism in the study; of the second he will find but a contorted shadow. So much of the man as fitted nicely with his doctrines, in the photographer's phrase, came out. But that large part which lay outside and beyond, for which he had found or sought no formula, on which perhaps his philosophy even looked askance, is wanting in my study, as it was wanting in the guide I followed. In some ways a less serious writer, in all ways a nobler man, the true Thoreau still remains to be depicted.

PREFACE

Villon.—I am tempted to regret that I ever wrote on this subject, not merely because the paper strikes me as too picturesque by half, but because I regarded Villon as a bad fellow. Others still think well of him, and can find beautiful and human traits where I saw nothing but artistic evil; and by the principle of the art, those should have written of the man, and not I. Where you see no good, silence is the best. Though this penitence comes too late, it may be well, at least, to give it expression.

The spirit of Villon is still living in the literature of France. Fat Peg is oddly of a piece with the work of Zola, the Goncourts, and the infinitely greater Flaubert; and, while similar in ugliness, still surpasses them in native power. The old author, breaking with an *éclat de voix*, out of his tongue-tied century, has not yet been touched on his own ground, and still gives us the most vivid and shocking impression of reality. Even if that were not worth doing at all, it would be worth doing as well as he had done it; for the pleasure we take in the author's skill repays us, or at least reconciles us to the baseness of his attitude. Fat Peg (*La Grosse Margot*) is typical of much; it is a piece of experience that has nowhere else been rendered into literature; and a kind of gratitude for the author's plainness mingles, as we read, with the nausea proper to the business. I shall quote here a verse of an old students' song, worth laying side by side with Villon's startling ballade. This singer, also, had an unworthy mistress, but he did not choose to share the wages of dishonor; and it is thus, with both wit and pathos, that he laments her fall:—

> Nunc plango florem
>   Ætatis teneræ
> Nitidiorem
>   Veneris sidere:
> Tunc columbinam
>   Mentis dulcedinem,
> Nunc serpentinam
>   Amaritudinem.
> Verbo rogantes
>   Removes ostio,
> Munera dantes
>   Foves cubiculo,

PREFACE

Illos abire præcipis
A quibus nihil accipis,
Cæcos claudosque recipis,
Viros illustres decipis
Cum melle venenosa.*

But our illustrious writer of ballades it was unnecessary to deceive; it was the flight of beauty alone, not that or honesty or honor, that he lamented in his song; and the nameless mediæval vagabond has the best of the comparison.
There is now a Villon Society in England; and Mr. John Payne has translated him entirely into English, a task of unusual difficulty. I regret to find that Mr. Payne and I are not always at one as to the author's meaning; in such cases I am bound to suppose that he is in the right, although the weakness of the flesh withholds me from anything beyond a formal submission. He is now upon a larger venture, promising us at last that complete ARABIAN NIGHTS to which we have all so long looked forward.

Charles of Orleans.—Perhaps I have done scanty justice to the charm of the old Duke's verses, and certainly he is too much treated as a fool. The period is not sufficiently remembered. What that period was, to what a blank of imbecility the human mind had fallen, can only be known to those who have waded in the chronicles. Excepting Commines and La Salle and Villon, I have read no author who did not appall me by his torpor; and even the trial of Joan of Arc, conducted as it was by chosen clerks, bears witness to a dreary, sterile folly,—a twilight of the mind peopled with childish phantoms. In relation to his contemporaries, Charles seems quite a lively character.

It remains for me to acknowledge the kindness of Mr. Henry Pyne, who, immediately on the appearance of the study, sent me his edition of the Debate between the Heralds: a courtesy from the expert to the amateur only too uncommon in these days.

Knox.—Knox, the second in order of interest among the reformers, lies dead and buried in the works of the learned

* *Gaudeamus: Carmina vagorum selecta.* Leipsic. Trübner. 1879.

PREFACE

and unreadable M'Crie. It remains for some one to break the tomb and bring him forth, alive again and breathing, in a human book. With the best intentions in the world, I have only added two more flagstones, ponderous like their predecessors, to the mass of obstruction that buries the reformer from the world, I have touched him in my turn with that "mace of death," which Carlyle has attributed to Dryasdust; and my two dull papers are, in the matter of dulness, worthy additions to the labors of M'Crie. Yet I believe they are worth reprinting in the interest of the next biographer of Knox. I trust his book may be a masterpiece; and I indulge the hope that my two studies may lend him a hint or perhaps spare him a delay in its composition.

Of the *Pepys* I can say nothing; for it has been too recently through my hands; and I still retain some of the heat of composition. Yet it may serve as a text for the last remark I have to offer. To Pepys I think I have been amply just; to the others, to Burns, Thoreau, Whitman, Charles of Orleans, even Villon, I have found myself in the retrospect ever too grudging of praise, ever too disrespectful in manner. It is not easy to see why I should have been most liberal to the man of least pretensions. Perhaps some cowardice withheld me from the proper warmth of tone; perhaps it is easier to be just to those nearer us in rank of mind. Such at least is the fact, which other critics may explain. For these were all men whom, for one reason or another, I loved; or when I did not love the men, my love was the greater to their books. I had read them and lived with them; for months they were continually in my thoughts; I seemed to rejoice in their joys and to sorrow with them in their griefs; and behold, when I came to write of them, my tone was sometimes hardly courteous and seldom wholly just.

R. L. S.

VICTOR HUGO'S ROMANCES

Après le roman pittoresque mais prosaïque de Walter Scott il restera un autre roman à créer, plus beau et plus complet encore selon nous. C'est le roman, à la fois drame et épopée, pittoresque mais poétique, réel mais idéal, vrai mais grand, qui enchâssera Walter Scott dans Homère.—Victor Hugo on *Quentin Durward*.

VICTOR HUGO'S romances occupy an important position in the history of literature; many innovations, timidly made elsewhere, have in them been carried boldly out to their last consequences; much that was indefinite in literary tendencies has attained to definite maturity; many things have come to a point and been distinguished one from the other; and it is only in the last romance of all, *Quatre Vingt Treize*, that this culmination is most perfect. This is in the nature of things. Men who are in any way typical of a stage of progress may be compared more justly to the hand upon the dial of the clock, which continues to advance as it indicates, than to the stationary milestone, which is only the measure of what is past. The movement is not arrested. That significant something by which the work of such a man differs from that of his predecessors, goes on disengaging itself and becoming more and more articulate and cognizable. The same principle of growth that carried his first book beyond the books of previous writers, carries his last book beyond his first. And just as the most imbecile production of any literary age gives us sometimes the very clew to comprehension we have sought long and vainly in contemporary masterpieces, so it may be the very weakest of an author's books that, coming in the sequel of many others, enables us at last to get hold of what underlies the whole of them—of that spinal marrow of significance that unites the work of his life into something organic and rational. This is what has been done by *Quatre Vingt*

FAMILIAR STUDIES

Treize for the earlier romances of Victor Hugo, and, through them, for a whole division of modern literature. We have here the legitimate continuation of a long and living literary tradition; and hence, so far, its explanation. When many lines diverge from each other in direction so slightly as to confuse the eye, we know that we have only to produce them to make the chaos plain: this is continually so in literary history; and we shall best understand the importance of Victor Hugo's romances if we think of them as some such prolongation of one of the main lines of literary tendency.

When we compare the novels of Walter Scott with those of the man of genius who preceded him, and whom he delighted to honor as a master in the art—I mean Henry Fielding—we shall be somewhat puzzled, at the first moment, to state the difference that there is between these two. Fielding has as much human science; has a far firmer hold upon the tiller of his story; has a keen sense of character, which he draws (and Scott often does so too) in a rather abstract and academical manner; and finally, is quite as humorous and quite as good-humored as the great Scotchman. With all these points of resemblance between the men, it is astonishing that their work should be so different. The fact is, that the English novel was looking one way and seeking one set of effects in the hands of Fielding; and in the hands of Scott it was looking eagerly in all ways and searching for all the effects that by any possibility it could utilize. The difference between these two men marks a great enfranchisement. With Scott the Romantic movement, the movement of an extended curiosity and an enfranchised imagination, has begun. This is a trite thing to say; but trite things are often very indefinitely comprehended: and this enfranchisement, in as far as it regards the technical change that came over modern prose romance, has never perhaps been explained with any clearness.

To do so, it will be necessary roughly to compare the two sets of conventions upon which plays and romances are

VICTOR HUGO

respectively based. The purposes of these two arts are so much alike, and they deal so much with the same passions and interests, that we are apt to forget the fundamental opposition of their methods. And yet such a fundamental opposition exists. In the drama the action is developed in great measure by means of things that remain outside of the art; by means of real things, that is, and not artistic conventions for things. This is a sort of realism that is not to be confounded with that realism in painting of which we hear so much. The realism in painting is a thing of purposes: this, that we have to indicate in the drama, is an affair of method. We have heard a story, indeed, of a painter in France who, when he wanted to paint a sea-beach, carried realism from his ends to his means, and plastered real sand upon his canvas; and that is precisely what is done in the drama. The dramatic author has to paint his beaches with real sand: real live men and women move about the stage; we hear real voices; what is feigned merely puts a sense upon what is; we do actually see a woman go behind a screen as Lady Teazle, and, after a certain interval, we do actually see her very shamefully produced again. Now all these things, that remain as they were in life, and are not transmuted into any artistic convention, are terribly stubborn and difficult to deal with; and hence there are for the dramatist many resultant limitations in time and space. These limitations in some sort approximate toward those of painting: the dramatic author is tied down, not indeed to a moment, but to the duration of each scene or act; he is confined to the stage, almost as the painter is confined within his frame. But the great restriction is this, that a dramatic author must deal with his actors, and with his actors alone. Certain moments of suspense, certain significant dispositions of personages, a certain logical growth of emotion, these are the only means at the disposal of the playwright. It is true that, with the assistance of the scene-painter, the costumer and the conductor of the orchestra, he may add to this something of pageant, something of sound and fury; but these are, for the dramatic writer, beside the mark, and do not

FAMILIAR STUDIES

come under the vivifying touch of his genius. When we turn to romance, we find this no longer. Here nothing is reproduced to our senses directly. Not only the main conception of the work, but the scenery, the appliances, the mechanism by which this conception is brought home to us, have been put through the crucible of another man's mind, and come out again, one and all, in the form of written words. With the loss of every degree of such realism as we have described, there is for art a clear gain of liberty and largeness of competence. Thus, painting, in which the round outlines of things are thrown on to a flat board, is far more free than sculpture, in which their solidity is preserved. It is by giving up these identities that art gains true strength. And so in the case of novels as compared with the stage. Continuous narration is the flat board on to which the novelist throws everything. And from this there results for him a great loss of vividness, but a great compensating gain in his power over the subject; so that he can now subordinate one thing to another in importance, and introduce all manner of very subtle detail, to a degree that was before impossible. He can render just as easily the flourish of trumpets before a victorious emperor and the gossip of country market women, the gradual decay of forty years of a man's life and the gesture of a passionate moment. He finds himself equally unable, if he looks at it from one point of view—equally able, if he looks at it from another point of view—to reproduce a color, a sound, an outline, a logical argument, a physical action. He can show his readers, behind and around the personages that for the moment occupy the foreground of his story, the continual suggestion of the landscape; the turn of the weather that will turn with it men's lives and fortunes, dimly foreshadowed on the horizon; the fatality of distant events, the stream of national tendency, the salient framework of causation. And all this thrown upon the flat board—all this entering, naturally and smoothly, into the texture of continuous intelligent narration.

This touches the difference between Fielding and Scott.

VICTOR HUGO

In the work of the latter, true to his character of a modern and a Romantic, we become suddenly conscious of the background. Fielding, on the other hand, although he had recognized that the novel was nothing else than an epic in prose, wrote in the spirit not of the epic, but of the drama. This is not, of course, to say that the drama was in any way incapable of a regeneration similar in kind to that of which I am now speaking with regard to the novel. The notorious contrary fact is sufficient to guard the reader against such a misconstruction. All that is meant is, that Fielding remained ignorant of certain capabilities which the novel possesses over the drama; or, at least, neglected and did not develop them. To the end he continued to see things as a playwright sees them. The world with which he dealt, the world he had realized for himself and sought to realize and set before his readers, was a world of exclusively human interest. As for landscape, he was content to underline stage directions, as it might be done in a play-book: Tom and Molly retire into a practicable wood. As for nationality and public sentiment, it is curious enough to think that Tom Jones is laid in the year forty-five, and that the only use he makes of the rebellion is to throw a troop of soldiers into his hero's way. It is most really important, however, to remark the change which has been introduced into the conception of character by the beginning of the Romantic movement and the consequent introduction into fiction of a vast amount of new material. Fielding tells us as much as he thought necessary to account for the actions of his creatures; he thought that each of these actions could be decomposed on the spot into a few simple personal elements, as we decompose a force in a question of abstract dynamics. The larger motives are all unknown to him; he had not understood that the nature of the landscape or the spirit of the times could be for anything in a story; and so, naturally and rightly, he said nothing about them. But Scott's instinct, the instinct of the man of an age profoundly different, taught him otherwise; and, in his work, the individual characters begin to occupy a comparatively small proportion of that canvas on which armies manœuvre, and great hills pile themselves upon each other's shoulders. Fielding's characters were always great to the full stature of a perfectly arbitrary will. Already in Scott we begin to have a sense of the subtle influences that moderate and qualify a man's personality; that personality is no longer thrown out in unnatural isolation, but is resumed into its place in the constitution of things.

It is this change in the manner of regarding men and their actions first exhibited in romance, that has since renewed and vivified history. For art precedes philosophy and even science. People must have noticed things and interested themselves in them before they begin to debate upon their causes or influence. And it is in this way that art is the pioneer of knowledge; those predilections of the artist he knows not why, those irrational acceptations and recognitions, reclaim, out of the world that we have not yet realized, ever another and another corner; and after the facts have been thus vividly brought before us and have had time to settle and arrange themselves in our minds, some day there will be found the man of science to stand up and give the explanation. Scott took an interest in many things in which Fielding took none; and for this reason, and no other, he introduced them into his romances. If he had been told what would be the nature of the movement that he was so lightly initiating, he would have been very incredulous and not a little scandalized. At the time when he wrote, the real drift of this new manner of pleasing people in fiction was not yet apparent; and, even now, it is only by looking at the romances of Victor Hugo that we are enabled to form any proper judgment in the matter. These books are not only descended by ordinary generation from the Waverley novels, but it is in them chiefly that we shall find the revolutionary tradition of Scott carried farther; that we shall find Scott himself, in so far as regards his conception of prose fiction and its purposes, surpassed in his own spirit, instead of tamely followed. We have here, as I said before, a line of literary tendency produced, and by this production definitely separated from others. When we come to Hugo, we see that

VICTOR HUGO

the deviation, which seemed slight enough and not very serious between Scott and Fielding, is indeed such a great gulf in thought and sentiment as only successive generations can pass over: and it is but natural that one of the chief advances that Hugo has made upon Scott is an advance in self-consciousness. Both men follow the same road; but where the one went blindly and carelessly, the other advances with all deliberation and forethought. There never was artist much more unconscious than Scott; and there have been not many more conscious than Hugo. The passage at the head of these pages shows how organically he had understood the nature of his own changes. He has, underlying each of the five great romances (which alone I purpose here to examine), two deliberate designs: one artistic, the other consciously ethical and intellectual. This is a man living in a different world from Scott, who professes sturdily (in one of his introductions) that he does not believe in novels having any moral influence at all; but still Hugo is too much of an artist to let himself be hampered by his dogmas; and the truth is that the artistic result seems, in at least one great instance, to have very little connection with the other, or directly ethical result.

The artistic result of a romance, what is left upon the memory by any really powerful and artistic novel, is something so complicated and refined that it is difficult to put a name upon it; and yet something as simple as nature. These two propositions may seem mutually destructive, but they are so only in appearance. The fact is that art is working far ahead of language as well as of science, realizing for us, by all manner of suggestions and exaggerations, effects for which as yet we have no direct name; nay, for which we may never perhaps have a direct name, for the reason that these effects do not enter very largely into the necessities of life. Hence alone is that suspicion of vagueness that often hangs about the purpose of a romance: it is clear enough to us in thought; but we are not used to consider anything clear until we are able to formulate it in words, and analytical language has not been sufficiently shaped to that end. We

FAMILIAR STUDIES

all know this difficulty in the case of a picture, simple and strong as may be the impression that it has left with us; and it is only because language is the medium of romance, that we are prevented from seeing that the two cases are the same. It is not that there is anything blurred or indefinite in the impression left with us, it is just because the impression is so very definite after its own kind, that we find it hard to fit it exactly with the expressions of our philosophical speech.

It is this idea which underlies and issues from a romance, this something which it is the function of that form of art to create, this epical value, that I propose chiefly to seek and, as far as may be, to throw into relief, in the present study. It is thus, I believe, that we shall see most clearly the great stride that Hugo has taken beyond his predecessors, and how, no longer content with expressing more or less abstract relations of man to man, he has set before himself the task of realizing, in the language of romance, much of the involution of our complicated lives.

This epical value is not to be found, let it be understood, in every so-called novel. The great majority are not works of art in anything but a very secondary signification. One might almost number on one's fingers the works in which such a supreme artistic intention has been in any way superior to the other and lesser aims, themselves more or less artistic, that generally go hand in hand with it in the conception of prose romance. The purely critical spirit is, in most novels, paramount. At the present moment we can recall one man only, for whose works it would have been equally possible to accomplish our present design: and that man is Hawthorne. There is a unity, an unwavering creative purpose, about some at least of Hawthorne's romances, that impresses itself on the most indifferent reader; and the very restrictions and weaknesses of the man served perhaps to strengthen the vivid and single impression of his works. There is nothing of this kind in Hugo: unity, if he attains to it, is indeed unity out of multitude; and it is the wonderful power of subordination and synthesis thus displayed, that

VICTOR HUGO

gives us the measure of his talent. No amount of mere discussion and statement, such as this, could give a just conception of the greatness of this power. It must be felt in the books themselves, and all that can be done in the present essay is to recall to the reader the more general features of each of the five great romances, hurriedly and imperfectly, as space will permit, and rather as a suggestion than anything more complete.

The moral end that the author had before him in the conception of *Notre Dame de Paris* was (he tells us) to "denounce" the external fatality that hangs over men in the form of foolish and inflexible superstition. To speak plainly, this moral purpose seems to have mighty little to do with the artistic conception; moreover it is very questionably handled, while the artistic conception is developed with the most consummate success. Old Paris lives for us with newness of life: we have ever before our eyes the city cut into three by the two arms of the river, the boat-shaped island "moored" by five bridges to the different shores, and the two unequal towns on either hand. We forget all that enumeration of palaces and churches and convents which occupies so many pages of admirable description, and the thoughtless reader might be inclined to conclude from this, that they were pages thrown away; but this is not so: we forget, indeed, the details, as we forget or do not see the different layers of paint on a completed picture; but the thing desired has been accomplished, and we carry away with us a sense of the "Gothic profile" of the city, of the "surprising forest of pinnacles and towers and belfries," and we know not what of rich and intricate and quaint. And throughout, Notre Dame has been held up over Paris by a height far greater than that of its twin towers: the Cathedral is present to us from the first page to the last; the title has given us the clew, and already in the Palace of Justice the story begins to attach itself to that central building by character after character. It is purely an effect of mirage; Notre Dame does not, in reality, thus dominate and stand out above the

FAMILIAR STUDIES

city; and any one who should visit it, in the spirit of the Scott-tourists to Edinburgh or the Trossachs, would be almost offended at finding nothing more than this old church thrust away into a corner. It is purely an effect of mirage, as we say; but it is an effect that permeates and possesses the whole book with astonishing consistency and strength. And then, Hugo has peopled this Gothic city, and, above all, this Gothic church, with a race of men even more distinctly Gothic than their surroundings. We know this generation already: we have seen them clustered about the worn capitals of pillars, or craning forth over the church-leads with the open mouths of gargoyles. About them all there is that sort of stiff quaint unreality, that conjunction of the grotesque, and even of a certain bourgeois smugness, with passionate contortion and horror, that is so characteristic of Gothic art. Esmeralda is somewhat an exception; she and the goat traverse the story like two children who have wandered in a dream. The finest moment of the book is when these two share with the two other leading characters, Dom Claude and Quasimodo, the chill shelter of the old cathedral. It is here that we touch most intimately the generative artistic idea of the romance: are they not all four taken out of some quaint moulding, illustrative of the Beatitudes, or the Ten Commandments, or the seven deadly sins? What is Quasimodo but an animated gargoyle? What is the whole book but the reanimation of Gothic art?

It is curious that in this, the earliest of the five great romances, there should be so little of that extravagance that latterly we have come almost to identify with the author's manner. Yet even here we are distressed by words, thoughts, and incidents that defy belief and alienate the sympathies. The scene of the *in pace*, for example, in spite of its strength, verges dangerously on the province of the penny novelist. I do not believe that Quasimodo rode upon the bell; I should as soon imagine that he swung by the clapper. And again the following two sentences, out of an otherwise admirable chapter, surely surpass what it has ever entered into the heart of any other man to imagine (vol. ii. p. 180): "Il

VICTOR HUGO

souffrait tant que par instants il s'arrachait des poignées de cheveux, *pour voir s' ils ne blanchissaient pas.*" And, p. 181: " Ses pensées étaient si insupportables qu'il prenait sa tête à deux mains et tâchait de l'arracher de ses épaules *pour la briser sur le pavé.*"

One other fault, before we pass on. In spite of the horror and misery that pervade all of his later work, there is in it much less of actual melodrama than here, and rarely, I should say never, that sort of brutality, that useless insufferable violence to the feelings, which is the last distinction between melodrama and true tragedy. Now, in *Notre Dame,* the whole story of Esmeralda's passion for the worthless archer is unpleasant enough; but when she betrays herself in her last hiding-place, herself and her wretched mother, by calling out to this sordid hero who has long since forgotten her—well, that is just one of those things that readers will not forgive; they do not like it, and they are quite right; life is hard enough for poor mortals, without having it indefinitely embittered for them by bad art.

We look in vain for any similar blemish in *Les Misérables.* Here, on the other hand, there is perhaps the nearest approach to literary restraint that Hugo has ever made: there is here certainly the ripest and most easy development of his powers. It is the moral intention of this great novel to awaken us a little, if it may be—for such awakenings are unpleasant—to the great cost of this society that we enjoy and profit by, to the labor and sweat of those who support the litter, civilization, in which we ourselves are so smoothly carried forward. People are all glad to shut their eyes; and it gives them a very simple pleasure when they can forget that our laws commit a million individual injustices, to be once roughly just in the general; that the bread that we eat, and the quiet of the family, and all that embellishes life and makes it worth having, have to be purchased by death— by the deaths of animals, and the deaths of men wearied out with labor, and the deaths of those criminals called tyrants and revolutionaries, and the deaths of those revolutionaries

FAMILIAR STUDIES

called criminals. It is to something of all this that Victor Hugo wishes to open men's eyes in *Les Misérables*; and this moral lesson is worked out in masterly coincidence with the artistic effect. The deadly weight of civilization to those who are below presses sensibly on our shoulders as we read. A sort of mocking indignation grows upon us as we find Society rejecting, again and again, the services of the most serviceable; setting Jean Valjean to pick oakum, casting Galileo into prison, even crucifying Christ. There is a haunting and horrible sense of insecurity about the book. The terror we thus feel is a terror for the machinery of law, that we can hear tearing, in the dark, good and bad between its formidable wheels with the iron stolidity of all machinery, human or divine. This terror incarnates itself sometimes and leaps horribly out upon us; as when the crouching mendicant looks up, and Jean Valjean, in the light of the street lamp, recognizes the face of the detective; as when the lantern of the patrol flashes suddenly through the darkness of the sewer; or as when the fugitive comes forth at last at evening, by the quiet riverside, and finds the police there also, waiting stolidly for vice and stolidly satisfied to take virtue instead. The whole book is full of oppression, and full of prejudice, which is the great cause of oppression. We have the prejudices of M. Gillenormand, the prejudices of Marius, the prejudices in revolt that defend the barricade, and the throned prejudices that carry it by storm. And then we have the admirable but ill-written character of Javert, the man who had made a religion of the police, and would not survive the moment when he learned that there was another truth outside the truth of laws; a just creation, over which the reader will do well to ponder.

With so gloomy a design this great work is still full of life and light and love. The portrait of the good Bishop is one of the most agreeable things in modern literature. The whole scene at Montfermeil is full of the charm that Hugo knows so well how to throw about children. Who can forget the passage where Cosette, sent out at night to draw water, stands in admiration before the illuminated booth,

VICTOR HUGO

and the huckster behind "lui faisait un peu l'effet d'être le Père éternel?" The pathos of the forlorn sabot laid trustingly by the chimney in expectation of the Santa Claus that was not, takes us fairly by the throat; there is nothing in Shakespeare that touches the heart more nearly. The loves of Cosette and Marius are very pure and pleasant, and we cannot refuse our affection to Gavroche, although we may make a mental reservation of our profound disbelief in his existence. Take it for all in all, there are few books in the world that can be compared with it. There is as much calm and serenity as Hugo has ever attained to; the melodramatic coarsenesses that disfigured *Notre Dame* are no longer present. There is certainly much that is painfully improbable; and again, the story itself is a little too well constructed; it produces on us the effect of a puzzle, and we grow incredulous as we find that every character fits again and again into the plot, and is, like the child's cube, serviceable on six faces; things are not so well arranged in life as all that comes to. Some of the digressions, also, seem out of place, and do nothing but interrupt and irritate. But when all is said, the book remains of masterly conception and of masterly development, full of pathos, full of truth, full of a high eloquence.

Superstition and social exigency having been thus dealt with in the first two members of the series, it remained for *Les Travailleurs de la Mer* to show man hand to hand with the elements, the last form of external force that is brought against him. And here once more the artistic effect and the moral lesson are worked out together, and are, indeed, one. Gilliat, alone upon the reef at his herculean task, offers a type of human industry in the midst of the vague "diffusion of forces into the illimitable," and the visionary development of "wasted labor" in the sea, and the winds, and the clouds. No character was ever thrown into such strange relief as Gilliat. The great circle of sea-birds that come wonderingly around him on the night of his arrival, strikes at once the note of his pre-eminence and isolation. He fills the whole reef with his indefatigable toil; this solitary spot in the ocean rings with the clamor of his anvil; we see him as he comes and goes, thrown out sharply against the clear background of the sea. And yet his isolation is not to be compared with the isolation of Robinson Crusoe, for example; indeed, no two books could be more instructive to set side by side than *Les Travailleurs* and this other of the old days before art had learned to occupy itself with what lies outside of human will. Crusoe was one sole centre of interest in the midst of a nature utterly dead and utterly unrealized by the artist; but this is not how we feel with Gilliat; we feel that he is opposed by a " dark coalition of forces," that an " immense animosity " surrounds him; we are the witnesses of the terrible warfare that he wages with " the silent inclemency of phenomena going their own way, and the great general law, implacable and passive "; " a conspiracy of the indifferency of things " is against him. There is not one interest on the reef, but two. Just as we recognize Gilliat for the hero, we recognize, as implied by this indifferency of things, this direction of forces to some purpose outside our purposes, yet another character who may almost take rank as the villain of the novel, and the two face up to one another blow for blow, feint for feint, until, in the storm, they fight it epically out, and Gilliat remains the victor;—a victor, however, who has still to encounter the octopus. I need say nothing of the grewsome, repulsive excellence of that famous scene; it will be enough to remind the reader that Gilliat is in pursuit of a crab when he is himself assaulted by the devil fish, and that this, in its way, is the last touch to the inner significance of the book; here, indeed, is the true position of man in the universe.

But in *Les Travailleurs*, with all its strength, with all its eloquence, with all the beauty and fitness of its main situations, we cannot conceal from ourselves that there is a thread of something that will not bear calm scrutiny. There is much that is disquieting about the storm, admirably as it begins. I am very doubtful whether it would be possible to keep the boat from foundering in such circumstances, by

VICTOR HUGO

any amount of breakwater and broken rock. I do not understand the way in which the waves are spoken of, and prefer just to take it as a loose way of speaking, and pass on. And lastly, how does it happen that the sea was quite calm next day? Is this great hurricane a piece of scene-painting after all? And when we have forgiven Gilliat's prodigies of strength (although, in soberness, he reminds us more of Porthos in the *Vicomte de Bragelonne* than is quite desirable), what is to be said to his suicide, and how are we to condemn in adequate terms that unprincipled avidity after effect, which tells us that the sloop disappeared over the horizon, and the head under the water, at one and the same moment? Monsieur Hugo may say what he will, but we know better; we know very well that they did not; a thing like that raises up a despairing spirit of opposition in a man's readers; they give him the lie fiercely, as they read. Lastly, we have here already some beginning of that curious series of English blunders, that makes us wonder if there are neither proof sheets nor judicious friends in the whole of France, and affects us sometimes with a sickening uneasiness as to what may be our own exploits when we touch upon foreign countries and foreign tongues. It is here that we shall find the famous "first of the fourth," and many English words that may be comprehensible perhaps in Paris. It is here that we learn that "laird" in Scotland is the same title as "lord" in England. Here, also, is an account of a Highland soldier's equipment, which we recommend to the lovers of genuine fun.

In *L'Homme qui Rit*, it was Hugo's object to "denounce" (as he would say himself) the aristocratic principle as it was exhibited in England; and this purpose, somewhat more unmitigatedly satiric than that of the two last, must answer for much that is unpleasant in the book. The repulsiveness of the scheme of the story, and the manner in which it is bound up with impossibilities and absurdities, discourage the reader at the outset, and it needs an effort to take it as seriously as it deserves. And yet when we judge it deliberately, it will be seen that, here again, the story is admirably adapted to the moral. The constructive ingenuity exhibited throughout is almost morbid. Nothing could be more happily imagined, as a *reductio ad absurdum* of the aristocratic principle, than the adventures of Gwynplaine, the itinerant mountebank, snatched suddenly out of his little way of life, and installed without preparation as one of the hereditary legislators of a great country. It is with a very bitter irony that the paper, on which all this depends, is left to float for years at the will of wind and tide. What, again, can be finer in conception than that voice from the people heard suddenly in the House of Lords, in solemn arraignment of the pleasures and privileges of its splendid occupants? The horrible laughter, stamped forever " by order of the king" upon the face of this strange spokesman of democracy, adds yet another feature of justice to the scene; in all time, travesty has been the argument of oppression: and, in all time, the oppressed might have made this answer: "If I am vile, is it not your system that has made me so?" This ghastly laughter gives occasion, moreover, for the one strain of tenderness running through the web of this unpleasant story: the love of the blind girl Dea for the monster. It is a most benignant providence that thus harmoniously brings together these two misfortunes; it is one of those compensations, one of those afterthoughts of a relenting destiny, that reconcile us from time to time to the evil that is in the world; the atmosphere of the book is purified by the presence of this pathetic love; it seems to be above the story somehow, and not of it, as the full moon over the night of some foul and feverish city.

There is here a quality in the narration more intimate and particular than is general with Hugo; but it must be owned, on the other hand, that the book is wordy, and even, now and then, a little wearisome. Ursus and his wolf are pleasant enough companions; but the former is nearly as much an abstract type as the latter. There is a beginning, also, of an abuse of conventional conversation, such as may be quite pardonable in the drama where needs must, but is

VICTOR HUGO

without excuse in the romance. Lastly, I suppose one must say a word or two about the weak points of this not immaculate novel; and if so, it will be best to distinguish at once. The large family of English blunders, to which we have alluded already in speaking of *Les Travailleurs*, are of a sort that is really indifferent in art. If Shakespeare makes his ships cast anchor by some seaport of Bohemia, if Hugo imagines Tom-Tim-Jack to be a likely nickname for an English sailor, or if either Shakespeare, or Hugo, or Scott, for that matter, be guilty of " figments enough to confuse the march of a whole history—anachronisms enough to overset all chronology," * the life of their creations, the artistic truth and accuracy of their work, is not so much as compromised. But when we come upon a passage like the sinking of the " Ourque " in this romance, we can do nothing but cover our face with our hands: the conscientious reader feels a sort of disgrace in the very reading. For such artistic falsehoods, springing from what I have called already an unprincipled avidity after effect, no amount of blame can be exaggerated; and above all, when the criminal is such a man as Victor Hugo. We cannot forgive in him what we might have passed over in a third-rate sensation novelist. Little as he seems to know of the sea and nautical affairs, he must have known very well that vessels do not go down as he makes the " Ourque " go down; he must have known that such a liberty with fact was against the laws of the game, and incompatible with all appearance of sincerity in conception or workmanship.

In each of these books, one after another, there has been some departure from the traditional canons of romance; but taking each separately, one would have feared to make too much of these departures, or to found any theory upon what was perhaps purely accidental. The appearance of *Quatre Vingt Treize* has put us out of the region of such doubt. Like a doctor who has long been hesitating how to classify an epidemic malady, we have come at last upon a case so

* Prefatory letter to *Peveril of the Peak.*

well marked that our uncertainty is at an end. It is a novel built upon " a sort of enigma," which was at that date laid before revolutionary France, and which is presented by Hugo to Tellmarch, to Lantenac, to Gauvain, and very terribly to Cimourdain, each of whom gives his own solution of the question, clement or stern, according to the temper of his spirit. That enigma was this: "Can a good action be a bad action? Does not he who spares the wolf kill the sheep?" This question, as I say, meets with one answer after another during the course of the book, and yet seems to remain undecided to the end. And something in the same way, although one character, or one set of characters, after another comes to the front and occupies our attention for the moment, we never identify our interest with any of these temporary heroes nor regret them after they are withdrawn. We soon come to regard them somewhat as special cases of a general law; what we really care for is something that they only imply and body forth to us. We know how history continues through century after century; how this king or that patriot disappears from its pages with his whole generation, and yet we do not cease to read, nor do we even feel as if we had reached any legitimate conclusion, because our interest is not in the men, but in the country that they loved or hated, benefited or injured. And so it is here: Gauvain and Cimourdain pass away, and we regard them no more than the lost armies of which we find the cold statistics in military annals; what we regard is what remains behind; it is the principle that put these men where they were, that filled them for a while with heroic inspiration, and has the power, now that they are fallen, to inspire others with the same courage. The interest of the novel centres about revolutionary France; just as the plot is an abstract judicial difficulty, the hero is an abstract historical force. And this has been done, not, as it would have been before, by the cold and cumbersome machinery of allegory, but with bold, straightforward realism, dealing only with the objective materials of art, and dealing with them so masterfully that the palest abstractions of thought come before us, and move

VICTOR HUGO

our hopes and fears, as if they were the young men and maidens of customary romance.

The episode of the mother and children in *Quatre Vingt Treize* is equal to anything that Hugo has ever written. There is one chapter in the second volume, for instance, called "*Sein guéri, cœur saignant,*" that is full of the very stuff of true tragedy, and nothing could be more delightful than the humors of the three children on the day before the assault. The passage on La Vendée is really great, and the scenes in Paris have much of the same broad merit. The book is full, as usual, of pregnant and splendid sayings. But when thus much is conceded by way of praise, we come to the other scale of the balance, and find this, also, somewhat heavy. There is here a yet greater over employment of conventional dialogue than in *L'Homme qui Rit;* and much that should have been said by the author himself, if it were to be said at all, he has most unwarrantably put into the mouths of one or other of his characters. We should like to know what becomes of the main body of the troop in the wood of La Saudraie during the thirty pages or so in which the foreguard lays aside all discipline, and stops to gossip over a woman and some children. We have an unpleasant idea forced upon us at one place, in spite of all the good-natured incredulity that we can summon up to resist it. Is it possible that Monsieur Hugo thinks they ceased to steer the corvette while the gun was loose? Of the chapter in which Lantenac and Halmalho are alone together in the boat, the less said the better; of course, if there were nothing else, they would have been swamped thirty times over during the course of Lantenac's harangue. Again, after Lantenac has landed, we have scenes of almost inimitable workmanship that suggest the epithet "statuesque" by their clear and trenchant outline; but the tocsin scene will not do, and the tocsin unfortunately pervades the whole passage, ringing continually in our ears with a taunting accusation of falsehood. And then, when we come to the place where Lantenac meets the Royalists, under the idea that he is going to meet the Republicans, it seems as if there were a hitch in the stage

FAMILIAR STUDIES

mechanism. I have tried it over in every way, and I cannot conceive any disposition that would make the scene possible as narrated.

Such then, with their faults and their signal excellences, are the five great novels.

Romance is a language in which many persons learn to speak with a certain appearance of fluency; but there are few who can ever bend it to any practical need, few who can ever be said to express themselves in it. It has become abundantly plain in the foregoing examination that Victor Hugo occupies a high place among those few. He has always a perfect command over his stories; and we see that they are constructed with a high regard to some ulterior purpose, and that every situation is informed with moral significance and grandeur. Of no other man can the same thing be said in the same degree. His romances are not to be confused with "the novel with a purpose" as familiar to the English reader: this is generally the model of incompetence; and we see the moral clumsily forced into every hole and corner of the story, or thrown externally over it like a carpet over a railing. Now the moral significance, with Hugo, is of the essence of the romance; it is the organizing principle. If you could somehow despoil *Les Misérables* or *Les Travailleurs* of their distinctive lesson, you would find that the story had lost its interest and the book was dead.

Having thus learned to subordinate his story to an idea, to make his art speak, he went on to teach it to say things heretofore unaccustomed. If you look back at the five books of which we have now so hastily spoken, you will be astonished at the freedom with which the original purposes of story-telling have been laid aside and passed by. Where are now the two lovers who descended the main watershed of all the Waverley novels, and all the novels that have tried to follow in their wake? Sometimes they are almost lost sight of before the solemn isolation of a man against the sea and sky, as in *Les Travailleurs;* sometimes, as in *Les Misérables*, they merely figure for awhile, as a beautiful episode in the epic of oppression; sometimes they are en-

VICTOR HUGO

tirely absent as in *Quatre Vingt Treize*. There is no hero in *Notre Dame*: in *Les Misérables* it is an old man: in *L'Homme qui Rit* it is a monster: in *Quatre Vingt Treize* it is the Revolution. Those elements that only began to show themselves timidly, as adjuncts, in the novels of Walter Scott, have usurped ever more and more of the canvas; until we find the whole interest of one of Hugo's romances centring around matter that Fielding would have banished from his altogether, as being out of the field of fiction. So we have elemental forces occupying nearly as large a place, playing (so to speak) nearly as important a *rôle*, as the man, Gilliat, who opposes and overcomes them. So we find the fortunes of a nation put upon the stage with as much vividness as ever before the fortunes of a village maiden or a lost heir; and the forces that oppose and corrupt a principle holding the attention quite as strongly as the wicked barons or dishonest attorneys of the past. Hence those individual interests that were supreme in Fielding, and even in Scott, stood out over everything else and formed as it were the spine of the story, figure here only as one set of interests among many sets, one force among many forces, one thing to be treated out of a whole world of things equally vivid and important. So that, for Hugo, man is no longer an isolated spirit without antecedent or relation here below, but a being involved in the action and reaction of natural forces, himself a centre of such action and reaction; or an unit in a great multitude, chased hither and thither by epidemic terrors and aspirations, and, in all seriousness, blown about by every wind of doctrine. This is a long way that we have travelled: between such work and the work of Fielding is there not, indeed, a great gulf in thought and sentiment?

Art, thus conceived, realizes for men a larger portion of life, and that portion one that it is more difficult for them to realize unaided; and, besides helping them to feel more intensely those restricted personal interests which are patent to all, it awakes in them some consciousness of those more general relations that are so strangely invisible to the aver-

age man in ordinary moods. It helps to keep man in
place in nature, and, above all, it helps him to understa
more intelligently the responsibilities of his place in society.
And in all this generalization of interest, we never miss those
small humanities that are at the opposite pole of excellence
in art; and while we admire the intellect that could see life
thus largely, we are touched with another sentiment for the
tender heart that slipped the piece of gold into Cosette's
sabot, that was virginally troubled at the fluttering of her
dress in the spring wind, or put the blind girl beside the
deformity of the laughing man. This, then, is the last
praise that we can award to these romances. The author
has shown a power of just subordination hitherto unequalled; and as, in reaching forward to one class of effects,
he has not been forgetful or careless of the other, his work
is more nearly complete work, and his art, with all its imperfections, deals more comprehensively with the materials of
life than that of any of his otherwise more sure and masterly
predecessors.

These five books would have made a very great fame for
any writer, and yet they are but one façade of the monument that Victor Hugo has erected to his genius. Everywhere we find somewhat the same greatness, somewhat the
same infirmities. In his poems and plays there are the same
unaccountable protervities that have already astonished us
in the romances. There, too, is the same feverish strength,
welding the fiery iron of his idea under forge-hammer repe-
titions—an emphasis that is somehow akin to weakness—a
strength that is a little epileptic. He stands so far above
all his contemporaries, and so incomparably excels them in
richness, breadth, variety, and moral earnestness, that we
almost feel as if he had a sort of right to fall oftener and
more heavily than others; but this does not reconcile us to
seeing him profit by the privilege so freely. We like to
have, in our great men, something that is above question;
we like to place an implicit faith in them, and see them always
on the platform of their greatness; and this, unhappily,
cannot be with Hugo. As Heine said long ago, his is

VICTOR HUGO

a genius somewhat deformed; but, deformed as it is, we accept it gladly; we shall have the wisdom to see where his foot slips, but we shall have the justice also to recognize in him one of the greatest artists of our generation, and, in many ways, one of the greatest artists of time. If we look back, yet once, upon these five romances, we see blemishes such as we can lay to the charge of no other man in the number of the famous; but to what other man can we attribute such sweeping innovations, such a new and significant presentment of the life of man, such an amount, if we merely think of the amount, of equally consummate performance?

SOME ASPECTS OF ROBERT BURNS

TO write with authority about another man, we must have fellow-feeling and some common ground of experience with our subject. We may praise or blame according as we find him related to us by the best or worst in ourselves; but it is only in virtue of some relationship that we can be his judges, even to condemn. Feelings which we share and understand enter for us into the tissue of the man's character; those to which we are strangers in our own experience we are inclined to regard as blots, exceptions, inconsistencies, and excursions of the diabolic; we conceive them with repugnance, explain them with difficulty, and raise our hands to heaven in wonder when we find them in conjunction with talents that we respect or virtues that we admire. David, king of Israel, would pass a sounder judgment on a man than either Nathaniel or David Hume. Now Principal Shairp's recent volume, although I believe no one will read it without respect and interest, has this one capital defect— that there is imperfect sympathy between the author and the subject, between the critic and the personality under criticism. Hence an inorganic, if not an incoherent, presentation of both the poems and the man. Of *Holy Willie's Prayer*, Principal Shairp remarks that "those who have loved most what was best in Burns's poetry must have regretted that it was ever written." To the *Jolly Beggars*, so far as my memory serves me, he refers but once; and then only to remark on the "strange, not to say painful," circumstance that the same hand which wrote the *Cotter's Saturday Night* should have stooped to write the *Jolly Beggars*. The *Saturday Night* may or may not be an admirable poem; but its significance is trebled, and the power and range of the poet first appear, when it is set beside the *Jolly Beggars*. To take a man's work piecemeal, except with the design of

ROBERT BURNS

elegant extracts, is the way to avoid, and not to perform, the critic's duty. The same defect is displayed in the treatment of Burns as a man, which is broken, apologetical, and confused. The man here presented to us is not that Burns, *teres atque rotundus*—a burly figure in literature, as, from our present vantage of time, we have begun to see him. This, on the other hand, is Burns as he may have appeared to a contemporary clergyman, whom we shall conceive to have been a kind and indulgent but orderly and orthodox person, anxious to be pleased, but too often hurt and disappointed by the behavior of his red-hot *protégé*, and solacing himself with the explanation that the poet was "the most inconsistent of men." If you are so sensibly pained by the misconduct of your subject, and so paternally delighted with his virtues, you will always be an excellent gentleman, but a somewhat questionable biographer. Indeed, we can only be sorry and surprised that Principal Shairp should have chosen a theme so uncongenial. When we find a man writing on Burns, who likes neither *Holy Willie*, nor the *Beggars*, nor the *Ordination*, nothing is adequate to the situation but the old cry of Géronte: "Que diable allait-il faire dans cette galère?" And every merit we find in the book, which is sober and candid in a degree unusual with biographies of Burns, only leads us to regret more heartily that good work should be so greatly thrown away.

It is far from my intention to tell over again a story that has been so often told; but there are certainly some points in the character of Burns that will bear to be brought out, and some chapters in his life that demand a brief rehearsal. The unity of the man's nature, for all its richness, has fallen somewhat out of sight in the pressure of new information and the apologetical ceremony of biographers. Mr. Carlyle made an inimitable bust of the poet's head of gold; may I not be forgiven if my business should have more to do with the feet, which were of clay?

FAMILIAR STUDIES

YOUTH

Any view of Burns would be misleading which passed over in silence the influences of his home and his father. That father, William Burnes, after having been for many years a gardener, took a farm, married, and, like an emigrant in a new country, built himself a house with his own hands. Poverty of the most distressing sort, with sometimes the near prospect of a jail, embittered the remainder of his life. Chill, backward, and austere with strangers, grave and imperious in his family, he was yet a man of very unusual parts and of an affectionate nature. On his way through life he had remarked much upon other men, with more result in theory than practice; and he had reflected upon many subjects as he delved the garden. His great delight was in solid conversation; he would leave his work to talk with the schoolmaster Murdoch; and Robert, when he came home late at night, not only turned aside rebuke but kept his father two hours beside the fire by the charm of his merry and vigorous talk. Nothing is more characteristic of the class in general, and William Burnes in particular, than the pains he took to get proper schooling for his boys, and, when that was no longer possible, the sense and resolution with which he set himself to supply the deficiency by his own influence. For many years he was their chief companion; he spoke with them seriously on all subjects as if they had been grown men; at night, when work was over, he taught them arithmetic; he borrowed books for them on history, science, and theology; and he felt it his duty to supplement this last—the trait is laughably Scottish—by a dialogue of his own composition, where his own private shade of orthodoxy was exactly represented. He would go to his daughter as she stayed afield herding cattle, to teach her the names of grasses and wild flowers, or to sit by her side when it thundered. Distance to strangers, deep family tenderness, love of knowledge, a narrow, precise, and formal reading of theology—everything we learn of him hangs well together, and builds

ROBERT BURNS

up a popular Scottish type. If I mention the name of Andrew Fairservice, it is only as I might couple for an instant Dugald Dalgetty with old Marshal Loudon, to help out the reader's comprehension by a popular but unworthy instance of a class. Such was the influence of this good and wise man that his household became a school to itself, and neighbors who came into the farm at meal-time would find the whole family, father, brothers, and sisters, helping themselves with one hand, and holding a book in the other. We are surprised at the prose style of Robert; that of Gilbert need surprise us no less; even William writes a remarkable letter for a young man of such slender opportunities. One anecdote marks the taste of the family. Murdoch brought *Titus Andronicus,* and, with such dominie elocution as we may suppose, began to read it aloud before this rustic audience; but when he had reached the passage where Tamora insults Lavinia, with one voice and " in an agony of distress" they refused to hear it to an end. In such a father and with such a home, Robert had already the making of an excellent education; and what Murdoch added, although it may not have been much in amount, was in character the very essence of a literary training. Schools and colleges, for one great man whom they complete, perhaps unmake a dozen; the strong spirit can do well upon more scanty fare.

Robert steps before us, almost from the first, in his complete character—a proud, headstrong, impetuous lad, greedy of pleasure, greedy of notice; in his own phrase " panting after distinction," and in his brother's " cherishing a particular jealousy of people who were richer or of more consequence than himself "; with all this, he was emphatically of the artist nature. Already he made a conspicuous figure in Tarbolton church, with the only tied hair in the parish, " and his plaid, which was of a particular color, wrapped in a particular manner round his shoulders." Ten years later, when a married man, the father of a family, a farmer, and an officer of Excise, we shall find him out fishing in masquerade, with fox-skin cap, belted great-coat, and great Highland broadsword. He liked dressing up, in fact, for its own sake.

FAMILIAR STUDIES

This is the spirit which leads to the extravagant array of Latin Quarter students, and the proverbial velveteen of the English landscape-painter; and, though the pleasure derived is in itself merely personal, it shows a man who is, to say the least of it, not pained by general attention and remark. His father wrote the family name *Burnes*; Robert early adopted the orthography *Burness* from his cousin in the Mearns; and in his twenty-eighth year changed it once more to *Burns*. It is plain that the last transformation was not made without some qualm; for in addressing his cousin he adheres, in at least one more letter, to spelling number two. And this, again, shows a man preoccupied about the manner of his appearance even down to the name, and little willing to follow custom. Again, he was proud, and justly proud of his powers in conversation. To no other man's have we the same conclusive testimony from different sources and from every rank of life. It is almost a commonplace that the best of his works was what he said in talk. Robertson the historian " scarcely ever met any man whose conversation displayed greater vigor "; the Duchess of Gordon declared that he " carried her off her feet "; and, when he came late to an inn, the servants would get out of bed to hear him talk. But, in these early days at least, he was determined to shine by any means. He made himself feared in the village for his tongue. He would crush weaker men to their faces, or even perhaps—for the statement of Sillar is not absolute—say cutting things of his acquaintances behind their back. At the church door, between sermons, he would parade his religious views amid hisses. These details stamped the man. He had no genteel timidities in the conduct of his life. He loved to force his personality upon the world. He would please himself, and shine. Had he lived in the Paris of 1830, and joined his lot with the Romantics, we can conceive him writing *Jehan* for *Jean*, swaggering in Gautier's red waistcoat, and horrifying the Bourgeois in a public café with paradox and gasconade.

A leading trait throughout his whole career was his desire to be in love. *Ne fait pas ce tour qui veut.* His affec-

ROBERT BURNS

tions were often enough touched, but perhaps never engaged. He was all his life on a voyage of discovery, but it does not appear conclusively that he ever touched the happy isle. A man brings to love a deal of ready-made sentiment, and even from childhood obscurely prognosticates the symptoms of this vital malady. Burns was formed for love; he had passion, tenderness, and a singular bent in the direction; he could foresee, with the intuition of an artist, what love ought to be; and he could not conceive a worthy life without it. But he had ill-fortune, and was besides so greedy after every shadow of the true divinity, and so much the slave of a strong temperament, that perhaps his nerve was relaxed and his heart had lost the power of self-devotion before an opportunity occurred. The circumstances of his youth doubtless counted for something in the result. For the lads of Ayrshire, as soon as the day's work was over and the beasts were stabled, would take the road, it might be in a winter tempest, and travel perhaps miles by moss and moorland to spend an hour or two in courtship. Rule 10 of the Bachelors' Club at Tarbolton provides that " every man proper for a member of this Society must be a professed lover of *one or more* of the female sex." The rich, as Burns himself points out, may have a choice of pleasurable occupations, but these lads had nothing but their " cannie hour at e'en." It was upon love and flirtation that this rustic society was built; gallantry was the essence of life among the Ayrshire hills as well as in the Court of Versailles; and the days were distinguished from each other by love-letters, meetings, tiffs, reconciliations, and expansions to the chosen confidant, as in a comedy of Marivaux. Here was a field for a man of Burns's indiscriminate personal ambition, where he might pursue his voyage of discovery in quest of true love, and enjoy temporary triumphs by the way. He was " constantly the victim of some fair enslaver "—at least, when it was not the other way about; and there were often underplots and secondary fair enslavers in the background. Many —or may we not say most?—of these affairs were entirely artificial. One, he tells us, he began out of " a vanity of

FAMILIAR STUDIES

showing his parts in courtship," for he piqued himself on his ability at a love-letter. But, however they began, these flames of his were fanned into a passion ere the end; and he stands unsurpassed in his power of self-deception, and positively without a competitor in the art, to use his own words, of "battering himself into a warm affection,"—a debilitating and futile exercise. Once he had worked himself into the vein, "the agitations of his mind and body" were an astonishment to all who knew him. Such a course as this, however pleasant to a thirsty vanity, was lowering to his nature. He sank more and more toward the professional Don Juan. With a leer of what the French call fatuity, he bids the belles of Mauchline beware of his seductions; and the same cheap self-satisfaction finds a yet uglier vent when he plumes himself on the scandal at the birth of his first bastard. We can well believe what we hear of his facility in striking up an acquaintance with women: he would have conquering manners; he would bear down upon his rustic game with the grace that comes of absolute assurance—the Richelieu of Lochlea or Mossgiel. In yet another manner did these quaint ways of courtship help him into fame. If he were great as principal, he was unrivalled as confidant. He could enter into a passion; he could counsel wary moves, being, in his own phrase, so old a hawk; nay, he could turn a letter for some unlucky swain, or even string a few lines of verse that should clinch the business and fetch the hesitating fair one to the ground. Nor, perhaps, was it only his "curiosity, zeal, and intrepid dexterity" that recommended him for a second in such affairs; it must have been a distinction to have the assistance and advice of *Rab the Ranter;* and one who was in no way formidable by himself might grow dangerous and attractive through the fame of his associate.

I think we can conceive him, in these early years, in that rough moorland country, poor among the poor with his seven pounds a year, looked upon with doubt by respectable elders, but for all that the best talker, the best letter-writer, the most famous lover and confidant, the laureate poet, and

ROBERT BURNS

the only man who wore his hair tied in the parish. He says he had then as high a notion of himself as ever after; and I can well believe it. Among the youth he walked *facile princeps*, an apparent god; and even if, from time to time, the Reverend Mr. Auld should swoop upon him with the thunders of the Church, and, in company with seven others, Rab the Ranter must figure some fine Sunday on the stool of repentance, would there not be a sort of glory, an infernal apotheosis, in so conspicuous a shame? Was not Richelieu in disgrace more idolized than ever by the dames of Paris? and when was the highwayman most acclaimed but on his way to Tyburn? Or, to take a simile from nearer home, and still more exactly to the point, what could even corporal punishment avail, administered by a cold, abstract, unearthly schoolmaster, against the influence and fame of the school's hero?

And now we come to the culminating point of Burns's early period. He began to be received into the unknown upper world. His fame soon spread from among his fellow-rebels on the benches, and began to reach the ushers and monitors of this great Ayrshire academy. This arose in part from his lax views about religion; for at this time that old war of the creeds and confessors, which is always grumbling from end to end of our poor Scotland, brisked up in these parts into a hot and virulent skirmish; and Burns found himself identified with the opposition party,—a clique of roaring lawyers and half-heretical divines, with wit enough to appreciate the value of the poet's help, and not sufficient taste to moderate his grossness and personality. We may judge of their surprise when *Holy Willie* was put into their hand; like the amorous lads of Tarbolton, they recognized in him the best of seconds. His satires began to go the round in manuscript; Mr. Aiken, one of the lawyers, " read him into fame "; he himself was soon welcome in many houses of a better sort, where his admirable talk, and his manners, which he had direct from his Maker, except for a brush he gave them at a country dancing school, completed what his poems had begun. We have a sight of him at his first visit to Adam-

FAMILIAR STUDIES

hill, in his ploughman's shoes, coasting around the carpet as though that were sacred ground. But he soon grew used to carpets and their owners; and he was still the superior of all of whom he encountered, and ruled the roost in conversation. Such was the impression made, that a young clergyman, himself a man of ability, trembled and became confused when he saw Robert enter the church in which he was to preach. It is not surprising that the poet determined to publish: he had now stood the test of some publicity, and under this hopeful impulse he composed in six winter months the bulk of his more important poems. Here was a young man who, from a very humble place, was mounting rapidly; from the cynosure of a parish, he had become the talk of a county; once the bard of rural courtships, he was now about to appear as a bound and printed poet in the world's bookshops.

A few more intimate strokes are necessary to complete the sketch. This strong young ploughman, who feared no competitor with the flail, suffered like a fine lady from sleeplessness and vapors; he would fall into the blackest melancholies, and be filled with remorse for the past and terror for the future. He was still not perhaps devoted to religion, but haunted by it; and at a touch of sickness prostrated himself before God in what I can only call unmanly penitence. As he had aspirations beyond his place in the world, so he had tastes, thoughts, and weaknesses to match. He loved to walk under a wood to the sound of a winter tempest; he had a singular tenderness for animals; he carried a book with him in his pocket when he went abroad, and wore out in this service two copies of the *Man of Feeling*. With young people in the field at work he was very long-suffering; and when his brother Gilbert spoke sharply to them—" O man, ye are no for young folk," he would say, and give the defaulter a helping hand and a smile. In the hearts of the men whom he met, he read as in a book; and, what is yet more rare, his knowledge of himself equalled his knowledge of others. There are no truer things said of Burns than what is to be found in his own letters. Country Don Juan as he was,

ROBERT BURNS

he had none of that blind vanity which values itself on what it is not; he knew his own strength and weakness to a hair: he took himself boldly for what he was, and except in moments of hypochondria, declared himself content.

THE LOVE STORIES

On the night of the Mauchline races, 1785, the young men and women of the place joined in a penny ball, according to their custom. In the same set danced Jean Armour, the master-mason's daughter, and our dark-eyed Don Juan. His dog (not the immortal Luath, but a successor unknown to fame, *caret quia vate sacro*), apparently sensible of some neglect, followed his master to and fro, to the confusion of the dancers. Some mirthful comments followed; and Jean heard the poet say to his partner—or, as I should imagine, laughingly launch the remark to the company at large— that " he wished he could get any of the lasses to like him as well as his dog." Some time after, as the girl was bleaching clothes on Mauchline green, Robert chanced to go by, still accompanied by his dog; and the dog, " scouring in long excursion," scampered with four black paws across the linen. This brought the two into conversation; when Jean, with a somewhat hoydenish advance, inquired if " he had yet got any of the lasses to like him as well as his dog?" It is one of the misfortunes of the professional Don Juan that his honor forbids him to refuse battle; he is in life like the Roman soldier upon duty, or like the sworn physician who must attend on all diseases. Burns accepted the provocation; hungry hope reawakened in his heart; here was a girl— pretty, simple at least, if not honestly stupid, and plainly not averse to his attentions; it seemed to him once more as if love might here be waiting him. Had he but known the truth! for this facile and empty-headed girl had nothing more in view than a flirtation; and her heart, from the first and on to the end of her story, was engaged by another man. Burns once more commenced the celebrated process of " battering himself into a warm affection "; and the proofs of his

FAMILIAR STUDIES

success are to be found in many verses of the period. Nor did he succeed with himself only; Jean, with her heart still elsewhere, succumbed to his fascination, and early in the next year the natural consequence became manifest. It was a heavy stroke for this unfortunate couple. They had trifled with life, and were now rudely reminded of life's serious issues. Jean awoke to the ruin of her hopes; the best she had now to expect was marriage with a man who was a stranger to her dearest thoughts; she might now be glad if she could get what she would never have chosen. As for Burns, at the stroke of the calamity he recognized that his voyage of discovery had led him into a wrong hemisphere—that he was not, and never had been, really in love with Jean. Hear him in the pressure of the hour. " Against two things," he writes, " I am as fixed as fate—staying at home, and owning her conjugally. The first, by heaven, I will not do! —the last, by hell, I will never do!" And then he adds, perhaps already in a more relenting temper: " If you see Jean, tell her I will meet her, so God help me in my hour of need." They met accordingly; and Burns, touched with her misery, came down from these heights of independence, and gave her a written acknowledgement of marriage. It is the punishment of Don Juanism to create continually false positions—relations in life which are wrong in themselves, and which it is equally wrong to break or to perpetuate. This was such a case. Worldly Wiseman would have laughed and gone his way; let us be glad that Burns was better counselled by his heart. When we discover that we can be no longer true, the next best is to be kind. I dare say he came away from that interview not very content, but with a glorious conscience; and as he went homeward, he would sing his favorite, " How are Thy servants blest, O Lord! " Jean, on the other hand, armed with her " lines," confided her position to the master-mason, her father, and his wife. Burns and his brother were then in a fair way to ruin themselves in their farm; the poet was an execrable match for any well-to-do country lass; and perhaps old Armour had an inkling of a previous attachment on his

ROBERT BURNS

daughter's part. At least, he was not so much incensed by her slip from virtue as by the marriage which had been designed to cover it. Of this he would not hear a word. Jean, who had besought the acknowledgment only to appease her parents, and not at all from any violent inclination to the poet, readily gave up the paper for destruction; and all parties imagined, although wrongly, that the marriage was thus dissolved. To a proud man like Burns here was a crushing blow. The concession which had been wrung from his pity was now publicly thrown back in his teeth. The Armour family preferred disgrace to his connection. Since the promise, besides, he had doubtless been busy "battering himself" back again into his affection for the girl; and the blow would not only take him in his vanity, but wound him at the heart.

He relieved himself in verse; but for such a smarting affront manuscript poetry was insufficient to console him. He must find a more powerful remedy in good flesh and blood, and after this discomfiture, set forth again at once upon his voyage of discovery in quest of love. It is perhaps one of the most touching things in human nature, as it is a commonplace of psychology, that when a man has just lost hope or confidence in one love, he is then most eager to find and lean upon another. The universe could not be yet exhausted; there must be hope and love waiting for him somewhere; and so, with his head down, this poor, insulted poet ran once more upon his fate. There was an innocent and gentle Highland nurserymaid at service in a neighboring family; and he had soon battered himself and her into a warm affection and a secret engagement. Jean's marriage lines had not been destroyed till March 13, 1786; yet all was settled between Burns and Mary Campbell by Sunday, May 14, when they met for the last time, and said farewell with rustic solemnities upon the banks of Ayr. They each wet their hands in a stream, and, standing one on either bank, held a Bible between them as they vowed eternal faith. Then they exchanged Bibles, on one of which Burns, for greater security, had inscribed texts as to the binding nature of an

FAMILIAR STUDIES

oath; and surely, if ceremony can do aught to fix the wandering affections, here were two people united for life. Mary came of a superstitious family, so that she perhaps insisted on these rites; but they must have been eminently to the taste of Burns at this period; for nothing would seem superfluous, and no oath great enough, to stay his tottering constancy.

Events of consequence now happened thickly in the poet's life. His book was announced; the Armours sought to summon him at law for the aliment of the child; he lay here and there in hiding to correct the sheets; he was under an engagement for Jamaica, where Mary was to join him as his wife; now, he had "orders within three weeks at latest to repair aboard the *Nancy*, Captain Smith"; now his chest was already on the road to Greenock; and now, in the wild autumn weather on the moorland, he measures verses of farewell:—

> "The bursting tears my heart declare;
> Farewell the bonny banks of Ayr!"

But the great master dramatist had secretly another intention for the piece; by the most violent and complicated solution, in which death and birth and sudden fame all play a part as interposing deities, the act-drop fell upon a scene of transformation. Jean was brought to bed of twins, and, by an amicable arrangement, the Burnses took the boy to bring up by hand, while the girl remained with her mother. The success of the book was immediate and emphatic; it put £20 at once into the author's purse; and he was encouraged upon all hands to go to Edinburgh and push his success in a second and larger edition. Third and last in this series of interpositions, a letter came one day to Mossgiel Farm for Robert. He went to the window to read it; a sudden change came over his face, and he left the room without a word. Years afterward, when the story began to leak out, his family understood that he had then learned the death of Highland Mary. Except in a few poems and a few dry indi-

ROBERT BURNS

cations purposely misleading as to date, Burns himself made no reference to this passage of his life; it was an adventure of which, for I think sufficient reasons, he desired to bury the details. Of one thing we may be glad: in after years he visited the poor girl's mother, and left her with the impression that he was " a real warm-hearted chield."

Perhaps a month after he received this intelligence, he set out for Edinburgh on a pony he had borrowed from a friend. The town that winter was " agog with the ploughman poet." Robertson, Dugald Stewart, Blair, " Duchess Gordon and all the gay world," were of his acquaintance. Such a revolution is not to be found in literary history. He was now, it must be remembered, twenty-seven years of age; he had fought since his early boyhood an obstinate battle against poor soil, bad seed, and inclement seasons, wading deep in Ayrshire mosses, guiding the plough in the furrow, wielding " the thresher's weary flingin'-tree "; and his education, his diet, and his pleasures, had been those of a Scotch countryman. Now he stepped forth suddenly among the polite and learned. We can see him as he then was, in his boots and buckskins, his blue boat and waistcoat striped with buff and blue, like a farmer in his Sunday best; the heavy ploughman's figure firmly planted on its burly legs; his face full of sense and shrewdness, and with a somewhat melancholy air of thought, and his large dark eye " literally glowing " as he spoke. " I never saw such another eye in a human head," says Walter Scott, " though I have seen the most distinguished men of my time." With men, whether they were lords or omnipotent critics, his manner was plain, dignified, and free from bashfulness or affectation. If he made a slip, he had the social courage to pass on and refrain from explanation. He was not embarrassed in this society, because he read and judged the men; he could spy snobbery in a titled lord; and, as for the critics, he dismissed their system in an epigram. " These gentlemen," said he, " remind me of some spinsters in my country who spin their thread so fine that it is neither fit for weft nor woof." Ladies, on the other hand, surprised him; he was scarce commander of him-

FAMILIAR STUDIES

self in their society; he was disqualified by his acquired nature as a Don Juan; and he, who had been so much at his ease with country lasses, treated the town dames to an extreme of deference. One lady, who met him at a ball, gave Chambers a speaking sketch of his demeanor. "His manner was not prepossessing, scarcely, she thinks, manly or natural. It seemed as if he affected a rusticity or *landertness*, so that when he said the music was 'bonnie, bonnie,' it was like the expression of a child." These would be company manners; and doubtless on a slight degree of intimacy the affectation would grow less. And his talk to women had always "a turn either to the pathetic or humorous, which engaged the attention particularly."

The Edinburgh magnates (to conclude this episode at once) behaved well to Burns from first to last. Were heaven-born genius to revisit us in similar guise, I am not venturing too far when I say that he need expect neither so warm a welcome nor such solid help. Although Burns was only a peasant, and one of no very elegant reputation as to morals, he was made welcome to their homes. They gave him a great deal of good advice, helped him to some five hundred pounds of ready money, and got him, as soon as he asked it, a place in the Excise. Burns, on his part, bore the elevation with perfect dignity; and with perfect dignity returned, when the time had come, into a country privacy of life. His powerful sense never deserted him, and from the first he recognized that his Edinburgh popularity was but an ovation and the affair of a day. He wrote a few letters in a high-flown, bombastic vein of gratitude; but in practice he suffered no man to intrude upon his self-respect. On the other hand, he never turned his back, even for a moment, on his old associates; and he was always ready to sacrifice an acquaintance to a friend, although the acquaintance were a duke. He would be a bold man who should promise similar conduct in equally exacting circumstances. It was, in short, an admirable appearance on the stage of life—socially successful, intimately self-respecting, and like a gentleman from first to last.

ROBERT BURNS

In the present study, this must only be taken by the way, while we return to Burns's love affairs. Even on the road to Edinburgh he had seized upon the opportunity of a flirtation, and had carried the "battering" so far that when next he moved from town, it was to steal two days with this anonymous fair one. The exact importance to Burns of this affair may be gathered from the song in which he commemorated its occurrence. "I love the dear lassie," he sings, "because she loves me"; or, in the tongue of prose: "Finding an opportunity, I did not hesitate to profit by it; and even now, if it returned, I should not hesitate to profit by it again." A love thus founded has no interest for mortal man. Meantime, early in the winter, and only once, we find him regretting Jean in his correspondence. "Because"—such is his reason—"because he does not think he will ever meet so delicious an armful again"; and then, after a brief excursion into verse, he goes straight on to describe a new episode in the voyage of discovery with the daughter of a Lothian farmer for a heroine. I must ask the reader to follow all these references to his future wife; they are essential to the comprehension of Burns's character and fate. In June, we find him back at Mauchline, a famous man. There, the Armour family greeted him with a "mean, servile compliance," which increased his former disgust. Jean was not less compliant; a second time the poor girl submitted to the fascination of the man whom she did not love, and whom she had so cruelly insulted little more than a year ago; and, though Burns took advantage of her weakness, it was in the ugliest and most cynical spirit, and with a heart absolutely indifferent. Judge of this by a letter written some twenty days after his return—a letter to my mind among the most degrading in the whole collection—a letter which seems to have been inspired by a boastful, libertine bagman. "I am afraid," it goes, "I have almost ruined one source, the principal one, indeed, of my former happiness—the eternal propensity I always had to fall in love. My heart no more glows with feverish rapture; I have no paradisiacal evening interviews." Even the process of "bat-

FAMILIAR STUDIES

tering" has failed him, you perceive. Still he had some one in his eye—a lady, if you please, with a fine figure and elegant manners, and who had "seen the politest quarters in Europe." "I frequently visited her," he writes, "and after passing regularly the intermediate degrees between the distant formal bow and the familiar grasp round the waist, I ventured, in my careless way, to talk of friendship in rather ambiguous terms; and after her return to ———, I wrote her in the same terms. Miss, construing my remarks further than even I intended, flew off in a tangent of female dignity and reserve, like a mounting lark in an April morning; and wrote me an answer which measured out very completely what an immense way I had to travel before I could reach the climate of her favors. But I am an old hawk at the sport, and wrote her such a cool, deliberate, prudent reply, as brought my bird from her aerial towerings, pop, down to my foot, like Corporal Trim's hat." I avow a carnal longing, after this transcription, to buffet the Old Hawk about the ears. There is little question that to this lady he must have repeated his addresses, and that he was by her (Miss Chalmers) eventually, though not at all unkindly, rejected. One more detail to characterize the period. Six months after the date of this letter, Burns, back in Edinburgh, is served with a writ *in meditatione fugæ,* on behalf of some Edinburgh fair one, probably of humble rank, who declared an intention of adding to his family.

About the beginning of December (1787), a new period opens in the story of the poet's random affections. He met at a tea party one Mrs. Agnes M'Lehose, a married woman of about his own age, who, with her two children, had been deserted by an unworthy husband. She had wit, could use her pen, and had read *Werther* with attention. Sociable, and even somewhat frisky, there was a good, sound human kernel in the woman; a warmth of love, strong dogmatic religious feeling, and a considerable, but not authoritative, sense of the proprieties. Of wnat biographers refer to daintily as "her somewhat voluptuous style of beauty," judging from the silhouette in Mr. Scott Douglas's invalu-

ROBERT BURNS

able edition, the reader will be fastidious if he does not approve. Take her for all in all, I believe she was the best woman Burns encountered. The pair took a fancy for each other on the spot; Mrs. M'Lehose, in her turn, invited him to tea; but the poet, in his character of the Old Hawk, preferred a *tête-à-tête*, excused himself at the last moment, and offered a visit instead. An accident confined him to his room for nearly a month, and this led to the famous Clarinda and Sylvander correspondence. It was begun in simple sport; they are already at their fifth or sixth exchange, when Clarinda writes: " It is really curious, so much *fun* passing between two persons who saw each other only *once;*" but it is hardly safe for a man and woman in the flower of their years to write almost daily, and sometimes in terms too ambiguous, sometimes in terms too plain, and generally in terms too warm, for mere acquaintance. The exercise partakes a little of the nature of battering, and danger may be apprehended when next they meet. It is difficult to give any account of this remarkable correspondence; it is too far away from us, and perhaps, not yet far enough, in point of time and manner; the imagination is baffled by these stilted literary utterances, warming, in bravura passages, into downright truculent nonsense. Clarinda has one famous sentence in which she bids Sylvander connect the thought of his mistress with the changing phases of the year; it was enthusiastically admired by the swain, but on the modern mind produces mild amazement and alarm. " Oh, Clarinda," writes Burns, " shall we not meet in a state—some yet unknown state—of being, where the lavish hand of Plenty shall minister to the highest wish of Benevolence, and where the chill north wind of Prudence shall never blow over the flowery field of Enjoyment? " The design may be that of an Old Hawk, but the style is more suggestive of a Bird of Paradise. It is sometimes hard to fancy they are not gravely making fun of each other as they write. Religion, poetry, love and charming sensibility, are the current topics. " I am delighted, charming Clarinda, with your honest enthusiasm for religion," writes Burns; and the pair enter-

FAMILIAR STUDIES

tained a fiction that this was their "favorite subject." "This is Sunday," writes the lady, "and not a word on our favorite subject. O fy! 'divine Clarinda!'" I suspect, although quite unconsciously on the part of the lady, who was bent on his redemption, they but used the favorite subject as a stalking-horse. In the meantime, the sportive acquaintance was ripening steadily into a genuine passion. Visits took place, and then became frequent. Clarinda's friends were hurt and suspicious; her clergyman interfered; she herself had smart attacks of conscience; but her heart had gone from her control; it was altogether his, and she "counted all things but loss—heaven excepted—that she might win and keep him." Burns himself was transported while in her neighborhood, but his transports somewhat rapidly declined during an absence. I am tempted to imagine that, womanlike, he took on the color of his mistress's feeling; that he could not but heat himself at the fire of her unaffected passion; but that, like one who should leave the hearth upon a winter's night, his temperature soon fell when he was out of sight, and in a word, though he could share the symptoms, that he had never shared the disease. At the same time, amid the fustian of the letters there are forcible and true expressions, and the love verses that he wrote upon Clarinda are among the most moving in the language.

We are approaching the solution. In mid-winter, Jean, once more in the family way, was turned out of doors by her family; and Burns had her received and cared for in the house of a friend. For he remained to the last imperfect in his character of Don Juan, and lacked the sinister courage to desert his victim. About the middle of February, (1788), he had to tear himself from his Clarinda and make a journey into the south west on business. Clarinda gave him two shirts for his little son. They were daily to meet in prayer at the appointed hour. Burns, too late for the post at Glasgow, sent her a letter by parcel that she might not have to wait. Clarinda on her part writes, this time with a beautiful simplicity: "I think the streets look deserted-like since Monday; and there's a certain insipidity in good kind folks

ROBERT BURNS

I once enjoyed not a little. Miss Wardrobe supped here on Monday. She once named you, which kept me from falling asleep. I drank your health in a glass of ale—as the lasses do, at Hallowe'en—' in to mysel'.' " Arrived at Mauchline, Burns installed Jean Armour in a lodging, and prevailed on Mrs. Armour to promise her help and countenance in the approaching confinement. This was kind at least; but hear his expressions: " I have taken her a room; I have taken her to my arms; I have given her a mahogany bed; I have given her a guinea. . . . I swore her privately and solemnly never to attempt any claim on me as a husband, even though anybody should persuade her she had such a claim— which she has not, neither during my life nor after my death. She did all this like a good girl." And then he took advantage of the situation. To Clarinda he wrote: " I this morning called for a certain woman. I am disgusted with her; I cannot endure her "; and he accused her of " tasteless insipidity, vulgarity of soul, and mercenary fawning." This was already in March; by the 13th of that month he was back in Edinburgh. On the 17th he wrote to Clarinda: " Your hopes, your fears, your cares, my love, are mine; so don't mind them. I will take you in my hand through the dreary wilds of this world, and scare away the ravening bird or beast that would annoy you." Again, on the 21st: " Will you open, with satisfaction and delight, a letter from the man who loves you, who has loved you, and who will love you, to death, through death, and for ever. . . . How rich am I to have such a treasure as you! . . . ' The Lord God knoweth,' and perhaps, ' Israel he shall know,' my love and your merit. Adieu, Clarinda! I am going to remember you in my prayers." By the 7th of April, seventeen days later, he had already decided to make Jean Armour publicly his wife.

A more astonishing stage-trick is not to be found. And yet his conduct is seen, upon a nearer examination, to be grounded both in reason and in kindness. He was now about to embark on a solid worldly career; he had taken a farm; the affair with Clarinda, however gratifying to his heart,

FAMILIAR STUDIES

was too contingent to offer any great consolation to a man like Burns, to whom marriage must have seemed the very dawn of hope and self-respect. This is to regard the question from its lowest aspect; but there is no doubt that he entered on this new period of his life with a sincere determination to do right. He had just helped his brother with a loan of a hundred and eighty pounds; should he do nothing for the poor girl whom he had ruined? It was true he could not do as he did without brutally wounding Clarinda; that was the punishment of his bygone fault; he was, as he truly says, " damned with the choice only of different species of error and misconduct." To be professional Don Juan, to accept the provocation of any lively lass upon the village green, may thus lead a man through a series of detestable words and actions, and land him at last in an undesired and most unsuitable union for life. If he had been strong enough to refrain or bad enough to persevere in evil; if he had only not been Don Juan at all, or been Don Juan altogether, there had been some possible road for him throughout this troublesome world; but a man, alas! who is equally at the call of his worse and better instincts, stands among changing events without foundation or resource.*

DOWNWARD COURSE

It may be questionable whether any marriage could have tamed Burns; but it is at least certain that there was no hope for him in the marriage he contracted. He did right, but then he had done wrong before; it was, as I said, one of those relations in life which it seems equally wrong to break or to perpetuate. He neither loved nor respected his wife. " God knows," he writes, " my choice was as random as blind man's buff." He consoles himself by the thought that he has acted kindly to her; that she " has the most sacred enthusiasm of attachment to him "; that she has a good figure; that she has a " wood-note wild," " her voice

* For the love affairs see, in particular, Mr. Scott Douglas's edition under the different dates.

ROBERT BURNS

rising with ease to B natural," no less. The effect on the reader is one of unmingled pity for both parties concerned. This was not the wife who (in his own words) could " enter into his favorite studies or relish his favorite authors "; this was not even a wife, after the affair of the marriage lines, in whom a husband could joy to place his trust. Let her manage a farm with sense, let her voice rise to B natural all day long, she would still be a peasant to her lettered lord, and an object of pity rather than of equal affection. She could now be faithful, she could now be forgiving, she could now be generous even to a pathetic and touching degree; but coming from one who was unloved, and who had scarce shown herself worthy of the sentiment, these were all virtues thrown away, which could neither change her husband's heart nor affect the inherent destiny of their relation. From the outset, it was a marriage that had no root in nature; and we find him, erelong, lyrically regretting Highland Mary, renewing correspondence with Clarinda in the warmest language, on doubtful terms with Mrs. Riddel, and on terms unfortunately beyond any question with Anne Park.

Alas! this was not the only ill circumstance in his future. He had been idle for some eighteen months, superintending his new edition, hanging on to settle with the publisher, travelling in the Highlands with Willie Nichol, or philandering with Mrs. M'Lehose; and in this period the radical part of the man had suffered irremediable hurt. He had lost his habits of industry, and formed the habit of pleasure. Apologetical biographers assure us of the contrary; but from the first, he saw and recognised the danger for himself; his mind, he writes, is " enervated to an alarming degree " by idleness and dissipation; and again, " my mind has been vitiated with idleness." It never fairly recovered. To business he could bring the required diligence and attention without difficulty; but he was thenceforward incapable, except in rare instances, of that superior effort of concentration which is required for serious literary work. He may be said, indeed, to have worked no more, and only amused himself with letters. The man who had written a volume

FAMILIAR STUDIES

of masterpieces in six months, during the remainder of his life rarely found courage for any more sustained effort than a song. And the nature of the songs is itself characteristic of these idle later years; for they are often as polished and elaborate as his earlier works were frank, and headlong, and colloquial; and this sort of verbal elaboration in short flights is, for a man of literary turn, simply the most agreeable of pastimes. The change in manner coincides exactly with the Edinburgh visit. In 1786 he had written the *Address to a Louse*, which may be taken as an extreme instance of the first manner; and already, in 1787, we come upon the rosebud pieces to Miss Cruikshank, which are extreme examples of the second. The change was, therefore, the direct and very natural consequence of his great change in life; but it is not the less typical of his loss of moral courage that he should have given up all larger ventures, nor the less melancholy that a man who first attacked literature with a hand that seemed capable of moving mountains, should have spent his later years in whittling cherry-stones.

Meanwhile, the farm did not prosper; he had to join to it the salary of an exciseman; at last he had to give it up, and rely altogether on the latter resource. He was an active officer; and, though he sometimes tempered severity with mercy, we have local testimony oddly representing the public feeling of the period, that, while " in everything else he was a perfect gentleman, when he met with anything seizable he was no better than any other gauger."

There is but one manifestation of the man in these last years which need delay us: and that was the sudden interest in politics which arose from his sympathy with the great French Revolution. His only political feeling had been hitherto a sentimental Jacobitism, not more or less respectable than that of Scott, Aytoun, and the rest of what George Borrow has nicknamed the " Charlie over the water " Scotchmen. It was a sentiment almost entirely literary and picturesque in its origin, built on ballads and the adventures of the Young Chevalier; and in Burns it is the more excusable, because he lay out of the way of active politics in his youth.

ROBERT BURNS

With the great French Revolution, something living, practical, and feasible appeared to him for the first time in this realm of human action. The young ploughman who had desired so earnestly to rise, now reached out his sympathies to a whole nation animated with the same desire. Already in 1788 we find the old Jacobitism hand in hand with the new popular doctrine, when, in a letter of indignation against the zeal of a Whig clergyman, he writes: " I dare say the American Congress in 1776 will be allowed to be as able and as enlightened as the English Convention was in 1688; and that their posterity will celebrate the centenary of their deliverance from us, as duly and sincerely as we do ours from the oppressive measures of the wrong-headed house of Stuart." As time wore on, his sentiments grew more pronounced and even violent; but there was a basis of sense and generous feeling to his hottest excess. What he asked was a fair chance for the individual in life; an open road to success and distinction for all classes of men. It was in the same spirit that he had helped to found a public library in the parish where his farm was situated, and that he sang his fervent snatches against tyranny and tyrants. Witness, were it alone, this verse:—

> "Here's freedom to him that wad read,
> Here's freedom to him that wad write;
> There's nane ever feared that the truth should be heard
> But them wham the truth wad indite."

Yet his enthusiasm for the cause was scarce guided by wisdom. Many stories are preserved of the bitter and unwise words he used in country coteries; how he proposed Washington's health as an amendment to Pitt's, gave as a toast " the last verse of the last chapter of Kings," and celebrated Dumouriez in a doggerel impromptu full of ridicule and hate. Now his sympathies would inspire him with *Scots, wha hae;* now involve him in a drunken broil with a loyal officer, and consequent apologies and explanations, hard to offer for a man of Burns's stomach. Nor was this the front of his offending. On February 27, 1792, he took part in the cap-

FAMILIAR STUDIES

ture of an armed smuggler, bought at the subsequent sale four carronades, and despatched them with a letter to the French Assembly. Letter and guns were stopped at Dover by the English officials; there was trouble for Burns with his superiors; he was reminded firmly, however delicately, that, as a paid official, it was his duty to obey and to be silent; and all the blood of this poor, proud, and falling man must have rushed to his head at the humiliation. His letter to Mr. Erskine, subsequently Earl of Mar, testifies, in its turgid, turbulent phrases, to a perfect passion of alarmed self-respect and vanity. He had been muzzled, and muzzled, when all was said, by his paltry salary as an exciseman; alas! had he not a family to keep? Already, he wrote, he looked forward to some such judgment from a hackney scribbler as this: "Burns, notwithstanding the *fanfaronnade* of independence to be found in his works, and after having been held forth to view and to public estimation as a man of some genius, yet, quite destitute of resources within himself to support his borrowed dignity, he dwindled into a paltry exciseman, and shrunk out the rest of his insignificant existence in the meanest of pursuits, and among the vilest of mankind." And then on he goes, in a style of rhodomontade, but filled with living indignation, to declare his right to a political opinion, and his willingness to shed his blood for the political birthright of his sons. Poor, perturbed spirit! He was indeed exercised in vain; those who share and those who differ from his sentiments about the Revolution, alike understand and sympathize with him in this painful strait; for poetry and human manhood are lasting like the race, and politics, which are but a wrongful striving after right, pass and change from year to year and age to age. The *Twa Dogs* has already outlasted the constitution of Siéyès and the policy of the Whigs; and Burns is better known among English-speaking races than either Pitt or Fox.

Meanwhile, whether as a man, a husband, or a poet, his steps led downward. He knew, knew bitterly, that the best was out of him; he refused to make another volume, for he

ROBERT BURNS

felt that it would be a disappointment; he grew petulantly alive to criticism, unless he was sure it reached him from a friend. For his songs, he would take nothing; they were all that he could do; the proposed Scotch play, the proposed series of Scotch tales in verse, all had gone to water; and in a fling of pain and disappointment, which is surely noble with the nobility of a viking, he would rather stoop to borrow than to accept money for these last and inadequate efforts of his muse. And this desperate abnegation rises at times near to the height of madness; as when he pretended that he had not written, but only found and published, his immortal *Auld Lang Syne*. In the same spirit he became more scrupulous as an artist; he was doing so little, he would fain do that little well; and about two months before his death, he asked Thompson to send back all his manuscripts for revisal, saying that he would rather write five songs to his taste than twice that number otherwise. The battle of his life was lost; in forlorn efforts to do well, in desperate submissions to evil, the last years flew by. His temper is dark and explosive, launching epigrams, quarrelling with his friends, jealous of young puppy officers. He tries to be a good father; he boasts himself a libertine. Sick, sad, and jaded, he can refuse no occasion of temporary pleasure, no opportunity to shine; and he who had once refused the invitations of lords and ladies is now whistled to the inn by any curious stranger. His death (July 21, 1796), in his thirty-seventh year, was indeed a kindly dispensation. It is the fashion to say he died of drink; many a man has drunk more and yet lived with reputation, and reached a good age. That drink and debauchery helped to destroy his constitution, and were the means of his unconscious suicide, is doubtless true; but he had failed in life, had lost his power of work, and was already married to the poor, unworthy, patient Jean, before he had shown his inclination to convivial nights, or at least before that inclination had become dangerous either to his health or his self-respect. He had trifled with life, and must pay the penalty. He had chosen to be Don Juan, he had grasped at temporary pleas-

FAMILIAR STUDIES

ures, and substantial happiness and solid industry had passed him by. He died of being Robert Burns, and there is no levity in such a statement of the case; for shall we not, one and all, deserve a similar epitaph?

WORKS

The somewhat cruel necessity which has lain upon me throughout this paper only to touch upon those points in the life of Burns where correction or amplification seemed desirable, leaves me little opportunity to speak of the works which have made his name so famous. Yet, even here, a few observations seem necessary.

At the time when the poet made his appearance and great first success, his work was remarkable in two ways. For, first, in an age when poetry had become abstract and conventional, instead of continuing to deal with shepherds, thunderstorms, and personifications, he dealt with the actual circumstances of his life, however matter-of-fact and sordid these might be. And, second, in a time when English versification was particularly stiff, lame, and feeble, and words were used with ultra-academical timidity, he wrote verses that were easy, racy, graphic, and forcible, and used language with absolute tact and courage as it seemed most fit to give a clear impression. If you take even those English authors whom we know Burns to have most admired and studied, you will see at once that he owed them nothing but a warning. Take Shenstone, for instance, and watch that elegant author as he tries to grapple with the facts of life. He has a description, I remember, of a gentleman engaged in sliding or walking on thin ice, which is a little miracle of incompetence. You see my memory fails me, and I positively cannot recollect whether his hero was sliding or walking; as though a writer should describe a skirmish, and the reader, at the end, be still uncertain whether it were a charge of cavalry or a slow and stubborn advance of foot. There could be no such ambiguity in Burns; his work is at the opposite pole from such indefinite and stam-

ROBERT BURNS

mering performances; and a whole lifetime passed in the study of Shenstone would only lead a man farther and farther from writing the *Address to a Louse*. Yet Burns, like most great artists, proceeded from a school and continued a tradition; only the school and tradition were Scotch, and not English. While the English language was becoming daily more pedantic and inflexible, and English letters more colorless and slack, there was another dialect in the sister country, and a different school of poetry tracing its descent, through King James I., from Chaucer. The dialect alone accounts for much; for it was then written colloquially, which kept it fresh and supple; and, although not shaped for heroic flights, it was a direct and vivid medium for all that had to do with social life. Hence, whenever Scotch poets left their laborious imitations of bad English verses, and fell back on their own dialect, their style would kindle, and they would write of their convivial and somewhat gross existences with pith and point. In Ramsay, and far more in the poor lad Fergusson, there was mettle, humor, literary courage, and a power of saying what they wished to say definitely and brightly, which in the latter case should have justified great anticipations. Had Burns died at the same age as Fergusson, he would have left us literally nothing worth remark. To Ramsay and to Fergusson, then, he was indebted in a very uncommon degree, not only following their tradition and using their measures, but directly and avowedly imitating their pieces. The same tendency to borrow a hint, to work on some one else's foundation, is notable in Burns from first to last, in the period of songwriting as well as in that of the early poems; and strikes one oddly in a man of such deep originality, who left so strong a print on all he touched, and whose work is so greatly distinguished by that character of "inevitability" which Wordsworth denied to Goethe.

When we remember Burns's obligations to his predecessors, we must never forget his immense advances on them. They had already "discovered" nature; but Burns discovered poetry—a higher and more intense way of thinking

FAMILIAR STUDIES

of the things that go to make up nature, a higher and more ideal key of words in which to speak of them. Ramsay and Fergusson excelled at making a popular—or shall we say vulgar?—sort of society verses, comical and prosaic, written, you would say, in taverns while a supper party waited for its laureate's word; but on the appearance of Burns, this coarse and laughing literature was touched to finer issues, and learned gravity of thought and natural pathos.

What he had gained from his predecessors was a direct speaking style, and to walk on his own feet instead of on academical stilts. There was never a man of letters with more absolute command of his means; and we may say of him, without excess, that his style was his slave. Hence that energy of epithet, so concise and telling, that a foreigner is tempted to explain it by some special richness or aptitude in the dialect he wrote. Hence that Homeric justice and completeness of description which gives us the very physiognomy of nature, in body and detail, as nature is. Hence, too, the unbroken literary quality of his best pieces, which keeps him from any slip into the weariful trade of word-painting, and presents everything, as everything should be presented by the art of words, in a clear, continuous medium of thought. Principal Shairp, for instance, gives us a paraphrase of one tough verse of the original; and for those who know the Greek poets only by paraphrase, this has the very quality they are accustomed to look for and admire in Greek. The contemporaries of Burns were surprised that he should visit so many celebrated mountains and waterfalls, and not seize the opportunity to make a poem. Indeed, it is not for those who have a true command of the art of words, but for peddling, professional amateurs, that these pointed occasions are most useful and inspiring. As those who speak French imperfectly are glad to dwell on any topic they may have talked upon or heard others talk upon before, because they know appropriate words for it in French, so the dabbler in verse rejoices to behold a waterfall, because he has learned the sentiment and knows appropriate words for

ROBERT BURNS

it in poetry. But the dialect of Burns was fitted to deal with any subject; and whether it was a stormy night, a shepherd's collie, a sheep struggling in the snow, the conduct of cowardly soldiers in the field, the gait and cogitations of a drunken man, or only a village cockcrow in the morning, he could find language to give it freshness, body, and relief. He was always ready to borrow the hint of a design, as though he had a difficulty in commencing—a difficulty, let us say, in choosing a subject out of a world which seemed all equally living and significant to him; but once he had the subject chosen, he could cope with nature single-handed, and make every stroke a triumph. Again, his absolute mastery in his art enabled him to express each and all of his different humors, and to pass smoothly and congruously from one to another. Many men invent a dialect for only one side of their nature—perhaps their pathos or their humor, or the delicacy of their senses—and, for lack of a medium, leave all the others unexpressed. You meet such an one, and find him in conversation full of thought, feeling, and experience, which he has lacked the art to employ in his writings. But Burns was not thus hampered in the practice of the literary art; he could throw the whole weight of his nature into his work, and impregnate it from end to end. If Doctor Johnson, that stilted and accomplished stylist, had lacked the sacred Boswell, what should we have known of him? and how should we have delighted in his acquaintance as we do? Those who spoke with Burns tell us how much we have lost who did not. But I think they exaggerate their privilege: I think we have the whole Burns in our possession set forth in his consummate verses.

It was by his style, and not by his matter, that he affected Wordsworth and the world. There is, indeed, only one merit worth considering in a man of letters—that he should write well; and only one damning fault—that he should write ill. We are little the better for the reflections of the sailor's parrot in the story. And so, if Burns helped to change the course of literary history, it was by his frank, direct, and masterly utterance, and not by his homely choice of subjects.

FAMILIAR STUDIES

That was imposed upon him, not chosen upon a principle. He wrote from his own experience, because it was his nature so to do, and the tradition of the school from which he proceeded was fortunately not opposed to homely subjects. But to these homely subjects he communicated the rich commentary of his nature; they were all steeped in Burns; and they interest us not in themselves, but because they have been passed through the spirit of so genuine and vigorous a man. Such is the stamp of living literature; and there was never any more alive than that of Burns.

What a gust of sympathy there is in him sometimes flowing out in byways hitherto unused, upon mice, and flowers, and the devil himself; sometimes speaking plainly between human hearts; sometimes ringing out in exultation like a peal of bells! When we compare the *Farmer's Salutation to his Auld Mare Maggie*, with the clever and inhumane production of half a century earlier, *The Auld Man's Mare's Dead*, we see in a nutshell the spirit of the change introduced by Burns. And as to its manner, who that has read it can forget how the collie, Luath, in the *Twa Dogs*, describes and enters into the merry-making in the cottage?

> "The luntin' pipe an' sneeshin' mill,
> Are handed round wi' richt guid will;
> The canty auld folks crackin' crouse,
> The young anes rantin' through the house—
> My heart has been sae fain to see them
> That I for joy hae barkit wi' them."

It was this ardent power of sympathy that was fatal to so many women, and, through Jean Armour, to himself at last. His humor comes from him in a stream so deep and easy that I will venture to call him the best of humorous poets. He turns about in the midst to utter a noble sentiment or a trenchant remark on human life, and the style changes and rises to the occasion. I think it is Principal Shairp who says, happily, that Burns would have been no Scotchman if he had not loved to moralize; neither, may we add, would he have been his father's son; but (what is worthy of

ROBERT BURNS

note) his moralizings are to a large extent the moral of his own career. He was among the least impersonal of artists. Except in the *Jolly Beggars*, he shows no gleam of dramatic instinct. Mr. Carlyle has complained that *Tam o' Shanter* is, from the absence of this quality, only a picturesque and external piece of work; and I may add that in the *Twa Dogs* it is precisely in the infringement of dramatic propriety that a great deal of the humor of the speeches depends for its existence and effect. Indeed, Burns was so full of his identity that it breaks forth on every page; and there is scarce an appropriate remark either in praise or blame of his own conduct, but he has put it himself into verse. Alas! for the tenor of these remarks! They are, indeed, his own pitiful apology for such a marred existence and talents so misused and stunted; and they seem to prove forever how small a part is played by reason in the conduct of man's affairs. Here was one, at least, who with unfailing judgment predicted his own fate; yet his knowledge could not avail him, and with open eyes he must fulfil his tragic destiny. Ten years before the end he had written his epitaph; and neither subsequent events, nor the critical eyes of posterity, have shown us a word in it to alter. And, lastly, has he not put in for himself the last unanswerable plea?—

> "Then gently scan your brother man,
>   Still gentler sister woman;
> Though they may gang a kennin wrang,
>   To step aside is human:
> One point must still be greatly dark——"

One? Alas! I fear every man and woman of us is "greatly dark" to all their neighbors, from the day of birth until death removes them, in their greatest virtues as well as in their saddest faults; and we, who have been trying to read the character of Burns, may take home the lesson and be gentle in our thoughts.

WALT WHITMAN

OF late years the name of Walt Whitman has been a good deal bandied about in books and magazines. It has become familiar both in good and ill repute. His works have been largely bespattered with praise by his admirers, and cruelly mauled and mangled by irreverent enemies. Now, whether his poetry is good or bad as poetry, is a matter that may admit of a difference of opinion without alienating those who differ. We could not keep the peace with a man who should put forward claims to taste and yet depreciate the choruses in *Samson Agonistes*; but, I think, we may shake hands with one who sees no more in Walt Whitman's volume, from a literary point of view, than a farrago of incompetent essays in a wrong direction. That may not be at all our own opinion. We may think that, when a work contains many unforgettable phrases, it cannot be altogether devoid of literary merit. We may even see passages of a high poetry here and there among its eccentric contents. But when all is said, Walt Whitman is neither a Milton nor a Shakespeare; to appreciate his works is not a condition necessary to salvation; and I would not disinherit a son upon the question, nor even think much the worse of a critic, for I should always have an idea what he meant.

What Whitman has to say is another affair from how he says it. It is not possible to acquit any one of defective intelligence, or else stiff prejudice, who is not interested by Whitman's matter and the spirit it represents. Not as a poet, but as what we must call (for lack of a more exact expression) a prophet, he occupies a curious and prominent position. Whether he may greatly influence the future or not, he is a notable symptom of the present. As a sign of the times, it would be hard to find his parallel. I should hazard a large wager, for instance, that he was not unaquainted

WALT WHITMAN

with the works of Herbert Spencer; and yet where, in all the history books, shall we lay our hands on two more incongruous contemporaries? Mr. Spencer so decorous—I had almost said, so dandy—in dissent; and Whitman, like a large shaggy dog, just unchained, scouring the beaches of the world and baying at the moon. And when was an echo more curiously like a satire, than when Mr. Spencer found his Synthetic Philosophy reverberated from the other shores of the Atlantic in the " barbaric yawp " of Whitman?

Whitman, it cannot be too soon explained, writes up to a system. He was a theorizer about society before he was a poet. He first perceived something wanting, and then sat down squarely to supply the want. The reader, running over his works, will find that he takes nearly as much pleasure in critically expounding his theory of poetry as in making poems. This is as far as it can be from the case of the spontaneous village minstrel dear to elegy, who has no theory whatever, although sometimes he may have fully as much poetry as Whitman. The whole of Whitman's work is deliberate and preconceived. A man born into a society comparatively new, full of conflicting elements and interests, could not fail, if he had any thoughts at all, to reflect upon the tendencies around him. He saw much good and evil on all sides, not yet settled down into some more or less unjust compromise as in older nations, but still in the act of settlement. And he could not but wonder what it would turn out; whether the compromise would be very just or very much the reverse, and give great or little scope for healthy human energies. From idle wonder to active speculation is but a step; and he seems to have been early struck with the inefficacy of literature and its extreme unsuitability to the conditions. What he calls " Feudal Literature " could have little living action on the tumult of American democracy; what he calls the " Literature of Wo," meaning the whole tribe of Werther and Byron, could have no action for good in any time or place. Both propositions, if art had none but a direct moral influence, would be true enough; and as this seems to be Whitman's view, they were true enough for him. He conceived the idea of a Literature which was to inhere in the life of the present; which was to be, first, human, and next, American; which was to be brave and cheerful as per contract; to give culture in a popular and poetical presentment; and, in so doing, catch and stereotype some democratic ideal of humanity which should be equally natural to all grades of wealth and education, and suited, in one of his favorite phrases, to "the average man." To the formation of some such literature as this his poems are to be regarded as so many contributions, one sometimes explaining, sometimes superseding, the other: and the whole together not so much a finished work as a body of suggestive hints. He does not profess to have built the castle, but he pretends he has traced the lines of the foundation. He has not made the poetry, but he flatters himself he has done something toward making the poets.

His notion of the poetic function is ambitious, and coincides roughly with what Schopenhauer has laid down as the province of the metaphysician. The poet is to gather together for men, and set in order, the materials of their existence. He is "The Answerer;" he is to find some way of speaking about life that shall satisfy, if only for the moment, man's enduring astonishment at his own position. And besides having an answer ready, it is he who shall provoke the question. He must shake people out of their indifference, and force them to make some election in this world, instead of sliding dully forward in a dream. Life is a business we are all apt to mismanage; either living recklessly from day to day, or suffering ourselves to be gulled out of our moments by the inanities of custom. We should despise a man who gave as little activity and forethought to the conduct of any other business. But in this, which is the one thing of all others, since it contains them all, we cannot see the forest for the trees. One brief impression obliterates another. There

WALT WHITMAN

is something stupefying in the recurrence of unimportant things. And it is only on rare provocations that we can rise to take an outlook beyond daily concerns, and comprehend the narrow limits and great possibilities of our existence. It is the duty of the poet to induce such moments of clear sight. He is the declared enemy of all living by reflex action, of all that is done betwixt sleep and waking, of all the pleasureless pleasurings and imaginary duties in which we coin away our hearts and fritter invaluable years. He has to electrify his readers into an instant unflagging activity, founded on a wide and eager observation of the world, and make them direct their ways by a superior prudence, which has little or nothing in common with the maxims of the copy-book. That many of us lead such lives as they would heartily disown after two hours' serious reflection on the subject is, I am afraid, a true, and, I am sure, a very galling thought. The Enchanted Ground of dead-alive respectability is next, upon the map, to the Beulah of considerate virtue. But there they all slumber and take their rest in the middle of God's beautiful and wonderful universe; the drowsy heads have nodded together in the same position since first their fathers fell asleep; and not even the sound of the last trumpet can wake them to a single active thought. The poet has a hard task before him to stir up such fellows to a sense of their own and other people's principles in life.

And it happens that literature is, in some ways, but an indifferent means to such an end. Language is but a poor bull's-eye lantern wherewith to show off the vast cathedral of the world; and yet a particular thing once said in words is so definite and memorable, that it makes us forget the absence of the many which remain unexpressed; like a bright window in a distant view, which dazzles and confuses our sight of its surroundings. There are not words enough in all Shakespeare to express the merest fraction of a man's experience in an hour. The speed of the eyesight and the hearing, and the continual industry of the mind, produce, in ten minutes, what it would require a laborious volume to shadow forth by comparisons and roundabout approaches.

FAMILIAR STUDIES

If verbal logic were sufficient, life would be as plain sailing as a piece of Euclid. But, as a matter of fact, we make a travesty of the simplest process of thought when we put it into words; for the words are all colored and forsworn, apply inaccurately, and bring with them, from former uses, ideas of praise and blame that have nothing to do with the question in hand. So we must always see to it nearly, that we judge by the realities of life and not by the partial terms that represent them in man's speech; and at times of choice, we must leave words upon one side, and act upon those brute convictions, unexpressed and perhaps inexpressible, which cannot be flourished in an argument, but which are truly the sum and fruit of our experience. Words are for communication, not for judgment. This is what every thoughtful man knows for himself, for only fools and silly schoolmasters push definitions over far into the domain of conduct; and the majority of women, not learned in these scholastic refinements, live all-of-a-piece and unconsciously, as a tree grows, without caring to put a name upon their acts or motives. Hence, a new difficulty for Whitman's scrupulous and argumentative poet; he must do more than waken up the sleepers to his words; he must persuade them to look over the book and at life with their own eyes.

This side of truth is very present to Whitman; it is this that he means when he tells us that "To glance with an eye confounds the learning of all times." But he is not unready. He is never weary of descanting on the undebatable conviction that is forced upon our minds by the presence of other men, of animals, or of inanimate things. To glance with an eye, were it only at a chair or a park railing, is by far a more persuasive process, and brings us to a far more exact conclusion, than to read the works of all the logicians extant. If both, by a large allowance, may be said to end in certainty, the certainty in the one case transcends the other to an incalculable degree. If people see a lion, they run away; if they only apprehend a deduction, they keep wandering around in an experimental humor. Now, how is the poet to convince like nature, and not like books? Is

WALT WHITMAN

there no actual piece of nature that he can show the man to his face, as he might show him a tree if they were walking together? Yes, there is one: the man's own thoughts. In fact, if the poet is to speak efficaciously, he must say what is already in his hearer's mind. That, alone, the hearer will believe; that, alone, he will be able to apply intelligently to the facts of life. Any conviction, even if it be a whole system or a whole religion, must pass into the condition of commonplace, or postulate, before it becomes fully operative. Strange excursions and high-flying theories may interest, but they cannot rule behavior. Our faith is not the highest truth that we perceive, but the highest that we have been able to assimilate into the very texture and method of our thinking. It is not, therefore, by flashing before a man's eyes the weapons of dialectic; it is not by induction, deduction, or construction; it is not by forcing him on from one stage of reasoning to another, that the man will be effectually renewed. He cannot be made to believe anything; but he can be made to see that he has always believed it. And this is the practical canon. It is when the reader cries, "Oh, I know!" and is, perhaps, half irritated to see how nearly the author has forestalled his own thoughts, that he is on the way to what is called in theology a Saving Faith.

Here we have the key to Whitman's attitude. To give a certain unity of ideal to the average population of America—to gather their activities about some conception of humanity that shall be central and normal, if only for the moment—the poet must portray that population as it is. Like human law, human poetry is simply declaratory. If any ideal is possible, it must be already in the thoughts of the people; and, by the same reason, in the thoughts of the poet, who is one of them. And hence Whitman's own formula: " The poet is individual—he is complete in himself: the others are as good as he; only he sees it, and they do not." To show them how good they are, the poet must study his fellow-countrymen and himself somewhat like a traveller on the hunt for his book of travels. There is a sense, of course, in which all true books are books of travel; and all genuine poets

FAMILIAR STUDIES

must run their risk of being charged with the traveller's exaggeration; for to whom are such books more surprising than to those whose own life is faithfully and smartly pictured? But this danger is all upon one side; and you may judiciously flatter the portrait without any likelihood of the sitter's disowning it for a faithful likeness. And so Whitman has reasoned: that by drawing at first hand from himself and his neighbors, accepting without shame the inconsistencies and brutalities that go to make up man, and yet treating the whole in a high, magnanimous spirit, he would make sure of belief, and at the same time encourage people forward by the means of praise.

II

We are accustomed nowadays to a great deal of puling over the circumstances in which we are placed. The great refinement of many poetical gentlemen has rendered them practically unfit for the jostling and ugliness of life, and they record their unfitness at considerable length. The bold and awful poetry of Job's complaint produces too many flimsy imitators; for there is always something consolatory in grandeur, but the symphony transposed for the piano becomes hysterically sad. This literature of woe, as Whitman calls it, this *Maladie de René*, as we like to call it in Europe, is in many ways a most humiliating and sickly phenomenon. Young gentlemen with three or four hundred a year of private means look down from a pinnacle of doleful experience on all the grown and hearty men who have dared to say a good word for life since the beginning of the world. There is no prophet but the melancholy Jaques, and the blue devils dance on all our literary wires.

It would be a poor service to spread culture, if this be its result, among the comparatively innocent and cheerful ranks of men. When our little poets have to be sent to look at the ploughman and learn wisdom, we must be careful how we tamper with our ploughmen. Where a man is not the best of circumstances preserves composure of mind, and relishes ale and tobacco, and his wife and children, in the intervals of dull and unremunerative labor; where a man in this predicament can afford a lesson by the way to what are called his intellectual superiors, there is plainly something to be lost, as well as something to be gained, by teaching him to think differently. It is better to leave him as he is than to teach him whining. It is better that he should go without the cheerful lights of culture, if cheerless doubt and paralyzing sentimentalism are to be the consequence. Let us, by all means, fight against that hide-bound stolidity of sensation and sluggishness of mind which blurs and decolorizes for poor natures the wonderful pageant of consciousness; let us teach people, as much as we can, to enjoy, and they will learn for themselves to sympathize; but let us see to it, above all, that we give these lessons in a brave, vivacious note, and build the man up in courage while we demolish its substitute, indifference.

Whitman is alive to all this. He sees that, if the poet is to be of any help, he must testify to the livableness of life. His poems, he tells us, are to be "hymns of the praise of things." They are to make for a certain high joy in living, or what he calls himself "a brave delight fit for freedom's athletes." And he has had no difficulty in introducing his optimism: it fitted readily enough with his system; for the average man is truly a courageous person and truly fond of living. One of Whitman's remarks upon this head is worth quotation, as he is there perfectly successful, and does precisely what he designs to do throughout: Takes ordinary and even commonplace circumstances; throws them out, by a happy turn of thinking, into significance and something like beauty; and tacks a hopeful moral lesson to the end.

"The passionate tenacity of hunters, woodmen, early risers, cultivators of gardens and orchards and fields [he says], the love of healthy women for the manly form, seafaring persons, drivers of horses, the passion for light and the open air,—all is an old unvaried sign of the unfailing perception of beauty, and of a residence of the poetic in outdoor people."

There seems to me something truly original in this choice

FAMILIAR STUDIES

of trite examples. You will remark how adroitly Whitman begins, hunters and woodmen being confessedly romantic. And one thing more. If he had said "the love of healthy men for the female form," he would have said almost a silliness; for the thing has never been dissembled out of delicacy, and is so obvious as to be a public nuisance. But by reversing it, he tells us something not unlike news; something that sounds quite freshly in words; and, if the reader be a man, gives him a moment of great self-satisfaction and spiritual aggrandizement. In many different authors you may find passages more remarkable for grammar, but few of a more ingenious turn, and none that could be more to the point in our connection. The tenacity of many ordinary people in ordinary pursuits is a sort of standing challenge to everybody else. If one man can grow absorbed in delving his garden, others may grow absorbed and happy over something else. Not to be upsides in this with any groom or gardener, is to be very meanly organized. A man should be ashamed to take his food if he has not alchemy enough in his stomach to turn some of it into intense and enjoyable occupation.

Whitman tries to reinforce this cheerfulness by keeping up a sort of outdoor atmosphere of sentiment. His book, he tells us, should be read "among the cooling influences of external nature"; and this recommendation, like that other famous one which Hawthorne prefixed to his collected tales, is in itself a character of the work. Every one who has been upon a walking or a boating tour, living in the open air, with the body in constant exercise and the mind in fallow, knows true ease and quiet. The irritating action of the brain is set at rest; we think in a plain, unfeverish temper; little things seem big enough, and great things no longer portentous; and the world is smilingly accepted as it is. This is the spirit that Whitman inculcates and parades. He thinks very ill of the atmosphere of parlors or libraries. Wisdom keeps school outdoors. And he has the art to recommend this attitude of mind by simply pluming himself upon it as a virtue; so that the reader, to keep the advantage

WALT WHITMAN

over his author which most readers enjoy, is tricked into professing the same view. And this spirit, as it is his chief lesson, is the greatest charm of his work. Thence, in spite of an uneven and emphatic key of expression, something trenchant and straightforward, something simple and surprising, distinguishes his poems. He has sayings that come home to one like the Bible. We fall upon Whitman, after the works of so many men who write better, with a sense of relief from strain, with a sense of touching nature, as when one passes out of the flaring, noisy thoroughfares of a great city into what he himself has called, with unexcelled imaginative justice of language, "the huge and thoughtful night." And his book in consequence, whatever may be the final judgment of its merit, whatever may be its influence on the future, should be in the hands of all parents and guardians as a specific for the distressing malady of being seventeen years old. Green-sickness yields to his treatment as to a charm of magic; and the youth, after a short course of reading, ceases to carry the universe upon his shoulders.

III

Whitman is not one of those who can be deceived by familiarity. He considers it just as wonderful that there are myriads of stars, as that one man should rise from the dead. He declares "a hair on the back of his hand just as curious as any special revelation." His whole life is to him what it was to Sir Thomas Browne, one perpetual miracle, Everything is strange, everything unaccountable, everything beautiful; from a bug to the moon, from the sight of the eyes to the appetite for food. He makes it his business to see things as if he saw them for the first time, and professes astonishment on principle. But he has no leaning toward mythology; avows his contempt for what he calls "unregenerate poetry;" and does not mean by nature

"The smooth walks, trimmed hedges, butterflies, posies, and nightingales of the English poets, but the whole orb, with its geologic history, the Kosmos, carrying fire and snow, that rolls through the illimitable areas, light as a feather though weighing billions of tons."

FAMILIAR STUDIES

Nor is this exhaustive; for in his character of idealist all impressions, all thoughts, trees and people, love and faith, astronomy, history, and religion, enter upon equal terms into his notion of the universe. He is not against religion; not, indeed against any religion. He wishes to drag with a larger net, to make a more comprehensive synthesis, than any or than all of them put together. In feeling after the central type of man, he must embrace all eccentricities; his cosmology must subsume all cosmologies, and the feelings that gave birth to them; his statement of facts must include all religion and all irreligion, Christ and Boodha, God and the devil. The world as it is, and the whole world as it is, physical, and spiritual, and historical, with its good and bad, with its manifold inconsistencies, is what he wishes to set forth, in strong, picturesque, and popular lineaments, for the understanding of the average man. One of his favorite endeavors is to get the whole matter into a nutshell; to knock the four corners of the universe, one after another, about his reader's ears; to hurry him, in breathless phrases, hither and thither, back and forward, in time and space; to focus all this about his own momentary personality; and then, drawing the ground from under his feet, as if by some cataclysm of nature, to plunge him into the unfathomable abyss sown with enormous suns and systems, and among the inconceivable numbers and magnitudes and velocities of the heavenly bodies. So that he concludes by striking into us some sense of that disproportion of things which Shelley has illuminated by the ironical flash of these eight words: The desire of the moth for the star.

The same truth, but to what a different purpose! Whitman's moth is mightily at his ease about all the planets in heaven, and cannot think too highly of our sublunary tapers. The universe is so large that imagination flags in the effort to conceive it; but here, in the meantime, is the world under our feet, a very warm and habitable corner. "The earth, that is sufficient; I do not want the constellations any nearer," he remarks. And again: "Let your soul stand cool and composed," says he, "before a million universes." It is the

WALT WHITMAN

language of a transcendental common sense, such as Thoreau held and sometimes uttered. But Whitman, who has a somewhat vulgar inclination for technical talk and the jargon of philosophy, is not content with a few pregnant hints; he must put the dots upon his i's; he must corroborate the songs of Apollo by some of the darkest talk of human metaphysic. He tells his disciples that they must be ready "to confront the growing arrogance of Realism." Each person is, for himself, the keystone and the occasion of this universal edifice. "Nothing, not God," he says, "is greater to one than oneself is"; a statement with an irreligious smack at the first sight; but like most startling sayings, a manifest truism on a second. He will give effect to his own character without apology; he sees "that the elementary laws never apologize." "I reckon," he adds, with quaint colloquial arrogance, "I reckon I behave no prouder than the level I plant my house by, after all." The level follows the law of its being; so, unrelentingly, will he; every thing, every person, is good in his own place and way; God is the maker of all, and all are in one design. For he believes in God, and that with a sort of blasphemous security. "No array of terms," quoth he, "no array of terms can say how much at peace I am about God and about death." There certainly never was a prophet who carried things with a higher hand; he gives us less a body of dogmas than a series of proclamations by the grace of God; and language, you will observe, positively fails him to express how far he stands above the highest human doubts and trepidations.

But next in order of truths to a person's sublime conviction of himself, comes the attraction of one person for another, and all that we mean by the word love:—

"The dear love of man for his comrade—the attraction of friend for friend,
Of the well-married husband and wife, of children and parents,
Of city for city and land for land."

The solitude of the most sublime idealist is broken in upon by other people's faces; he sees a look in their eyes

FAMILIAR STUDIES

that corresponds to something in his own heart; there comes a tone in their voices which convicts him of a startling weakness for his fellow-creatures. While he is hymning the *ego* and commercing with God and the universe, a woman goes below his window; and at the turn of her skirt or the color of her eyes, Icarus is recalled from heaven by the run. Love is so startlingly real that it takes rank upon an equal footing of reality with the consciousness of personal existence. We are as heartily persuaded of the identity of those we love as of our own identity. And so sympathy pairs with self-assertion, the two gerents of human life on earth; and Whitman's ideal man must not only be strong, free and self-reliant in himself, but his freedom must be bounded and his strength perfected by the most intimate, eager, and long-suffering love for others. To some extent this is taking away with the left hand what has been so generously given with the right. Morality has been ceremoniously extruded from the door only to be brought in again by the window. We are told, on one page, to do as we please; and on the next we are sharply upbraided for not having done as the author pleases. We are first assured that we are the finest fellows in the world in our own right; and then it appears that we are only fine fellows in so far as we practise a most quixotic code of morals. The disciple who saw himself in clear ether a moment before is plunged down again among the fogs and complications of duty. And this is all the more overwhelming because Whitman insists not only on love between sex and sex, and between friends of the same sex, but in the field of the less intense political sympathies; and his ideal man must not only be a generous friend but a conscientious voter into the bargain.

His method somewhat lessens the difficulty. He is not, the reader will remember, to tell us how good we ought to be, but to remind us how good we are. He is to encourage us to be free and kind, by proving that we are free and kind already. He passes our corporate life under review, to show that it is upheld by the very virtues of which he makes himself the advocate. " There is no object so soft," he says

WALT WHITMAN

somewhere in his big, plain way, " there is no object so soft but it makes a hub for the wheel'd universe." Rightly understood, it is on the softest of all objects, the sympathetic heart, that the wheel of society turns easily and securely as on a perfect axle. There is no room, of course, for doubt or discussion, about conduct, where every one is to follow the law of his being with exact compliance. Whitman hates doubt, deprecates discussion, and discourages to his utmost the craving, carping sensibilities of the conscience. We are to imitate, to use one of his absurd and happy phrases, " the satisfaction and aplomb of animals." If he preaches a sort of ranting Christianity in morals, a fit consequent to the ranting optimism of his cosmology, it is because he declares it to be the original deliverance of the human heart; or at least, for he would be honestly historical in method, of the human heart as at present Christianized. His is a morality without a prohibition; his policy is one of encouragement all round. A man must be a born hero to come up to Whitman's standard in the practice of any of the positive virtues; but of a negative virtue, such as temperance or chastity, he has so little to say, that the reader need not be surprised if he drops a word or two upon the other side. He would lay down nothing that would be a clog; he would prescribe nothing that cannot be done ruddily, in a heat. The great point is to get people under way. To the faithful Whitmanite this would be justified by the belief that God made all, and that all was good; the prophet, in this doctrine, has only to cry " Tally-ho," and mankind will break into a gallop on the road to El Dorado. Perhaps, to another class of minds, it may look like the result of the somewhat cynical reflection that you will not make a kind man out of one who is unkind by any precepts under heaven; tempered by the belief that, in natural circumstances, the large majority is well disposed. Thence it would follow, that if you can only get every one to feel more warmly and act more courageously, the balance of results will be for good.

So far, you see, the doctrine is pretty coherent as a doctrine; as a picture of man's life it is incomplete and misleading, although eminently cheerful. This he is himself the first to acknowledge; for if he is prophetic in anything, it is in his noble disregard of consistency. "Do I contradict myself?" he asks somewhere; and then pat comes the answer, the best answer ever given in print, worthy of a sage, or rather of a woman: "Very well, then, I contradict myself!" with this addition, not so feminine and perhaps not altogether so satisfactory: "I am large—I contain multitudes." Life, as a matter of fact, partakes largely of the nature of tragedy. The gospel according to Whitman, even if it be not so logical, has this advantage over the gospel according to Pangloss, that it does not utterly disregard the existence of temporal evil. Whitman accepts the fact of disease and wretchedness like an honest man; and instead of trying to qualify it in the interest of his optimism, sets himself to spur people up to be helpful. He expresses a conviction, indeed, that all will be made up to the victims in the end; that "what is untried and afterward" will fail no one, not even "the old man who has lived without purpose and feels it with bitterness worse than gall." But this is not to palliate our sense of what is hard or melancholy in the present. Pangloss, smarting under one of the worst things that ever was supposed to come from America, consoled himself with the reflection that it was the price we have to pay for cochineal. And with that murderous parody, logical optimism and the praises of the best of possible words went irrevocably out of season, and have been no more heard of in the mouths of reasonable men. Whitman spares us all allusions to the cochineal; he treats evil and sorrow in a spirit almost as of welcome; as an old sea-dog might have welcomed the sight of the enemy's topsails off the Spanish Main. There, at least, he seems to say, is something obvious to be done. I do not know many better things in literature than the brief pictures,—brief and vivid like things seen by lightning,—with which he tries to stir up the world's heart upon the side of mercy. He braces us, on the one hand, with examples of heroic duty and helpfulness; on the other, he touches us with pitiful instances of people needing help. He

WALT WHITMAN

knows how to make the heart beat at a brave story; to inflame us with just resentment over the hunted slave; to stop our mouths for shame when he tells of the drunken prostitute. For all the afflicted, all the weak, all the wicked, a good word is said in a spirit which I can only call one of ultra-Christianity; and however wild, however contradictory, it may be in parts, this at least may be said for his book, as it may be said of the Christian Gospels, that no one will read it, however respectable, but he gets a knock upon his conscience; no one, however fallen, but he finds a kindly and supporting welcome.

IV

Nor has he been content with merely blowing the trumpet for the battle of well-doing; he has given to his precepts the authority of his own brave example. Naturally a grave, believing man, with little or no sense of humor, he has succeeded as well in life as in his printed performances. The spirit that was in him has come forth most eloquently in his actions. Many who have only read his poetry have been tempted to set him down as an ass, or even as a charlatan; but I never met any one who had known him personally who did not profess a solid affection and respect for the man's character. He practises as he professes; he feels deeply that Christian love for all men, that toleration, that cheerful delight in serving others, which he often celebrates in literature with a doubtful measure of success. And perhaps, out of all his writings, the best and the most human and convincing passages are to be found in " these soil'd and creas'd little livraisons, each composed of a sheet or two of paper, folded small to carry in the pocket, and fastened with a pin," which he scribbed during the war by the bedside of the wounded or in the excitement of great events. They are hardly literature in the formal meaning of the word; he has left his jottings for the most part as he made them; a homely detail, a word from the lips of a dying soldier, a business memorandum, the copy of a letter—short, straightforward

FAMILIAR STUDIES

to the point, with none of the trappings of composition; but they breathe a profound sentiment, they give us a vivid look at one of the sides of life, and they make us acquainted with a man whom it is an honor to love.

Whitman's intense Americanism, his unlimited belief in the future of These States (as, with reverential capitals, he loves to call them), made the war a period of great trial to his soul. The new virtue, Unionism, of which he is the sole inventor, seemed to have fallen into premature unpopularity. All that he loved, hoped, or hated, hung in the balance. And the game of war was not only momentous to him in its issues; it sublimated his spirit by its heroic displays, and tortured him intimately by the spectacle of its horrors. It was a theatre, it was a place of education, it was like a season of religious revival. He watched Lincoln going daily to his work; he studied and fraternized with young soldiery passing to the front; above all, he walked the hospitals, reading the Bible, distributing clean clothes, or apples, or tobacco; a patient, helpful, reverend man, full of kind speeches.

His memoranda of this period are almost bewildering to read. From one point of view they seem those of a district visitor; from another, they look like the formless jottings of an artist in the picturesque. More than one woman, on whom I tried the experiment, immediately claimed the writer for a fellow-woman. More than one literary purist might identify him as a shoddy newspaper correspondent without the necessary faculty of style. And yet the story touches home; and if you are of the weeping order of mankind, you will certainly find your eyes fill with tears, of which you have no reason to be ashamed. There is only one way to characterize a work of this order, and that is to quote. Here is a passage from a letter to a mother, unknown to Whitman, whose son died in hospital:—

"Frank, as far as I saw, had everything requisite in surgical treatment, nursing, etc. He had watches much of the time. He was so good and well-behaved, and affectionate, I myself liked him very much. I was in the habit of coming in afternoons and sitting by him, and he liked to have me—liked to put out his arm and lay his hand on my knee— would keep it so a long while. Toward the last he was more restless

WALT WHITMAN

and flighty at night—often fancied himself with his regiment—by his talk sometimes seem'd as if his feelings were hurt by being blamed by his officers for something he was entirely innocent of—said 'I never in my life was thought capable of such a thing, and never was.' At other times he would fancy himself talking as it seem'd to children or such like, his relatives, I suppose, and giving them good advice; would talk to them a long while. All the time he was out of his head not one single bad word, or thought, or idea escaped him. It was remark'd that many a man's conversation in his senses was not half so good as Frank's delirium.

" He was perfectly willing to die—he had become very weak, and had suffer'd a good deal, and was perfectly resign'd, poor boy. I do not know his past life, but I feel as if it must have been good. At any rate what I saw of him here, under the most trying circumstances, with a painful wound, and among strangers, I can say that he behaved so brave, so composed, and so sweet and affectionate, it could not be surpassed. And now, like many other noble and good men, after serving his country as a soldier, he has yielded up his young life at the very outset in her service. Such things are gloomy—yet there is a text, 'God doeth all things well,' the meaning of which, after due time, appears to the soul.

" I thought perhaps a few words, though from a stranger, about your son, from one who was with him at the last, might be worth while, for I loved the young man, though I but saw him immediately to lose him."

It is easy enough to pick holes in the grammar of this letter, but what are we to say of its profound goodness and tenderness? It is written as though he had the mother's face before his eyes, and saw her wincing in the flesh at every word. And what, again, are we to say of its sober truthfulness, not exaggerating, not running to phrases, not seeking to make a hero out of what was only an ordinary but good and brave young man? Literary reticence is not Whitman's stronghold; and this reticence is not literary, but humane; it is not that of a good artist but that of a good man. He knew that what the mother wished to hear about was Frank; and he told her about her Frank as he was.

Something should be said of Whitman's style, for style is of the essence of thinking. And where a man is so critically deliberate as our author, and goes solemnly about his poetry for an ulterior end, every indication is worth notice.

FAMILIAR STUDIES

He has chosen a rough, unrhymed, lyrical verse; sometimes instinct with a fine processional movement; often so rugged and careless that it can only be described by saying that he has not taken the trouble to write prose. I believe myself that it was selected principally because it was easy to write, although not without recollections of the marching measures of some of the prose in our English Old Testament. According to Whitman, on the other hand, " the time has arrived to essentially break down the barriers of form between Prose and Poetry . . . for the most cogent purposes of those great inland states, and for Texas, and California, and Oregon ";—a statement which is among the happiest achievements of American humor. He calls his verses " recitatives," in easily followed allusion to a musical form. " Easily-written, loose-fingered chords," he cries, " I feel the thrum of your climax and close." Too often, I fear, he is the only one who can perceive the rhythm; and in spite of Mr. Swinburne, a great part of his work considered as verse is poor bald stuff. Considered, not as verse, but as speech, a great part of it is full of strange and admirable merits. The right detail is seized; the right word, bold and trenchant, is thrust into its place. Whitman has small regard to literary decencies, and is totally free from literary timidities. He is neither afraid of being slangy nor of being dull; nor, let me add, of being ridiculous. The result is a most surprising compound of plain grandeur, sentimental affectation, and downright nonsense. It would be useless to follow his detractors and give instances of how bad he can be at his worst; and perhaps it would be not much wiser to give extracted specimens of how happily he can write when he is at his best. These come in to most advantage in their own place; owing something, it may be, to the offset of their curious surroundings. And one thing is certain, that no one can appreciate Whitman's excellences until he has grown accustomed to his faults. Until you are content to pick poetry out of his pages almost as you must pick it out of a Greek play in Bohn's translation, your gravity will be continually upset, your ears perpetually disappointed, and the

WALT WHITMAN

whole book will be no more to you than a particularly flagrant production by the Poet Close.

A writer of this uncertain quality was, perhaps, unfortunate in taking for thesis the beauty of the world as it now is, not only on the hill-tops, but in the factory; not only by the harbor full of stately ships, but in the magazine of the hopelessly prosaic hatter. To show beauty in common things is the work of the rarest tact. It is not to be done by the wishing. It is easy to posit as a theory, but to bring it home to men's minds is the problem of literature, and is only accomplished by rare talent, and in comparatively rare instances. To bid the whole world stand and deliver, with a dogma in one's right hand by way of pistol; to cover reams of paper in a galloping, headstrong vein; to cry louder and louder over everything as it comes up, and make no distinction in one's enthusiasm over the most incomparable matters; to prove one's entire want of sympathy for the jaded, literary palate, by calling, not a spade a spade, but a hatter a hatter, in a lyrical apostrophe;—this, in spite of all the airs of inspiration, is not the way to do it. It may be very wrong, and very wounding to a respectable branch of industry, but the word "hatter" cannot be used seriously in emotional verse; not to understand this, is to have no literary tact; and I would, for his own sake, that this were the only inadmissible expression with which Whitman had bedecked his pages. The book teems with similar comicalities; and, to a reader who is determined to take it from that side only, presents a perfect carnival of fun.

A good deal of this is the result of theory playing its usual vile trick upon the artist. It is because he is a democrat that Whitman must have in the hatter. If you may say Admiral, he reasons, why may you not say Hatter? One man is as good as another, and it is the business of the "great poet" to show poetry in the life of the one as well as the other. A most incontrovertible sentiment surely, and one which nobody would think of controverting, where—and here is the point—where any beauty has been shown. But how, where that is not the case? where the hatter is simply

FAMILIAR STUDIES

introduced, as God made him and as his fellow-men have miscalled him, at the crisis of a high-flown rhapsody? And what are we to say, where a man of Whitman's notable capacity for putting things in a bright, picturesque, and novel way, simply gives up the attempt, and indulges, with apparent exultation, in an inventory of trades or implements, with no more color or coherence than so many index-words out of a dictionary? I do not know that we can say anything, but that it is a prodigiously amusing exhibition for a line or so. The worst of it is, that Whitman must have known better. The man is a great critic, and, so far as I can make out, a good one; and how much criticism does it require to know that capitulation is not description, or that fingering on a dumb keyboard, with whatever show of sentiment and execution, is not at all the same thing as discoursing music? I wish I could believe he was quite honest with us; but, indeed, who was ever quite honest who wrote a book for a purpose? It is a flight beyond the reach of human magnanimity.

One other point, where his means failed him, must be touched upon, however shortly. In his desire to accept all facts loyally and simply, it fell within his programme to speak at some length and with some plainness on what is, for I really do not know what reason, the most delicate of subjects. Seeing in that one of the most serious and interesting parts of life, he was aggrieved that it should be looked upon as ridiculous or shameful. No one speaks of maternity with his tongue in his cheek; and Whitman made a bold push to set the sanctity of fatherhood beside the sanctity of motherhood, and introduce this also among the things that can be spoken of without either a blush or a wink. But the Philistines have been too strong; and, to say truth, Whitman has rather played the fool. We may be thoroughly conscious that his end is improving; that it would be a good thing if a window were opened on these close privacies of life; that on this subject, as on all others, he now and then lets fall a pregnant saying. But we are not satisfied. We feel that he was not the man for so difficult an enterprise. He loses our

WALT WHITMAN

sympathy in the character of a poet by attracting too much of our attention in that of a Bull in a China Shop. And where, by a little more art, we might have been solemnized ourselves, it is too often Whitman alone who is solemn in the face of an audience somewhat indecorously amused.

VI

Lastly, as most important, after all, to human beings in our disputable state, what is that higher prudence which was to be the aim and issue of these deliberate productions?

Whitman is too clever to slip into a succinct formula. If he could have adequately said his say in a single proverb, it is to be presumed he would not have put himself to the trouble of writing several volumes. It was his programme to state as much as he could of the world with all its contradictions, and leave the upshot with God who planned it. What he has made of the world and the world's meanings is to be found at large in his poems. These altogether give his answers to the problems of belief and conduct; in many ways righteous and high-spirited, in some ways loose and contradictory. And yet there are two passages from the preface to the *Leaves of Grass* which do pretty well condense his teaching on all essential points, and yet preserve a measure of his spirit.

"This is what you shall do [he says in the one], love the earth, and sun, and animals, despise riches, give alms to every one that asks, stand up for the stupid and crazy, devote your income and labor to others, hate tyrants, argue not concerning God, have patience and indulgence toward the people, take off your hat to nothing known or unknown, or to any man or number of men; go freely with powerful uneducated persons, and with the young, and mothers of families, read these leaves [his own works] in the open air every season of every year of your life; re-examine all you have been told at school or church, or in any book, and dismiss whatever insults your own soul."

"The prudence of the greatest poet [he adds in the other—and the greatest poet is, of course, himself] knows that the young man who composedly perilled his life and lost it, has done exceeding well for himself; while the man who has not perilled his life, and retains it to old age in riches and ease, has perhaps achieved nothing for himself

FAMILIAR STUDIES

worth mentioning; and that only that person has no great prudence to learn, who has learnt to prefer real long-lived things, and favors body and soul the same, and perceives the indirect surely following the direct, and what evil or good he does leaping onward and waiting to meet him again, and who in his spirit, in any emergency whatever, neither hurries nor avoids death."

There is much that is Christian in these extracts, startlingly Christian. Any reader who bears in mind Whitman's own advice and "dismisses whatever insults his own soul" will find plenty that is bracing, brightening, and chastening to reward him for a little patience at first. It seems hardly possible that any being should get evil from so healthy a book as the *Leaves of Grass*, which is simply comical wherever it falls short of nobility; but if there be any such, who cannot both take and leave, who cannot let a single opportunity pass by without some unworthy and unmanly thought, I should have as great difficulty, and neither more nor less, in recommending the works of Whitman as in lending them Shakespeare, or letting them go abroad outside of the grounds of a private asylum.

HENRY DAVID THOREAU

HIS CHARACTER AND OPINIONS

THOREAU'S thin, penetrating, big-nosed face, even in a bad woodcut, conveys some hint of the limitations of his mind and character. With his almost acid sharpness of insight, with his almost animal dexterity in act, there went none of that large, unconscious geniality of the world's heroes. He was not easy, not ample, not urbane, not even kind; his enjoyment was hardly smiling, or the smile was not broad enough to be convincing; he had no waste lands nor kitchen-midden in his nature, but was all improved and sharpened to a point. "He was bred to no profession," says Emerson; "he never married; he lived alone; he never went to church; he never voted; he refused to pay a tax to the State; he ate no flesh, he drank no wine, he never knew the use of tobacco; and, though a naturalist, he used neither trap nor gun. When asked at dinner what dish he preferred, he answered, 'the nearest.'" So many negative superiorities begin to smack a little of the prig. From his later works he was in the habit of cutting out the humorous passages, under the impression that they were beneath the dignity of his moral muse; and there we see the prig stand public and confessed. It was "much easier," says Emerson acutely, much easier for Thoreau to say *no* than *yes*; and that is a characteristic which depicts the man. It is a useful accomplishment to be able to say *no*, but surely it is the essence of amiability to prefer to say *yes* where it is possible. There is something wanting in the man who does not hate himself whenever he is constrained to say no. And there was

FAMILIAR STUDIES

a great deal wanting in this born dissenter. He was almost shockingly devoid of weaknesses; he had not enough of them to be truly polar with humanity; whether you call him demi-god or demi-man, he was at least not altogether one of us, for he was not touched with a feeling of our infirmities. The world's heroes have room for all positive qualities, even those which are disreputable, in the capacious theatre of their dispositions. Such can live many lives; while a Thoreau can live but one, and that only with perpetual foresight.

He was no ascetic, rather an Epicurean of the nobler sort; and he had this one great merit, that he succeeded so far as to be happy. "I love my fate to the core and rind," he wrote once; and even while he lay dying, here is what he dictated (for it seems he was already too feeble to control the pen): "You ask particularly after my health. I *suppose* that I have not many months to live, but of course know nothing about it. I may say that I am enjoying existence as much as ever, and regret nothing." It is not given to all to bear so clear a testimony to the sweetness of their fate, nor to any without courage and wisdom; for this world in itself is but a painful and uneasy place of residence, and lasting happiness, at least to the self-conscious, comes only from within. Now Thoreau's content and ecstasy in living was, we may say, like a plant that he had watered and tended with womanish solicitude; for there is apt to be something unmanly, something almost dastardly, in a life that does not move with dash and freedom, and that fears the bracing contact of the world. In one word, Thoreau was a skulker. He did not wish virtue to go out of him among his fellow-men, but slunk into a corner to hoard it for himself. He left all for the sake of certain virtuous self-indulgences. It is true that his tastes were noble; that his ruling passion was to keep himself unspotted from the world; and that his luxuries were all of the same healthy order as cold tubs and early rising. But a man may be both coldly cruel in the pursuit of goodness, and morbid even in the pursuit of health. I cannot lay my hands on the passage in which he explains his abstinence from tea and coffee, but I am sure I have the

HENRY DAVID THOREAU

meaning correctly. It is this: He thought it bad economy and worthy of no true virtuoso to spoil the natural rapture of the morning with such muddy stimulants; let him but see the sun rise, and he was already sufficiently inspirited for the labors of the day. That may be reason good enough to abstain from tea; but when we go on to find the same man, on the same or similar grounds, abstain from nearly everything that his neighbors innocently and pleasurably use, and from the rubs and trials of human society itself into the bargain, we recognize that valetudinarian healthfulness which is more delicate than sickness itself. We need have no respect for a state of artificial training. True health is to be able to do without it. Shakespeare, we can imagine, might begin the day upon a quart of ale, and yet enjoy the sunrise to the full as much as Thoreau, and commemorate his enjoyment in vastly better verses. A man who must separate himself from his neighbors' habits in order to be happy, is in much the same case with one who requires to take opium for the same purpose. What we want to see is one who can breast into the world, do a man's work, and still preserve his first and pure enjoyment of existence.

Thoreau's faculties were of a piece with his moral shyness; for they were all delicacies. He could guide himself about the woods on the darkest night by the touch of his feet. He could pick up at once an exact dozen of pencils by the feeling, pace distances with accuracy, and gauge cubic contents by the eye. His smell was so dainty that he could perceive the fœtor of dwelling-houses as he passed them by at night; his palate so unsophisticated that, like a child, he disliked the taste of wine—or perhaps, living in America, had never tasted any that was good; and his knowledge of nature was so complete and curious that he could have told the time of year, within a day or so, by the aspect of the plants. In his dealings with animals, he was the original of Hawthorne's Donatello. He pulled the woodchuck out of its hole by the tail; the hunted fox came to him for protection; wild squirrels have been seen to nestle in his waistcoat; he would thrust his arm into a pool and bring forth a bright, panting fish,

FAMILIAR STUDIES

lying undismayed in the palm of his hand. There were few things that he could not do. He could make a house, a boat, a pencil, or a book. He was a surveyor, a scholar, a natural historian. He could run, walk, climb, skate, swim, and manage a boat. The smallest occasion served to display his physical accomplishment; and a manufacturer, from merely observing his dexterity with the window of a railway carriage, offered him a situation on the spot. "The only fruit of much living," he observes, "is the ability to do some slight thing better." But such was the exactitude of his senses, so alive was he in every fibre, that it seems as if the maxim should be changed in his case, for he could do most things with unusual perfection. And perhaps he had an approving eye to himself when he wrote: "Though the youth at last grows indifferent, the laws of the universe are not indifferent, *but are forever on the side of the most sensitive.*"

II

Thoreau had decided, it would seem, from the very first to lead a life of self-improvement: the needle did not tremble as with richer natures, but pointed steadily north; and as he saw duty and inclination in one, he turned all his strength in that direction. He was met upon the threshold by a common difficulty. In this world, in spite of its many agreeable features, even the most sensitive must undergo some drudgery to live. It is not possible to devote your time to study and meditation without what are quaintly but happily denominated private means; these absent, a man must contrive to earn his bread by some service to the public such as the public cares to pay him for; or, as Thoreau loved to put it, Apollo must serve Admetus. This was to Thoreau even a sourer necessity than it is to most; there was a love of freedom, a strain of the wild man, in his nature, that rebelled with violence against the yoke of custom; and he was so eager to cultivate himself and to be happy in his own society, that he could consent with difficulty even to the interruptions

HENRY DAVID THOREAU

of friendship. "*Such are my engagements to myself* that I dare not promise," he once wrote in answer to an invitation; and the italics are his own. Marcus Aurelius found time to study virtue, and between whiles to conduct the imperial affairs of Rome; but Thoreau is so busy improving himself, that he must think twice about a morning call. And now imagine him condemned for eight hours a day to some uncongenial and unmeaning business! He shrank from the very look of the mechanical in life; all should, if possible, be sweetly spontaneous and swimmingly progressive. Thus he learned to make lead-pencils, and, when he had gained the best certificate and his friends began to congratulate him on his establishment in life, calmly announced that he should never make another. "Why should I?" said he; "I would not do again what I have done once." For when a thing has once been done as well as it wants to be, it is of no further interest to the self-improver. Yet in after years, and when it became needful to support his family, he returned patiently to this mechanical art—a step more than worthy of himself.

The pencils seem to have been Apollo's first experiment in the service of Admetus; but others followed. "I have thoroughly tried school-keeping," he writes, "and found that my expenses were in proportion, or rather out of proportion, to my income; for I was obliged to dress and train, not to say think and believe, accordingly, and I lost my time into the bargain. As I did not teach for the benefit of my fellowmen, but simply for a livelihood, this was a failure. I have tried trade, but I found that it would take ten years to get under way in that, and that then I should probably be on my way to the devil." Nothing, indeed, can surpass his scorn for all so-called business. Upon that subject gall squirts from him at a touch. "The whole enterprise of this nation is not illustrated by a thought," he writes; "it is not warmed by a sentiment; there is nothing in it for which a man should lay down his life, nor even his gloves." And again: "If our merchants did not most of them fail, and the banks too, my faith in the old laws of this world would be staggered. The statement that ninety-six in a hundred doing such business surely break down is perhaps the sweetest fact that statistics have revealed." The wish was probably father to the figures; but there is something enlivening in a hatred of so genuine a brand, hot as Corsican revenge and sneering like Voltaire.

Pencils, school-keeping, and trade being thus discarded one after another, Thoreau, with a stroke of strategy, turned the position. He saw his way to get his board and lodging for practically nothing; and Admetus never got less work out of any servant since the world began. It was his ambition to be an Oriental philosopher; but he was always a very Yankee sort of Oriental. Even in the peculiar attitude in which he stood to money, his system of personal economics, as we may call it, he displayed a vast amount of truly down-East calculation, and he adopted poverty like a piece of business. Yet his system is based on one or two ideas which, I believe, come naturally to all thoughtful youths, and are only pounded out of them by city uncles. Indeed, something essentially youthful distinguishes all Thoreau's knock-down blows at current opinion. Like the posers of a child, they leave the orthodox in a kind of speechless agony. These know the thing is nonsense. They are sure there must be an answer, yet somehow cannot find it. So it is with his system of economy. He cuts through the subject on so new a plane that the accepted arguments apply no longer; he attacks it in a new dialect where there are no catchwords ready made for the defender; after you have been boxing for years on a polite, gladiatorial convention, here is an assailant who does not scruple to hit below the belt.

"The cost of a thing," says he, "is *the amount of what I will call life* which is required to be exchanged for it, immediately or in the long run." I have been accustomed to put it to myself, perhaps more clearly, that the price we have to pay for money is paid in liberty. Between these two ways of it, at least, the reader will probably not fail to find a third definition of his own; and it follows, on one or other, that a man may pay too dearly for his livelihood, by

HENRY DAVID THOREAU

giving, in Thoreau's terms, his whole life for it, or, in mine, bartering for it the whole of his available liberty, and becoming a slave till death. There are two questions to be considered—the quality of what we buy, and the price we have to pay for it. Do you want a thousand a year, a two thousand a year, or a ten thousand a year livelihood? and can you afford the one you want? It is a matter of taste; it is not in the least degree a question of duty, though commonly supposed so. But there is no authority for that view anywhere. It is nowhere in the Bible. It is true that we might do a vast amount of good if we were wealthy, but it is also highly improbable; not many do; and the art of growing rich is not only quite distinct from that of doing good, but the practice of the one does not at all train a man for practising the other. "Money might be of great service to me," writes Thoreau; "but the difficulty now is that I do not improve my opportunities, and therefore I am not prepared to have my opportunities increased." It is a mere illusion that, above a certain income, the personal desires will be satisfied and leave a wider margin for the generous impulse. It is as difficult to be generous, or anything else, except perhaps a member of Parliament, on thirty thousand as on two hundred a year.

Now Thoreau's tastes were well defined. He loved to be free, to be master of his times and seasons, to indulge the mind rather than the body; he preferred long rambles to rich dinners, his own reflections to the consideration of society, and an easy, calm, unfettered, active life among green trees to dull toiling at the counter of a bank. And such being his inclination he determined to gratify it. A poor man must save off something; he determined to save off his livelihood. "When a man has attained those things which are necessary to life," he writes, "there is another alternative than to obtain the superfluities; *he may adventure on life now*, his vacation from humbler toil having commenced." Thoreau would get shelter, some kind of covering for his body, and necessary daily bread; even these he should get as cheaply as possible; and then, his vacation from humbler

FAMILIAR STUDIES

toil having commenced, devote himself to Oriental philosophers, the study of nature, and the work of self-improvement.

Prudence, which bids us all go to the ant for wisdom and hoard against the day of sickness, was not a favorite with Thoreau. He preferred that other, whose name is so much misappropriated: Faith. When he had secured the necessaries of the moment, he would not reckon up possible accidents or torment himself with trouble for the future. He had no toleration for the man "who ventures to live only by the aid of the mutual insurance company, which has promised to bury him decently." He would trust himself a little to the world. "We may safely trust a good deal more than we do," says he. "How much is not done by us! or what if we had been taken sick?" And then, with a stab of satire, he describes contemporary mankind in a phrase: "All the day long on the alert, at night we unwillingly say our prayers and commit ourselves to uncertainties." It is not likely that the public will be much affected by Thoreau, when they blink the direct injunctions of the religion they profess; and yet, whether we will or no, we make the same hazardous ventures; we back our own health and the honesty of our neighbors for all that we are worth; and it is chilling to think how many must lose their wager.

In 1845, twenty-eight years old, an age by which the liveliest have usually declined into some conformity with the world, Thoreau, with a capital of something less than five pounds and a borrowed axe, walked forth into the woods by Walden Pond, and began his new experiment in life. He built himself a dwelling, and returned the axe, he says with characteristic and workman-like pride, sharper than when he borrowed it; he reclaimed a patch, where he cultivated beans, peas, potatoes, and sweet corn; he had his bread to bake, his farm to dig, and for the matter of six weeks in the summer he worked at surveying, carpentry, or some other of his numerous dexterities, for hire. For more than five years, this was all that he required to do for his support, and he had the winter and most of the summer at his entire

HENRY DAVID THOREAU

disposal. For six weeks of occupation, a little cooking and a little gentle hygienic gardening, the man, you may say, had as good as stolen his livelihood. Or we must rather allow that he had done far better; for the thief himself is continually and busily occupied; and even one born to inherit a million will have more calls upon his time than Thoreau. Well might he say, "What old people tell you you cannot do, you try and find you can." And how surprising is his conclusion: "I am convinced that *to maintain oneself on this earth is not a hardship, but a pastime*, if we will live simply and wisely; *as the pursuits of simpler nations are still the sports of the more artificial.*"

When he had enough of that kind of life, he showed the same simplicity in giving it up as in beginning it. There are some who could have done the one, but, vanity forbidding, not the other; and that is perhaps the story of the hermits; but Thoreau made no fetich of his own example, and did what he wanted squarely. And five years is long enough for an experiment and to prove the success of transcendental Yankeeism. It is not his frugality which is worthy of note; for, to begin with, that was inborn, and therefore inimitable by others who are differently constituted; and again, it was no new thing, but has often been equalled by poor Scotch students at the universities. The point is the sanity of his view of life, and the insight with which he recognized the position of money, and thought out for himself the problem of riches and a livelihood. Apart from his eccentricities, he had perceived, and was acting on, a truth of universal application. For money enters in two different characters into the scheme of life. A certain amount, varying with the number and empire of our desires, is a true necessary to each one of us in the present order of society; but beyond that amount, money is a commodity to be bought or not to be bought, a luxury in which we may either indulge or stint ourselves, like any other. And there are many luxuries that we may legitimately prefer to it, such as a grateful conscience, a country life, or the woman of our inclination. Trite, flat, and obvious as this conclusion may appear, we have only to look round us in society to see how scantily it has been recognized; and perhaps even ourselves, after a little reflection, may decide to spend a trifle less for money, and indulge ourselves a trifle more in the article of freedom.

III

"To have done anything by which you earned money merely," says Thoreau, "is to be" (have been, he means) "idle and worse." There are two passages in his letters, both, oddly enough, relating to firewood, which must be brought together to be rightly understood. So taken, they contain between them the marrow of all good sense on the subject of work in its relation to something broader than mere livelihood. Here is the first: "I suppose I have burned up a good-sized tree to-night—and for what? I settled with Mr. Tarbell for it the other day; but that wasn't the final settlement. I got off cheaply from him. At last one will say: 'Let us see, how much wood did you burn, sir?' And I shall shudder to think that the next question will be, 'What did you do while you were warm?'" Even after we have settled with Admetus in the person of Mr. Tarbell, there comes, you see, a further question. It is not enough to have earned our livelihood. Either the earning itself should have been serviceable to mankind, or something else must follow. To live is sometimes very difficult, but it is never meritorious in itself; and we must have a reason to allege to our own conscience why we should continue to exist upon this crowded earth. If Thoreau had simply dwelt in his house at Walden, a lover of trees, birds, and fishes, and the open air and virtue, a reader of wise books, an idle, selfish self-improver, he would have managed to cheat Admetus, but, to cling to metaphor, the devil would have had him in the end. Those who can avoid toil altogether and dwell in the Arcadia of private means, and even those who can, by abstinence, reduce the necessary amount of it to some six weeks a year, having the more liberty, have only the higher

HENRY DAVID THOREAU

moral obligation to be up and doing in the interest of man. The second passage is this: "There is a far more important and warming heat, commonly lost, which precedes the burning of the wood. It is the smoke of industry, which is incense. I had been so thoroughly warmed in body and spirit, that when at length my fuel was housed, I came near selling it to the ashman, as if I had extracted all its heat." Industry is, in itself and when properly chosen, delightful and profitable to the worker; and when your toil has been a pleasure, you have not, as Thoreau says, "earned money merely," but money, health, delight, and moral profit, all in one. "We must heap up a great pile of doing for a small diameter of being," he says in another place; and then exclaims, "How admirably the artist is made to accomplish his self-culture by devotion to his art!" We may escape uncongenial toil, only to devote ourselves to that which is congenial. It is only to transact some higher business that even Apollo dare play the truant from Admetus. We must all work for the sake of work; we must all work, as Thoreau says again, in any "absorbing pursuit—it does not much matter what, so it be honest"; but the most profitable work is that which combines into one continued effort the largest proportion of the powers and desires of a man's nature; that into which he will plunge with ardor, and from which he will desist with reluctance; in which he will know the weariness of fatigue, but not that of satiety; and which will be ever fresh, pleasing and stimulating to his taste. Such work holds a man together, braced at all points; it does not suffer him to doze or wander; it keeps him actively conscious of himself, yet raised among superior interests; it gives him the profit of industry with the pleasures of a pastime. This is what his art should be to the true artist, and that to a degree unknown in other and less intimate pursuits. For other professions stand apart from the human business of life; but an art has its seat at the centre of the artist's doings and sufferings, deals directly with his experiences, teaches him the lessons of his own fortunes and mishaps, and becomes a part of his biography. So says Goethe;

FAMILIAR STUDIES

"Spät erklingt was früh erklang;
Glück und Unglück wird Gesang."

Now Thoreau's art was literature; and it was one of which he had conceived most ambitiously. He loved and believed in good books. He said well, "Life is not habitually seen from any common platform so truly and unexaggerated as in the light of literature." But the literature he loved was of the heroic order. "Books, not which afford us a cowering enjoyment, but in which each thought is of unusual daring; such as an idle man cannot read, and a timid one would not be entertained by, which even make us dangerous to existing institutions—such I call good books." He did not think them easy to be read. "The heroic books," he says, "even if printed in the character of our mother-tongue, will always be in a language dead to degenerate times; and we must laboriously seek the meaning of each word and line, conjecturing a larger sense than common use permits out of what wisdom and valor and generosity we have." Nor does he suppose that such books are easily written. "Great prose, of equal elevation, commands our respect more than great verse," says he, "since it implies a more permanent and level height, a life more pervaded with the grandeur of the thought. The poet often only makes an irruption, like the Parthian, and is off again, shooting while he retreats; but the prose writer has conquered like a Roman and settled colonies." We may ask ourselves, almost with dismay, whether such works exist at all but in the imagination of the student. For the bulk of the best of books is apt to be made up with ballast; and those in which energy of thought is combined with any stateliness of utterance may be almost counted on the fingers. Looking round in English for a book that should answer Thoreau's two demands of a style like poetry and sense that shall be both original and inspiriting, I come to Milton's *Areopagitica*, and can name no other instance for the moment. Two things at least are plain: that if a man will condescend to nothing more commonplace in the way of reading, he must not look to have a large

HENRY DAVID THOREAU

ary; and that if he proposes himself to write in a similar
1, he will find his work cut out for him.
Thoreau composed seemingly while he walked, or at least
rcise and composition were with him intimately connected;
we are told that " the length of his walk uniformly made
length of his writing." He speaks in one place of
lainness and vigor, the ornaments of style," which is
her too paradoxical to be comprehensively true. In an-
er he remarks: " As for style of writing, if one has any-
1g to say it drops from him simply as a stone falls to the
und." We must conjecture a very large sense indeed for
phrase " if one has anything to say." When truth flows
m a man, fittingly clothed in style and without conscious
rt, it is because the effort has been made and the work
ctically completed before he sat down to write. It is only
of fulness of thinking that expression drops perfect like
ipe fruit; and when Thoreau wrote so nonchalantly at his
k, it was because he had been vigorously active during his
k. For neither clearness, compression, nor beauty of
guage, come to any living creature till after a busy and a
longed acquaintance with the subject on hand. Easy
ters are those who, like Walter Scott, choose to remain
tented with a less degree of perfection than is legitimately
hin the compass of their powers. We hear of Shakespeare
l his clean manuscript; but in face of the evidence of the
le itself and of the various editions of *Hamlet*, this merely
ves that Messrs. Hemming and Condell were unac-
unted with the common enough phenomenon called a fair
y. He who would recast a tragedy already given to the
rld must frequently and earnestly have revised details in
study. Thoreau himself, and in spite of his protesta-
s, is an instance of even extreme research in one direc-
; and his effort after heroic utterance is proved not only
the occasional finish, but by the determined exaggeration
his style. " I trust you realize what an exaggerator I
—that I lay myself out to exaggerate," he writes. And
in, hinting at the explanation: " Who that has heard a
in of music feared lest he should speak extravagantly

FAMILIAR STUDIES

any more forever?" And yet once more, in his essay on Carlyle, and this time with his meaning well in hand: "No truth, we think, was ever expressed but with this sort of emphasis, that for the time there seemed to be no other." Thus Thoreau was an exaggerative and a parabolical writer, not because he loved the literature of the East, but from a desire that people should understand and realize what he was writing. He was near the truth upon the general question; but in his own particular method, it appears to me, he wandered. Literature is not less a conventional art than painting or sculpture; and it is the least striking, as it is the most comprehensive of the three. To hear a strain of music, to see a beautiful woman, a river, a great city, or a starry night, is to make a man despair of his Lilliputian arts in language. Now, to gain that emphasis which seems denied to us by the very nature of the medium, the proper method of literature is by selection, which is a kind of negative exaggeration. It is the right of the literary artist, as Thoreau was on the point of seeing, to leave out whatever does not suit his purpose. Thus we extract the pure gold; and thus the well-written story of a noble life becomes, by its very omissions, more thrilling to the reader. But to go beyond this, like Thoreau, and to exaggerate directly, is to leave the saner classical tradition, and to put the reader on his guard. And when you write the whole for the half, you do not express your thought more forcibly, but only express a different thought which is not yours.

Thoreau's true subject was the pursuit of self-improvement combined with an unfriendly criticism of life as it goes on in our societies; it is there that he best displays the freshness and surprising trenchancy of his intellect; it is there that his style becomes plain and vigorous, and therefore, according to his own formula, ornamental. Yet he did not care to follow this vein singly, but must drop into it by the way in books of a different purport. *Walden, or Life in the Woods, A Week on the Concord and Merrimack Rivers, The Maine Woods,*—such are the titles he affects. He was probably reminded by his delicate critical perception that the

HENRY DAVID THOREAU

true business of literature is with narrative; in reasoned narrative, and there alone, that art enjoys all its advantages, and suffers least from its defects. Dry precept and disembodied disquisition, as they can only be read with an effort of abstraction, can never convey a perfectly complete or a perfectly natural impression. Truth, even in literature, must be clothed with flesh and blood, or it cannot tell its whole story to the reader. Hence the effect of anecdote on simple minds; and hence good biographies and works of high, imaginative art, are not only far more entertaining, but far more edifying, than books of theory or precept. Now Thoreau could not clothe his opinions in the garment of art, for that was not his talent; but he sought to gain the same elbow-room for himself, and to afford a similar relief to his readers, by mingling his thoughts with a record of experience.

Again, he was a lover of nature. The quality which we should call mystery in a painting, and which belongs so particularly to the aspect of the external world and to its influence upon our feelings, was one which he was never weary of attempting to reproduce in his books. The seeming significance of nature's appearances, their unchanging strangeness to the senses, and the thrilling response which they waken in the mind of man, continued to surprise and stimulate his spirits. It appeared to him, I think, that if we could only write near enough to the facts, and yet with no pedestrian calm, but ardently, we might transfer the glamour of reality direct upon our pages; and that, if it were once thus captured and expressed, a new and instructive relation might appear between men's thoughts and the phenomena of nature. This was the eagle that he pursued all his life long, like a schoolboy with a butterfly net. Hear him to a friend: " Let me suggest a theme for you—to state to yourself precisely and completely what that walk over the mountains amounted to for you, returning to this essay again and again until you are satisfied that all that was important in your experience is in it. Don't suppose that you can tell it precisely the first dozen times you try,

FAMILIAR STUDIES

but at 'em again; especially when, after a sufficient pause, you suspect that you are touching the heart or summit of the matter, reiterate your blows there, and account for the mountain to yourself. Not that the story need be long, but it will take a long while to make it short." Such was the method, not consistent for a man whose meanings were to " drop from him as a stone falls to the ground." Perhaps the most successful work that Thoreau ever accomplished in this direction is to be found in the passages relating to fish in the *Week*. These are remarkable for a vivid truth of impression and a happy suitability of language, not frequently surpassed.

Whatever Thoreau tried to do was tried in fair, square prose, with sentences solidly built, and no help from bastard rhythms. Moreover, there is a progression—I cannot call it a progress—in his work toward a more and more strictly prosaic level, until at last he sinks into the bathos of the prosy. Emerson mentions having once remarked to Thoreau: " Who would not like to write something which all can read, like *Robinson Crusoe?* and who does not see with regret that his page is not solid with a right materialistic treatment which delights everybody?" I must say in passing that it is not the right materialistic treatment which delights the world in *Robinson*, but the romantic and philosophic interest of the fable. The same treatment does quite the reverse of delighting us when it is applied, in *Colonel Jack*, to the management of a plantation. But I cannot help suspecting Thoreau to have been influenced either by this identical remark or by some other closely similar in meaning. He began to fall more and more into a detailed materialistic treatment; he went into the business doggedly, as one who should make a guide-book; he not only chronicled what had been important in his own experience, but whatever might have been important in the experience of anybody else; not only what had affected him, but all that he saw or heard. His ardor had grown less, or perhaps it was inconsistent with a right materialistic treatment to display such emotions as he felt; and, to complete the eventful change, he

HENRY DAVID THOREAU

chose, from a sense of moral dignity, to gut these later works of the saving quality of humor. He was not one of those authors who have learned, in his own words, "to leave out their dulness." He inflicts his full quantity upon the reader in such books as *Cape Cod*, or *The Yankee in Canada*. Of the latter he confessed that he had not managed to get much of himself into it. Heaven knows he had not, nor yet much of Canada, we may hope. "Nothing," he says somewhere, "can shock a brave man but dulness." Well, there are few spots more shocking to the brave than the pages of *The Yankee in Canada*.

There are but three books of his that will be read with much pleasure: the *Week*, *Walden*, and the collected letters. As to his poetry, Emerson's word shall suffice for us, it is so accurate and so prettily said: "The thyme and marjoram are not yet honey." In this, as in his prose, he relied greatly on the goodwill of the reader, and wrote throughout in faith. It was an exercise of faith to suppose that many would understand the sense of his best work, or that any could be exhilarated by the dreary chronicling of his worst. "But," as he says, "the gods do not hear any rude or discordant sound, as we learn from the echo; and I know that the nature toward which I launch these sounds is so rich that it will modulate anew and wonderfully improve my rudest strain."

IV

"What means the fact," he cries, "that a soul which has lost all hope for itself can inspire in another listening soul such an infinite confidence in it, even while it is expressing its despair?" The question is an echo and an illustration of the words last quoted; and it forms the key-note of his thoughts on friendship. No one else, to my knowledge, has spoken in so high and just a spirit of the kindly relations; and I doubt whether it be a drawback that these lessons should come from one in many ways so unfitted to be a teacher in this branch. The very coldness and egoism of his own intercourse gave him a clearer insight into the in-

FAMILIAR STUDIES

tellectual basis of our warm, mutual tolerations; and testimony to their worth comes with added force from one who was solitary and disobliging, and of whom a friend remarked, with equal wit and wisdom, "I love Henry, but I cannot like him."

He can hardly be persuaded to make any distinction between love and friendship; in such rarefied and freezing air, upon the mountain-tops of meditation, had he taught himself to breathe. He was, indeed, too accurate an observer not to have remarked that "there exists already a natural disinterestedness and liberality" between men and women; yet, he thought, "friendship is no respecter of sex." Perhaps there is a sense in which the words are true; but they were spoken in igorance; and perhaps we shall have put the matter most correctly, if we call love a foundation for a nearer and freer degree of friendship than can be possible without it. For there are delicacies, eternal between persons of the same sex, which are melted and disappear in the warmth of love.

To both, if they are to be right, he attributes the same nature and condition. "We are not what we are," says he, "nor do we treat or esteem each other for such, but for what we are capable of being." "A friend is one who incessantly pays us the compliment of expecting all the virtues from us, and who can appreciate them in us." "The friend asks no return but that his friend will religiously accept and wear and not disgrace his apotheosis of him." "It is the merit and preservation of friendship that it takes place on a level higher than the actual characters of the parties would seem to warrant." This is to put friendship on a pedestal indeed; and yet the root of the matter is there; and the last sentence, in particular, is like a light in a dark place, and makes many mysteries plain. We are different with different friends; yet if we look closely we shall find that every such relation reposes on some particular apotheosis of oneself; with each friend, although we could not distinguish it in words from any other, we have at least one special reputation to preserve: and it is thus that we run, when mortified,

HENRY DAVID THOREAU

to our friend or the woman that we love, not to hear ourselves called better, but to be better men in point of fact. We seek this society to flatter ourselves with our own good conduct. And hence any falsehood in the relation, any incomplete or perverted understanding, will spoil even the pleasure of these visits. Thus says Thoreau again: "Only lovers know the value of truth." And yet again: "They ask for words and deeds, when a true relation is word and deed."

But it follows that since they are neither of them so good as the other hopes, and each is, in a very honest manner, playing a part above his powers, such an intercourse must often be disappointing to both. "We may bid farewell sooner than complain," says Thoreau, "for our complaint is too well grounded to be uttered." "We have not so good a right to hate any as our friend."

> "It were treason to our love
> And a sin to God above,
> One iota to abate
> Of a pure, impartial hate."

Love is not blind, nor yet forgiving. "O yes, believe me," as the song says, "Love has eyes!" The nearer the intimacy, the more cuttingly do we feel the unworthiness of those we love; and because you love one, and would die for that love to-morrow, you have not forgiven, and you never will forgive, that friend's misconduct. If you want a person's faults, go to those who love him. They will not tell you, but they know. And herein lies the magnanimous courage of love, that it endures this knowledge without change.

It required a cold, distant personality like that of Thoreau, perhaps, to recognize and certainly to utter this truth; for a more human love makes it a point of honor not to acknowledge those faults of which it is most conscious. But his point of view is both high and dry. He has no illusions; he does not give way to love any more than to hatred, but preserves them both with care like valuable curiosities. A more bald-headed picture of life, if I may so express my-

FAMILIAR STUDIES

self, has seldom been presented. He is an egoist; he does not remember, or does not think it worth while to remark, that, in these near intimacies, we are ninety-nine times disappointed in our beggarly selves for once that we are disappointed in our friend; that it is we who seem most frequently undeserving of the love that unites us; and that it is by our friend's conduct that we are continually rebuked and yet strengthened for a fresh endeavor. Thoreau is dry, priggish, and selfish. It is profit he is after in these intimacies; moral profit, certainly, but still profit to himself. "If you will be the sort of friend I want," he remarks naïvely, "my education cannot dispense with your society." His education! as though a friend were a dictionary. And with all this, not one word about pleasure, or laughter, or kisses, or any quality of flesh and blood. It was not inappropriate, surely, that he had such close relations with the fish. We can understand the friend already quoted, when he cried: "As for taking his arm, I would as soon think of taking the arm of an elm-tree!"

As a matter of fact he experienced but a broken enjoyment in his intimacies. He says he has been perpetually on the brink of the sort of intercourse he wanted, and yet never completely attained it. And what else had he to expect when he would not, in a happy phrase of Carlyle's, "nestle down into it"? Truly, so it will be always if you only stroll in upon your friends as you might stroll in to see a cricket match; and even then not simply for the pleasure of the thing, but with some after-thought of self-improvement, as though you had come to the cricket match to bet. It was his theory that people saw each other too frequently, so that their curiosity was not properly whetted, nor had they anything fresh to communicate; but friendship must be something else than a society for mutual improvement—indeed, it must only be that by the way, and to some extent unconsciously; and if Thoreau had been a man instead of a manner of elm-tree, he would have felt that he saw his friends too seldom, and have reaped benefits unknown to his philosophy from a more sustained and easy intercourse. We might

HENRY DAVID THOREAU

remind him of his own words about love: "We should have no reserve; we should give the whole of ourselves to that business. But commonly men have not imagination enough to be thus employed about a human being, but must be coopering a barrel, forsooth." Ay, or reading Oriental philosophers. It is not the nature of the rival occupation, it is the fact that you suffer it to be a rival, that renders loving intimacy impossible. Nothing is given for nothing in this world; there can be no true love, even on your own side, without devotion; devotion is the exercise of love, by which it grows; but if you will give enough of that, if you will pay the price in a sufficient "amount of what you call life," why then, indeed, whether with wife or comrade, you may have months and even years of such easy, natural, pleasurable, and yet improving intercourse as shall make time a moment and kindness a delight.

The secret of his retirement lies not in misanthropy, of which he had no tincture, but part in his engrossing design of self-improvement and part in the real deficiencies of social intercourse. He was not so much difficult about his fellow human beings as he could not tolerate the terms of their association. He could take to a man for any genuine qualities, as we see by his admirable sketch of the Canadian woodcutter in *Walden;* but he would not consent, in his own words, to "feebly fabulate and paddle in the social slush." It seemed to him, I think, that society is precisely the reverse of friendship, in that it takes place on a lower level than the characters of any of the parties would warrant us to expect. The society talk of even the most brilliant man is of greatly less account than what you will get from him in (as the French say) a little committee. And Thoreau wanted geniality; he had not enough of the superficial, even at command; he could not swoop into a parlor and, in the naval phrase, "cut out" a human being from that dreary port; nor had he inclination for the task. I suspect he loved books and nature as well and near as warmly as he loved his fellow-creatures,—a melancholy, lean degeneration of the human character.

FAMILIAR STUDIES

"As for the dispute about solitude and society," he thus sums up: "Any comparison is impertinent. It is an idling down on the plain at the base of the mountain instead of climbing steadily to its top. Of course you will be glad of all the society you can get to go up with? Will you go to glory with me? is the burden of the song. It is not that we love to be alone, but that we love to soar, and when we do soar the company grows thinner and thinner till there is none at all. It is either the tribune on the plain, a sermon on the mount, or a very private ecstasy still higher up. Use all the society that will abet you." But surely it is no very extravagant opinion that it is better to give than to receive, to serve than to use our companions; and above all, where there is no question of service upon either side, that it is good to enjoy their company like a natural man. It is curious and in some ways dispiriting that a writer may be always best corrected out of his own mouth; and so, to conclude, here is another passage from Thoreau which seems aimed directly at himself: "Do not be too moral; you may cheat yourself out of much life so. . . . *All fables, indeed, have their morals; but the innocent enjoy the story.*"

"The only obligation," says he, "which I have a right to assume is to do at any time what I think right." "Why should we ever go abroad, even across the way, to ask a neighbor's advice?" "There is a nearer neighbor within, who is incessantly telling us how we should behave. *But we wait for the neighbor without to tell us of some false, easier way.*" "The greater part of what my neighbors call good I believe in my soul to be bad." To be what we are, and to become what we are capable of becoming, is the only end of life. It is "when we fall behind ourselves" that "we are cursed with duties and the neglect of duties." "I love the wild," he says, "not less than the good." And again: "The life of a good man will hardly improve us more than the life of a freebooter, for the inevitable laws appear as plainly in

HENRY DAVID THOREAU

the infringement as in the observance, and " (mark this) " *our lives are sustained by a nearly equal expense of virtue of some kind.*" Even although he were a prig, it will be owned he could announce a startling doctrine. " As for doing good," he writes elsewhere, " that is one of the professions that are full. Moreover, I have tried it fairly, and, strange as it may seem, am satisfied that it does not agree with my constitution. Probably I should not conscientiously and deliberately forsake my particular calling to do the good which society demands of me, to save the universe from annihilation; and I believe that a like but infinitely greater steadfastness elsewhere is all that now preserves it. If you should ever be betrayed into any of these philanthropies, do not let your left hand know what your right hand does, for it is not worth knowing." Elsewhere he returns upon the subject, and explains his meaning thus: " If I ever *did* a man any good in their sense, of course it was something exceptional and insignificant compared with the good or evil I am constantly doing by being what I am."

There is a rude nobility, like that of a barbarian king, in this unshaken confidence in himself and indifference to the wants, thoughts, or sufferings of others. In his whole works I find no trace of pity. This was partly the result of theory, for he held the world too mysterious to be criticised, and asks conclusively: "What right have I to grieve who have not ceased to wonder?" But it sprang still more from constitutional indifference and superiority; and he grew up healthy, composed, and unconscious from among life's horrors, like a green bay-tree from a field of battle. It was from this lack in himself that he failed to do justice to the spirit of Christ; for while he could glean more meaning from individual precepts than any score of Christians, yet he conceived life in such a different hope, and viewed it with such contrary emotions, that the sense and purport of the doctrine as a whole seems to have passed him by or left him unimpressed. He could understand the idealism of the Christian view, but he was himself so unaffectedly unhuman that he did not recognize the human intention and essence of that

FAMILIAR STUDIES

teaching. Hence he complained that Christ did not leave us a rule that was proper and sufficient for this world, not having conceived the nature of the rule that was laid down; for things of that character that are sufficiently unacceptable become positively non-existent to the mind. But perhaps we shall best appreciate the defect in Thoreau by seeing it supplied in the case of Whitman. For the one, I feel confident, is the disciple of the other; it is what Thoreau clearly whispered that Whitman so uproariously bawls; it is the same doctrine, but with how immense a difference! the same argument, but used to what a new conclusion! Thoreau had plenty of humor until he tutored himself out of it, and so forfeited that best birthright of a sensible man; Whitman, in that respect, seems to have been sent into the world naked and unashamed; and yet by a strange consummation, it is the theory of the former that is arid, abstract, and claustral. Of these two philosophies so nearly identical at bottom, the one pursues Self-improvement—a churlish, mangy dog; the other is up with the morning, in the best of health, and following the nymph Happiness, buxom, blithe, and debonair. Happiness, at least, is not solitary; it joys to communicate; it loves others, for it depends on them for its existence; it sanctions and encourages to all delights that are not unkind in themselves; if it lived to a thousand, it would not make excision of a single humorous passage; and while the self-improver dwindles toward the prig, and, if he be not of an excellent constitution, may even grow deformed into an Obermann, the very name and appearance of a happy man breathe of good-nature, and help the rest of us to live.

In the case of Thoreau, so great a show of doctrine demands some outcome in the field of action. If nothing were to be done but build a shanty beside Walden Pond, we have heard altogether too much of these declarations of independence. That the man wrote some books is nothing to the purpose, for the same has been done in a suburban villa. That he kept himself happy is perhaps a sufficient excuse, but it is disappointing to the reader. We may be unjust, but when a man despises commerce and philanthropy alike,

HENRY DAVID THOREAU

and has views of good so soaring that he must take himself apart from mankind for their cultivation, we will not be content without some striking act. It was not Thoreau's fault if he were not martyred; had the occasion come, he would have made a noble ending. As it is, he did once seek to interfere in the world's course; he made one practical appearance on the stage of affairs; and a strange one it was, and strangely characteristic of the nobility and the eccentricity of the man. It was forced on him by his calm but radical opposition to negro slavery. "Voting for the right is doing nothing for it," he saw; "it is only expressing to men feebly your desire that it should prevail." For his part, he would not "for an instant recognize that political organization for *his* government which is the *slave's* government also." "I do not hesitate to say," he adds, "that those who call themselves Abolitionists should at once effectually withdraw their support, both in person and property, from the government of Massachusetts." That is what he did: in 1843 he ceased to pay the poll-tax. The highway-tax he paid, for he said he was as desirous to be a good neighbor as to be a bad subject; but no more poll-tax to the State of Massachusetts. Thoreau had now seceded, and was a polity unto himself; or, as he explains it with admirable sense, "In fact, I quietly declare war with the State after my fashion, though I will still make what use and get what advantage of her I can, as is usual in such cases." He was put in prison; but that was a part of his design. "Under a government which imprisons any unjustly, the true place for a just man is also a prison. I know this well, that if one thousand, if one hundred, if ten men whom I could name —ay, if *one* HONEST man, in this State of Massachusetts, *ceasing to hold slaves*, were actually to withdraw from this copartnership, and be locked up in the county jail therefor, it would be the abolition of slavery in America. For it matters not how small the beginning may seem to be; what is once well done is done forever." Such was his theory of civil disobedience.

And the upshot? A friend paid the tax for him; con-

FAMILIAR STUDIES

tinued year by year to pay it in the sequel; and Thoreau was free to walk the woods unmolested. It was a *fiasco*, but to me it does not seem laughable; even those who joined in the laughter at the moment would be insensibly affected by this quaint instance of a good man's horror for injustice. We may compute the worth of that one night's imprisonment as outweighing half a hundred voters at some subsequent election: and if Thoreau had possessed as great a power of persuasion as (let us say) Falstaff, if he had counted a party however small, if his example had been followed by a hundred or by thirty of his fellows, I cannot but believe it would have greatly precipitated the era of freedom and justice. We feel the misdeeds of our country with so little fervor, for we are not witnesses to the suffering they cause; but when we see them wake in active horror in our fellow-man, when we see a neighbor prefer to lie in prison rather than be so much as passively implicated in their perpetration, even the dullest of us will begin to realize them with a quicker pulse.

Not far from twenty years later, when Captain John Brown was taken at Harper's Ferry, Thoreau was the first to come forward in his defence. The committees wrote to him unanimously that his action was premature. "I did not send to you for advice," said he, " but to announce that I was to speak." I have used the word " defence "; in truth he did not seek to defend him, even declared it would be better for the good cause that he should die; but he praised his action as I think Brown would have liked to hear it praised.

Thus this singularly eccentric and independent mind, wedded to a character of so much strength, singleness, and purity, pursued its own path of self-improvement for more than half a century, part gymnosophist, part backwoodsman; and thus did it come twice, though in a subaltern attitude, into the field of political history.

NOTE.—For many facts in the above essay, among which I may mention the incident of the squirrel, I am indebted to *Thoreau: His Life and Aims*, by J. A. Page, or, as is well known, Dr. Japp.

YOSHIDA-TORAJIRO

THE name at the head of this page is probably unknown to the English reader, and yet I think it should become a household word like that of Garibaldi or John Brown. Some day soon, we may expect to hear more fully the details of Yoshida's history, and the degree of his influence in the transformation of Japan; even now there must be Englishmen acquainted with the subject, and perhaps the appearance of this sketch may elicit something more complete and exact. I wish to say that I am not, rightly speaking, the author of the present paper: I tell the story on the authority of an intelligent Japanese gentleman, Mr. Taiso Masaki; who told it me with an emotion that does honor to his heart; and though I have taken some pains, and sent my notes to him to be corrected, this can be no more than an imperfect outline.

Yoshida-Torajiro was son to the hereditary military instructor of the house of Choshu. The name you are to pronounce with an equality of accent on the different syllables, almost as in French, the vowels as in Italian, but the consonants in the English manner—except the *j*, which has the French sound, or, as it has been cleverly proposed to write it, the sound of *zh*. Yoshida was very learned in Chinese letters, or, as we might say, in the classics, and in his father's subject; fortification was among his favorite studies, and he was a poet from his boyhood. He was born to a lively and intelligent patriotism; the condition of Japan was his great concern; and while he projected a better future, he lost no opportunity of improving his knowledge of her present state. With this end he was continually travelling in his youth, going on foot and sometimes with three days' provision on his back, in the brave, self-helpful manner of all heroes. He kept a full diary while he was thus upon his journeys, but

FAMILIAR STUDIES

it is feared that these notes have been destroyed. If their value were in any respect such as we have reason to expect from the man's character, this would be a loss not easy to exaggerate. It is still wonderful to the Japanese how far he contrived to push these explorations; a cultured gentleman of that land and period would leave a complimentary poem wherever he had been hospitably entertained; and a friend of Mr. Masaki, who was likewise a great wanderer, has found such traces of Yoshida's passage in very remote regions of Japan.

Politics is perhaps the only profession for which no preparation is thought necessary; but Yoshida considered otherwise, and he studied the miseries of his fellow-countrymen with as much attention and research as though he had been going to write a book instead of merely to propose a remedy. To a man of his intensity and singleness, there is no question but that this survey was melancholy in the extreme. His dissatisfaction is proved by the eagerness with which he threw himself into the cause of reform; and what would have discouraged another braced Yoshida for his task. As he professed the theory of arms, it was firstly the defences of Japan that occupied his mind. The external feebleness of that country was then illustrated by the manners of overriding barbarians, and the visits of big barbarian war ships: she was a country beleaguered. Thus the patriotism of Yoshida took a form which may be said to have defeated itself: he had it upon him to keep out these all-powerful foreigners, whom it is now one of his chief merits to have helped to introduce; but a man who follows his own virtuous heart will be always found in the end to have been fighting for the best. One thing leads naturally to another in an awakened mind, and that with an upward progress from effect to cause. The power and knowledge of these foreigners were things inseparable; by envying them their military strength, Yoshida came to envy them their culture; from the desire to equal them in the first, sprang his desire to share with them in the second; and thus he is found treating in the same book of a new scheme to strengthen the defences

YOSHIDA-TORAJIRO

of Kioto and of the establishment, in the same city, of a university of foreign teachers. He hoped, perhaps, to get the good of other lands without their evil; to enable Japan to profit by the knowledge of the barbarians, and still keep her inviolate with her own arts and virtues. But whatever was the precise nature of his hope, the means by which it was to be accomplished were both difficult and obvious. Some one with eyes and understanding must break through the official cordon, escape into the new world, and study this other civilization on the spot. And who could be better suited for the business? It was not without danger, but he was without fear. It needed preparation and insight; and what had he done since he was a child but prepare himself with the best culture of Japan, and acquire in his excursions the power and habit of observing?

He was but twenty-two, and already all this was clear in his mind, when news reached Choshu that Commodore Perry was lying near to Yeddo. Here, then, was the patriot's opportunity. Among the Samurai of Choshu, and in particular among the councillors of the Daimio, his general culture, his views, which the enlightened were eager to accept, and, above all, the prophetic charm, the radiant persuasion of the man, had gained him many and sincere disciples. He had thus a strong influence at the Provincial Court; and so he obtained leave to quit the district, and, by way of a pretext, a privilege to follow his profession in Yeddo. Thither he hurried, and arrived in time to be too late: Perry had weighed anchor, and his sails had vanished from the waters of Japan. But Yoshida, having put his hand to the plough, was not the man to go back; he had entered upon this business, and, please God, he would carry it through; and so he gave up his professional career and remained in Yeddo to be at hand against the next opportunity. By this behavior he put himself into an attitude toward his superior, the Daimio of Choshu, which I cannot thoroughly explain. Certainly, he became a *Ronyin*, a broken man, a feudal outlaw; certainly he was liable to be arrested if he set foot upon his native province; yet I am cautioned that " he did not really break his allegiance," but only so far separated himself as that the prince could no longer be held accountable for his late vassal's conduct. There is some nicety of feudal custom here that escapes my comprehension.

In Yeddo, with this nondescript political status, and cut off from any means of livelihood, he was joyfully supported by those who sympathized with his design. One was Sákuma-Shozan, hereditary retainer of one of the Shogun's councillors, and from him he got more than money or than money's worth. A steady, respectable man, with an eye to the world's opinion, Sákuma was one of those who, if they cannot do great deeds in their own person, have yet an ardor of admiration for those who can, that recommends them to the gratitude of history. They aid and abet greatness more, perhaps, than we imagine. One thinks of them in connection with Nicodemus, who visited our Lord by night. And Sákuma was in a position to help Yoshida more practically than by simple countenance; for he could read Dutch, and was eager to communicate what he knew.

While the young Ronyin thus lay studying in Yeddo, news came of a Russian ship at Nagasaki. No time was to be lost. Sákuma contributed "a long copy of encouraging verses"; and off set Yoshida on foot for Nagasaki. His way lay through his own province of Choshu; but, as the highroad to the south lay apart from the capital, he was able to avoid arrest. He supported himself, like a *trouvère*, by his proficiency in verse. He carried his works along with him, to serve as an introduction. When he reached a town he would inquire for the house of any one celebrated for swordsmanship, or poetry, or some of the other acknowledged forms of culture; and there, on giving a taste of his skill, he would be received and entertained, and leave behind him, when he went away, a compliment in verse. Thus he travelled through the Middle Ages on his voyage of discovery into the nineteenth century. When he reached Nagasaki he was once more too late. The Russians were gone. But he made a profit on his journey in spite of fate, and stayed awhile to pick up scraps of knowledge from the Dutch interpreters—

YOSHIDA-TORAJIRO

a low class of men, but one that had opportunities; and then, still full of purpose, returned to Yeddo on foot, as he had come. It was not only his youth and courage that supported him under these successive disappointments, but the continual affluence of new disciples. The man had the tenacity of a Bruce or a Columbus, with a pliability that was all his own. He did not fight for what the world would call success; but for "the wages of going on." Check him off in a dozen directions, he would find another outlet and break forth. He missed one vessel after another, and the main work still halted; but so long as he had a single Japanese to enlighten and prepare for the better future, he could still feel that he was working for Japan. Now, he had scarce returned from Nagasaki, when he was sought out by a new inquirer, the most promising of all. This was a common soldier, of the Hemming class, a dyer by birth, who had heard vaguely * of Yoshida's movements, and had become filled with wonder as to their design. This was a far different inquirer from Sákuma-Shozan, or the councillors of the Daimio of Choshu. This was no two-sworded gentleman, but the common stuff of the country, born in low traditions and unimproved by books; and yet that influence, that radiant persuasion that never failed Yoshida in any circumstance of his short life, enchanted, enthralled, and converted the common soldier, as it had done already with the elegant and learned. The man instantly burned up into a true enthusiasm; his mind had been only waiting for a teacher; he grasped in a moment the profit of these new ideas; he, too, would go to foreign, outlandish parts, and bring back the knowledge that was to strengthen and renew Japan; and in the meantime, that he might be the better prepared, Yoshida set himself to teach, and he to learn, the Chinese literature. It is an episode most

* Yoshida, when on his way to Nagasaki, met the soldier and talked with him by the roadside; they then parted, but the soldier was so much struck by the words he heard, that on Yoshida's return he sought him out and declared his intention of devoting his life to the good cause. I venture, in the absence of the writer, to insert this correction, having been present when the story was told by Mr. Masaki.—F. J. And I, there being none to settle the difference, must reproduce both versions. —R. L. S.

FAMILIAR STUDIES

honorable to Yoshida, and yet more honorable still to the soldier, and to the capacity and virtue of the common people of Japan.

And now, at length, Commodore Perry returned to Simoda. Friends crowded round Yoshida with help, counsels, and encouragement. One presented him with a great sword, three feet long and very heavy, which, in the exultation of the hour, he swore to carry throughout all his wanderings, and to bring back—a far-travelled weapon—to Japan. A long letter was prepared in Chinese for the American officers; it was revised and corrected by Sákuma, and signed by Yoshida, under the name of Urinaki-Manji, and by the soldier under that of Ichigi-Koda. Yoshida had supplied himself with a profusion of materials for writing; his dress was literally stuffed with paper which was to come back again enriched with his observations, and make a great and happy kingdom of Japan. Thus equipped, this pair of emigrants set forward on foot from Yeddo, and reached Simoda about nightfall. At no period within history can travel have presented to any European creature the same face of awe and terror as to these courageous Japanese. The descent of Ulysses into hell is a parallel more near the case than the boldest expedition in the Polar circles. For their act was unprecedented; it was criminal; and it was to take them beyond the pale of humanity into a land of devils. It is not to be wondered at if they were thrilled by the thought of their unusual situation; and perhaps the soldier gave utterance to the sentiment of both when he sang, " in Chinese singing " (so that we see he had already profited by his lessons), these two appropriate verse:

"We do not know where we are to sleep to-night,
In a thousand miles of desert where we can see no human smoke."

In a little temple, hard by the sea-shore, they lay down to repose; sleep overtook them as they lay; and when they awoke, "the east was already white" for their last morning in Japan. They seized a fisherman's boat and rowed out—Perry lying far to sea because of the two tides. Their very

YOSHIDA-TORAJIRO

manner of boarding was significant of determination; for they had no sooner caught hold upon the ship than they kicked away their boat to make return impossible. And now you would have thought that all was over. But the Commodore was already in treaty with the Shogun's Government; it was one of the stipulations that no Japanese was to be aided in escaping from Japan; and Yoshida and his followers were handed over as prisoners to the authorities at Simoda. That night he who had been to explore the secrets of the barbarian slept, if he might sleep at all, in a cell too short for lying down at full length, and too low for standing upright. There are some disappointments too great for commentary.

Sákuma, implicated by his handwriting, was sent into his own province in confinement, from which he was soon released. Yoshida and the soldier suffered a long and miserable period of captivity, and the latter, indeed, died while yet in prison, of a skin disease. But such a spirit as that of Yoshida-Torajiro is not easily made or kept a captive; and that which cannot be broken by misfortune you shall seek in vain to confined in a Bastille. He was indefatigably active, writing reports to Government and treatises for dissemination. These latter were contraband; and yet he found no difficulty in their distribution, for he always had the jailer on his side. It was in vain that they kept changing him from one prison to another; Government by that plan only hastened the spread of new ideas; for Yoshida had only to arrive to make a convert. Thus, though he himself was laid by the heels, he confirmed and extended his party in the State.

At last, after many lesser transferences, he was given over from the prisons of the Shogun to those of his own superior, the Daimio of Choshu. I conceive it possible that he may then have served out his time for the attempt to leave Japan, and was now resigned to the provincial Government on a lesser count, as a Ronyin or feudal rebel. But, however that may be, the change was of great importance to Yoshida; for by the influence of his admirers in the Daimio's council, he was allowed the privilege, underhand, of dwelling in his

FAMILIAR STUDIES

own house. And there, as well to keep up communication with his fellow-reformers as to pursue his work of education, he received boys to teach. It must not be supposed that he was free; he was too marked a man for that; he was probably assigned to some small circle, and lived, as we should say, under police surveillance; but to him, who had done so much from under lock and key, this would seem a large and profitable liberty.

It was at this period that Mr. Masaki was brought into personal contact with Yoshida; and hence, through the eyes of a boy of thirteen, we get one good look at the character and habits of the hero. He was ugly and laughably disfigured with the small-pox; and while nature had been so niggardly with him from the first, his personal habits were even sluttish. His clothes were wretched; when he ate or washed he wiped his hands upon his sleeves; and as his hair was not tied more than once in the two months, it was often disgusting to behold. With such a picture, it is easy to believe that he never married. A good teacher, gentle in act, although violent and abusive in speech, his lessons were apt to go over the heads of his scholars, and to leave them gaping, or more often laughing. Such was his passion for study that he even grudged himself natural repose; and when he grew drowsy over his books he would, if it was summer, put mosquitoes up his sleeve; and, if it was winter, take off his shoes and run barefoot on the snow. His handwriting was exceptionally villainous; poet though he was, he had no taste for what was elegant; and in a country where to write beautifully was not the mark of a scrivener but an admired accomplishment for gentlemen, he suffered his letters to be jolted out of him by the press of matter and the heat of his convictions. He would not tolerate even the appearance of a bribe; for bribery lay at the root of much that was evil in Japan, as well as in countries nearer home; and once when a merchant brought him his son to educate, and added, as was customary,* a little private sweetener, Yoshida dashed

* I understood that the merchant was endeavoring surreptitiously to obtain for his son instruction to which he was not entitled.—F. J.

YOSHIDA-TORAJIRO

the money in the giver's face, and launched into such an outbreak of indignation as made the matter public in the school. He was still, when Masaki knew him, much weakened by his hardships in prison; and the presentation sword, three feet long, was too heavy for him to wear without distress; yet he would always gird it on when he went to dig in his garden. That is a touch which qualifies the man. A weaker nature would have shrunk from the sight of what only commemorated a failure. But he was of Thoreau's mind, that if you can " make your failure tragical by courage, it will not differ from success." He could look back without confusion to his enthusiastic promise. If events had been contrary, and he found himself unable to carry out that purpose—well, there was but the more reason to be brave and constant in another; if he could not carry the sword into barbarian lands, it should at least be witness to a life spent entirely for Japan.

This is the sight we have of him as he appeared to schoolboys, but not related in the schoolboy spirit. A man so careless of the graces must be out of court with boys and women. And, indeed, as we have all been more or less to school, it will astonish no one that Yoshida was regarded by his scholars as a laughing-stock. The schoolboy has a keen sense of humor. Heroes he learns to understand and to admire in books; but he is not forward to recognize the heroic under the traits of any contemporary man, and least of all in a brawling, dirty, and eccentric teacher. But as the years went by, and the scholars of Yoshida continued in vain to look around them for the abstractly perfect, and began more and more to understand the drift of his instructions, they learned to look back upon their comic schoolmaster as upon the noblest of mankind.

The last act of this brief and full existence was already near at hand. Some of his work was done; for already there had been Dutch teachers admitted into Nagasaki, and the country at large was keen for the new learning. But though the renaissance had begun, it was impeded and dangerously threatened by the power of the Shogun. His minister—the same who was afterward assassinated in the snow in

FAMILIAR STUDIES

the very midst of his bodyguard—not only held back pupils from going to the Dutchmen, but by spies and detectives, by imprisonment and death, kept thinning out of Japan the most intelligent and active spirits. It is the old story of a power upon its last legs—learning to the Bastile, and courage to the block; when there are none left but sheep and donkeys, the State will have been saved. But a man must not think to cope with a revolution; nor a minister, however fortified with guards, to hold in check a country that had given birth to such men as Yoshida and his soldier follower. The violence of the ministerial Tarquin only served to direct attention to the illegality of his master's rule; and people began to turn their allegiance from Yeddo and the Shogun to the long-forgotten Mikado, in his seclusion at Kioto. At this juncture, whether in consequence or not, the relations between these two rulers became strained; and the Shogun's minister set forth for Kioto to put another affront upon the rightful sovereign. The circumstance was well fitted to precipitate events. It was a piece of religion to defend the Mikado; it was a plain piece of political righteousness to oppose a tyrannical and bloody usurpation. To Yoshida the moment for action seemed to have arrived. He was himself still confined in Choshu. Nothing was free but his intelligence; but with that he sharpened a sword for the Shogun's minister. A party of his followers were to waylay the tyrant at a village on the Yeddo and Kioto road, present him with a petition, and put him to the sword. But Yoshida and his friends were closely observed; and the too great expedition of two of the conspirators, a boy of eighteen and his brother, wakened the suspicion of the authorities, and led to a full discovery of the plot and the arrest of all who were concerned.

In Yeddo, to which he was taken, Yoshida was thrown again into a strict confinement. But he was not left destitute of sympathy in this last hour of trial. In the next cell lay one Kusákabé, a reformer from the southern highlands of Satzuma. They were in prison for different plots indeed, but for the same intention; they shared the same beliefs and

YOSHIDA-TORAJIRO

the same aspirations for Japan; many and long were the conversations they held through the prison wall, and dear was the sympathy that soon united them. It fell first to the lot of Kusákabé to pass before the judges; and when sentence had been pronounced he was led toward the place of death below Yoshida's window. To turn the head would have been to implicate his fellow-prisoner; but he threw him a look from his eye, and bade him farewell in a loud voice, with these two Chinese verses:—

"It is better to be a crystal and be broken,
Than to remain perfect like a tile upon the housetop."

So Kusákabé, from the highlands of Satzuma, passed out of the theatre of this world. His death was like an antique worthy's.

A little after, and Yoshida too must appear before the Court. His last scene was of a piece with his career, and fitly crowned it. He seized on the opportunity of a public audience, confessed and gloried in his design, and, reading his auditors a lesson in the history of their country, told at length the illegality of the Shogun's power and the crimes by which its exercise was sullied. So, having said his say for once, he was led forth and executed, thirty-one years old.

A military engineer, a bold traveller (at least in wish), a poet, a patriot, a schoolmaster, a friend to learning, a martyr to reform,—there are not many men, dying at seventy, who have served their country in such various characters. He was not only wise and provident in thought, but surely one of the fieriest of heroes in execution. It is hard to say which is most remarkable—his capacity for command, which subdued his very jailers; his hot, unflagging zeal; or his stubborn superiority to defeat. He failed in each particular enterprise that he attempted; and yet we have only to look at his country to see how complete has been his general success. His friends and pupils made the majority of leaders in that final Revolution, now some twelve years old; and many of them are, or were until the other day,

FAMILIAR STUDIES

high placed among the rulers of Japan. And when we see all round us these brisk intelligent students, with their strange foreign air, we should never forget how Yoshida marched afoot from Choshu to Yeddo, and from Yeddo to Nagasaki, and from Nagasaki back again to Yeddo; how he boarded the American ship, his dress stuffed with writing material; nor how he languished in prison, and finally gave his death, as he had formerly given all his life and strength and leisure, to gain for his native land that very benefit which she now enjoys so largely. It is better to be Yoshida and perish than to be only Sákuma and yet save the hide. Kusákabé, of Satzuma, has said the word: it is better to be a crystal and be broken.

I must add a word; for I hope the reader will not fail to perceive that this is as much the story of a heroic people as that of a heroic man. It is not enough to remember Yoshida; we must not forget the common soldier, nor Kusákabé, nor the boy of eighteen, Nomura, of Choshu, whose eagerness betrayed the plot. It is exhilarating to have lived in the same days with these great-hearted gentlemen. Only a few miles from us, to speak by the proportion of the universe, while I was droning over my lessons, Yoshida was goading himself to be wakeful with the stings of the mosquito; and, while you were grudging a penny income tax, Kusákabé was stepping to death with a noble sentence on his lips.

FRANÇOIS VILLON, STUDENT, POET, AND HOUSEBREAKER

PERHAPS one of the most curious revolutions in literary history is the sudden bull's-eye light cast by M. Longnon on the obscure existence of François Villon.* His book is not remarkable merely as a chapter of biography exhumed after four centuries. To readers of the poet it will recall, with a flavor of satire, that characteristic passage in which he bequeaths his spectacles—with a humorous reservation of the case—to the hospital for blind paupers known as the Fifteen-Score. Thus equipped, let the blind paupers go and separate the good from the bad in the cemetery of the Innocents! For his own part the poet can see no distinction. Much have the dead people made of their advantages. What does it matter now that they have lain in state beds and nourished portly bodies upon cakes and cream! Here they all lie, to be trodden in the mud; the large estate and the small, sounding virtue and adroit or powerful vice, in very much the same condition; and a bishop not to be distinguished from a lamplighter with even the strongest spectacles.

Such was Villon's cynical philosophy. Four hundred years after his death, when surely all danger might be considered at an end, a pair of critical spectacles have been applied to his own remains; and though he left behind him a sufficiently ragged reputation from the first, it is only after these four hundred years that his delinquencies have been finally tracked home, and we can assign him to his proper place among the good or wicked. It is a staggering thought, and one that affords a fine figure of the imperishability of men's acts, that the stealth of the private inquiry office can be carried so far back into the dead and dusty past.

* *Étude Biographique sur François Villon.* Paris: H. Menu.

FAMILIAR STUDIES

We are not so soon quit of our concerns as Villon fancied. In the extreme of dissolution, when not so much as a man's name is remembered, when his dust is scattered to the four winds, and perhaps the very grave and the very graveyard where he was laid to rest have been forgotten, desecrated, and buried under populous towns,—even in this extreme let an antiquary fall across a sheet of manuscript, and the name will be recalled, the old infamy will pop out into daylight like a toad out of a fissure in the rock, and the shadow of the shade of what was once a man will be heartily pilloried by his descendants. A little while ago and Villon was almost totally forgotten; then he was revived for the sake of his verses; and now he is being revived with a vengeance in the detection of his misdemeanors. How unsubstantial is this projection of a man's existence, which can lie in abeyance for centuries and then be brushed up again and set forth for the consideration of posterity by a few dips in an antiquary's inkpot! This precarious tenure of fame goes a long way to justify those (and they are not few) who prefer cakes and cream in the immediate present.

A WILD YOUTH

François de Montcorbier, *alias* François des Loges, *alias* François Villon, *alias* Michel Mouton, Master of Arts in the University of Paris, was born in that city in the summer of 1431. It was a memorable year for France on other and higher considerations. A great-hearted girl and a poor-hearted boy made, the one her last, the other his first appearance on the public stage of that unhappy country. On the 30th of May the ashes of Joan of Arc were thrown into the Seine, and on the 2d of December our Henry Sixth made his Joyous Entry dismally enough into disaffected and depopulating Paris. Sword and fire still ravaged the open country. On a single April Saturday twelve hundred persons, besides children, made their escape out of the starving capital. The hangman, as is not uninteresting to note in connection with Master Francis, was kept hard at work in 1431; on the last of April and on the 4th of May alone,

FRANÇOIS VILLON

sixty-two bandits swung from Paris gibbets.* A more confused or troublous time it would have been difficult to select for a start in life. Not even a man's nationality was certain; for the people of Paris there was no such thing as a Frenchman. The English were the English indeed, but the French were only the Armagnacs, whom, with Joan of Arc at their head, they had beaten back from under their ramparts not two years before. Such public sentiment as they had centred about their dear Duke of Burgundy, and the dear Duke had no more urgent business than to keep out of their neighborhood. . . . At least, and whether he liked it or not, our disreputable troubadour was tubbed and swaddled as a subject of the English crown.

We hear nothing of Villon's father except that he was poor and of mean extraction. His mother was given piously, which does not imply very much in an old Frenchwoman, and quite uneducated. He had an uncle, a monk in an abbey at Angers, who must have prospered beyond the family average, and was reported to be worth five or six hundred crowns. Of this uncle and his money-box the reader will hear once more. In 1448 Francis became a student of the University of Paris; in 1450 he took the degree of Bachelor, and in 1452 that of Master of Arts. His *bourse*, or the sum paid weekly for his board, was of the amount of two sous. Now two sous was about the price of a pound of salt butter in the bad times of 1417; it was the price of half-a-pound in the worse times of 1419; and in 1444, just four years before Villon joined the University, it seems to have been taken as the average wage for a day's manual labor.† In short, it cannot have been a very profuse allowance to keep a sharp-set lad in breakfast and supper for seven mortal days; and Villon's share of the cakes and pastry and general good cheer, to which he is never weary of referring, must have been slender from the first.

The educational arrangements of the University of Paris were, to our way of thinking, somewhat incomplete. Worldly

Bourgeois de Paris, ed. Panthéon, pp. 688, 689.
† *Bourgeois*, pp. 627, 636, and 725.

and monkish elements were presented in a curious confusion, which the youth might disentangle for himself. If he had an opportunity, on the one hand, of acquiring much hair-drawn divinity and a taste for formal disputation, he was put in the way of much gross and flaunting vice upon the other. The lecture room of a scholastic doctor was sometimes under the same roof with establishments of a very different and peculiarly unedifying order. The students had extraordinary privileges, which by all accounts they abused extraordinarily. And, while some condemned themselves to an almost sepulchral regularity and seclusion, others fled the schools, swaggered in the street " with their thumbs in their girdle," passed the night in riot, and behaved themselves as the worthy forerunners of Jehan Frollo in the romance of *Notre Dame de Paris.* Villon tells us himself that he was among the truants, but we hardly needed his avowal. The burlesque erudition in which he sometimes indulged implies no more than the merest smattering of knowledge; whereas his acquaintance with blackguard haunts and industries could only have been acquired by early and consistent impiety and idleness. He passed his degrees, it is true; but some of us who have been to modern universities will make their own reflections on the value of the test. As for his three pupils, Colin Laurent, Girard Gossouyn, and Jehan Marceau—if they were really his pupils in any serious sense —what can we say but God help them! And sure enough, by his own description, they turned out as ragged, rowdy, and ignorant as was to be looked for from the views and manners of their rare preceptor.

At some time or other, before or during his university career, the poet was adopted by Master Guillaume de Villon, chaplain of Saint Benoît-le-Bétourné near the Sorbonne. From him he borrowed the surname by which he is known to posterity. It was most likely from his house, called the *Porte Rouge,* and situated in a garden in the cloister of Saint Benoît, that Master Francis heard the bell of the Sorbonne ring out the Angelus while he was finishing his *Small Testament* at Christmastide in 1546. Toward this

FRANÇOIS VILLON

benefactor he usually gets credit for a respectable display of gratitude. But with his trap and pitfall style of writing, it is easy to make too sure. His sentiments are about as much to be relied on as those of a professional beggar; and in this, as in so many other matters, he comes toward us whining and piping the eye, and goes off again with a whoop and his finger to his nose. Thus, he calls Guillaume de Villon his "more than father," thanks him with a great show of sincerity for having helped him out of many scrapes, and bequeaths him his portion of renown. But the portion of renown which belonged to a young thief, distinguished (if, at the period when he wrote this legacy, he was distinguished at all) for having written some more or less obscene and scurrilous ballads, must have been little fitted to gratify the self-respect or increase the reputation of a benevolent ecclesiastic. The same remark applies to a subsequent legacy of the poet's library, with specification of one work which was plainly neither decent nor devout. We are thus left on the horns of a dilemma. If the chaplain was a godly, philanthropic personage, who had tried to graft good principles and good behavior on this wild slip of an adopted son, these jesting legacies would obviously cut him to the heart. The position of an adopted son toward his adoptive father is one full of delicacy; where a man lends his name he looks for great consideration. And this legacy of Villon's portion of renown may be taken as the mere fling of an unregenerate scapegrace who has wit enough to recognize in his own shame the readiest weapon of offence against a prosy benefactor's feelings. The gratitude of Master Francis figures, on this reading, as a frightful *minus* quantity. If, on the other hand, those jests were given and taken in good humor, the whole relation between the pair degenerates into the unedifying complicity of a debauched old chaplain and a witty and dissolute young scholar. At this rate the house with the red door may have rung with the most mundane minstrelsy; and it may have been below its roof that Villon, through a hole in the plaster, studied, as he tells us, the leisures of a rich ecclesiastic.

FAMILIAR STUDIES

It was, perhaps, of some moment in the poet's life that he should have inhabited the cloister of Saint Benoît. Three of the most remarkable among his early acquaintances are Catherine de Vausselles, for whom he entertained a short-lived affection and an enduring and most unmanly resentment; Regnier de Montigny, a young blackguard of good birth: and Colin de Cayeux, a fellow with a marked aptitude for picking locks. Now we are on a foundation of mere conjecture, but it is at least curious to find that two of the canons of Saint Benoît answered respectively to the names of Pierre de Vaucel and Étienne de Montigny, and that there was a householder called Nicolas de Cayeux in a street—the Rue des Poirées—in the immediate neighborhood of the cloister. M. Longnon is almost ready to identify Catherine as the niece of Pierre; Regnier as the nephew of Étienne, and Colin as the son of Nicolas. Without going so far, it must be owned that the approximation of names is significant. As we go on to see the part played by each of these persons in the sordid melodrama of the poet's life, we shall come to regard it as even more notable. Is it not Clough who has remarked that, after all, everything lies in juxtaposition? Many a man's destiny has been settled by nothing apparently more grave than a pretty face on the opposite side of the street and a couple of bad companions round the corner.

Catherine de Vausselles (or de Vaucel—the change is within the limits of Villon's license) had plainly delighted in the poet's conversation; near neighbors or not, they were much together; and Villon made no secret of his court, and suffered himself to believe that his feeling was repaid in kind. This may have been an error from the first, or he may have estranged her by subsequent misconduct or temerity. One can easily imagine Villon an impatient wooer. One thing, at least, is sure: that the affair terminated in a manner bitterly humiliating to Master Francis. In presence of his lady-love, perhaps under her window and certainly with her connivance, he was unmercifully thrashed by one Noë le Joly—beaten, as he says himself, like dirty linen on the

FRANÇOIS VILLON

washing-board. It is characteristic that his malice had notably increased between the time when he wrote the *Small Testament* immediately on the back of the occurrence, and the time when he wrote the *Large Testament* five years after. On the latter occasion nothing is too bad for his "damsel with the twisted nose," as he calls her. She is spared neither hint nor accusation, and he tells his messenger to accost her with the vilest insults. Villon, it is thought, was out of Paris when these amenities escaped his pen; or perhaps the strong arm of Noë le Joly would have been again in requisition. So ends the love story, if love story it may properly be called. Poets are not necessarily fortunate in love; but they usually fall among more romantic circumstances and bear their disappointment with a better grace.

The neighborhood of Regnier de Montigny and Colin de Cayeux was probably more influential on his after life than the contempt of Catherine. For a man who is greedy of all pleasures, and provided with little money and less dignity of character, we may prophesy a safe and speedy voyage downward. Humble or even truckling virtue may walk unspotted in this life. But only those who despise the pleasures can afford to despise the opinion of the world. A man of a strong, heady temperament, like Villon, is very differently tempted. His eyes lay hold on all provocations greedily, and his heart flames up at a look into imperious desire; he is snared and broached to by anything and everything, from a pretty face to a piece of pastry in a cookshop window; he will drink the rinsing of the wine cup, stay the latest at the tavern party; tap at the lit windows, follow the sound of singing, and beat the whole neighborhood for another reveller, as he goes reluctantly homeward; and grudge himself every hour of sleep as a black, empty period in which he cannot follow after pleasure. Such a person is lost if he have not dignity, or, failing that, at least pride, which is its shadow and in many ways its substitute. Master Francis, I fancy, would follow his own eager instincts without much spiritual struggle. And we soon find him fallen among thieves in sober, literal earnest, and counting as acquaintances

FAMILIAR STUDIES

the most disreputable people he could lay his hands on: fellows who stole ducks in Paris Moat; sergeants of the criminal court, and archers of the watch; blackguards who slept at night under the butchers' stalls, and for whom the aforesaid archers peered about carefully with lanterns; Regnier de Montigny, Colin de Cayeux, and their crew, all bound on a favoring breeze toward the gallows; the disorderly abbess of Port Royal, who went about at fair time with soldiers and thieves, and conducted her abbey on the queerest principles; and most likely Perette Mauger, the great Paris receiver of stolen goods, not yet dreaming, poor woman! of the last scene of her career when Henry Cousin, executor of the high justice, shall bury her, alive and most reluctant, in front of the new Montigny gibbet.* Nay, our friend soon began to take a foremost rank in this society. He could string off verses, which is always an agreeable talent; and he could make himself useful in many other ways. The whole ragged army of Bohemia, and whosoever loved good cheer without at all loving to work and pay for it, are addressed in contemporary verses as the "Subjects of François Villon." He was a good genius to all hungry and unscrupulous persons; and became the hero of a whole legendary cycle of tavern tricks and cheateries. At best, these were doubtful levities, rather too thievish for a schoolboy, rather too gamesome for a thief. But he would not linger long in this equivocal border land. He must soon have complied with his surroundings. He was one who would go where the cannikin clinked, not caring who should pay; and from supping in the wolves' den, there is but a step to hunting with the pack. And here, as I am on the chapter of his degradation, I shall say all I mean to say about its darkest expression, and be done with it for good. Some charitable critics see no more than a *jeu d'esprit*, a graceful and trifling exercise of the imagination, in the grimy ballad of Fat Peg (*Grosse Margot*). I am not able to follow these gentlemen to this polite extreme. Out of all Villon's works that ballad stands forth in flaring reality, gross and ghastly,

* *Chronique Scandaleuse*, ed. Panthéon, p. 237.

FRANÇOIS VILLON

as a thing written in a contraction of disgust. M. Longnon shows us more and more clearly at every page that we are to read our poet literally, that his names are the names of real persons, and the events he chronicles were actual events. But even if the tendency of criticism had run the other way, this ballad would have gone far to prove itself. I can well understand the reluctance of worthy persons in this matter; for of course it is unpleasant to think of a man of genius as one who held, in the words of Marina to Boult—

> "A place, for which the pained'st fiend
> Of hell would not in reputation change."

But beyond this natural unwillingness, the whole difficulty of the case springs from a highly virtuous ignorance of life. Paris now is not so different from the Paris of then; and the whole of the doings of Bohemia are not written in the sugar-candy pastorals of Murger. It is really not at all surprising that a young man of the fifteenth century, with a knack of making verses, should accept his bread upon disgraceful terms. The race of those who do is not extinct; and some of them to this day write the prettiest verses imaginable. . . . After this, it were impossible for Master Francis to fall lower: to go and steal for himself would be an admirable advance from every point of view, divine or human.

And yet it is not as a thief, but as a homicide, that he makes his first appearance before angry justice. On June 5, 1455, when he was about twenty-four, and had been Master of Arts for a matter of three years, we behold him for the first time quite definitely. Angry justice had, as it were, photographed him in the act of his homicide; and M. Longnon, rummaging among old deeds, has turned up the negative and printed it off for our instruction. Villon had been supping—copiously we may believe—and sat on a stone bench in front of the Church of St. Benoît, in company with a priest called Gilles and a woman of the name of Isabeau. It was nine o'clock, a mighty late hour for the period, and

FAMILIAR STUDIES

evidently a fine summer's night. Master Francis carried a mantle, like a prudent man, to keep him from the dews (*serain*), and had a sword below it dangling from his girdle. So these three dallied in front of St. Benoît, taking their pleasure (*pour soy esbatre*). Suddenly there arrived upon the scene a priest, Philippe Chermoye or Sermaise, also with sword and cloak, and accompanied by one Master Jehan le Mardi. Sermaise, according to Villon's account, which is all we have to go upon, came up blustering and denying God; as Villon rose to make room for him upon the bench, thrust him rudely back into his place; and finally drew his sword and cut open his lower lip, by what I should imagine was a very clumsy stroke. Up to this point, Villon professes to have been a model of courtesy, even of feebleness: and the brawl, in his version, reads like the fable of the wolf and the lamb. But now the lamb was roused; he drew his sword, stabbed Sermaise in the groin, knocked him on the head with a big stone, and then, leaving him to his fate, went away to have his own lip doctored by a barber of the name of Fouquet. In one version, he says that Gilles, Isabeau, and Le Mardi ran away at the first high words, and that he and Sermaise had it out alone; in another, Le Mardi is represented as returning and wresting Villon's sword from him: the reader may please himself. Sermaise was picked up, lay all that night in the prison of Saint Benoît, where he was examined by an official of the Châtelet and expressly pardoned Villon, and died on the following Saturday in the Hôtel Dieu.

This, as I have said, was in June. Not before January of the next year could Villon extract a pardon from the king; but, while his hand was in, he got two. One is for " François des Loges, *alias* (*autrement dit*) de Villon "; and the other runs in the name of François de Montcorbier. Nay, it appears there was a further complication; for in the narrative of the first of these documents, it is mentioned that he passed himself off upon Fouquet, the barber-surgeon, as one Michel Mouton. M. Longnon has a theory that this unhappy accident with Sermaise was the cause of Villon's

FRANÇOIS VILLON

subsequent irregularities; and that up to that moment he had been the pink of good behavior. But the matter has to my eyes a more dubious air. A pardon necessary for Des Loges and another for Montcorbier? and these two the same person? and one or both of them known by the *alias* of Villon, however honestly come by? and lastly, in the heat of the moment, a fourth name thrown out with an assured countenance? A ship is not to be trusted that sails under so many colors. This is not the simple bearing of innocence. No—the young master was already treading crooked paths; already, he would start and blench at a hand upon his shoulder, with the look we know so well in the face of Hogarth's Idle Apprentice; already, in the blue devils, he would see Henry Cousin, the executor of high justice, going in dolorous procession toward Montfaucon, and hear the wind and the birds crying around Paris gibbet.

A GANG OF THIEVES

In spite of the prodigious number of people who managed to get hanged, the fifteenth century was by no means a bad time for criminals. A great confusion of parties and great dust of fighting favored the escape of private housebreakers and quiet fellows who stole ducks in Paris Moat. Prisons were leaky; and as we shall see, a man with a few crowns in his pocket and perhaps some acquaintance among the officials, could easily slip out and become once more a free marauder. There was no want of a sanctuary where he might harbor until troubles blew by; and accomplices helped each other with more or less good faith. Clerks, above all, had remarkable facilities for a criminal way of life; for they were privileged, except in cases of notorious incorrigibility, to be plucked from the hands of rude secular justice and tried by a tribunal of their own. In 1402, a couple of thieves, both clerks of the University, were condemned to death by the Provost of Paris. As they were taken to Montfaucon, they kept crying "high and clearly" for their benefit of clergy, but were none the less pitilessly

FAMILIAR STUDIES

hanged and gibbeted. Indignant Alma Mater interfered before the king; and the Provost was deprived of all royal offices, and condemned to return the bodies and erect a great stone cross, on the road from Paris to the gibbet, graven with the effigies of these two holy martyrs.* We shall hear more of the benefit of clergy; for after this the reader will not be surprised to meet with thieves in the shape of tonsured clerks, or even priests and monks.

To a knot of such learned pilferers our poet certainly belonged; and by turning over a few more of M. Longnon's negatives, we shall get a clear idea of their character and doings. Montigny and De Cayeux are names already known; Guy Tabary, Petit-Jehan, Dom Nicholas, little Thibault, who was both clerk and goldsmith, and who made picklocks and melted plate for himself and his companions—with these the reader has still to become acquainted. Petit-Jehan and De Cayeux were handy fellows and enjoyed a useful preeminence in honor of their doings with the picklock. "*Dictus des Cahyeus est fortis operator crochetorum,*" says Tabary's interrogation, "*sed dictus Petit-Jehan, ejus socius, est forcius operator.*" But the flower of the flock was little Thibault; it was reported that no lock could stand before him; he had a persuasive hand; let us salute capacity wherever we may find it. Perhaps the term *gang* is not quite properly applied to the persons whose fortunes we are now about to follow; rather they were independent malefactors, socially intimate, and occasionally joining together for some serious operation, just as modern stockjobbers form a syndicate for an important loan. Nor were they at all particular to any branch of misdoing. They did not scrupulously confine themselves to a single sort of theft, as I hear is common among modern thieves. They were ready for anything, from pitch-and-toss to manslaughter. Montigny, for instance, had neglected neither of these extremes, and we find him accused of cheating at games of hazard on the one hand, and on the other of the murder of one Thepenin Pensete in a house by the Cemetery of St. John. If time had

* Monstrelet: *Panthéon Littéraire*, p. 96.

FRANÇOIS VILLON

only spared us some particulars, might not this last have furnished us with the matter of a grisly winter's tale?

At Christmas-time in 1456, readers of Villon will remember that he was engaged on the *Small Testament*. About the same period, *circa festum nativitatis Domini*, he took part in a memorable supper at the Mule Tavern, in front of the Church of St. Mathurin. Tabary, who seems to have been very much Villon's creature, had ordered the supper in the course of the afternoon. He was a man who had had troubles in his time and languished in the Bishop of Paris's prisons on a suspicion of picking locks; confiding, convivial, not very astute—who had copied out a whole improper romance with his own right hand. This supper-party was to be his first introduction to De Cayeux and Petit-Jehan, which was probably a matter of some concern to the poor man's muddy wits; in the sequel, at least, he speaks of both with an undisguised respect, based on professional inferiority in the matter of picklocks. Dom Nicolas, a Picardy monk, was the fifth and last at table. When supper had been despatched and fairly washed down, we may suppose, with white Baigneux or red Beaune, which were favorite wines among the fellowship, Tabary was solemnly sworn over to secrecy on the night's performances; and the party left the Mule and proceeded to an unoccupied house belonging to Robert de Saint-Simon. This, over a low wall, they entered without difficulty. All but Tabary took off their upper garments; a ladder was found and applied to the high wall which separated Saint-Simon's house from the court of the College of Navarre; the four fellows in their shirt-sleeves (as we might say) clambered over in a twinkling; and Master Guy Tabary remained alone beside the overcoats. From the court the burglars made their way into the vestry of the chapel, where they found a large chest, strengthened with iron bands and closed with four locks. One of these locks they picked, and then, by levering up the corner, forced the other three. Inside was a small coffer, of walnut wood, also barred with iron, but fastened with only three locks, which were all comfortably picked by way of the keyhole.

FAMILIAR STUDIES

In the walnut coffer—a joyous sight by our thieves' lantern—were five hundred crowns of gold. There was some talk of opening the aumries, where, if they had only known, a booty eight or nine times greater lay ready to their hand; but one of the party (I have a humorous suspicion it was Dom Nicolas, the Picardy monk) hurried them away. It was ten o'clock when they mounted the ladder; it was about midnight before Tabary beheld them coming back. To him they gave ten crowns, and promised a share of a two-crown dinner on the morrow; whereat we may suppose his mouth watered. In course of time, he got wind of the real amount of their booty and understood how scurvily he had been used; but he seems to have borne no malice. How could he, against such superb operators as Petit-Jehan and De Cayeux; or a person like Villon, who could have made a new improper romance out of his own head, instead of merely copying an old one with mechanical right hand?

The rest of the winter was not uneventful for the gang. First they made a demonstration against the Church of St. Mathurin after chalices, and were ignominiously chased away by barking dogs. Then Tabary fell out with Casin Chollet, one of the fellows who stole ducks in Paris Moat, who subsequently became a sergeant of the Châtelet and distinguished himself by misconduct, followed by imprisonment and public castigation, during the wars of Louis Eleventh. The quarrel was not conducted with a proper regard to the king's peace, and the pair publicly belabored each other until the police stepped in, and Master Tabary was cast once more into the prisons of the Bishop. While he still lay in durance, another job was cleverly executed by the band in broad daylight, at the Augustine Monastery. Brother Guillaume Coiffier was beguiled by an accomplice to St. Mathurin to say mass; and, during his absence, his chamber was entered and five or six hundred crowns in money and some silver plate successfully abstracted. A melancholy man was Coiffier on his return! Eight crowns from this adventure were forwarded by little Thibault to the incarcerated Tabary; and with these he bribed the jailer and reappeared in Paris tav-

FRANÇOIS VILLON

erns. Some time before, or shortly after this, Villon set out for Angers, as he had promised in the *Small Testament*. The object of this excursion was not merely to avoid the presence of his cruel mistress or the strong arm of Noë le Joly, but to plan a deliberate robbery on his uncle the monk. As soon as he had properly studied the ground, the others were to go over in force from Paris—picklocks and all—and away with my uncle's strongbox! This throws a comical sidelight on his own accusation against his relatives, that they had " forgotten natural duty " and disowned him because he was poor. A poor relation is a distasteful circumstance at the best, but a poor relation who plans deliberate robberies against those of his blood, and trudges hundreds of weary leagues to put them into execution, is surely a little on the wrong side of toleration. The uncle at Angers may have been monstrously undutiful; but the nephew from Paris was upsides with him.

On the 23d April, that venerable and discreet person, Master Pierre Marchand, Curate and Prior of Paray-le-Monial, in the diocese of Chartres, arrived in Paris and put up at the sign of the Three Chandeliers, in the Rue de la Huchette. Next day, or the day after, as he was breakfasting at the sign of the Armchair, he fell into talk with two customers, one of whom was a priest and the other our friend Tabary. The idiotic Tabary became mighty confidential as to his past life. Pierre Marchand, who was an acquaintance of Guillaume Coiffier's and had sympathized with him over his loss, pricked up his ears at the mention of picklocks, and led on the transcriber of improper romances from one thing to another, until they were fast friends. For picklocks the Prior of Paray professed a keen curiosity; but Tabary, upon some late alarm, had thrown all his into the Seine. Let that be no difficulty, however, for was there not little Thibault, who could make them of all shapes and sizes, and to whom Tabary, smelling an accomplice, would be only too glad to introduce his new acquaintance? On the morrow, accordingly, they met; and Tabary, after having first wet his whistle at the Prior's expense, led him to Notre Dame

FAMILIAR STUDIES

and presented him to four or five " young companions," who were keeping sanctuary in the church. They were all clerks, recently escaped, like Tabary himself, from the episcopal prisons. Among these we may notice Thibault, the operator, a little fellow of twenty-six, wearing long hair behind. The Prior expressed, through Tabary, his anxiety to become their accomplice and altogether such as they were (*de leur sorte et de leurs complices*). Mighty polite they showed themselves, and made him many fine speeches in return. But for all that, perhaps because they had longer heads than Tabary, perhaps because it is less easy to wheedle men in a body, they kept obstinately to generalities and gave him no information as to their exploits, past, present, or to come. I suppose Tabary groaned under this reserve; for no sooner were he and the Prior out of the church than he fairly emptied his heart to him, gave him full details of many hanging matters in the past, and explained the future intentions of the band. The scheme of the hour was to rob another Augustine monk, Robert de la Porte, and in this the Prior agreed to take a hand with simulated greed. Thus, in the course of two days, he had turned this wineskin of a Tabary inside out. For a while longer the farce was carried on; the Prior was introduced to Petit-Jehan, whom he describes as a little, very smart man of thirty, with a black beard and a short jacket; an appointment was made and broken in the de la Porte affair; Tabary had some breakfast at the Prior's charge and leaked out more secrets under the influence of wine and friendship; and then all of a sudden, on the 17th of May, an alarm sprang up, the Prior picked up his skirts and walked quietly over to the Châtelet to make a deposition, and the whole band took to their heels and vanished out of Paris and the sight of the police.

Vanish as they like, they all go with a clog about their feet. Sooner or later, here or there, they will be caught in the fact, and ignominiously sent home. From our vantage of four centuries afterward, it is odd and pitiful to watch the order in which the fugitives are captured and dragged in.

FRANÇOIS VILLON

Montigny was the first. In August of that same year, he was laid by the heels on many grievous counts; sacrilegious robberies, frauds, incorrigibility, and that bad business about Thevenin Pensete in the house by the Cemetery of St. John. He was reclaimed by the ecclesiastical authorities as a clerk; but the claim was rebutted on the score of incorrigibility, and ultimately fell to the ground; and he was condemned to death by the Provost of Paris. It was a very rude hour for Montigny, but hope was not yet over.

He was a fellow of some birth; his father had been king's pantler; his sister, probably married to some one about the Court, was in the family way, and her health would be endangered if the execution was proceeded with. So down comes Charles the Seventh with letters of mercy, commuting the penalty to a year in a dungeon on bread and water, and a pilgrimage to the shrine of St. James in Galicia. Alas! the document was incomplete; it did not contain the full tale of Montigny's enormities; it did not recite that he had been denied benefit of clergy, and it said nothing about Thevenin Pensete. Montigny's hour was at hand. Benefit of clergy, honorable descent from king's pantler, sister in the family way, royal letters of commutation—all were of no avail. He had been in prison in Rouen, in Tours, in Bordeaux, and four times already in Paris; and out of all these he had come scathless; but now he must make a little excursion as far as Montfaucon with Henry Cousin, executor of high justice. There let him swing among the carrion crows.

About a year later, in July, 1458, the police laid hands on Tabary. Before the ecclesiastical commissary he was twice examined, and, on the latter occasion, put to the question ordinary and extraordinary. What a dismal change from pleasant suppers at the Mule, where he sat in triumph with expert operators and great wits! He is at the lees of life, poor rogue; and those fingers which once transcribed improper romances are now agonizingly stretched upon the rack. We have no sure knowledge, but we may have a

FAMILIAR STUDIES

shrewd guess of the conclusion. Tabary, the admirer, would go the same way as those whom he admired.

The last we hear of is Colin de Cayeux. He was caught in autumn, 1460, in the great Church of St. Leu d'Esserens, which makes so fine a figure in the pleasant Oise valley between Creil and Beaumont. He was reclaimed by no less than two bishops; but the Procureur for the Provost held fast by incorrigible Colin. 1460 was an ill-starred year: for justice was making a clean sweep of " poor and indigent persons, thieves, cheats, and lockpickers," in the neighborhood of Paris;* and Colin de Cayeux, with many others, was condemned to death and hanged.†

VILLON AND THE GALLOWS

Villon was still absent on the Angers expedition when the Prior of Paray sent such a bombshell among his accomplices; and the dates of his return and arrest remain undiscoverable. M. Campaux plausibly enough opined for the autumn of 1457, which would make him closely follow on Montigny, and the first of those denounced by the Prior to fall into the toils. We may suppose, at least, that it was not long thereafter; we may suppose him competed for between lay and clerical Courts; and we may suppose him alternately pert and impudent, humble and fawning, in his defence. But at the end of all supposing, we come upon some nuggets of fact. For first, he was put to the question by water. He who had tossed off so many cups of white Baigneux or red Beaune, now drank water through linen folds, until his bowels were flooded and his heart stood still. After so much raising of the elbow, so much outcry of fictitious thirst, here at last was enough drinking for a life-

* *Chron. Scand.* ut supra.
† Here and there, principally in the order of events, this article differs from M. Longnon's own reading of his material. The ground on which he defers the execution of Montigny and De Cayeux beyond the date of their trials seems insufficient. There is a law of parsimony for the construction of historical documents; simplicity is the first duty of narration; and hanged they were.

FRANÇOIS VILLON

time. Truly, of our pleasant vices, the gods make whips to scourge us. And secondly he was condemned to be hanged. A man may have been expecting a catastrophe for years, and yet find himself unprepared when it arrives. Certainly, Villon found, in this legitimate issue of his career, a very staggering and grave consideration. Every beast, as he says, clings bitterly to a whole skin. If everything is lost, and even honor, life still remains; nay, and it becomes, like the ewe lamb in Nathan's parable, as dear as all the rest. "Do you fancy," he asks, in a lively ballad, "that I had not enough philosophy under my hood to cry out: 'I appeal'? If I had made any bones about the matter, I should have been planted upright in the fields, by the St. Denis Road"—Montfaucon being on the way to St. Denis. An appeal to Parliament, as we saw in the case of Colin de Cayeux, did not necessarily lead to an acquittal or a commutation; and, while the matter was pending, our poet had ample opportunity to reflect on his position. Hanging is a sharp argument, and to swing with many others on the gibbet adds a horrible corollary for the imagination. With the aspect of Montfaucon he was well acquainted; indeed, as the neighborhood appears to have been sacred to junketing and nocturnal picnics of wild young men and women, he had probably studied it under all varieties of hour and weather. And now, as he lay in prison waiting the mortal push, these different aspects crowded back on his imagination with a new and startling significance; and he wrote a ballad, by way of epitaph for himself and his companions, which remains unique in the annals of mankind. It is, in the highest sense, a piece of his biography:—

> "La pluye nous a debuez et lavez,
> Et le soleil desseches et noirciz;
> Pies, corbeaulx, nous ont les yeux cavez,
> Et arrachez la barbe et les sourcilz.
> Jamais, nul temps, nous ne sommes rassis;
> Puis çà puis là, comme le vent varie,
> A son plaisir sans cesser nous charie,
> Plus becquetez d' oiseaulx que dez à couldre.
> Ne soyez donc de nostre confrairie,
> Mais priez Dieu que tous nous vueille absouldre."

FAMILIAR STUDIES

Here is some genuine thieves' literature after so much that was spurious; sharp as an etching, written with a shuddering soul. There is an intensity of consideration in the piece that shows it to be the transcript of familiar thoughts. It is the quintessence of many a doleful nightmare on the straw, when he felt himself swing helpless in the wind, and saw the birds turn about him, screaming and menacing his eyes.

And, after all, the Parliament changed his sentence into one of banishment; and to Roussillon in Dauphiny, our poet must carry his woes without delay. Travellers between Lyons and Marseilles may remember a station on the line, some way below Vienne, where the Rhone fleets seaward between vine-clad hills. This was Villon's Siberia. It would be a little warm in summer perhaps, and a little cold in winter in that draughty valley between two great mountain fields; but what with the hills, and the racing river, and the fiery Rhone wines, he was little to be pitied on the conditions of his exile. Villon, in a remarkably bad ballad, written in a breath, heartily thanked and fulsomely belauded the Parliament; the *envoi*, like the proverbial postscript of a lady's letter, containing the pith of his performance in a request for three days' delay to settle his affairs and bid his friends farewell. He was probably not followed out of Paris, like Antoine Fradin, the popular preacher, another exile of a few years later, by weeping multitudes;* but I dare say one or two rogues of his acquaintance would keep him company for a mile or so on the south road, and drink a bottle with him before they turned. For banished people, in those days, seem to have set out on their own responsibility, in their own guard, and at their own expense. It was no joke to make one's way from Paris to Roussillon alone and penniless in the fifteenth century. Villon says he left a rag of his tails on every bush. Indeed, he must have had many a weary tramp, many a slender meal, and many a to-do with blustering captains of the Ordonnance. But with one of his light fingers, we may

* *Chron. Scand.,* p. 338.

FRANÇOIS VILLON

fancy that he took as good as he gave; for every rag of his tail, he would manage to indemnify himself upon the population in the shape of food, or wine, or ringing money; and his route would be traceable across France and Burgundy by housewives and inn-keepers lamenting over petty thefts, like the track of a single human locust. A strange figure he must have cut in the eyes of the good country people: this ragged, blackguard city poet, with a smack of the Paris student, and a smack of the Paris street arab, posting along the highways, in rain or sun, among the green fields and vineyards. For himself, he had no taste for rural loveliness; green fields and vineyards would be mighty indifferent to Master Francis; but he would often have his tongue in his cheek at the simplicity of rustic dupes, and often, at city gates, he might stop to contemplate the gibbet with its swinging bodies, and hug himself on his escape.

How long he stayed at Roussillon, how far he became the protégé of the Bourbons, to whom that town belonged, or when it was that he took part, under the auspices of Charles of Orleans, in a rhyming tournament to be referred to once again in the pages of the present volume, are matters that still remain in darkness, in spite of M. Longnon's diligent rummaging among archives. When we next find him, in summer, 1461, alas! he is once more in durance: this time at Méun-sur-Loire, in the prisons of Thibault d'Aussigny, Bishop of Orleans. He had been lowered in a basket into a noisome pit, where he lay, all summer, gnawing hard crusts and railing upon fate. His teeth, he says, were like the teeth of a rake: a touch of haggard portraiture all the more real for being excessive and burlesque, and all the more proper to the man for being a caricature of his own misery. His eyes were "bandaged with thick walls." It might blow hurricanes overhead; the lightning might leap in high heaven; but no word of all this reached him in his noisome pit. "Il n'entre, ou gist, n'escler ni tourbillon." Above all, he was fevered with envy and anger at the freedom of others; and his heart flowed over into curses as he thought of Thibault d'Aussigny, walking the streets in God's sunlight, and blessing people with extended fingers. So much we find sharply lined in his own poems. Why he was cast again into prison—how he had again managed to shave the gallows—this we know not, nor, from the destruction of authorities, are we ever likely to learn. But on October 2d, 1461, or some day immediately preceding, the new King, Louis Eleventh, made his joyous entry into Méun. Now it was a part of the formality on such occasions for the new King to liberate certain prisoners; and so the basket was let down into Villon's pit, and hastily did Master Francis scramble in, and was most joyfully hauled up, and shot out, blinking and tottering, but once more a free man, into the blessed sun and wind. Now or never is the time for verses! Such a happy revolution would turn the head of a stocking-weaver, and set him jingling rhymes. And so—after a voyage to Paris, where he finds Montigny and De Cayeux clattering their bones upon the gibbet, and his three pupils roystering in Paris streets, "with their thumbs under their girdles,"—down sits Master Francis to write his *Large Testament*, and perpetuate his name in a sort of glorious ignominy.

THE LARGE TESTAMENT

Of this capital achievement and, with it, of Villon's style in general, it is here the place to speak. The *Large Testament* is a hurly-burly of cynical and sentimental reflections about life, jesting legacies to friends and enemies, and, interspersed among these, many admirable ballades, both serious and absurd. With so free a design, no thought that occurred to him would need to be dismissed without expression; and he could draw at full length the portrait of his own bedevilled soul, and of the bleak and blackguardly world which was the theatre of his exploits and sufferings. If the reader can conceive something between the slap-dash inconsequence of Byron's *Don Juan* and the racy humorous gravity and brief noble touches that distinguish the vernacu-

FRANÇOIS VILLON

lar poems of Burns, he will have formed some idea of Villon's style. To the latter writer—except in the ballades, which are quite his own, and can be paralleled from no other language known to me—he bears a particular resemblance. In common with Burns he has a certain rugged compression, a brutal vivacity of epithet, a homely vigor, a delight in local personalities, and an interest in many sides of life, that are often despised and passed over by more effete and cultured poets. Both also, in their strong, easy colloquial way, tend to become difficult and obscure; the obscurity in the case of Villon passing at times into the absolute darkness of cant language. They are perhaps the only two great masters of expression who keep sending their readers to a glossary.

"Shall we not dare to say of a thief," asks Montaigne, "that he has a handsome leg?" It is a far more serious claim that we have to put forward in behalf of Villon. Beside that of his contemporaries, his writing, so full of color, so eloquent, so picturesque, stands out in an almost miraculous isolation. If only one or two of the chroniclers could have taken a leaf out of his book, history would have been a pastime, and the fifteenth century as present to our minds as the age of Charles Second. This gallows-bird was the one great writer of his age and country, and initiated modern literature for France. Boileau, long ago, in the period of perukes and snuff-boxes, recognized him as the first articulate poet in the language; and if we measure him, not by priority of merit, but living duration of influence, not on a comparison with obscure forerunners, but with great and famous successors, we shall install this ragged and disreputable figure in a far higher niche in glory's temple than was ever dreamed of by the critic. It is, in itself, a memorable fact that, before 1542, in the very dawn of printing, and while modern France was in the making, the works of Villon ran through seven different editions. Out of him flows much of Rabelais; and through Rabelais, directly and indirectly, a deep, permanent, and growing inspiration. Not only his style, but his callous pertinent way of looking upon the sordid and ugly sides of life, becomes every day a more specific feature in the literature of France. And only the other year, a work of some power appeared in Paris, and appeared with infinite scandal, which owed its whole inner significance and much of its outward form to the study of our rhyming thief.

The world to which he introduces us is, as before said, blackguardly and bleak. Paris swarms before us, full of famine, shame, and death; monks and the servants of great lords hold high wassail upon cakes and pastry; the poor man licks his lips before the baker's window; people with patched eyes sprawl all night under the stalls; chuckling Tabary transcribes an improper romance; bare-bosomed lasses and ruffling students swagger in the streets; the drunkard goes stumbling homeward; the graveyard is full of bones; and away on Montfaucon, Colin de Cayeux and Montigny hang draggled in the rain. Is there nothing better to be seen than sordid misery and worthless joys? Only where the poor old mother of the poet kneels in church below painted windows, and makes tremulous supplication to the Mother of God.

In our mixed world, full of green fields and happy lovers, where not long before, Joan of Arc had led one of the highest and noblest lives in the whole story of mankind, this was all worth chronicling that our poet could perceive. His eyes were indeed sealed with his own filth. He dwelt all his life in a pit more noisome than the dungeon at Méun. In the moral world, also, there are large phenomena not cognizable out of holes and corners. Loud winds blow, speeding home deep-laden ships and sweeping rubbish from the earth; the lightning leaps and cleans the face of heaven; high purposes and brave passions shake and sublimate men's spirits; and meanwhile, in the narrow dungeon of his soul, Villon is mumbling crusts and picking vermin.

Along with this deadly gloom of outlook, we must take another characteristic of his work: its unrivalled insincerity. I can give no better similitude of this quality than I have given already: that he comes up with a whine, and runs away with a whoop and his finger to his nose. His pathos is that of a professional mendicant who should happen to be a man

FRANÇOIS VILLON

of genius; his levity that of a bitter street arab, full of bread. On a first reading, the pathetic passages preoccupy the reader, and he is cheated out of an alms in the shape of sympathy. But when the thing is studied the illusion fades away; in the transitions, above all, we can detect the evil, ironical temper of the man; and instead of a flighty work, where many crude but genuine feelings tumble together for the mastery as in the lists of a tournament, we are tempted to think of the *Large Testament* as of one long-drawn epical grimace, pulled by a merry-andrew, who has found a certain despicable eminence over human respect and human affections by perching himself astride upon the gallows. Between these two views, at best, all temperate judgments will be found to fall; and rather, as I imagine, toward the last.

There were two things on which he felt with perfect, and, in one case, even threatening sincerity.

The first of these was an undisguised envy of those richer than himself. He was forever drawing a parallel, already exemplified from his own words, between the happy life of the well-to-do and the miseries of the poor. Burns, too proud and honest not to work, continued through all reverses to sing of poverty with a light, defiant note. Béranger waited till he was himself beyond the reach of want before writing the *Old Vagabond* or *Jacques*. Samuel Johnson, although he was very sorry to be poor, " was a great arguer for the advantages of poverty " in his ill days. Thus it is that brave men carry their crosses, and smile with the fox burrowing in their vitals. But Villon, who had not the courage to be poor with honesty, now whiningly implores our sympathy, now shows his teeth upon the dung-heap with an ugly snarl. He envies bitterly, envies passionately. Poverty, he protests, drives men to steal, as hunger makes the wolf sally from the forest. The poor, he goes on, will always have a carping word to say, or, if that outlet be denied, nourish rebellious thoughts. It is a calumny on the noble army of the poor. Thousands in a small way of life, ay, and even in the smallest, go through life with tenfold as much honor and dignity and peace of mind, as the rich gluttons

FAMILIAR STUDIES

whose dainties and state-beds awakened Villon's covetous temper. And every morning's sun sees thousands who pass whistling to their toil. But Villon was the "mauvais pauvre" defined by Victor Hugo, and, in its English expression, so admirably stereotyped by Dickens. He was the first wicked sans-culotte. He is the man of genius with the mole-skin cap. He is mighty pathetic and beseeching here in the street, but I would not go down a dark road with him for a large consideration.

The second of the points on which he was genuine and emphatic was common to the Middle Ages; a deep and somewhat snivelling conviction of the transitory nature of this life and the pity and horror of death. Old age and the grave, with some dark and yet half-sceptical terror of an after-world—these were ideas that clung about his bones like a disease. An old ape, as he says, may play all the tricks in its repertory, and none of them will tickle an audience into good humour. "Tousjours vieil synge est desplaisant." It is not the old jester who receives most recognition at a tavern party, but the young fellow, fresh and handsome, who knows the new slang, and carries off his vice with a certain air. Of this, as a tavern jester himself, he would be pointedly conscious. As for the women with whom he was best acquainted, his reflections on their old age, in all their harrowing pathos, shall remain in the original for me. Horace has disgraced himself to something the same tune; but what Horace throws out with an ill-favored laugh, Villon dwells on with an almost maudlin whimper.

It is in death that he finds his truest inspiration; in the swift and sorrowful change that overtakes beauty; in the strange revolution by which great fortunes and renowns are diminished to a handful of churchyard dust; and in the utter passing away of what was once lovable and mighty. It is in this that the mixed texture of his thought enables him to reach such poignant and terrible effects, and to enhance pity with ridicule, like a man cutting capers to a funeral march. It is in this, also, that he rises out of himself into the higher spheres of art. So, in the ballade by which he is best known

FRANÇOIS VILLON

he rings the changes on names that once stood for beautiful and queenly women, and are now no more than letters and a legend. "Where are the snows of yester year?" runs the burden. And so, in another not so famous, he passes in review the different degrees of bygone men, from the holy Apostles and the golden Emperor of the East, down to the heralds, pursuivants, and trumpeters, who also bore their part in the world's pageantries and ate greedily at great folks' tables: all this to the refrain of "So much carry the winds away!" Probably, there was some melancholy in his mind for a yet lower grade, and Montigny and Colin de Cayeux clattering their bones on Paris gibbet. Alas, and with so pitiful an experience of life, Villon can offer us nothing but terror and lamentation about death! No one has ever more skilfully communicated his own disenchantment; no one ever blown a more ear-piercing note of sadness. This unrepentant thief can attain neither to Christian confidence, nor to the spirit of the bright Greek saying, that whom the gods love die early. It is a poor heart, and a poorer age, that cannot accept the conditions of life with some heroic readiness.

. . . . .

The date of the *Large Testament* is the last date in the poet's biography. After having achieved that admirable and despicable performance, he disappears into the night from whence he came. How or when he died, whether decently in bed or trussed up to a gallows, remains a riddle for foolhardy commentators. It appears his health had suffered in the pit at Méun; he was thirty years of age and quite bald; with the notch in his under lip where Sermaise had struck him with the sword, and what wrinkles the reader may imagine. In default of portraits, this is all I have been able to piece together, and perhaps even the baldness should be taken as a figure of his destitution. A sinister dog, in all likelihood, but with a look in his eye, and the loose flexile mouth that goes with wit and an overweening sensual temperament. Certainly the sorriest figure on the rolls of fame.

CHARLES OF ORLEANS

FOR one who was no great politician, nor (as men go) especially wise, capable or virtuous, Charles of Orleans is more than usually enviable to all who love that better sort of fame which consists in being known not widely, but intimately. " To be content that time to come should know there was such a man, not caring whether they knew more of him, or to subsist under naked denominations, without deserts or noble acts," is, says Sir Thomas Browne, a frigid ambition. It is to some more specific memory that youth looks forward in its vigils. Old kings are sometimes disinterred in all the emphasis of life, the hands untainted by decay, the beard that had so often wagged in camp or senate still spread upon the royal bosom; and in busts and pictures, some similitude of the great and beautiful of former days is handed down. In this way, public curiosity may be gratified, but hardly any private aspiration after fame. It is not likely that posterity will fall in love with us, but not impossible that it may respect or sympathize; and so a man would rather leave behind him the portrait of his spirit than a portrait of his face, *figura animi magis quam corporis.* Of those who have thus survived themselves most completely, left a sort of personal seduction behind them in the world, and retained, after death, the art of making friends, Montaigne and Samuel Johnson certainly stand first. But we have portraits of all sorts of men, from august Cæsar to the king's dwarf; and all sorts of portraits, from a Titian treasured in the Louvre to a profile over the grocer's chimney-shelf. And so in a less degree, but no less truly, than the spirit of Montaigne lives on in the delightful Essays, that of Charles of Orleans survives in a few old songs and old account-books; and it is still in the choice of the reader

CHARLES OF ORLEANS

to make this duke's acquaintance, and, if their humors suit, become his friend.

His birth—if we are to argue from a man's parents—was above his merit. It is not merely that he was the grandson of one king, the father of another, and the uncle of a third; but something more specious was to be looked for from the son of his father, Louis de Valois, Duke of Orleans, brother to the mad king Charles VI., lover of Queen Isabel, and the leading patron of art and one of the leading politicians in France. And the poet might have inherited yet higher virtues from his mother, Valentina of Milan, a very pathetic figure of the age, the faithful wife of an unfaithful husband, and the friend of a most unhappy king. The father, beautiful, eloquent, and accomplished, exercised a strange fascination over his contemporaries; and among those who dip nowadays into the annals of the time there are not many— and these few are little to be envied—who can resist the fascination of the mother. All mankind owe her a debt of gratitude because she brought some comfort into the life of the poor madman who wore the crown of France.

Born (May, 1391) of such a noble stock, Charles was to know from the first all favors of nature and art. His father's gardens were the admiration of his contemporaries; his castles were situated in the most agreeable parts of France, and sumptuously adorned. We have preserved, in an inventory of 1403, the description of tapestried rooms where Charles may have played in childhood.* "A green room, with the ceiling full of angels, and the *dossier* of shepherds and shepherdesses seeming (*faisant contenance*) to eat nuts and cherries. A room of gold, silk and worsted, with a device of little children in a river, and the sky full of birds. A room of green tapestry, showing a knight and lady at chess in a pavilion. Another green room, with shepherdesses

* Champollion-Figeac's *Louis et Charles d'Orléans*, p. 348.

FAMILIAR STUDIES

in a trellised garden worked in gold and silk. A carpet representing cherry-trees, where there is a fountain, and a lady gathering cherries in a basin." These were some of the pictures over which his fancy might busy itself of an afternoon, or at morning as he lay awake in bed. With our deeper and more logical sense of life, we can have no idea how large a space in the attention of mediæval men might be occupied by such figured hangings on the wall. There was something timid and purblind in the view they had of the world. Morally, they saw nothing outside of traditional axioms; and little of the physical aspect of things entered vividly into their mind, beyond what was to be seen on church windows and the walls and floors of palaces. The reader will remember how Villon's mother conceived of heaven and hell and took all her scanty stock of theology from the stained glass that threw its light upon her as she prayed. And there is a scarcely a detail of external effect in the chronicles and romances of the time, but might have been borrowed at second hand from a piece of tapestry. It was a stage in the history of mankind which we may see paralleled, to some extent, in the first infant school, where the representations of lions and elephants alternate round the wall with more verses and trite presentments of the lesser virtues. So that to live in a house of many pictures was tantamount, for the time, to a liberal education in itself.

At Charles's birth an order of knighthood was inaugurated in his honor. At nine years old, he was a squire; at eleven, he had the escort of a chaplain and a schoolmaster; at twelve, his uncle the king made him a pension of twelve thousand livres d'or.* He saw the most brilliant and the most learned persons of France, in his father's Court; and would not fail to notice that these brilliant and learned persons were one and all engaged in rhyming. Indeed, if it is difficult to realize the part played by pictures, it is perhaps even more difficult to realize that played by verses in the polite and active history of the age. At the siege of Pontoise, English

* D'Héricault's admirable *Memoir*, prefixed to his edition of Charles's works, vol. i. p. xi.

CHARLES OF ORLEANS

and French exchanged defiant ballades over the walls.* If a scandal happened, as in the loathsome thirty-third story of the *Cent Nouvelles Nouvelles*, all the wits must make rondels and chansonettes, which they would hand from one to another with an unmanly sneer. Ladies carried their favorite's ballades in their girdles.† Margaret of Scotland, all the world knows already, kissed Alain Chartier's lips in honor of the many virtuous thoughts and golden sayings they had uttered; but it is not so well known, that this princess was herself the most industrious of poetasters, that she is supposed to have hastened her death by her literary vigils, and sometimes wrote as many as twelve rondels in the day.‡ It was in rhyme, even, that the young Charles should learn his lessons. He might get all manner of instruction in the truly noble art of the chase, not without a smack of ethics by the way, from the compendious didactic poem of Gace de la Bigne. Nay, and it was in rhyme that he should learn rhyming: in the verses of his father's Maître d'Hôtel, Eustache Deschamps, which treated of "l'art de dictier et de faire chançons, ballades, virelais et rondeaux," along with many other matters worth attention, from the courts of Heaven to the misgovernment of France.§ At this rate, all knowledge is to be had in a goody, and the end of it is an old song. We need not wonder when we hear from Monstrelet that Charles was a very well-educated person. He could string Latin texts together by the hour, and make ballades and rondels better than Eustache Deschamps himself. He had seen a mad king who would not change his clothes, and a drunken emperor who could not keep his hand from the wine-cup. He had spoken a great deal with jesters and fiddlers, and with the profligate lords who helped his father to waste the revenues of France. He had seen ladies dance on into broad daylight, and much burning of torches and waste of dainties and good wine.|| And when all is said,

* Vallet de Viriville, *Charles VII. et son Epoque*, ii. 428, note 2.
† See Lecoy de la Marche, *Le Roi René*, i. 167.
‡ Vallet, *Charles VII.*, ii. 85, 86, note 2.
§ Champollion-Figeac, 193-198.
|| *Ibid.* 209.

FAMILIAR STUDIES

it was no very helpful preparation for the battle of life. "I believe Louis XI.," writes Comines, "would not have saved himself, if he had not been very differently brought up from such other lords as I have seen educated in this country; for these were taught nothing but to play the jackanapes with finery and fine words." * I am afraid Charles took such lessons to heart, and conceived of life as a season principally for junketing and war. His view of the whole duty of man, so empty, vain, and wearisome to us, was yet sincerely and consistently held. When he came in his ripe years to compare the glory of two kingdoms, England and France, it was on three points only,—pleasures, valor, and riches,—that he cared to measure them; and in the very outset of that tract he speaks of the life of the great as passed, " whether in arms, as in assaults, battles, and sieges, or in jousts and tournaments, in high and stately festivities and in funeral solemnities." †

When he was no more than thirteen, his father had him affianced to Isabella, virgin-widow of our Richard II. and daughter of his uncle Charles VI.; and, two years after (June 29, 1406), the cousins were married at Compiègne, he fifteen, she seventeen years of age. It was in every way a most desirable match. The bride brought five hundred thousand francs of dowry. The ceremony was of the utmost magnificence, Louis of Orleans figuring in crimson velvet, adorned with no less than seven hundred and ninety-five pearls, gathered together expressly for this occasion. And no doubt it must have been very gratifying for a young gentleman of fifteen, to play the chief part in a pageant so gayly put upon the stage. Only, the bridegroom might have been a little older; and, as ill-luck would have it, the bride was of

* The student will see that there are facts cited, and expressions borrowed, in this paragraph, from a period extending over almost the whole of Charles's life, instead of being confined entirely to his boyhood. As I do not believe there was any change, so I do not believe there is any anachronism involved.

† *The Debate between the Heralds of France and England*, translated and admirably edited by Mr. Henry Pyne. For the attribution of this tract to Charles, the reader is referred to Mr. Pyne's conclusive argument.

CHARLES OF ORLEANS

this way of thinking, and would not be consoled for the loss of her title as queen, or the contemptible age of her new husband. *Pleuroit fort ladite Isabeau;* the said Isabella wept copiously.* It is fairly debatable whether Charles was much to be pitied when, three years later (September, 1409), this odd marriage was dissolved by death. Short as it was, however, this connection left a lasting stamp upon his mind; and we find that, in the last decade of his life, and after he had remarried for perhaps the second time, he had not yet forgotten or forgiven the violent death of Richard II. "Ce mauvais cas"—that ugly business, he writes, has yet to be avenged.

The marriage festivity was on the threshold of evil days. The great rivalry between Louis of Orleans and John the Fearless, Duke of Burgundy, had been forsworn with the most reverend solemnities. But the feud was only in abeyance, and John of Burgundy still conspired in secret. On November 23, 1407—in that black winter when the frost lasted six-and-sixty days on end—a summons from the king reached Louis of Orleans at the Hôtel Barbette, where he had been supping with Queen Isabel. It was seven or eight in the evening, and the inhabitants of the quarter were abed. He set forth in haste, accompanied by two squires riding on one horse, a page, and a few varlets running with torches. As he rode, he hummed to himself and trifled with his glove. And so riding, he was beset by the bravoes of his enemy and slain. My lord of Burgundy set an ill precedent in this deed, as he found some years after on the bridge of Montereau; and even in the meantime he did not profit quietly by his rival's death. The horror of the other princes seems to have perturbed himself; he avowed his guilt in the council, tried to brazen it out, finally lost heart and fled at full gallop, cutting bridges behind him, toward Bapaume and Lille. And so there we have the head of one faction, who had just made himself the most formidable man in France, engaged in a remarkably hurried journey, with black care on the pillion. And meantime, on the other side, the widowed duchess came to Paris in appropriate mourning,

*Des Ursins.

FAMILIAR STUDIES

to demand justice for her husband's death. Charles VI., who was then in a lucid interval, did probably all that he could, when he raised up the kneeling suppliant with kisses and smooth words. Things were at a dead-lock. The criminal might be in the sorriest fright, but he was still the greatest of vassals. Justice was easy to ask and not difficult to promise; how it was to be executed was another question. No one in France was strong enough to punish John of Burgundy; and perhaps no one, except the widow, very sincere in wishing to punish him.

She, indeed, was eaten up of zeal; but the intensity of her eagerness wore her out; and she died about a year after the murder, of grief and indignation, unrequited love and unsatisfied resentment. It was during the last months of her life that this fiery and generous woman, seeing the soft hearts of her own children, looked with envy on a certain natural son of her husband's destined to become famous in the sequel as the Bastard of Orleans, or the brave Dunois. "*You were stolen from me,*" she said; "it is you who are fit to avenge your father." These are not the words of ordinary mourning, or of an ordinary woman. It is a saying, over which Balzac would have rubbed his episcopal hands. That the child who was to avenge her husband had not been born out of her body, was a thing intolerable to Valentina of Milan; and the expression of this singular and tragic jealousy is preserved to us by a rare chance, in such straightforward and vivid words as we are accustomed to hear only on the stress of actual life, or in the theatre. In history—where we see things as in a glass darkly, and the fashion of former times is brought before us, deplorably adulterated and defaced, fitted to very vague and pompous words, and strained through many men's minds of everything personal or precise—this speech of the widowed duchess startles a reader, somewhat as the footprint startled Robinson Crusoe. A human voice breaks in upon the silence of the study, and the student is aware of a fellow-creature in his world of documents. With such a clew in hand, one may imagine how this wounded lioness would spur and exasperate

CHARLES OF ORLEANS

resentment of her children, and what would be the last
·ds of counsel and command she left behind her.
Vith these instances of his dying mother—almost a voice
m the tomb—still tingling in his ears, the position of
ing Charles of Orleans, when he was left at the head of
t great house, was curiously similar to that of Shake-
are's Hamlet. The times were out of joint; here was a
rdered father to avenge on a powerful murderer; and
e, in both cases, a lad of inactive disposition born to set
se matters right. Valentina's commendation of Dunois
olved a judgment on Charles, and that judgment was
ctly correct. Whoever might be, Charles was not the
a to avenge his father. Like Hamlet, this son of a dear
her murdered was sincerely grieved at heart. Like Ham-
too, he could unpack his heart with words, and wrote a
st eloquent letter to the king, complaining that what was
ied to him would not be denied " to the lowest born and
rest man on earth." Even in his private hours he strove
preserve a lively recollection of his injury, and keep up
native hue of resolution. He had gems engraved with
propriate legends, hortatory or threatening: "*Dieu le
!*," God knows it; or " *Souvenez-vous de—*" Remember.*
is only toward the end that the stories begin to differ;
l in some points the historical version is the more tragic.
mlet only stabbed a silly old councillor behind the arras;
arles of Orleans trampled France for five years under the
fs of his banditti. The miscarriage of Hamlet's ven-
nce was confined, at widest, to the palace; the ruin
ught by Charles of Orleans was broad as France.
Yet the first act of the young duke is worthy of honorable
ition. Prodigal Louis had made enormous debts; and
re is a story extant, to illustrate how lightly he himself
arded these commercial obligations. It appears that
is, after a narrow escape he made in a thunder-storm,
l a smart access of penitence, and announced he would
r his debts on the following Sunday. More than eight
dred creditors presented themselves, but by that time
devil was well again, and they were shown the door

* Michelet, iv. App. 179, p. 337.

FAMILIAR STUDIES

with more gayety than politeness. A time when such cyn[i]cal dishonesty was possible for a man of culture is not, i[t] will be granted, a fortunate epoch for creditors. When th[e] original debtor was so lax, we may imagine how an hei[r] would deal with the incumbrances of his inheritance. On th[e] death of Philip the Forward, father of that John the Fear[less] whom we have seen at work, the widow went through th[e] ceremony of a public renunciation of goods; taking off he[r] purse and girdle, she left them on the grave, and thus, b[y] one notable act cancelled her husband's debts and defame[d] his honor. The conduct of young Charles of Orleans wa[s] very different. To meet the joint liabilities of his fathe[r] and mother (for Valentina also was lavish), he had to sell o[r] pledge a quantity of jewels; and yet he would not tak[e] advantage of a pretext, even legally valid, to diminish th[e] amount. Thus, one Godefroi Lefèvre, having disburse[d] many odd sums for the late duke, and received or kept n[o] vouchers, Charles ordered that he should be believed upo[n] his oath.* To a modern mind this seems as honorable to hi[s] father's memory as if John the Fearless had been hange[d] as high as Haman. And as things fell out, except a recanta-tion from the University of Paris, which had justified th[e] murder out of party feeling, and various other purely pape[r] reparations, this was about the outside of what Charles wa[s] to effect in that direction. He lived five years, and grew up from sixteen to twenty-one, in the midst of the most horribl[e] civil war, or series of civil wars that ever devastated France; and from first to last his wars were ill-starred, or else hi[s] victories useless. Two years after the murder (March 1409), John the Fearless having the upper hand for the moment, a shameful and useless reconciliation took place, by the king's command, in the church of Our Lady at Chartres. The advocate of the Duke of Burgundy stated that Louis of Orleans had been killed " for the good of the king's person and realm." Charles and his brothers, with tears of shame, under protest, *pour ne pas desobéir au roi*, forgave their father's murderer, and swore peace upon the missal. It was, as I say, a shameful and useless ceremony;

* Champollion-Figeac, pp. 279-82.

CHARLES OF ORLEANS

ery greffier, entering it in his register, wrote in the
in, "*Pax, pax, inquit Propheta, et non est pax.*" *
es was soon after allied with the abominable Bernard
nagnac, even betrothed or married to a daughter of
alled by a name that sounds like a contradiction in
, Bonne d'Armagnac. From that time forth, through-
ll this monstrous period—a very nightmare in the his-
of France—he is no more than a stalking-horse for the
ious Gascon. Sometimes the smoke lifts, and you can
im for the twinkling of an eye, a very pale figure; at
noment there is a rumor he will be crowned king; at
er, when the uproar has subsided, he will be heard still
g out for justice; and the next (1412), he is showing
lf to the applauding populace on the same horse with
of Burgundy. But these are exceptional seasons, and,
he most part, he merely rides at the Gascon's bridle
devastated France. His very party go, not by the
of Orleans, but by the name of Armagnac. Paris is
e hands of the butchers: the peasants have taken to
oods. Alliances are made and broken as if in a country
e; the English called in, now by this one, now by the
. Poor people sing in church, with white faces and la-
ible music: "*Domine Jesu, parce populo tuo, dirige in
pacis principes.*" And the end and upshot of the whole
· for Charles of Orleans is another peace with John
'earless. France is once more tranquil, with the tran-
ty of ruin; he may ride home again to Blois, and look,
what countenance he may, on those gems he had got
ived in the early days of his resentment, "*Souvenez-
de—*" Remember! He has killed Polonius, to be sure;
he king is never a penny the worse.

II

om the battle of Agincourt (October, 1415) dates the
d period of Charles's life. The English reader will
nber the name of Orleans in the play of *Henry V.*;
· is at least odd that we can trace a resemblance between

165   * Michelet, iv. pp. 123-4.

the puppet and the original. The interjection, "I have heard a sonnet begin so to one's mistress" (Act iii. scene 7), may very well indicate one who was already an expert in that sort of trifle; and the game of proverbs he plays with the Constable in the same scene, would be quite in character for a man who spent many years of his life capping verses with his courtiers. Certainly, Charles was in the great battle with five hundred lances (say three thousand men), and there he was made prisoner as he led the van. According to one story, some ragged English archer shot him down; and some diligent English Pistol, hunting ransoms on the field of battle, extracted him from under a heap of bodies and retailed him to our King Henry. He was the most important capture of the day, and used with all consideration. On the way to Calais, Henry sent him a present of bread and wine (and bread, you will remember, was an article of luxury in the English camp), but Charles would neither eat nor drink. Thereupon, Henry came to visit him in his quarters. "Noble cousin," said he, "how are you?" Charles replied that he was well. "Why, then, do you neither eat nor drink?" And then with some asperity, as I imagine, the young duke told him that "truly he had no inclination for food." And our Henry improved the occasion with something of a snuffle, assuring his prisoner that God had fought against the French on account of their manifold sins and transgressions. Upon this there supervened the agonies of a rough sea passage; and many French lords, Charles, certainly, among the number, declared they would rather endure such another defeat than such another sore trial on shipboard. Charles, indeed, never forgot his sufferings. Long afterward, he declared his hatred to a seafaring life, and willingly yielded to England the empire of the seas, "because there is danger and loss of life, and God knows what pity when it storms; and sea-sickness is for many people hard to bear; and the rough life that must be led is little suitable for the nobility:"* which, of all babyish utterances that ever fell from any public man, may

Debate between the Heralds.

CHARLES OF ORLEANS

surely bear the bell. Scarcely disembarked, he followed his victor, with such wry face as we may fancy, through the streets of holiday London. And then the doors closed upon his last day of garish life for more than a quarter of a century. After a boyhood passed in the dissipations of a luxurious court or in the camp of war, his ears still stunned and his cheeks still burning from his enemies' jubilations; out of all this ringing of English bells and singing of English anthems, from among all these shouting citizens in scarlet cloaks, and beautiful virgins attired in white, he passed into the silence and solitude of a political prison.*

His captivity was not without alleviations. He was allowed to go hawking, and he found England an admirable country for the sport; he was a favorite with English ladies, and admired their beauty; and he did not lack for money, wine, or books; he was honorably imprisoned in the strongholds of great nobles, in Windsor Castle and the Tower of London. But when all is said, he was a prisoner for five-and-twenty years. For five-and-twenty years he could not go where he would, or do what he liked, or speak with any but his jailers. We may talk very wisely of alleviations; there is only one alleviation for which the man would thank you: he would thank you to open the door. With what regret Scottish James I. bethought him (in the next room perhaps to Charles) of the time when he rose " as early as the day." What would he not have given to wet his boots once more with morning dew, and follow his vagrant fancy among the meadows? The only alleviation to the misery of constraint lies in the disposition of the prisoner. To each one this place of discipline brings his own lesson. It stirs Latude or Baron Trenck into heroic action; it is a hermitage for pious and conformable spirits. Béranger tells us he found prison life, with its regular hours and long evenings, both pleasant and profitable. The *Pilgrim's Progress* and *Don Quixote* were begun in prison. It was after they were become (to use the words of one of them), " Oh, worst imprisonment—the dungeon of themselves!" that Homer and Milton worked so hard and so well for the profit of

*Sir H. Nicholas, *Agincourt*.

FAMILIAR STUDIES

mankind. In the year 1415 Henry V. had two distin
prisoners, French Charles of Orleans and Scottish J.
who whiled away the hours of their captivity with r]
Indeed, there can be no better pastime for a lonely m
the mechanical exercise of verse. Such intricate f(
Charles had been used to from childhood, the balla
its scanty rhymes; the rondel, with the recurrence
the whole, then of half the burden, in thirteen versi
to have been invented for the prison and the sick-be
common Scotch saying, on the sight of anything opei
finical, "he must have had little to do that made
might be put as epigraph on all the song books of old
Making such sorts of verse belongs to the same (
pleasures as guessing acrostics or "burying proverl
is almost purely formal, almost purely verbal.]
be done gently and gingerly. It keeps the mind occ
long time, and never so intently as to be distressii
anything like strain is against the very nature of th
Sometimes things go easily, the refrains fall into the
as if of their own accord, and it becomes something
nature of an intellectual tennis; you must make you
as the rhymes will go, just as you must strike your
your adversary played it. So that these forms are
rather for those who wish to make verses, than for th
wish to express opinions. Sometimes, on the othe:
difficulties arise: rival verses come into a man's he
fugitive words elude his memory. Then it is that he
at the same time the deliberate pleasures of a coni
comparing wines, and the ardor of the chase. He mi
been sitting all day long in prison with folded han
when he goes to bed, the retrospect will seem anima'
eventful.

Besides confirming himself as an habitual maker of
Charles acquired some new opinions during his ca
He was perpetually reminded of the change that]
fallen him. He found the climate of England c(
"prejudicial to the human frame"; he had a gre
tempt for English fruit and English beer; even t

CHARLES OF ORLEANS

ires were unpleasing in his eyes.* He was rooted up from among his friends and customs and the places that had known him. And so in this strange land he began to learn the love of his own. Sad people all the world over are like to be moved when the wind is in some particular quarter. So Burns preferred when it was in the west, and blew to him from his mistress; so the girl in the ballade, looking south to Yarrow, thought it might carry a kiss betwixt her and her gallant; and so we find Charles singing of the " pleasant wind that comes from France." † One day, at " Dover-on-the-Sea," he looked across the straits, and saw the sandhills about Calais. And it happened to him, he tells us in a ballade, to remember his happiness over there in the past; and he was both sad and merry at the recollection, and could not have his fill of gazing on the shores of France.‡ Although guilty of unpatriotic acts, he had never been exactly unpatriotic in feeling. But his sojourn in England gave, for the time at least, some consistency to what had been a very weak and ineffectual prejudice. He must have been under the influence of more than usually solemn considerations, when he proceeded to turn Henry's puritanical homily after Agincourt into a ballade, and reproach France, and himself by implication, with pride, gluttony, idleness, unbridled covetousness, and sensuality.§ For the moment, he must really have been thinking more of France than of Charles of Orleans.

And another lesson he learned. He who was only to be released in case of peace, begins to think upon the disadvantages of war. "Pray for peace," is his refrain: a strange enough subject for the ally of Bernard d'Armagnac.‖ But this lesson was plain and practical; it had one side in particular that was specially attractive for Charles; and he did not hesitate to explain it in so many words. 'Everybody," he writes—I translate roughly—" everybody hould be much inclined to peace, for everybody has a deal o gain by it." ¶

Debate between the Heralds. † Works (ed. d'Héricault), i. 43.
‡ Works (ed d'Héricault), i. 143. § *Ibid.* 190.
‖ *Ibid.* 144. ¶ *Ibid.* 158.

FAMILIAR STUDIES

Charles made laudable endeavors to acquire English, and even learned to write a rondel in that tongue of quite average mediocrity.* He was for some time billeted on the unhappy Suffolk, who received fourteen shillings and fourpence a day for his expenses; and from the fact that Suffolk afterward visited Charles in France while he was negotiating the marriage of Henry VI., as well as the terms of that nobleman's impeachment, we may believe there was some not unkindly intercourse between the prisoner and his jailer: a fact of considerable interest when we remember that Suffolk's wife was the granddaughter of the poet Geoffrey Chaucer.† Apart from this, and a mere catalogue of dates and places, only one thing seems evident in the story of Charles's captivity. It seems evident that, as these five-and-twenty years drew on, he became less and less resigned. Circumstances were against the growth of such a feeling. One after another of his fellow-prisoners was ransomed and went home. More than once he was himself permitted to visit France; where he worked on abortive treaties and showed himself more eager for his own deliverance than for the profit of his native land. Resignation may follow after a reasonable time upon despair; but if a man is persecuted by a series of brief and irritating hopes, his mind no more attains to a settled frame of resolution, than his eye would grow familiar with a night of thunder and lightning. Years after, when he was speaking at the trial of that Duke of Alençon, who began life so hopefully as the boyish favorite of Joan of Arc, he sought to prove that captivity was a harder punishment than death. "For I have had experience myself," he said; "and in my prison of England, for the weariness, danger, and displeasure in which I then lay, I have many a time wished I had been slain at the battle where they took me." ‡ This is a flourish, if you will, but it is something more. His spirit would sometimes rise up in a

* M. Champollion-Figeac gives many in his editions of Charles's works, most (as I should think) of very doubtful authenticity, or worse.
† Rymer, x. 564. D'Héricault's *Memoir*, p. xli. Gairdner's *Paston Letters*, i. 27, 99.
‡ Champollion-Figeac, 377,

'170

CHARLES OF ORLEANS

fine anger against the petty desires and contrarieties of life. He would compare his own condition with the quiet and dignified estate of the dead; and aspire to lie among his comrades on the field of Agincourt, as the Psalmist prayed to have the wings of a dove and dwell in the uttermost parts of the sea. But such high thoughts came to Charles only in a flash.

John the Fearless had been murdered in his turn on the bridge of Montereau so far back as 1419. His son, Philip the Good—partly to extinguish the feud, partly that he might do a popular action, and partly, in view of his ambitious schemes, to detach another great vassal from the throne of France—had taken up the cause of Charles of Orleans, and negotiated diligently for his release. In 1433 a Burgundian embassy was admitted to an interview with the captive duke, in the presence of Suffolk. Charles shook hands most affectionately with the ambassadors. They asked after his health. "I am well enough in body," he replied, "but far from well in mind. I am dying of grief at having to pass the best days of my life in prison, with none to sympathize." The talk falling on the chances of peace, Charles referred to Suffolk if he were not sincere and constant in his endeavors to bring it about. "If peace depended on me," he said, "I should procure it gladly, were it to cost me my life seven days after." We may take this as showing what a large price he set, not so much on peace, as on seven days of freedom. Seven days!—he would make them seven years in the employment. Finally, he assured the ambassadors of his good will to Philip of Burgundy; squeezed one of them by the hand and nipped him twice in the arm to signify things unspeakable before Suffolk; and two days after sent them Suffolk's barber, one Jean Carnet, a native of Lille, to testify more freely of his sentiments. "As I speak French," said the emissary, "the Duke of Orleans is more familiar with me than with any other of the household; and I can bear witness he never said anything against Duke Philip."* It will be remembered that this person, with whom he was so anxious to stand well, was no other

* Dom Plancher, iv. 178-9.

FAMILIAR STUDIES

than his hereditary enemy, the son of his father's murderer. But the honest fellow bore no malice, indeed not he. He began exchanging ballades with Philip, whom he apostrophizes as his companion, his cousin, and his brother. He assures him that, soul and body, he is altogether Burgundian; and protests that he has given his heart in pledge to him. Regarded as the history of a vendetta, it must be owned that Charles's life has points of some originality. And yet there is an engaging frankness about these ballades which disarms criticism.* You see Charles throwing himself headforemost into the trap; you hear Burgundy, in his answers, begin to inspire him with his own prejudices, and draw melancholy pictures of the misgovernment of France. But Charles's own spirits are so high and so amiable, and he is so thoroughly convinced his cousin is a fine fellow, that one's scruples are carried away in the torrent of his happiness and gratitude. And his would be a sordid spirit who would not clap hands at the consummation (November, 1440); when Charles, after having sworn on the Sacrament that he would never again bear arms against England, and pledged himself body and soul to the unpatriotic faction in his own country, set out from London with a light heart and a damaged integrity.

In the magnificent copy of Charles's poems, given by our Henry VII. to Elizabeth of York on the occasion of their marriage, a large illumination figures at the head of one of the pages, which, in chronological perspective, is almost a history of his imprisonment. It gives a view of London with all its spires, the river passing through the old bridge and busy with boats. One side of the White Tower has been taken out, and we can see, as under a sort of shrine, the paved room where the duke sits writing. He occupies a high-backed bench in front of a great chimney; red and black ink are before him; and the upper end of the apartment is guarded by many halberdiers, with the red cross of England on their breast. On the next side of the tower he appears again, leaning out of window and gazing on the river; doubtless there blows just then " a pleasant wind

* Works, I. 157-63.

CHARLES OF ORLEANS

from out the land of France," and some ship comes up the river: "the ship of good news." At the door we find him yet again; this time embracing a messenger, while a groom stands by holding two saddled horses. And yet further to the left, a cavalcade defiles out of the tower; the duke is on his way at last toward "the sunshine of France."

III

During the five-and-twenty years of his captivity, Charles had not lost in the esteem of his fellow-countrymen. For so young a man, the head of so great a house, and so numerous a party, to be taken prisoner as he rode in the vanguard of France, and stereotyped for all men in this heroic attitude, was to taste untimeously the honors of the grave. Of him, as of the dead, it would be ungenerous to speak evil; what little energy he had displayed would be remembered with piety, when all that he had done amiss was courteously forgotten. As English folk looked for Arthur; as Danes awaited the coming of Ogier; as Somersetshire peasants or sergeants of the Old Guard expected the return of Monmouth or Napoleon; the countrymen of Charles of Orleans looked over the straits toward his English prison with desire and confidence. Events had so fallen out while he was rhyming ballades, that he had become the type of all that was most truly patriotic. The remnants of his old party had been the chief defenders of the unity of France. His enemies of Burgundy had been notoriously favorers and furtherers of English domination. People forgot that his brother still lay by the heels for an unpatriotic treaty with England, because Charles himself had been taken prisoner patriotically fighting against it. That Henry V. had left special orders against his liberation, served to increase the wistful pity with which he was regarded. And when, in defiance of all contemporary virtue, and against express pledges, the English carried war into their prisoner's fief, not only France, but all thinking men in Christendom, were roused to indignation against the oppressors, and sym-

FAMILIAR STUDIES

pathy with the victim. It was little wonder if he came to bulk somewhat largely in the imagination of the best of those at home. Charles le Boutteillier, when (as the story goes) he slew Clarence at Beaugé, was only seeking an exchange for Charles of Orleans.* It was one of Joan of Arc's declared intentions to deliver the captive duke. If there was no other way, she meant to cross the seas and bring him home by force. And she professed before her judges a sure knowledge that Charles of Orleans was beloved of God.†

Alas! it was not at all as a deliverer that Charles returned to France. He was nearly fifty years old. Many changes had been accomplished since, at twenty-three, he was taken on the field of Agincourt. But of all these he was profoundly ignorant, or had only heard of them in the discolored reports of Philip of Burgundy. He had the ideas of a former generation, and sought to correct them by the scandal of a factious party. With such qualifications he came back eager for the domination, the pleasures, and the display that befitted his princely birth. A long disuse of all political activity combined with the flatteries of his new friends to fill him with an overweening conceit of his own capacity and influence. If aught had gone wrong in his absence, it seemed quite natural men should look to him for its redress. Was not King Arthur come again?

The Duke of Burgundy received him with politic honors. He took his guest by his foible for pageantry, all the easier as it was a foible of his own; and Charles walked right out of prison into much the same atmosphere of trumpeting and bell-ringing as he had left behind when he went in. Fifteen days after his deliverance he was married to Mary of Cleves, at St. Omer. The marriage was celebrated with the usual pomp of the Burgundian court; there were joustings, and illuminations, and animals that spouted wine; and many nobles dined together, *comme en brigade*, and were served abundantly with many rich and curious dishes.‡ It must have reminded Charles not a little of his first marriage at

* Vallet's *Charles VII.*, i. 251.   † *Procès de Jeanne d'Arc*, 133-55.
‡ Monstrelet.   174

CHARLES OF ORLEANS

Compiègne; only then he was two years the junior of his bride, and this time he was five-and-thirty years her senior. It will be a fine question which marriage promises more: for a boy of fifteen to lead off with a lass of seventeen, or a man of fifty to make a match of it with a child of fifteen. But there was something bitter in both. The lamentations of Isabella will not have been forgotten. As for Mary, she took up with one Jaquet de la Lain, a sort of muscular Methody of the period, with a huge appetite for tournaments, and a habit of confessing himself the last thing before he went to bed.* With such a hero, the young duchess's amours were most likely innocent; and in all other ways she was a suitable partner for the duke, and well fitted to enter into his pleasures.

When the festivities at St. Omer had come to an end, Charles and his wife set forth by Ghent and Tournay. The towns gave him offerings of money as he passed through, to help in the payment of his ransom. From all sides, ladies and gentlemen thronged to offer him their services; some gave him their sons for pages, some archers for a bodyguard; and by the time he reached Tournay, he had a following of 800 horse. Everywhere he was received as though he had been the King of France.† If he did not come to imagine himself something of the sort, he certainly forgot the existence of any one with a better claim to the title. He conducted himself on the hypothesis that Charles VII. was another Charles VI. He signed with enthusiasm that treaty of Arras, which left France almost at the discretion of Burgundy. On December 18 he was still no farther than Bruges, where he entered into a private treaty with Philip; and it was not until January 14, ten weeks after he disembarked in France, and attended by a ruck of Burgundian gentlemen, that he arrived in Paris and offered to present himself before Charles VII. The king sent word that he might come, if he would, with a small retinue, but not with his present following; and the duke, who was

* Vallet's *Charles VII.*, iii. chap. i. But see the chronicle that bears Jaquet's name: a lean and dreary book.
† Monstrelet.

mightily on his high horse after all the ovations he had received, took the king's attitude amiss, and turned aside into Touraine, to receive more welcome and more presents, and be convoyed by torchlight into faithful cities.

And so you see, here was King Arthur home again, and matters nowise mended in consequence. The best we can says is, that this last stage of Charles's public life was of no long duration. His confidence was soon knocked out of him in the contact with others. He began to find he was an earthen vessel among many vessels of brass; he began to be shrewdly aware that he was no King Arthur. In 1442, at Limoges, he made himself the spokesman of the malcontent nobility. The king showed himself humiliatingly indifferent to his counsels, and humiliatingly generous toward his necessities. And there, with some blushes, he may be said to have taken farewell of the political stage. A feeble attempt on the county of Asti is scarce worth the name of exception. Thenceforward let Ambition wile whom she may into the turmoil of events, our duke will walk cannily in his well-ordered garden, or sit by the fire to touch the slender reed.*

IV

If it were given each of us to transplant his life wherever he pleased in time or space, with all the ages and all the countries of the world to choose from, there would be quite an instructive diversity of taste. A certain sedentary majority would prefer to remain where they were. Many would choose the Renaissance; many some stately and simple period of Grecian life; and still more elect to pass a few years wandering among the villages of Palestine with an inspired conductor. For some of our quaintly vicious contemporaries, we have the decline of the Roman Empire and the reign of Henry III. of France. But there are others not quite so vicious, who yet cannot look upon the world with perfect gravity, who have never taken the categorical imperative to wife, and have more taste for what is com-

* D'Héricault's *Memoir*, xl, xli. Vallet, *Charles VI.*, ii. 435.

CHARLES OF ORLEANS

fortable than for what is magnanimous and high; and I can imagine some of these casting their lot in the Court of Blois during the last twenty years of the life of Charles of Orleans.

The duke and duchess, their staff of officers and ladies, and the high-born and learned persons who were attracted to Blois on a visit, formed a society for killing time and perfecting each other in various elegant accomplishments, such as we might imagine for an ideal watering-place in the Delectable Mountains. The company hunted and went on pleasure-parties; they played chess, tables, and many other games. What we now call the history of the period passed, I imagine, over the heads of these good people much as it passes over our own. News reached them, indeed, of great and joyful import. William Peel received eight livres and five sous from the duchess, when he brought the first tidings that Rouen was recaptured from the English.* A little later and the duke sang, in a truly patriotic vein, the deliverance of Guyenne and Normandy.† They were liberal of rhymes and largesse, and welcomed the prosperity of their country much as they welcomed the coming of spring, and with no more thought of collaborating toward the event. Religion was not forgotten in the Court of Blois. Pilgrimages were agreeable and picturesque excursions. In those days a well-served chapel was something like a good vinery in our own, an opportunity for display and the source of mild enjoyments. There was probably something of his rooted delight in pageantry, as well as a good deal of gentle piety, in the feelings with which Charles gave a dinner every Friday to thirteen poor people, served them himself, and washed their feet with his own hands.‡ Solemn affairs would interest Charles and his courtiers from their trivial side. The duke perhaps cared less for the deliverance of Guyenne and Normandy than for his own verses on the occasion; just as Dr. Russell's correspondence in *The Times* was among the most material parts of the Crimean War for that talented correspondent. And I think it scarcely cynical to suppose

* Champollion-Figeac, 368. † Works, i. 115.
‡ D'Héricault's *Memior*, xlv.

that religion as well as patriotism was principally cultivated as a means of filling up the day.

It was not only messengers fiery red with haste and charged with the destiny of nations, who were made welcome at the gates of Blois. If any man of accomplishment came that way, he was sure of an audience, and something for his pocket. The courtiers would have received Ben Jonson like Drummond of Hawthornden, and a good pugilist like Captain Barclay. They were catholic, as none but the entirely idle can be catholic. It might be Pierre, called Dieu d'amours, the juggler; or it might be three high English minstrels; or the two men, players of ghitterns, from the kingdom of Scotland, who sang the destruction of the Turks; or again Jehan Rognelet, player of instruments of music, who played and danced with his wife and two children; they would each be called into the castle to give a taste of his proficiency before my lord the duke.* Sometimes the performance was of a more personal interest, and produced much the same sensations as are felt on an English green on the arrival of a professional cricketer, or round an English billiard table during a match between Roberts and Cooke. This was when Jehan Nègre, the Lombard, came to Blois and played chess against all these chess-players, and won much money from my lord and his intimates; or when Baudet Harenc of Chalons made ballades before all these ballade-makers.†

It will not surprise the reader to learn they were all makers of ballades and rondels. To write verses for May day, seems to have been as much a matter of course, as to ride out with the cavalcade that went to gather hawthorn. The choice of Valentines was a standing challenge, and the courtiers pelted each other with humorous and sentimental verses as in a literary carnival. If an indecorous adventure befell our friend Maistre Estienne le Gout, my lord the duke would turn it into the funniest of rondels, all the rhymes being the names of the cases of nouns or the moods of verbs; and Maistre Estienne would make reply in similar fashion, seeking to prune the story of its more humiliating episodes. If

* Champollion-Figeac, 881, 361.
† Champollion-Figeac, 359, 361.

CHARLES OF ORLEANS

Frédet was too long away from Court, a rondel went to upbraid him; and it was in a rondel that Frédet would excuse himself. Sometimes two or three, or as many as a dozen, would set to work on the same refrain, the same idea, or in the same macaronic jargon. Some of the poetasters were heavy enough; others were not wanting in address; and the duchess herself was among those who most excelled. On one occasion eleven competitors made a ballade on the idea,

"I die of thirst beside the fountain's edge"
(Je meurs de soif emprès de la fontaine).

These eleven ballades still exist; and one of them arrests the attention rather from the name of the author than from any special merit in itself. It purports to be the work of François Villon; and so far as a foreigner can judge (which is indeed a small way), it may very well be his. Nay, and if any one thing is more probable than another, in the great *tabula rasa*, or unknown land, which we are fain to call the biography of Villon, it seems probable enough that he may have gone upon a visit to Charles of Orleans. Where Master Baudet Harenc, of Chalons, found a sympathetic, or perhaps a derisive audience (for who can tell nowadays the degree of Baudet's excellence in his art?), favor would not be wanting for the greatest ballade-maker of all time. Great as would seem the incongruity, it may have pleased Charles to own a sort of kinship with ragged singers, and whimsically regard himself as one of the confraternity of poets. And he would have other grounds of intimacy with Villon. A room looking upon Windsor gardens is a different matter from Villon's dungeon at Méun; yet each in his own degree had been tried in prison. Each in his own way also, loved the good things of this life and the service of the Muses. But the same gulf that separated Burns from his Edinburgh patrons would separate the singer of Bohemia from the rhyming duke. And it is hard to imagine that Villon's training among thieves, loose women, and vagabond students, had fitted him to move in a society of any

FAMILIAR STUDIES

dignity and courtliness. Ballades are very admirable things; and a poet is doubtless a most interesting visitor. But among the courtiers of Charles, there would be considerable regard for the proprieties of etiquette; and even a duke will sometimes have an eye to his teaspoons. Moreover, as a poet, I can conceive he may have disappointed expectation. It need surprise nobody if Villon's ballade on the theme,

"I die of thirst beside the fountain's edge,"

was but a poor performance. He would make better verses on the lee-side of a flagon at the sign of the Pomme du Pin, than in a cushioned settle in the halls of Blois.

Charles liked change of place. He was often, not so much travelling as making a progress; now to join the king for some great tournament; now to visit King René, at Tarascon, where he had a study of his own and saw all manner of interesting things—oriental curios, King René painting birds, and, what particularly pleased him, Triboulet, the dwarf jester, whose skull-cap was no bigger than an orange.* Sometimes the journeys were set about on horseback in a large party, with the *fourriers* sent forward to prepare a lodging at the next stage. We find almost Gargantuan details of the provision made by these officers against the duke's arrival, of eggs and butter and bread, cheese and peas and chickens, pike and bream and barbel, and wine both white and red.† Sometimes he went by water in a barge, playing chess or tables with a friend in the pavilion, or watching other vessels as they went before the wind.‡ Children ran along the banks, as they do to this day on the Crinan Canal; and when Charles threw in money, they would dive and bring it up.§ As he looked on at

* Lecoy de la Marche, *Roi René*, ii. 155, 177.
† Champollion-Figeac, chaps. v. and vi.
‡ *Ibid.* 364; Works, i. 172.
§ Champollion-Figeac, 364: "Jeter de l'argent aux petis enfans qui estoient au long de Bourbon, pour les faire nonner en l'eau et aller querre l'argent au fond."

180

CHARLES OF ORLEANS

their exploits, I wonder whether that room of gold and silk and worsted came back into his memory, with the device of little children in a river, and the sky full of birds?

He was a bit of a book-fancier, and had vied with his brother Angoulême in bringing back the library of their grandfather Charles V., when Bedford put it up for sale in London.* The duchess had a library of her own; and we hear of her borrowing romances from ladies in attendance on the blue-stocking Margaret of Scotland.† Not only were books collected, but new books were written at the Court of Blois. The widow of one Jean Fougère, a bookbinder, seems to have done a number of odd commissions for the bibliophilous count. She it was who received three vellum-skins to bind the duchess's Book of Hours, and who was employed to prepare parchment for the use of the duke's scribes. And she it was who bound in vermillion leather the great manuscript of Charles's own poems, which was presented to him by his secretary, Anthony Astesan, with the text in one column, and Astesan's Latin version in the other.‡

Such tastes, with the coming of years, would doubtless take the place of many others. We find in Charles's verse much semi-ironical regret for other days, and resignation to growing infirmities. He who had been " nourished in the schools of love," now sees nothing either to please or displease him. Old age has imprisoned him within doors, where he means to take his ease, and let younger fellows bestir themselves in life. He had written (in earlier days, we may presume) a bright and defiant little poem in praise of solitude. If they would but leave him alone with his own thoughts and happy recollections, he declared it was beyond the power of melancholy to affect him. But now, when his animal strength has so much declined that he sings the discomforts of winter instead of the inspirations of spring, and he has no longer any appetite for life, he confesses he is wretched when alone, and, to keep his mind from grievous

* Champollion-Figeac, 887.
† *Nouvelle Biographie Didot*, art. " Marie de Clèves." Vallet *Charles VII.*, iii. 85, note 1.
‡ Champollion-Figeac, 383, 384-386.

FAMILIAR STUDIES

thoughts, he must have many people around him, laughing, talking, and singing.*
While Charles was thus falling into years, the order of things, of which he was the outcome and ornament, was growing old along with him. The semi-royalty of the princes of the blood was already a thing of the past; and when Charles VII. was gathered to his fathers, a new king reigned in France, who seemed every way the opposite of royal. Louis XI. had aims that were incomprehensible, and virtues that were inconceivable to his contemporaries. But his contemporaries were able enough to appreciate his sordid exterior and his cruel and treacherous spirit. To the whole nobility of France he was a fatal and unreasonable phenomenon. All such courts as that of Charles at Blois, or his friend René's in Provence, would soon be made impossible; interference was the order of the day; hunting was already abolished; and who should say what was to go next? Louis, in fact, must have appeared to Charles primarily in the light of a kill-joy. I take it, when missionaries land in South Sea Islands and lay strange embargo on the simplest things in life, the islanders will not be much more puzzled and irritated than Charles of Orleans at the policy of the Eleventh Louis. There was one thing, I seem to apprehend, that had always particularly moved him; and that was, any proposal to punish a person of his acquaintance. No matter what treason he may have made or meddled with, an Alençon or an Armagnac was sure to find Charles reappear from private life, and do his best to get him pardoned. He knew them quite well. He had made rondels with them. They were charming people in every way. There must certainly be some mistake. Had not he himself made anti-national treaties almost before he was out of his nonage? And for the matter of that, had not every one else done the like? Such are some of the thoughts by which he might explain to himself his aversion to such extremities; but it was on a deeper basis that the feeling probably reposed. A man of his temper could not fail to be impressed at the thought of disastrous revolutions in the fortunes of those he knew.

Works, ii. 57, 258.

CHARLES OF ORLEANS

He would feel painfully the tragic contrast, when those who had everything to make life valuable were deprived of life itself. And it was shocking to the clemency of his spirit, that sinners should be hurried before their Judge without a fitting interval for penitence and satisfaction. It was this feeling which brought him at last, a poor, purblind bluebottle of the later autumn, into collision with " the universal spider," Louis XI. He took up the defence of the Duke of Brittany at Tours. But Louis was then in no humor to hear Charles's texts and Latin sentiments; he had his back to the wall, the future of France was at stake; and if all the old men in the world had crossed his path, they would have had the rough side of his tongue like Charles of Orleans. I have found nowhere what he said, but it seems it was monstrously to the point, and so rudely conceived that the old duke never recovered the indignity. He got home as far as Amboise, sickened, and died two days after (Jan. 4, 1465), in the seventy-fourth year of his age. And so a whiff of pungent prose stopped the issue of melodious rondels to the end of time.

The futility of Charles' public life was of a piece throughout. He never succeeded in any single purpose he set before him; for his deliverance from England, after twenty-five years of failure and at the cost of dignity and consistency, it would be ridiculously hyperbolical to treat as a success. During the first part of his life he was the stalking horse of Bernard d'Armagnac; during the second, he was the passive instrument of English diplomatists; and before he was well entered on the third, he hastened to become the dupe and catspaw of Burgundian treason. On each of these occasions, a strong and not dishonorable personal motive determined his behavior. In 1407 and the following years, he had his father's murder uppermost in his mind. During his English captivity, that thought was displaced by a more immediate desire for his own liberation. In 1440 a senti-

FAMILIAR STUDIES

ment of gratitude to Philip of Burgundy blinded him to all else, and led him to break with the tradition of his party and his own former life. He was born a great vassal, and he conducted himself like a private gentleman. He began life in a showy and brilliant enough fashion, by the light of a petty personal chivalry. He was not without some tincture of patriotism; but it was resolvable into two parts: a preference for life among his fellow-countrymen, and a barren point of honor. In England, he could comfort himself by the reflection that "he had been taken while loyally doing his devoir," without any misgiving as to his conduct in the previous years, when he had prepared the disaster of Agincourt by wasteful feud. This unconsciousness of the larger interests is perhaps most happily exampled out of his own mouth. When Alençon stood accused of betraying Normandy into the hands of the English, Charles made a speech in his defence, from which I have already quoted more than once. Alençon, he said, had professed a great love and trust toward him: "yet did he give no great proof thereof, when he sought to betray Normandy; whereby he would have made me lose an estate of 10,000 livres a year, and might have occasioned the destruction of the kingdom and of all us Frenchmen." These are the words of one, mark you, against whom Gloucester warned the English Council because of his "great subtility and cautelous disposition." It is not hard to excuse the impatience of Louis XI., if such stuff was foisted on him by way of political deliberation.

This incapacity to see things with any greatness, this obscure and narrow view, was fundamentally characteristic of the man as well as of the epoch. It is not even so striking in his public life, where he failed, as in his poems, where he notably succeeded. For wherever we might expect a poet to be unintelligent, it certainly would not be in his poetry. And Charles is unintelligent even there. Of all authors whom a modern may still read and read over again with pleasure, he has perhaps the least to say. His poems seem to bear testimony rather to the fashion of rhyming, which

CHARLES OF ORLEANS

distinguished the age, than to any special vocation in the man himself. Some of them are drawing-room exercises, and the rest seem made by habit. Great writers are struck with something in nature or society, with which they become pregnant and longing; they are possessed with an idea, and cannot be at peace until they have put it outside of them in some distinct embodiment. But with Charles literature was an object rather than a means; he was one who loved bandying words for its own sake; the rigidity of intricate metrical forms stood him in lieu of precise thought; instead of communicating truth, he observed the laws of a game; and when he had no one to challenge at chess or rackets, he made verses in a wager against himself. From the very idleness of the man's mind, and not from intensity of feeling, it happens that all his poems are more or less autobiographical. But they form an autobiography singularly bald and uneventful. Little is therein recorded besides sentiments. Thoughts, in any true sense, he had none to record. And if we can gather that he had been a prisoner in England, that he had lived in the Orleannese, and that he hunted and went in parties of pleasure, I believe it is about as much definite experience as is to be found in all these five hundred pages of autobiographical verse. Doubtless, we find here and there a complaint on the progress of the infirmities of age. Doubtless, he feels the great change of the year, and distinguishes winter from spring; winter as the time of snow and the fireside; spring as the return of grass and flowers, the time of St. Valentine's day and a beating heart. And he feels love after a fashion. Again and again, we learn that Charles of Orleans is in love, and hear him ring the changes through the whole gamut of dainty and tender sentiment. But there is never a spark of passion; and heaven alone knows whether there was any real woman in the matter, or the whole thing was an exercise in fancy. If these poems were indeed inspired by some living mistress, one would think he had never seen, never heard, and never touched her. There is nothing in any one of these so numerous love-songs to indicate who or what the lady was. Was she dark or fair,

FAMILIAR STUDIES

passionate or gentle like himself, witty or simple? Was it always one woman? or are there a dozen here immortalized in cold indistinction? The old English translator mentions gray eyes in his version of one of the amorous rondels; so far as I remember, he was driven by some emergency of the verse; but in the absence of all sharp lines of character and anything specific, we feel for the moment a sort of surprise, as though the epithet were singularly happy and unusual, or as though we had made our escape from cloud-land into something tangible and sure. The measure of Charles's indifference to all that now preoccupies and excites a poet, is best given by a positive example. If, besides the coming of spring, any one external circumstance may be said to have struck his imagination, it was the despatch of *fourriers*, while on a journey, to prepare the night's lodging. This seems to be his favorite image; it reappears like the upas-tree in the early work of Coleridge: we may judge with what childish eyes he looked upon the world, if one of the sights which most impressed him was that of a man going to order dinner.

Although they are not inspired by any deeper motive than the common run of contemporaneous drawing-room verses, those of Charles of Orleans are executed with inimitable lightness and delicacy of touch. They deal with floating and colorless sentiments, and the writer is never greatly moved, but he seems always genuine. He makes no attempt to set off thin conceptions with a multiplicity of phrases. His ballades are generally thin and scanty of import; for the ballade presented too large a canvas, and he was preoccupied by technical requirements. But in the rondel he has put himself before all competitors by a happy knack and a prevailing distinction of manner. He is very much more of a duke in his verses than in his absurd and inconsequential career as a statesman; and how he shows himself a duke is precisely by the absence of all pretension, turgidity, or emphasis. He turns verses, as he would have come into the king's presence, with a quiet accomplishment of grace.

Théodore de Banville, the youngest poet of a famous gen-

CHARLES OF ORLEANS

eration now nearly extinct, and himself a sure and finished artist, knocked off, in his happiest vein, a few experiments in imitation of Charles of Orleans. I would recommend these modern rondels to all who care about the old duke, not only because they are delightful in themselves, but because they serve as a contrast to throw into relief the peculiarities of their model. When De Banville revives a forgotten form of verse—and he has already had the honor of reviving the ballade—he does it in the spirit of a workman choosing a good tool wherever he can find one, and not at all in that of the dilettante, who seeks to renew bygone forms of thought and make historic forgeries. With the ballade this seemed natural enough; for in connection with ballades the mind recurs to Villon, and Villon was almost more of a modern than De Banville himself. But in the case of the rondel, a comparison is challenged with Charles of Orleans, and the difference between two ages and two literatures is illustrated in a few poems of thirteen lines. Something, certainly, has been retained of the old movement; the refrain falls in time like a well-played bass; and the very brevity of the thing, by hampering and restraining the greater fecundity of the modern mind, assists the imitation. But De Banville's poems are full of form and color; they smack racily of modern life, and own small kindred with the verse of other days, when it seems as if men walked by twilight, seeing little, and that with distracted eyes, and instead of blood, some thin and spectral fluid circulated in their veins. They might gird themselves for battle, make love, eat and drink, and acquit themselves manfully in all the external parts of life; but of the life that is within, and those processes by which we render ourselves an intelligent account of what we feel and do, and so represent experience that we for the first time make it ours, they had only a loose and troubled possession. They beheld or took part in great events, but there was no answerable commotion in their reflective being; and they passed throughout turbulent epochs in a sort of ghostly quiet and abstraction. Feeling seems to have been strangely disproportioned to the occasion, and

FAMILIAR STUDIES

words were laughably trivial and scanty to set forth the feeling even such as it was. Juvenal des Ursins chronicles calamity after calamity, with but one comment for them all: that "it was great pity." Perhaps, after too much of our florid literature, we find an adventitious charm in what is so different; and while the big drums are beaten every day by perspiring editors over the loss of a cock-boat or the rejection of a clause, and nothing is heard that is not proclaimed with sound of trumpet, it is not wonderful if we retire with pleasure into old books, and listen to authors who speak small and clear, as if in a private conversation. Truly this is so with Charles of Orleans. We are pleased to find a small man without the buskin, and obvious sentiments stated without affectation. If the sentiments are obvious, there is all the more chance we may have experienced the like. As we turn over the leaves, we may find ourselves in sympathy with some one or other of these staid joys and smiling sorrows. If we do we shall be strangely pleased, for there is a genuine pathos in these simple words, and the lines go with a lilt, and sing themselves to music of their own.

SAMUEL PEPYS

IN two books a fresh light has recently been thrown on the character and position of Samuel Pepys. Mr. Mynors Bright has given us a new transcription of the Diary, increasing it in bulk by near a third, correcting many errors, and completing our knowledge of the man in some curious and important points. We can only regret that he has taken liberties with the author and the public. It is no part of the duties of the editor of an established classic to decide what may or may not be " tedious to the reader." The book is either an historical document or not, and in condemning Lord Braybrooke Mr. Bright condemns himself. As for the time-honored phrase, " unfit for publication," without being cynical, we may regard it as the sign of a precaution more or less commercial; and we may think, without being sordid, that when we purchase six huge and distressingly expensive volumes, we are entitled to be treated rather more like scholars and rather less like children. But Mr. Bright may rest assured: while we complain, we are still grateful. Mr. Wheatley, to divide our obligation, brings together, clearly and with no lost words, a body of illustrative material. Sometimes we might ask a little more; never, I think, less. And as a matter of fact, a great part of Mr. Wheatley's volume might be transferred, by a good editor of Pepys, to the margin of the text, for it is precisely what the reader wants.

In the light of these two books, at least, we have now to read our author. Between them they contain all we can expect to learn for, it may be, many years. Now, if ever, we should be able to form some notion of that unparalleled figure in the annals of mankind—unparalleled for three good reasons: first, because he was a man known to his contemporaries in a halo of almost historical pomp, and to his remote descendants with an indecent familiarity, like a tap-room comrade; second, because he has outstripped all competitors in the art or virtue of a conscious honesty about oneself; and, third, because, being in many ways a very ordinary person, he has yet placed himself before the public eye with such a fulness and such an intimacy of detail as might be envied by a genius like Montaigne. Not then for his own sake only, but as a character in a unique position, endowed with a unique talent, and shedding a unique light upon the lives of the mass of mankind, he is surely worthy of prolonged and patient study.

THE DIARY

That there should be such a book as Pepys's Diary is incomparably strange. Pepys, in a corrupt and idle period, played the man in public employments, toiling hard and keeping his honor bright. Much of the little good that is set down to James the Second comes by right to Pepys; and if it were little for a king, it is much for a subordinate. To his clear, capable head was owing somewhat of the greatness of England on the seas. In the exploits of Hawke, Rodney, or Nelson, this dead Mr. Pepys of the Navy Office had some considerable share. He stood well by his business in the appalling plague of 1666. He was loved and respected by some of the best and wisest men in England. He was President of the Royal Society; and when he came to die, people said of his conduct in that solemn hour—thinking it needless to say more—that it was answerable to the greatness of his life. Thus he walked in dignity, guards of soldiers sometimes attending him in his walks, subalterns bowing before his periwig; and when he uttered his thoughts they were suitable to his state and services. On February 8, 1668, we find him writing to Evelyn, his mind bitterly occupied with the late Dutch war, and some thoughts of the different story of the repulse of the Great Armada: "Sir, you will not wonder at the backwardness of my thanks for the present you made me, so many days since, of the Pros-

SAMUEL PEPYS

ct of the Medway, while the Hollander rode master in it,
 en I have told you that the sight of it hath led me to
ch reflections on my particular interest, by my employ-
ent, in the reproach due to that miscarriage, as have given
 e little less disquiet than he is fancied to have who found
 s face in Michael Angelo's hell. The same should serve
e also in excuse for my silence in celebrating your mastery
 own in the design and draught, did not indignation rather
 an courtship urge me so far to commend them, as to wish
 e furniture of our House of Lords changed from the story
 : '88 to that of '67 [of Evelyn's designing], till the pravity
 : this were reformed to the temper of that age, wherein God
lmighty found his blessings more operative than, I fear, he
 oth in ours his judgments."

This is a letter honorable to the writer, where the
eaning rather than the words is eloquent. Such was
 e account he gave of himself to his contemporaries;
 ich thoughts he chose to utter, and in such language:
iving himself out for a grave and patriotic public servant.
 Ve turn to the same date in the Diary by which he is known,
fter two centuries, to his descendants. The entry begins in
he same key with the letter, blaming the " madness of the
Iouse of Commons " and " the base proceedings, just the
pitome of all our public proceedings in this age, of
 he House of Lords "; and then, without the least transition,
his is how our diarist proceeds: " To the Strand, to my
ookseller's, and there bought an idle, rogueish French book,
 'escholle des Filles, which I have bought in plain binding,
voiding the buying of it better bound, because I resolve, as
 on as I have read it, to burn it, that it may not stand in
 e list of books, nor among them, to disgrace them, if it
 ould be found." Even in our day, when responsibility is
 much more clearly apprehended, the man who wrote the
tter would be notable; but what about the man, I do not
 y who bought a roguish book, but who was ashamed of
 ing so, yet did it, and recorded both the doing and the
ame in the pages of his daily journal?

We all, whether we write or speak, must somewhat drape

ourselves when we address our fellows; at a given moment we apprehend our character and acts by some particular side; we are merry with one, grave with another, as befits the nature and demands of the relation. Pepys's letter to Evelyn would have little in common with that other one to Mrs. Knipp which he signed by the pseudonym of *Dapper Dicky;* yet each would be suitable to the character of his correspondent. There is no untruth in this, for man, being a Protean animal, swiftly shares and changes with his company and surroundings; and these changes are the better part of his education in the world. To strike a posture once for all, and to march through life like a drum-major, is to be highly disagreeable to others and a fool for oneself into the bargain. To Evelyn and to Knipp we understand the double facing; but to whom was he posing in the Diary, and what, in the name of astonishment, was the nature of the pose? Had he suppressed all mention of the book, or had he bought it, gloried in the act, and cheerfully recorded his glorification, in either case we should have made him out. But no; he is full of precautions to conceal the "disgrace" of the purchase, and yet speeds to chronicle the whole affair in pen and ink. It is a sort of anomaly in human action, which we can exactly parallel from another part of the Diary.

Mrs. Pepys had written a paper of her too just complaints against her husband, and written it in plain and very pungent English. Pepys, in an agony lest the world should come to see it, brutally seizes and destroys the tell-tale document; and then—you disbelieve your eyes—down goes the whole story with unsparing truth and in the cruellest detail. It seems he has no design but to appear respectable, and here he keeps a private book to prove he was not. You are at first faintly reminded of some of the vagaries of the morbid religious diarist; but at a moment's thought the resemblance disappears. The design of Pepys is not at all to edify; it is not from repentance that he chronicles his peccadilloes, for he tells us when he does repent, and, to be just to him, there often follows some improvement.

SAMUEL PEPYS

Again, the sins of the religious diarist are of a very formal pattern, and are told with an elaborate whine. But in Pepys you come upon good, substantive misdemeanors; beams in his eye of which he alone remains unconscious; healthy outbreaks of the animal nature, and laughable subterfuges to himself that always command belief and often engage the sympathies.

Pepys was a young man for his age, came slowly to himself in the world, sowed his wild oats late, took late to industry, and preserved till nearly forty the headlong gusto of a boy. So, to come rightly at the spirit in which the Diary was written, we must recall a class of sentiments which with most of us are over and done before the age of twelve. In our tender years we still preserve a freshness of surprise at our prolonged existence; events make an impression out of all proportion to their consequence; we are unspeakably touched by our own past adventures, and look forward to our future personality with sentimental interest. It was something of this, I think, that clung to Pepys. Although not sentimental in the abstract, he was sweetly sentimental about himself. His own past clung about his heart, an evergreen. He was the slave of an association. He could not pass by Islington, where his father used to carry him to cakes and ale, but he must light at the " King's Head " and eat and drink "for remembrance of the old house sake." He counted it good fortune to lie a night at Epsom to renew his old walks, " where Mrs. Hely and I did use to walk and talk, with whom I had the first sentiments of love and pleasure in a woman's company, discourse and taking her by the hand, she being a pretty woman." He goes about weighing up the *Assurance*, which lay near Woolwich under water, and cries in a parenthesis, " Poor ship, that I have been twice merry in, in Captain Holland's time "; and after revisiting the *Naseby*, now changed into the *Charles*, he confesses " it was a great pleasure to myself to see the ship that I began my good fortune in." The stone that he was cut for he preserved in a case; and to the Turners he kept alive such gratitude for their assistance that for years, and after

FAMILIAR STUDIES

he had begun to mount himself into higher zones, he continued to have that family to dinner on the anniversary of the operation. Not Hazlitt nor Rousseau had a more romantic passion for their past, although at times they might express it more romantically; and if Pepys shared with them this childish fondness, did not Rousseau, who left behind him the *Confessions*, or Hazlitt, who wrote the *Liber Amoris*, and loaded his essays with loving personal detail, share with Pepys in his unwearied egotism? For the two things go hand in hand; or, to be more exact, it is the first that makes the second either possible or pleasing.

But, to be quite in sympathy with Pepys, we must return once more to the experience of children. I can remember to have written, in the fly-leaf of more than one book, the date and the place where I then was—if, for instance, I was ill in bed or sitting in a certain garden; these were jottings for my future self; if I should chance on such a note in after years, I thought it would cause me a particular thrill to recognize myself across the intervening distance. Indeed, I might come upon them now, and not be moved one tittle—which shows that I have comparatively failed in life, and grown older than Samuel Pepys. For in the Diary we can find more than one such note of perfect childish egotism; as when he explains that his candle is going out, "which makes me write thus slobberingly"; or as in this incredible particularity, " To my study, where I only wrote thus much of this day's passages to this *, and so out again "; or lastly, as here, with more of circumstance: " I staid up till the bellman came by with his bell under my window, *as I was writing of this very line*, and cried, ' Past one of the clock, and a cold, frosty, windy morning.' " Such passages are not to be misunderstood. The appeal to Samuel Pepys years hence is unmistakable. He desires that dear, though unknown, gentleman keenly to realize his predecessor; to remember why a passage was uncleanly written; to recall (let us fancy, with a sigh) the tones of the bellman, the chill of the early, windy morning, and the very line his own romantic self was scribing at the moment. The man, you will perceive, was making reminiscences—a sort of pleasure by ricochet, which comforts many in distress, and turns some others into sentimental libertines: and the whole book, if you will but look at it in that way, is seen to be a work of art to Pepys's own address.

Here, then, we have the key to that remarkable attitude preserved by him throughout his Diary, to that unflinching —I had almost said, that unintelligent—sincerity which makes it a miracle among human books. He was not unconscious of his errors—far from it; he was often startled into shame, often reformed, often made and broke his vows of change. But whether he did ill or well, he was still his own unequalled self; still that entrancing *ego* of whom alone he cared to write; and still sure of his own affectionate indulgence, when the parts should be changed, and the writer come to read what he had written. Whatever he did, or said, or thought, or suffered, it was still a trait of Pepys, a character of his career; and as, to himself, he was more interesting than Moses or than Alexander, so all should be faithfully set down. I have called his Diary a work of art. Now when the artist has found something, word or deed, exactly proper to a favorite character in play or novel, he will neither suppress nor diminish it, though the remark be silly or the act mean. The hesitation of Hamlet, the credulity of Othello, the baseness of Emma Bovary, or the irregularities of Mr. Swiveller, caused neither disappointment nor disgust to their creators. And so with Pepys and his adored protagonist: adored not blindly, but with trenchant insight and enduring, human toleration. I have gone over and over the greater part of the Diary; and the points where, to the most suspicious scrutiny, he has seemed not perfectly sincere, are so few, so doubtful, and so petty, that I am ashamed to name them. It may be said that we all of us write such a diary in airy characters upon our brain; but I fear there is a distinction to be made; I fear that as we render to our consciousness an account of our daily fortunes and behavior, we too often weave a tissue of romantic compliments and dull excuses; and even if Pepys were the ass and coward that men call him, we must take rank as sillier and more cowardly than he. The bald truth about oneself, what we are all too timid to admit when we are not too dull to see it, that was what he saw clearly and set down unsparingly.

It is improbable that the Diary can have been carried on in the same single spirit in which it was begun. Pepys was not such an ass, but he must have perceived, as he went on, the extraordinary nature of the work he was producing. He was a great reader, and he knew what other books were like. It must, at least, have crossed his mind that some one might ultimately decipher the manuscript, and he himself, with all his pains and pleasures, be resuscitated in some later day; and the thought, although discouraged, must have warmed his heart. He was not such an ass, besides, but he must have been conscious of the deadly explosives, the gun-cotton and the giant powder, he was hoarding in his drawer. Let some contemporary light upon the Journal, and Pepys was plunged forever in social and political disgrace. We can trace the growth of his terrors by two facts. In 1660, while the Diary was still in its youth, he tells about it, as a matter of course, to a lieutenant in the navy; but in 1669, when it was already near an end, he could have bitten his tongue out, as the saying is, because he had let slip his secret to one so grave and friendly as Sir William Coventry. And from two other facts I think we may infer that he had entertained, even if he had not acquiesced in, the thought of a far-distant publicity. The first is of capital importance: the Diary was not destroyed. The second—that he took unusual precautions to confound the cipher in "rogueish" passages—proves, beyond question, that he was thinking of some other reader besides himself. Perhaps while his friends were admiring the "greatness of his behavior" at the approach of death, he may have had a twinkling hope of immortality. *Mens cujusque is est quisque*, said his chosen motto; and, as he had stamped his mind with every crook and foible in the pages of the Diary, he might feel that what he left behind him was indeed him-

SAMUEL PEPYS

self. There is perhaps no other instance so remarkable of the desire of man for publicity and an enduring name. The greatness of his life was open, yet he longed to communicate its smallness also; and, while contemporaries bowed before him, he must buttonhole posterity with the news that his periwig was once alive with nits. But this thought, although I cannot doubt he had it, was neither his first nor his deepest; it did not color one word that he wrote; and the Diary, for as long as he kept it, remained what it was when he began, a private pleasure for himself. It was his bosom secret; it added a zest to all his pleasures; he lived in and for it, and might well write these solemn words, when he closed that confidant forever: "And so I betake myself to that course which is almost as much as to see myself go into the grave; for which, and all the discomforts that will accompany my being blind, the good God prepare me."

A LIBERAL GENIUS

Pepys spent part of a certain winter Sunday, when he had taken physic, composing "a song in praise of a liberal genius (such as I take my own to be) to all studies and pleasures." The song was unsuccessful, but the Diary is, in a sense, the very song that he was seeking; and his portrait by Hales, so admirably reproduced in Mynors Bright's edition, is a confirmation of the Diary. Hales, it would appear, had known his business; and though he put his sitter to a deal of trouble, almost breaking his neck "to have the portrait full of shadows," and draping him in an Indian gown hired expressly for the purpose, he was preoccupied about no merely picturesque effects, but to portray the essence of the man. Whether we read the picture by the Diary or the Diary by the picture, we shall at least agree that Hales was among the number of those who can "surprise the manners in the face." Here we have a mouth pouting, moist with desires; eyes greedy, protuberant, and yet apt for weeping too; a nose great alike in character and dimensions; and altogether a most fleshly, melting countenance. The face is attractive by its promise of reciprocity. I have used the word *greedy*, but the reader must not suppose that he can change it for that closely kindred one of *hungry*, for there is here no aspiration, no waiting for better things, but an animal joy in all that comes. It could never be the face of an artist; it is the face of a *viveur*—kindly, pleased and pleasing, protected from excess and upheld in contentment by the shifting versatility of his desires. For a single desire is more rightly to be called a lust; but there is health in a variety, where one may balance and control another.

The whole world, town or country, was to Pepys a garden of Armida. Wherever he went, his steps were winged with the most eager expectation; whatever he did, it was done with the most lively pleasure. An insatiable curiosity in all the shows of the world and all the secrets of knowledge, filled him brimful of the longing to travel, and supported him in the toils of study. Rome was the dream of his life; he was never happier than when he read or talked of the Eternal City. When he was in Holland, he was "with child" to see any strange thing. Meeting some friends and singing with them in a palace near The Hague, his pen fails him to express his passion of delight, "the more so because in a heaven of pleasure and in a strange country." He must go to see all famous executions. He must needs visit the body of a murdered man, defaced "with a broad wound," he says, "that makes my hand now shake to write of it." He learned to dance, and was "like to make a dancer." He learned to sing, and walked about Gray's Inn Fields "humming to myself (which is now my constant practice) the trillo." He learned to play the lute, the flute, the flageolet, and the theorbo, and it was not the fault of his intention if he did not learn the harpsichord or the spinet. He learned to compose songs, and burned to give forth "a scheme and theory of music not yet ever made in the world." When he heard "a fellow whistle like a bird exceeding well," he promised to return another day and

SAMUEL PEPYS

give an angel for a lesson in the art. Once, he writes, "I took the Bezan back with me, and with a brave gale and tide reached up that night to the Hope, taking great pleasure in learning the seamen's manner of singing when they sound the depths." If he found himself rusty in his Latin grammar, he must fall to it like a schoolboy. He was a member of Harrington's Club till its dissolution, and of the Royal Society before it had received the name. Boyle's *Hydrostatics* was "of infinite delight" to him, walking in Barnes Elms. We find him comparing Bible concordances, a captious judge of sermons, deep in Descartes and Aristotle. We find him, in a single year, studying timber and the measurement of timber; tar and oil, hemp, and the process of preparing cordage; mathematics and accounting; the hull and the rigging of ships from a model; and "looking and improving himself of the (naval) stores with"—hark to the fellow!—" great delight." His familiar spirit of delight was not the same with Shelley's; but how true it was to him through life! He is only copying something, and behold, he "takes great pleasure to rule the lines, and have the capital words wrote with red ink"; he has only had his coal-cellar emptied and cleaned, and behold, "it do please him exceedingly." A hog's harslett is "a piece of meat he loves." He cannot ride home in my Lord Sandwich's coach, but he must exclaim, with breathless gusto, "his noble, rich coach." When he is bound for a supper party, he anticipates a "glut of pleasure." When he has a new watch, "to see my childishness," says he, "I could not forbear carrying it in my hand and seeing what o'clock it was an hundred times." To go to Vauxhall, he says, and "to hear the nightingales and other birds, hear fiddles, and there a harp and here a Jew's trump, and here laughing, and there fine people walking, is mighty divertising." And the nightingales, I take it, were particularly dear to him; and it was again "with great pleasure" that he paused to hear them as he walked to Woolwich, while the fog was rising and the April sun broke through.

He must always be doing something agreeable, and, by

FAMILIAR STUDIES

preference, two agreeable things at once. In his house he had a box of carpenter's tools, two dogs, an eagle, a canary, and a blackbird that whistled tunes, lest, even in that full life, he should chance upon an empty moment. If he had to wait for a dish of poached eggs, he must put in the time by playing on the flageolet; if a sermon were dull, he must read in the book of Tobit or divert his mind with sly advances on the nearest women. When he walked, it must be with a book in his pocket to beguile the way in case the nightingales were silent; and even along the streets of London, with so many pretty faces to be spied for and dignitaries to be saluted, his trail was marked by little debts "for wine, pictures, etc.," the true headmark of a life intolerant of any joyless passage. He had a kind of idealism in pleasure; like the princess in the fairy story, he was conscious of a rose-leaf out of place. Dearly as he loved to talk, he could not enjoy nor shine in a conversation when he thought himself unsuitably dressed. Dearly as he loved eating, he "knew not how to eat alone"; pleasure for him must heighten pleasure; and the eye and ear must be flattered like the palate ere he avow himself content. He had no zest in a good dinner when it fell to be eaten "in a bad street and in a periwig-maker's house"; and a collation was spoiled for him by indifferent music. His body was indefatigable, doing him yeoman's service in this breathless chase of pleasure. On April 11, 1662, he mentions that he went to bed "weary, *which I seldom am*"; and already over thirty, he would sit up all night cheerfully to see a comet. But it is never pleasure that exhausts the pleasure-seeker; for in that career, as in all others, it is failure that kills. The man who enjoys so wholly and bears so impatiently the slightest widowhood from joy, is just the man to lose a night's rest over some paltry question of his right to fiddle on the leads, or to be "vexed to the blood" by a solecism in his wife's attire; and we find in consequence that he was always peevish when he was hungry, and that his head "aked mightily" after a dispute. But nothing could divert him from his aim in life; his remedy

SAMUEL PEPYS

in care was the same as his delight in prosperity; it was with pleasure, and with pleasure only, that he sought to drive out sorrow; and, whether he was jealous of his wife or skulking from a bailiff, he would equally take refuge in the theatre. There, if the house be full and the company noble, if the songs be tunable, the actors perfect, and the play diverting, this odd hero of the secret Diary, this private self-adorer, will speedily be healed of his distresses.

Equally pleased with a watch, a coach, a piece of meat, a tune upon the fiddle, or a fact in hydrostatics, Pepys was pleased yet more by the beauty, the worth, the mirth, or the mere scenic attitude in life of his fellow-creatures. He shows himself throughout a sterling humanist. Indeed, he who loves himself, not in idle vanity, but with a plenitude of knowledge, is the best equipped of all to love his neighbors. And perhaps it is in this sense that charity may be most properly said to begin at home. It does not matter what quality a person has: Pepys can appreciate and love him for it. He "fills his eyes" with the beauty of Lady Castlemaine; indeed, he may be said to dote upon the thought of her for years; if a woman be good-looking and not painted, he will walk miles to have another sight of her; and even when a lady by a mischance spat upon his clothes, he was immediately consoled when he had observed that she was pretty. But, on the other hand, he is delighted to see Mrs. Pett upon her knees, and speaks thus of his Aunt James: "a poor, religious, well-meaning, good soul, talking of nothing but God Almighty, and that with so much innocence that mightily pleased me." He is taken with Pen's merriment and loose songs, but not less taken with the sterling worth of Coventry. He is jolly with a drunken sailor, but listens with interest and patience, as he rides the Essex roads, to the story of a Quaker's spiritual trials and convictions. He lends a critical ear to the discourse of kings and royal dukes. He spends an evening at Vauxhall with "Killigrew and young Newport—loose company," says he, "but worth a man's being in for once, to know the nature of it, and their manner of talk and lives." And when a rag-boy lights him home, he examines him about his business and other ways of livelihood for destitute children. This is almost half-way to the beginning of philanthropy; had it only been the fashion, as it is at present, Pepys had perhaps been a man famous for good deeds. And it is through this quality that he rises, at times, superior to his surprising egotism; his interest in the love affairs of others is, indeed, impersonal; he is filled with concern for my Lady Castlemaine, whom he only knows by sight, shares in her very jealousies, joys with her in her successes; and it is not untrue, however strange it seems in his abrupt presentment, that he loved his maid Jane because she was in love with his man Tom.

Let us hear him, for once, at length: " So the women and W. Hewer and I walked upon the Downes, where a flock of sheep was; and the most pleasant and innocent sight that ever I saw in my life. We found a shepherd and his little boy reading, far from any houses or sight of people, the Bible to him; so I made the boy read to me, which he did with the forced tone that children do usually read, that was mighty pretty; and then I did give him something, and went to the father, and talked with him. He did content himself mightily in my liking his boy's reading, and did bless God for him, the most like one of the old patriarchs that ever I saw in my life, and it brought those thoughts of the old age of the world in my mind for two or three days after. We took notice of his woollen knit stockings of two colors mixed, and of his shoes shod with iron, both at the toe and heels, and with great nails in the soles of his feet, which was mighty pretty; and taking notice of them, 'Why,' says the poor man, 'the downes, you see, are full of stones, and we are faine to shoe ourselves thus; and these,' says he, 'will make the stones fly till they ring before me.' I did give the poor man something, for which he was mighty thankful, and I tried to cast stones with his horne crooke. He values his dog mightily, that would turn a sheep any way which he would have him, when he goes to fold them; told me there was about eighteen score

SAMUEL PEPYS

ep in his flock, and that he hath four shillings a week the
r round for keeping of them; and Mrs. Turner, in the
mon fields here, did gather one of the prettiest nosegays
t ever I saw in my life."
And so the story rambles on to the end of that day's
asuring; with cups of milk, and glowworms, and people
king at sundown with their wives and children, and all
way home Pepys still dreaming "of the old age of the
rld" and the early innocence of man. This was how
walked through life, his eyes and ears wide open, and his
id, you will observe, not shut; and thus he observed the
·s, the speech, and the manners of his fellow-men, with
ise fidelity of detail and yet a lingering glamour of
nance.
[t was "two or three days after" that he extended this
ısage in the pages of his Journal, and the style has thus
benefit of some reflection. It is generally supposed that,
a writer, Pepys must rank at the bottom of the scale of
rit. But a style which is indefatigably lively, telling, and
turesque through six large volumes of everyday experience,
ich deals with the whole matter of a life, and yet is rarely
ırisome, which condescends to the most fastidious par-
ılars, and yet sweeps all away in the forthright current
the narrative,—such a style may be ungrammatical, it
y be inelegant, it may be one tissue of mistakes, but it
ı never be devoid of merit. The first and the true func-
ı of the writer has been thoroughly performed through-
:; and though the manner of his utterance may be
ldishly awkward, the matter has been transformed and
imilated by his unfeigned interest and delight. The
ito of the man speaks out fierily after all these years. For
difference between Pepys and Shelley, to return to that
f whimsical approximation, is one of quality but not one
degree; in his sphere, Peyps felt as keenly, and his is
true prose of poetry—prose because the spirit of the
n was narrow and earthly, but poetry because he was
ightedly alive. Hence, in such a passage as this about
Epsom shepherd, the result upon the reader's mind is

FAMILIAR STUDIES

entire conviction and unmingled pleasure. So, you feel, the thing fell out, not otherwise; and you would no more change it than you would change a sublimity of Shakespeare's, a homely touch of Bunyan's, or a favored reminiscence of your own.

There never was a man nearer being an artist, who yet was not one. The tang was in the family; while he was writing the journal for our enjoyment in his comely house in Navy Gardens, no fewer than two of his cousins were tramping the fens, kit under arm, to make music to the country girls. But he himself, though he could play so many instruments and pass judgment in so many fields of art, remained an amateur. It is not given to any one so keenly to enjoy, without some greater power to understand. That he did not like Shakespeare as an artist for the stage may be a fault, but it is not without either parallel or excuse. He certainly admired him as a poet; he was the first beyond mere actors on the rolls of that innumerable army who have got "To be or not to be" by heart. Nor was he content with that; it haunted his mind; he quoted it to himself in the pages of the Diary, and, rushing in where angels fear to tread, he set it to music. Nothing, indeed, is more notable than the heroic quality of the verses that our little sensualist in a periwig chose out to marry with his own mortal strains. Some gust from brave Elizabethan times must have warmed his spirit, as he sat tuning his sublime theorbo. "To be or not to be. Whether 'tis nobler"— "Beauty retire, thou dost my pity move"—"It is decreed, nor shall thy fate, O Rome":—open and dignified in the sound, various and majestic in the sentiment, it was no inapt, as it was certainly no timid, spirit that selected such a range of themes. Of "Gaze not on Swans," I know no more than these four words; yet that also seems to promise well. It was, however, on a probable suspicion, the work of his master, Mr. Berkenshaw—as the drawings that figure at the breaking up of a young ladies' seminary are the work of the professor attached to the establishment. Mr. Berkenshaw was not altogether happy in his pupil. The

SAMUEL PEPYS

amateur cannot usually rise into the artist, some leaven of the world still clogging him; and we find Pepys behaving like a pickthank to the man who taught him composition. In relation to the stage, which he so warmly loved and understood, he was not only more hearty, but more generous to others. Thus he encounters Colonel Reames, " a man," says he, " who understands and loves a play as well as I, and I love him for it." And again, when he and his wife had seen a most ridiculously insipid piece, " Glad we were," he writes, " that Betterton had no part in it." It is by such a zeal and loyalty to those who labor for his delight that the amateur grows worthy of the artist. And it should be kept in mind that, not only in art, but in morals, Pepys rejoiced to recognize his betters. There was not one speck of envy in the whole human-hearted egotist.

RESPECTABILITY

When writers inveigh against respectability, in the present degraded meaning of the word, they are usually suspected of a taste for clay pipes and beer cellars; and their performances are thought to hail from the *Owl's Nest* of the comedy. They have something more, however, in their eye than the dulness of a round million dinner parties that sit down yearly in old England. For to do anything because others do it, and not because the thing is good, or kind, or honest in its own right, is to resign all moral control and captaincy upon yourself, and go post-haste to the devil with the greater number. We smile over the ascendency of priests; but I had rather follow a priest than what they call the leaders of society. No life can better than that of Pepys illustrate the dangers of this respectable theory of living. For what can be more untoward than the occurrence, at a critical period and, while the habits are still pliable, of such a sweeping transformation as the return of Charles the Second? Round went the whole fleet of England on the other tack; and while a few tall pintas, Milton or Pen, still sailed a lonely course by the stars and their

FAMILIAR STUDIES

own private compass, the cock-boat, Pepys, must go about with the majority among " the stupid starers and the loud huzzas."

The respectable are not led so much by any desire of applause as by a positive need for countenance. The weaker and the tamer the man, the more will he require this support; and any positive quality relieves him, by just so much, of this dependence. In a dozen ways, Pepys was quite strong enough to please himself without regard for others; but his positive qualities were not coextensive with the field of conduct; and in many parts of life he followed, with gleeful precision, in the footprints of the contemporary Mrs. Grundy. In morals, particularly, he lived by the countenance of others; felt a slight from another more keenly than a meanness in himself; and then first repented when he was found out. You could talk of religion or morality to such a man; and by the artist side of him, by his lively sympathy and apprehension, he could rise, as it were dramatically, to the significance of what you said. All that matter in religion which has been nicknamed other-worldliness was strictly in his gamut; but a rule of life that should make a man rudely virtuous, following right in good report and ill report, was foolishness and a stumbling-block to Pepys. He was much thrown across the Friends; and nothing can be more instructive than his attitude toward these most interesting people of that age. I have mentioned how he conversed with one as he rode; when he saw some brought from a meeting under arrest, " I would to God," said he, " they would either conform, or be more wise and not be catched "; and to a Quaker in his own office he extended a timid though effectual protection. Meanwhile there was growing up next door to him that beautiful nature, William Pen. It is odd that Pepys condemned him for a fop; odd, though natural enough when you see Pen's portrait, that Pepys was jealous of him with his wife. But the cream of the story is when Pen publishes his *Sandy Foundation Shaken*, and Pepys has it read aloud by his wife. " I find it," he says, " so well writ as, I think, it is too good for

SAMUEL PEPYS

him ever to have writ it; and it is a serious sort of book, and *not fit for everybody to read.*" Nothing is more galling to the merely respectable than to be brought in contact with religious ardor. Pepys had his own foundation, sandy enough, but dear to him from practical considerations, and he would read the book with true uneasiness of spirit; for conceive the blow if, by some plaguy accident, this Pen were to convert him! It was a different kind of doctrine that he judged profitable for himself and others. "A good sermon of Mr. Gifford's at our church, upon 'Seek ye first the kingdom of heaven.' A very excellent and persuasive, good and moral sermon. He showed, like a wise man, that righteousness is a surer moral way of being rich than sin and villainy." It is thus that respectable people desire to have their Greathearts address them, telling, in mild accents, how you may make the best of both worlds, and be a moral hero without courage, kindness, or troublesome reflection; and thus the Gospel, cleared of Eastern metaphor, becomes a manual of worldly prudence, and a handy-book for Pepys and the successful merchant.

The respectability of Pepys was deeply grained. He has no idea of truth except for the Diary. He has no care that a thing shall be, if it but appear; gives out that he has inherited a good estate, when he has seemingly got nothing but a lawsuit; and is pleased to be thought liberal when he knows he has been mean. He is conscientiously ostentatious. I say conscientiously, with reason. He could never have been taken for a fop, like Pen, but arrayed himself in a manner nicely suitable to his position. For long he hesitated to assume the famous periwig; for a public man should travel gravely with the fashions, not foppishly before, nor dowdily behind, the central movement of his age. For long he durst not keep a carriage; that, in his circumstances, would have been improper; but a times comes, with the growth of his fortune, when the impropriety has shifted to the other side, and he is "ashamed to be seen in a hackney." Pepys talked about being "a Quaker or some very melancholy thing"; for my part, I can imagine nothing

FAMILIAR STUDIES

so melancholy, because nothing half so silly, as to be concerned about such problems. But so respectability and the duties of society haunt and burden their poor devotees; and what seems at first the very primrose path of life, proves difficult and thorny like the rest. And the time comes to Pepys, as to all the merely respectable, when he must not only order his pleasures, but even clip his virtuous movements, to the public patter of the age. There was some juggling among officials to avoid direct taxation; and Pepys, with a noble impulse, growing ashamed of this dishonesty, designed to charge himself with £1000; but finding none to set him an example, "nobody of our ablest merchants" with this moderate liking for clean hands, he judged it "not decent"; he feared it would "be thought vain glory"; and, rather than appear singular, cheerfully remained a thief. One able merchant's countenance, and Pepys had dared to do an honest act! Had he found one brave spirit, properly recognized by society, he might have gone far as a disciple. Mrs. Turner, it is true, can fill him full of sordid scandal, and make him believe, against the testimony of his senses, that Pen's venison pasty stank like the devil; but, on the other hand, Sir William Coventry can raise him by a word into another being. Pepys, when he is with Coventry, talks in the vein of an old Roman. What does he care for office or emolument? "Thank God, I have enough of my own," says he, " to buy me a good book and a good fiddle, and I have a good wife." And again, we find this pair projecting an old age when an ungrateful country shall have dismissed them from the field of public service; Coventry living retired in a fine house, and Pepys dropping in, "it may be, to read a chapter of Seneca."

Under this influence, the only good one in his life, Pepys continued zealous and, for the period, pure in his employment. He would not be "bribed to be unjust," he says, though he was "not so squeamish as to refuse a present after," suppose the king to have received no wrong. His new arrangement for the victualling of Tangier, he tells us with honest complacency, will save the king a thousand

SAMUEL PEPYS

and gain Pepys three hundred pounds a year,—a statement which exactly fixes the degree of the age's enlightenment. But for his industry and capacity no praise can be too high. It was an unending struggle for the man to stick to his business in such a garden of Armida as he found this life; and the story of his oaths, so often broken, so courageously renewed, is worthy rather of admiration than the contempt it has received.

Elsewhere, and beyond the sphere of Coventry's influence, we find him losing scruples and daily complying further with the age. When he began the Journal, he was a trifle prim and puritanic; merry enough, to be sure, over his private cups, and still remembering Magdalene ale and his acquaintance with Mrs. Ainsworth of Cambridge. But youth is a hot season with all; when a man smells April and May he is apt at times to stumble; and, in spite of a disordered practice, Pepys's theory, the better things that he approved and followed after, we may even say were strict. Where there was "tag, rag, and bobtail, dancing, singing, and drinking," he felt "ashamed, and went away"; and when he slept in church, he prayed God forgive him. In but a little while we find him with some ladies keeping each other awake "from spite," as though not to sleep in church were an obvious hardship; and yet later he calmly passes the time of service, looking about him, with a perspective glass, on all the pretty women. His favorite ejaculation, "Lord!" occurs but once that I have observed in 1660, never in '61, twice in '62, and at least five times in '63; after which the "Lords" may be said to pullulate like herrings, with here and there a solitary "damned," as it were a whale among the shoal. He and his wife, once filled with dudgeon by some innocent freedoms at a marriage, are soon content to go pleasuring with my Lord Brouncker's mistress, who was not even, by his own account, the most discreet of mistresses. Tag, rag, and bobtail, dancing, singing, and drinking, become his natural element; actors and actresses and drunken, roaring courtiers are to be found in his society; until the man grew so involved with Saturnalian manners and companions that he was shot almost unconsciously into the grand domestic crash of 1668.

That was the legitimate issue and punishment of years of staggering walk and conversation. The man who has smoked his pipe for half a century in a powder magazine finds himself at last the author and the victim of a hideous disaster. So with our pleasant-minded Pepys and his peccadilloes. All of a sudden, as he still trips dexterously enough among the dangers of a double-faced career, thinking no great evil, humming to himself the trillo, Fate takes the further conduct of that matter from his hands, and brings him face to face with the consequences of his acts. For a man still, after so many years, the lover, although not the constant lover, of his wife,—for a man, besides, who was so greatly careful of appearances,—the revelation of his infidelities was a crushing blow. The tears that he shed, the indignities that he endured, are not to be measured. A vulgar woman, and now justly incensed, Mrs. Pepys spared him no detail of suffering. She was violent, threatening him with the tongs; she was careless of his honor, driving him to insult the mistress whom she had driven him to betray and to discard; worst of all, she was hopelessly inconsequent, in word and thought and deed, now lulling him with reconciliations, and anon flaming forth again with the original anger. Pepys had not used his wife well; he had wearied her with jealousies, even while himself unfaithful; he had grudged her clothes and pleasures, while lavishing both upon himself; he had abused her in words; he had bent his fist at her in anger; he had once blacked her eye; and it is one of the oddest particulars in that odd Diary of his, that, while the injury is referred to once in passing, there is no hint as to the occasion or the manner of the blow. But now, when he is in the wrong, nothing can exceed the long-suffering affection of this impatient husband. While he was still sinning and still undiscovered, he seems not to have known a touch of penitence stronger than what might lead him to take his wife to the theatre, or for an airing, or to give her a new dress, by way of compensation. Once found

SAMUEL PEPYS

out, however, and he seems to himself to have lost all claim to decent usage. It is perhaps the strongest instance of his externality. His wife may do what she pleases, and though he may groan, it will never occur to him to blame her; he has no weapon left but tears and the most abject submission. We should perhaps have respected him more had he not given way so utterly—above all, had he refused to write, under his wife's dictation, an insulting letter to his unhappy fellow-culprit, Miss Willet; but somehow I believe we like him better as he was.

The death of his wife, following so shortly after, must have stamped the impression of this episode upon his mind. For the remaining years of his long life we have no Diary to help us, and we have seen already how little stress is to be laid upon the tenor of his correspondence; but what with the recollection of the catastrophe of his married life, what with the natural influence of his advancing years and reputation, it seems not unlikely that the period of gallantry was at an end for Pepys; and it is beyond a doubt that he sat down at last to an honored and agreeable old age among his books and music, the correspondent of Sir Isaac Newton, and, in one instance at least, the poetical counsellor of Dryden. Through all this period, that Diary which contained the secret memoirs of his life, with all its inconsistencies and escapades, had been religiously preserved; nor when he came to die, does he appear to have provided for its destruction. So we may conceive him faithful to the end to all his dear and early memories; still mindful of Mrs. Hely in the woods at Epsom; still lighting at Islington for a cup of kindness to the dead; still, if he heard again that air that once so much disturbed him, thrilling at the recollection of the love that bound him to his wife.

JOHN KNOX AND HIS RELATIONS TO WOMEN

I—THE CONTROVERSY ABOUT FEMALE RULE

WHEN first the idea became widely spread among men that the Word of God, instead of being truly the foundation of all existing institutions, was rather a stone which the builders had rejected, it was but natural that the consequent havoc among received opinions should be accompanied by the generation of many new and lively hopes for the future. Somewhat as in the early days of the French Revolution, men must have looked for an immediate and universal improvement in their condition. Christianity, up to that time, had been somewhat of a failure politically. The reason was now obvious, the capital flaw was detected, the sickness of the body politic traced at last to its efficient cause. It was only necessary to put the Bible thoroughly into practice, to set themselves strenuously to realize in life the Holy Commonwealth, and all abuses and iniquities would surely pass away. Thus, in a pageant played at Geneva in the year 1523, the world was represented as a sick man at the end of his wits for help, to whom his doctor recommends Lutheran specifics.*

The Reformers themselves had set their affections in a different world, and professed to look for the finished result of their endeavors on the other side of death. They took no interest in politics as such; they even condemned political action as Antichristian: notably, Luther in the case of the Peasants' War. And yet, as the purely religious question was inseparably complicated with political difficulties, and they had to make opposition, from day to day, against principalities and powers, they were led, one after

* Gaberel's *Eglise de Genève*, i. 88.

JOHN KNOX

another, and again and again, to leave the sphere which was more strictly their own, and meddle, for good and evil, with the affairs of State. Not much was to be expected from interference in such a spirit. Whenever a minister found himself galled or hindered, he would be inclined to suppose some contravention of the Bible. Whenever Christian liberty was restrained (and Christian liberty for each individual would be about coextensive with what he wished to do), it was obvious that the State was Antichristian. The great thing, and the one thing, was to push the Gospel and the Reformers' own interpretation of it. Whatever helped was good; whatever hindered was evil; and if this simple classification proved inapplicable over the whole field, it was no business of his to stop and reconcile incongruities. He had more pressing concerns on hand; he had to save souls; he had to be about his Father's business. This short-sighted view resulted in a doctrine that was actually Jesuitical in application. They had no serious ideas upon politics, and they were ready, nay, they seemed almost bound, to adopt and support whichever ensured for the moment the greatest benefit to the souls of their fellow-men. They were dishonest in all sincerity. Thus Labitte, in the introduction to a book * in which he exposes the hypocritical democracy of the Catholics under the League, steps aside for a moment to stigmatize the hypocritical democracy of the Protestants. And nowhere was this expediency in political questions more apparent than about the question of female sovereignty. So much was this the case that one James Thomasius, of Leipsic, wrote a little paper † about the religious partialities of those who took part in the controversy, in which some of these learned disputants cut a very sorry figure.

Now Knox has been from the first a man well hated; and it is somewhat characteristic of his luck that he figures here in the very forefront of the list of partial scribes who trimmed their doctrine with the wind in all good conscience,

* *La Démocratie chez les Prédicateurs de la Ligue.*
† *Historia affectuum se immiscentium controversiæ de gynæcocratia.* It is in his collected prefaces, Leipsic, 1683.

FAMILIAR STUDIES

and were political weathercocks out of conviction. Not only has Thomasius mentioned him, but Bayle has taken the hint from Thomasius, and dedicated a long note to the matter at the end of his article on the Scotch Reformer. This is a little less than fair. If any one among the evangelists of that period showed more serious political sense than another, it was assuredly Knox; and even in this very matter of female rule, although I do not suppose any one nowadays will feel inclined to endorse his sentiments, I confess I can make great allowance for his conduct. The controversy, besides, has an interest of its own, in view of later controversies.

John Knox, from 1556 to 1559, was resident in Geneva, as minister, jointly with Goodman, of a little church of English refugees. He and his congregation were banished from England by one woman, Mary Tudor, and proscribed in Scotland by another, the Regent Mary of Guise. The coincidence was tempting: here were many abuses centring about one abuse; here was Christ's Gospel persecuted in the two kingdoms by one anomalous power. He had not far to go to find the idea that female government was anomalous. It was an age, indeed, in which women, capable and incapable, played a conspicuous part upon the stage of European history; and yet their rule, whatever may have been the opinion of here and there a wise man or enthusiast, was regarded as an anomaly by the great bulk of their contemporaries. It was defended as an anomaly. It, and all that accompanied and sanctioned it, was set aside as a single exception; and no one thought of reasoning down from queens and extending their privileges to ordinary women. Great ladies, as we know, had the privilege of entering into monasteries and cloisters, otherwise forbidden to their sex. As with one thing, so with another. Thus, Margaret of Navarre wrote books with great acclamation, and no one, seemingly, saw fit to call her conduct in question; but Mademoiselle de Gournay, Montaigne's adopted daughter, was in a controversy with the world as to whether a woman might be an author without incongruity. Thus, too,

JOHN KNOX

we have Théodore Agrippa d'Aubigné writing to his daughters about the learned women of his century, and cautioning them, in conclusion, that the study of letters was unsuited to ladies of a middling station, and should be reserved for princesses.* And once more, if we desire to see the same principle carried to ludicrous extreme, we shall find that Reverend Father in God the Abbot of Brantôme, claiming, on the authority of some lord of his acquaintance, a privilege, or rather a duty, of free love for great princesses, and carefully excluding other ladies from the same gallant dispensation.† One sees the spirit in which these immunities were granted; and how they were but the natural consequence of that awe for courts and kings that made the last writer tell us, with simple wonder, how Catherine de Medici would "laugh her fill just like another" over the humors of pantaloons and zanies. And such servility was, of all things, what would touch most nearly the republican spirit of Knox. It was not difficult for him to set aside this weak scruple of loyalty. The lantern of his analysis did not always shine with a very serviceable light; but he had the virtue, at least, to carry it into many places of fictitious holiness, and was not abashed by the tinsel divinity that hedged kings and queens from his contemporaries. And so he could put the proposition in the form already mentioned: there was Christ's Gospel persecuted in the two kingdoms by one anomalous power; plainly, then, the "regiment of women" was Antichristian. Early in 1558 he communicated this discovery to the world, by publishing at Geneva his notorious book—*The First Blast of the Trumpet against the Monstrous Regiment of Women.*‡

As a whole, it is a dull performance; but the preface, as is usual with Knox, is both interesting and morally fine. Knox was not one of those who are humble in the hour of triumph; he was aggressive even when things were at their worst. He had a grim reliance in himself, or rather in his mission; if he were not sure that he was a great man,

---

* *Œuvres de d'Aubigné*, i. 449.   † *Dames Illustres*, pp. 358-360.
‡ Works of John Knox, iv. 349.

FAMILIAR STUDIES

he was at least sure that he was one set apart to do great things. And he judged simply that whatever passed in his mind, whatever moved him to flee from persecution instead of constantly facing it out, or, as here, to publish and withhold his name from the title-page of a critical work, would not fail to be of interest, perhaps of benefit, to the world. There may be something more finely sensitive in the modern humor, that tends more and more to withdraw a man's personality from the lessons he inculcates or the cause that he has espoused; but there is a loss herewith of wholesome responsibility; and when we find in the works of Knox, as in the Epistles of Paul, the man himself standing nakedly forward, courting and anticipating criticism, putting his character, as it were, in pledge for the sincerity of his doctrine, we had best waive the question of delicacy, and make our acknowledgments for a lesson of courage, not unnecessary in these days of anonymous criticism, and much light, otherwise unattainable, on the spirit in which great movements were initiated and carried forward. Knox's personal revelations are always interesting; and, in the case of the "First Blast," as I have said, there is no exception to the rule. He begins by stating the solemn responsibility of all who are watchmen over God's flock; and all are watchmen (he goes on to explain, with that fine breadth of spirit that characterizes him even when, as here, he shows himself most narrow), all are watchmen "whose eyes God doth open, and whose conscience he pricketh to admonish the ungodly." And with the full consciousness of this great duty before him, he sets himself to answer the scruples of timorous or worldly-minded people. How can a man repent, he asks, unless the nature of his transgression is made plain to him? "And therefore I say," he continues, "that of necessity it is that this monstriferous empire of women (which among all enormities that this day do abound upon the face of the whole earth, is most detestable and damnable) be openly and plainly declared to the world, to the end that some may repent and be saved." To those who think the doctrine useless, because it cannot be expected to amend

JOHN KNOX

those princes whom it would dispossess if once accepted, he makes answer in a strain that shows him at his greatest.[1] After having instanced how the rumor of Christ's censures found its way to Herod in his own court, " even so," he continues, " may the sound of our weak trumpet, by the support of some wind (blow it from the south, or blow it from the north, it is of no matter), come to the ears of the chief offenders. *But whether it do or not, yet dare we not cease to blow as God will give strength. For we are debtors to more than to princes, to wit, to the great multitude of our brethren*, of whom, no doubt, a great number have heretofore offended by error and ignorance."

It is for the multitude, then, he writes; he does not greatly hope that his trumpet will be audible in palaces, or that crowned women will submissively discrown themselves at his appeal; what he does hope, in plain English, is to encourage and justify rebellion; and we shall see, before we have done, that he can put his purpose into words as roundly as I can put it for him. This he sees to be a matter of much hazard; he is not " altogether so brutish and insensible, but that he has laid his account what the finishing of the work may cost." He knows that he will find many adversaries, since " to the most part of men, lawful and godly appeareth whatsoever antiquity hath received." He looks for opposition, " not only of the ignorant multitude, but of the wise, politic, and quiet spirits of the earth." He will be called foolish, curious, despiteful, and a sower of sedition; and one day, perhaps, for all he is now nameless, he may be attainted of treason. Yet he has " determined to obey God, notwithstanding that the world shall rage thereat." Finally, he makes some excuse for the anonymous appearance of this first instalment: it is his purpose thrice to blow the trumpet in this matter, if God so permit; twice he intends to do it without name; but at the last blast to take the odium upon himself, that all others may be purged.

Thus he ends the preface, and enters upon his argument with a secondary title: " The First Blast to awake Women degenerate." We are in the land of assertion without de-

FAMILIAR STUDIES

lay. That a woman should bear rule, superiority, dominion or empire over any realm, nation, or city, he tells us, is repugnant to nature, contumely to God, and a subversion of good order. Women are weak, frail, impatient, feeble, and foolish. God has denied to woman wisdom to consider, or providence to foresee, what is profitable to a commonwealth. Women have been ever lightly esteemed; they have been denied the tutory of their own sons, and subjected to the unquestionable sway of their husbands; and surely it is irrational to give the greater where the less has been withheld, and suffer a woman to reign supreme over a great kingdom who would be allowed no authority by her own fireside. He appeals to the Bible; but though he makes much of the first transgression and certain strong texts in Genesis and Paul's Epistles, he does not appeal with entire success. The cases of Deborah and Huldah can be brought into no sort of harmony with his thesis. Indeed, I may say that, logically, he left his bones there; and that it is but the phantom of an argument that he parades thenceforward to the end. Well was it for Knox that he succeeded no better; it is under this very ambiguity about Deborah that we shall find him fain to creep for shelter before he is done with the regiment of women. After having thus exhausted Scripture, and formulated its teaching in the somewhat blasphemous maxim that the man is placed above the woman, even as God above the angels, he goes on triumphantly to adduce the testimonies of Tertullian, Augustine, Ambrose, Basil, Chrysostom, and the Pandects; and having gathered this little cloud of witnesses about him, like pursuivants about a herald, he solemnly proclaims all reigning women to be traitoresses and rebels against God; discharges all men thenceforward from holding any office under such monstrous regiment, and calls upon all the lieges with one consent to "*study to repress the inordinate pride and tyranny*" of queens. If this is not treasonable teaching, one would be glad to know what is; and yet, as if he feared he had not made the case plain enough against himself, he goes on to deduce the startling corollary that all

JOHN KNOX

oaths of allegiance must be incontinently broken. If it was sin thus to have sworn even in ignorance, it were obstinate sin to continue to respect them after fuller knowledge. Then comes the peroration, in which he cries aloud against the cruelties of that cursed Jezebel of England—that horrible monster Jezebel of England; and after having predicted sudden destruction to her rule and to the rule of all crowned women, and warned all men that if they presume to defend the same when any " noble heart " shall be raised up to vindicate the liberty of his country, they shall not fail to perish themselves in the ruin, he concludes with a last rhetorical flourish: " And therefore let all men be advertised, for THE TRUMPET HATH ONCE BLOWN."

The capitals are his own. In writing, he probably felt the want of some such reverberation of the pulpit under strong hands as he was wont to emphasize his spoken utterances withal; there would seem to him a want of passion in the orderly lines of type; and I suppose we may take the capitals as a mere substitute for the great voice with which he would have given it forth, had we heard it from his own lips. Indeed, as it is, in this little strain of rhetoric about the trumpet, this current allusion to the fall of Jericho, that alone distinguishes his bitter and hasty production, he was probably right, according to all artistic canon, thus to support and accentuate in conclusion the sustained metaphor of a hostile proclamation. It is curious, by the way, to note how favorite an image the trumpet was with the Reformer. He returns to it again and again; it is the Alpha and Omega of his rhetoric; it is to him what a ship is to the stage sailor; and one would almost fancy he had begun the world as a trumpeter's apprentice. The partiality is surely characteristic. All his life long he was blowing summonses before various Jerichos, some of which fell duly, but not all. Wherever he appears in history his speech is loud, angry, and hostile; there is no peace in his life, and little tenderness; he is always sounding hopefully to the front for some rough enterprise. And as his voice had something of the trumpet's hardness, it had something also of the trumpet's warlike inspiration. So Randolph, possibly fresh from the sound of the Reformer's preaching, writes of him to Cecil:—" Where your honor exhorteth us to stoutness, I assure you the voice of one man is able, in an hour, to put more life in us than six hundred trumpets continually blustering in our ears." *

Thus was the proclamation made. Nor was it long in wakening all the echoes of Europe. What success might have attended it, had the question decided been a purely abstract question, it is difficult to say. As it was, it was to stand or fall, not by logic, but by political needs and sympathies. Thus, in France, his doctrine was to have some future, because Protestants suffered there under the feeble and treacherous regency of Catherine de' Medici; and thus it was to have no future anywhere else, because the Protestant interest was bound up with the prosperity of Queen Elizabeth. This stumbling-block lay at the very threshold of the matter; and Knox, in the text of the " First Blast," had set everybody the wrong example and gone to the ground himself. He finds occasion to regret " the blood of innocent Lady Jane Dudley." But Lady Jane Dudley, or Lady Jane Grey, as we call her, was a would-be traitoress and rebel against God, to use his own expressions. If, therefore, political and religious sympathy led Knox himself into so grave a partiality, what was he to expect from his disciples? If the trumpet gave so ambiguous a sound, who could heartily prepare himself for the battle? The question whether Lady Jane Dudley was an innocent martyr, or a traitoress against God, whose inordinate pride and tyranny had been effectually repressed, was thus left altogether in the wind; and it was not, perhaps, wonderful if many of Knox's readers concluded that all right and wrong in the matter turned upon the degree of the sovereign's orthodoxy and possible helpfulness to the Reformation. He should have been the more careful of such an ambiguity of meaning, as he must have known well the lukewarm indifference and dishonesty of his fellow-reformers in political matters. He had already, in 1556 or 1557, talked the matter over

* M'Crie's *Life of Knox*, ii. 41.

JOHN KNOX

with his great master, Calvin, in "a private conversation"; and the interview * must have been truly distasteful to both parties. Calvin, indeed, went a far way with him in theory, and owned that the "government of women was a deviation from the original and proper order of nature, to be ranked, no less than slavery, among the punishments consequent upon the fall of man." But, in practice, their two roads separated. For the Man of Geneva saw difficulties in the way of the Scripture proof in the cases of Deborah and Huldah, and in the prophecy of Isaiah that queens should be the nursing mothers of the Church. And as the Bible was not decisive, he thought the subject should be let alone, because "by custom and public consent and long practice, it has been established that realms and principalities may descend to females by hereditary right, and it would not be lawful to unsettle governments which are ordained by the peculiar providence of God." I imagine Knox's ears must have burned during this interview. Think of him listening dutifully to all this—how it would not do to meddle with anointed kings—how there was a peculiar providence in these great affairs; and then think of his own peroration, and the "noble heart" whom he looks for "to vindicate the liberty of his country"; or his answer to Queen Mary, when she asked him who he was, to interfere in the affairs of Scotland:—"Madame, a subject born within the same!" Indeed, the two doctors who differed at this private conversation represented, at the moment, two principles of enormous import in the subsequent history of Europe. In Calvin we have represented that passive obedience, that toleration of injustice and absurdity, that holding back of the hand from political affairs as from something unclean, which lost France, if we are to believe M. Michelet, for the Reformation; a spirit necessarily fatal in the long run to the existence of any sect that may profess it; a suicidal doctrine that survives among us to this day in narrow views of personal duty, and the low political morality of many virtuous men. In Knox, on the other hand, we see fore-

* Described by Calvin in a letter to Cecil, Knox's Works, vol. iv.

FAMILIAR STUDIES

shadowed the whole Puritan Revolution and the scaffold of Charles I.

There is little doubt in my mind that this interview was what caused Knox to print his book without a name.* It was a dangerous thing to contradict the Man of Geneva, and doubly so, surely, when one had had the advantage of correction from him in a private conversation; and Knox had his little flock of English refugees to consider. If they had fallen into bad odor at Geneva, where else was there left to flee to? It was printed, as I said, in 1558; and, by a singular *mal-à-propos*, in that same year Mary died, and Elizabeth succeeded to the throne of England. And just as the accession of Catholic Queen Mary had condemned female rule in the eyes of Knox, the accession of Protestant Queen Elizabeth justified it in the eyes of his colleagues. Female rule ceases to be an anomaly, not because Elizabeth can "reply to eight ambassadors in one day in their different languages," but because she represents for the moment the political future of the Reformation. The exiles troop back to England with songs of praise in their mouths. The bright occidental star, of which we have all read in the Preface to the Bible, had risen over the darkness of Europe. There is a thrill of hope through the persecuted Churches of the Continent. Calvin writes to Cecil, washing his hands of Knox and his political heresies. The sale of the "First Blast" is prohibited in Geneva; and along with it the bold book of Knox's colleague, Goodman—a book dear to Milton—where female rule was briefly characterized as a "monster in nature and disorder among men." † Any who may ever have doubted, or been for a moment led away by Knox or Goodman, or their own wicked imaginations, are now more than convinced. They have seen the occidental star. Aylmer, with his eye set greedily on a possible bishopric, and "the better to obtain the favor of the new Queen," ‡ sharpens his pen to confound Knox by logic.

* It was anonymously published, but no one seems to have been in doubt about its authorship; he might as well have set his name to it, for all the good he got by holding it back.
† Knox's Works, iv. 358.   ‡ Strype's *Aylmer*, p. 16.

JOHN KNOX

What need? He has been confounded by facts. "Thus what had been to the refugees of Geneva as the very word of God, no sooner were they back in England than, behold! it was the word of the devil." *

Now, what of the real sentiments of these loyal subjects of Elizabeth? They professed a holy horror for Knox's position: let us see if their own would please a modern audience any better, or was, in substance, greatly different.

John Aylmer, afterward Bishop of London, published an answer to Knox, under the title of *An Harbour for Faithful and true Subjects against the late Blown Blast, concerning the government of Women.*† And certainly he was a thought more acute, a thought less precipitate and simple, than his adversary. He is not to be led away by such captious terms as *natural* and *unnatural*. It is obvious to him that a woman's disability to rule is not natural in the same sense in which it is natural for a stone to fall or fire to burn. He is doubtful, on the whole, whether this disability be natural at all; nay, when he is laying it down that a woman should not be a priest, he shows some elementary conception of what many of us now hold to be the truth of the matter. "The bringing-up of women," he says, "is commonly such" that they cannot have the necessary qualifications, "for they are not brought up in learning in schools, nor trained in disputation." And even so, he can ask, "Are there not in England women, think you, that for learning and wisdom could tell their household and neighbors as good a tale as any Sir John there?" For all that, his advocacy is weak. If women's rule is not unnatural in a sense preclusive of its very existence, it is neither so convenient nor so profitable as the government of men. He holds England to be specially suitable for the government of women, because there the governor is more limited and restrained by the other members of the constitution than in other places;

---

* It may interest the reader to know that these (so says Thomasius) are the "ipsissima verba Schlusselburgii."
† I am indebted for a sight of this book to the kindness of Mr. David Laing, the editor of Knox's Works.

FAMILIAR STUDIES

and this argument has kept his book from being altogether forgotten. It is only in hereditary monarchies that he will offer any defence of the anomaly. "If rulers were to be chosen by lot or suffrage, he would not that any woman should stand in the election, but men only." The law of succession of crowns was a law to him, in the same sense as the law of evolution is a law to Mr. Herbert Spencer; and the one and the other counsels his readers, in a spirit suggestively alike, not to kick against the pricks or seek to be more wise than He who made them.* If God has put a female child into the direct line of inheritance, it is God's affair. His strength will be perfected in her weakness. He makes the Creator address the objectors in this not very flattering vein:—" I, that could make Daniel, a sucking babe, to judge better than the wisest lawyers; a brute beast to reprehend the folly of a prophet; and poor fishers to confound the great clerks of the world—cannot I make a woman to be a good ruler over you?" This is the last word of his reasoning. Although he was not altogether without Puritanic leaven, shown particularly in what he says of the incomes of Bishops, yet it was rather loyalty to the old order of things than any generous belief in the capacity of women, that raised up for them this clerical champion. His courtly spirit contrasts singularly with the rude, bracing republicanism of Knox. "Thy knee shall bow," he says, "thy cap shall off, thy tongue shall speak reverently of thy sovereign." For himself, his tongue is even more than reverent. Nothing can stay the issue of his eloquent adulation. Again and again, "the remembrance of Elizabeth's virtues" carries him away; and he has to hark back again to find the scent of his argument. He is repressing his vehement adoration throughout, until, when the end comes, and he feels his business at an end, he can indulge himself to his heart's content in indiscriminate laudation of his royal mistress. It is humorous to think that this illustrious lady, whom he here praises, among many other excellences, for the simplicity of her attire and the "marvellous meekness of her stomach," threatened him, years after, in no

* *Social Statics*, p. 64, etc.

JOHN KNOX

very meek terms, for a sermon against female vanity in dress, which she held as a reflection on herself.*
Whatever was wanting here in respect for women generally, there was no want of respect for the Queen; and one cannot very greatly wonder if these devoted servants looked askance, not upon Knox only, but on his little flock, as they came back to England tainted with disloyal doctrine. For them, as for him, the occidental star rose somewhat red and angry. As for poor Knox, his position was the saddest of all. For the juncture seemed to him of the highest importance; it was the nick of time, the flood-water of opportunity. Not only was there an opening for him in Scotland, a smouldering brand of civil liberty and religious enthusiasm which it should be for him to kindle into flame with his powerful breath; but he had his eye seemingly on an object of even higher worth. For now, when religious sympathy ran so high that it could be set against national aversion, he wished to begin the fusion together of England and Scotland, and to begin it at the sore place. If once the open wound were closed at the Border, the work would be half done. Ministers placed at Berwick and such places might seek their converts equally on either side of the march; old enemies would sit together to hear the gospel of peace, and forget the inherited jealousies of many generations in the enthusiasm of a common faith; or—let us say better—a common heresy. For people are not most conscious of brotherhood when they continue languidly together in one creed, but when, with some doubt, with some danger perhaps, and certainly not without some reluctance, they violently break with the tradition of the past, and go forth from the sanctuary of their fathers to worship under the bare heaven. A new creed, like a new country, is an unhomely place of sojourn; but it makes men lean on one another and join hands. It was on this that Knox relied to begin the union of the English and the Scotch. And he had, perhaps, better means of judging than any even of his contemporaries. He knew the temper of both nations; and already

* Hallam's *Const. Hist. of England*, i. 225, note m.

during his two years' chaplaincy at Berwick, he had seen his scheme put to the proof. But whether practicable or not, the proposal does him much honor. That he should thus have sought to make a love match of it between the two peoples, and tried to win their inclination toward a union instead of simply transferring them, like so many sheep, by a marriage or testament, or private treaty, is thoroughly characteristic of what is best in the man. Nor was this all. He had, besides, to assure himself of English support, secret or avowed, for the Reformation party in Scotland; a delicate affair, trenching upon treason. And so he had plenty to say to Cecil, plenty that he did not care to " commit to paper, neither yet to the knowledge of many." But his miserable publication had shut the doors of England in his face. Summoned to Edinburgh by the confederate lords, he waited at Dieppe, anxiously praying for leave to journey through England. The most dispiriting tidings reach him. His messengers, coming from so obnoxious a quarter, narrowly escape imprisonment. His old congregation are coldly received, and even begin to look back again to their place of exile with regret. "My First Blast," he writes ruefully, " has blown from me all my friends of England." And then he adds, with a snarl, " The Second Blast, I fear, shall sound somewhat more sharp, except men be more moderate than I hear they are." * But the threat is empty; there will never be a second blast—he has had enough of that trumpet. Nay, he begins to feel uneasily that, unless he is to be rendered useless for the rest of his life, unless he is to lose his right arm and go about his great work maimed and impotent, he must find some way of making his peace with England and the indignant Queen. The letter just quoted was written on the 6th of April, 1559; and on the 10th, after he had cooled his heels for four days more about the streets of Dieppe, he gave in altogether, and writes a letter of capitulation to Cecil. In this letter,† which he kept back until the 22d, still hoping that things would come right of

* Knox to Mrs. Locke, 6th April, 1559. Works, vi. 14.
† Knox to Sir William Cecil, 10th April, 1559. Works, ii. 16, or vi. 15.

JOHN KNOX

themselves, he censures the great secretary for having "followed the world in the way of perdition," characterizes him as "worthy of hell," and threatens him, if he be not found simple, sincere, and fervent in the cause of Christ's gospel, that he shall "taste of the same cup that politic heads have drunken in before him." This is all, I take it, out of respect for the Reformer's own position; if he is going to be humiliated, let others be humiliated first; like a child who will not take his medicine until he has made his nurse and his mother drink of it before him. "But I have, say you, written a treasonable book against the regiment and empire of women. . . . The writing of that book I will not deny; but to prove it treasonable I think it shall be hard. . . . It is hinted that my book shall be written against. If so be, sir, I greatly doubt they shall rather hurt nor [than] mend the matter." And here comes the terms of capitulation; for he does not surrender unconditionally, even in this sore strait: "And yet if any," he goes on, "think me enemy to the person, or yet to the regiment of her whom God hath now promoted, they are utterly deceived in me, *for the miraculous work of God, comforting his afflicted by means of an infirm vessel, I do acknowledge, and the power of His most potent hand I will obey. More plainly to speak, if Queen Elizabeth shall confess, that the extraordinary dispensation of God's great mercy maketh that lawful unto her which both nature and God's law do deny to all women*, then shall none in England be more willing to maintain her lawful authority than I shall be. But if (God's wondrous work set aside) she ground (as God forbid) the justness of her title upon consuetude, laws, or ordinances of men, then "—Then Knox will denounce her? Not so; he is more politic nowadays—then, he "greatly fears" that her ingratitude to God will not go long without punishment.

His letter to Elizabeth, written some few months later, was a mere amplification of the sentences quoted above. She must base her title entirely upon the extraordinary providence of God; but if she does this, "if thus, in God's presence, she humbles herself, so will he with tongue and pen justify her authority, as the Holy Ghost hath justified the same in Deborah, that blessed mother in Israel." * And so, you see, his consistency is preserved; he is merely applying the doctrine of the " First Blast." The argument goes thus: The regiment of women, is as before noted in our work, repugnant to nature, contumely to God, and a subversion of good order. It has nevertheless pleased God to raise up, as exceptions to this law, first Deborah, and afterward Elizabeth Tudor—whose regiment we shall proceed to celebrate.

There is no evidence as to how the Reformer's explanations were received, and indeed it is most probable that the letter was never shown to Elizabeth at all. For it was sent under cover of another to Cecil, and as it was not of a very courtly conception throughout, and was, of all things, what would most excite the Queen's uneasy jealousy about her title, it is like enough that the secretary exercised his discretion (he had Knox's leave in this case, and did not always wait for that, it is reputed) to put the letter harmlessly away beside other valueless or unpresentable State Papers. I wonder very much if he did the same with another,† written two years later, after Mary had come into Scotland, in which Knox almost seeks to make Elizabeth an accomplice with him in the matter of the " First Blast." The Queen of Scotland is going to have that work refuted, he tells her; and " though it were but foolishness in him to prescribe unto her Majesty what is to be done," he would yet remind her that Mary is neither so much alarmed about her own security, nor so generously interested in Elizabeth's, " that she would take such pains, *unless her crafty counsel in so doing shot at a further mark.*" There is something really ingenious in this letter; it showed Knox in the double capacity of the author of the " First Blast " and the faithful friend of Elizabeth; and he combines them there so naturally, that one would scarcely imagine the two to be incongruous.

Twenty days later he was defending his intemperate publication to another queen—his own queen, Mary Stuart.

* Knox to Queen Elizabeth, July 20th, 1559. Works, vi. 47, or ii. 26.
† Knox to Queen Elizabeth, August 6th, 1561. Works, vi. 126.

JOHN KNOX

This was on the first of those three interviews which he has preserved for us with so much dramatic vigor in the picturesque pages of his history. After he had avowed the authorship in his usual haughty style, Mary asked: "You think, then, that I have no just authority?" The question was evaded. "Please your Majèsty," he answered, "that learned men in all ages have had their judgments free, and most commonly disagreeing from the common judgment of the world; such also have they published by pen and tongue; and yet notwithstanding they themselves have lived in the common society with others, and have borne patiently with the errors and imperfections which they could not amend." Thus did "Plato the philosopher": thus will do John Knox. "I have communicated my judgment to the world: if the realm finds no inconvenience from the regiment of a woman, that which they approve, shall I not further disallow than within my own breast; but shall be as well content to live under your Grace, as Paul was to live under Nero. And my hope is, that so long as ye defile not your hands with the blood of the saints of God, neither I nor my book shall hurt either you or your authority." All this is admirable in wisdom and moderation, and, except that he might have hit upon a comparison less offensive than that with Paul and Nero, hardly to be bettered. Having said thus much, he feels he needs say no more; and so, when he is further pressed, he closes that part of the discussion with an astonishing sally. If he has been content to let this matter sleep, he would recommend her Grace to follow his example with thankfulness of heart; it is grimly to be understood which of them has most to fear if the question should be reawakened. So the talk wandered to other subjects. Only, when the Queen was summoned at last to dinner ("for it was afternoon") Knox made his salutation in this form of words: "I pray God, Madam, that you may be as much blessed within the Commonwealth of Scotland, if it be the pleasure of God, as ever Deborah was in the Commonwealth of Israel."* Deborah again.

But he was not yet done with the echoes of his own "First

* Knox's Works, ii. 278-280.

FAMILIAR STUDIES

Blast." In 1571, when he was already near his end, the old controversy was taken up in one of a series of anonymous libels against the Reformer affixed, Sunday after Sunday, to the church door. The dilemma was fairly enough stated. Either his doctrine is false, in which case he is a "false doctor" and seditious; or, if it be true, why does he "avow and approve the contrare, I mean that regiment in the Queen of England's person; which he avoweth and approveth, not only praying for the maintenance of her estate, but also procuring her aid and support against his own native country?" Knox answered the libel, as his wont was, next Sunday, from the pulpit. He justified the "First Blast" with all the old arrogance; there is no drawing back there. The regiment of women is repugnant to nature, contumely to God, and a subversion of good order, as before. When he prays for the maintenance of Elizabeth's estate, he is only following the example of those prophets of God who warned and comforted the wicked kings of Israel; or of Jeremiah, who bade the Jews pray for the prosperity of Nebuchadnezzar. As for the Queen's aid, there is no harm in that: *quia* (these are his own words) *quia omnia munda mundis:* because to the pure all things are pure. One thing, in conclusion, he "may not pretermit"; to give the lie in the throat to his accuser, where he charges him with seeking support against his native country. "What I have been to my country," said the old Reformer, "what I have been to my country, albeit this unthankful age will not know, yet the ages to come will be compelled to bear witness to the truth. And thus I cease, requiring of all men that have anything to oppone against me, that he may [they may] do it so plainly, as that I may make myself and all my doings manifest to the world. For to me it seemeth a thing unreasonable, that, in this my decrepit age, I shall be compelled to fight against shadows, and howlets that dare not abide the light." *

Now, in this, which may be called his *Last Blast*, there

* Calderwood's *History of the Kirk of Scotland*, edition of the Wodrow Society, iii. 51-54.

JOHN KNOX

s as sharp speaking as any in the " First Blast " itself. He
s of the same opinion to the end, you see, although he has
been obliged to cloak and garble that opinion for political
ends. He has been tacking indeed, and he has indeed been
seeking the favor of a queen; but what man ever sought a
queen's favor with a more virtuous purpose, or with as
little courtly policy? The question of consistency is delicate,
and must be made plain. Knox never changed his opinion
about female rule, but lived to regret that he had published
that opinion. Doubtless he had many thoughts so far out
of the range of public sympathy, that he could only keep
them to himself, and, in his own words, bear patiently with
the errors and imperfections that he could not amend. For
example, I make no doubt myself, that, in his own heart, he
did hold the shocking dogma attributed to him by more than
one calumniator; and that, had the time been ripe, had there
been aught to gain by it, instead of all to lose, he would
have been the first to assert that Scotland was elective instead
of hereditary—" elective as in the days of paganism," as
one Thevet says in holy horror.* And yet, because the time
was not ripe, I find no hint of such an idea in his collected
works. Now, the regiment of women was another matter
that he should have kept to himself; right or wrong, his
opinion did not fit the moment; right or wrong, as Aylmer
puts it, " the *Blast* was blown out of season." And this it
was that he began to perceive after the accession of Elizabeth; not that he had been wrong, and that female rule was
a good thing, for he had said from the first that " the felicity of some women in their empires " could not change the
law of God and the nature of created things; not this, but
that the regiment of women was one of those imperfections
of society which must be borne with because yet they cannot
be remedied. The thing had seemed so obvious to him, in
his sense of unspeakable masculine superiority, and his
fine contempt for what is only sanctioned by antiquity and
common consent, he had imagined that, at the first hint, men
would arise and shake off the debasing tyranny. He found

* Bayle's *Historical Dictionary*, art. Knox, remark G.

FAMILIAR STUDIES

himself wrong, and he showed that he could be moderate in his own fashion, and understood the spirit of true compromise. He came round to Calvin's position, in fact, but by a different way. And it derogates nothing from the merit of this wise attitude that it was the consequence of a change of interest. We are all taught by interest; and if the interest be not merely selfish, there is no wiser preceptor under heaven, and perhaps no sterner.

Such is the history of John Knox's connection with the controversy about female rule. In itself, this is obviously an incomplete study; not fully to be understood, without a knowledge of his private relations with the other sex, and what he thought of their position in domestic life. This shall be dealt with in another paper.

JOHN KNOX AND HIS RELATIONS TO WOMEN

II—PRIVATE LIFE

TO those who know Knox by hearsay only, I believe the matter of this paper will be somewhat astonishing. For the hard energy of the man in all public matters has possessed the imagination of the world; he remains for posterity in certain traditional phrases, browbeating Queen Mary, or breaking beautiful carved work in abbeys and cathedrals, that had long smoked themselves out and were no more than sorry ruins, while he was still quietly teaching children in a country gentleman's family. It does not consist with the common acceptation of his character to fancy him much moved, except with anger. And yet the language of passion came to his pen as readily, whether it was a passion of denunciation against some of the abuses that vexed his righteous spirit, or of yearning for the society of an absent friend. He was vehement in affection as in doctrine. I will not deny that there may have been, along with his vehemence, something shifty, and for the moment only; that, like many men, and many Scotchmen, he saw the world and his own heart, not so much under any very steady, equable light, as by extreme flashes of passion, true for the moment, but not true in the long run. There does seem to me to be something of this traceable in the Reformer's utterances: precipitation and repentance, hardy speech and action somewhat circumspect, a strong tendency to see himself in a heroic light and to place a ready belief in the disposition of the moment. Withal he had considerable confidence in himself, and in the uprightness of his own disciplined emotions, underlying much sincere aspiration after spiritual humility. And it is this confidence that

FAMILIAR STUDIES

makes his intercourse with women so interesting to a modern. It would be easy, of course, to make fun of the whole affair, to picture him strutting vaingloriously among these inferior creatures, or compare a religious friendship in the sixteenth century with what was called, I think, a literary friendship in the eighteenth. But it is more just and profitable to recognize what there is sterling and human underneath all his theoretical affectations of superiority. Women, he has said in his "First Blast," are "weak, frail, impatient, feeble, and foolish"; and yet it does not appear that he was himself any less dependent than other men upon the sympathy and affection of these weak, frail, impatient, feeble, and foolish creatures; it seems even as if he had been rather more dependent than most.

Of those who are to act influentially on their fellows, we should expect always something large and public in their way of life, something more or less urbane and comprehensive in their sentiment for others. We should not expect to see them spend their sympathy in idyls, however beautiful. We should not seek them among those who, if they have but a wife to their bosom, ask no more of womankind, just as they ask no more of their own sex, if they can find a friend or two for their immediate need. They will be quick to feel all the pleasures of our association—not the great ones alone, but all. They will know not love only, but all those other ways in which man and woman mutually make each other happy—by sympathy, by admiration, by the atmosphere they bear about them—down to the mere impersonal pleasure of passing happy faces in the street. For, through all this gradation, the difference of sex makes itself pleasurably felt. Down to the most lukewarm courtesies of life, there is a special chivalry due and a special pleasure received, when the two sexes are brought ever so lightly into contact. We love our mothers otherwise than we love our fathers; a sister is not as a brother to us; and friendship between man and woman, be it never so unalloyed and innocent, is not the same as friendship between man and man. Such friendship is not even possible for all. To conjoin

JOHN KNOX

tenderness for a woman that is not far short of passionate with such disinterestedness and beautiful gratuity of affection as there is between friends of the same sex, requires no ordinary disposition in the man. For it either would presuppose quite womanly delicacy of perception, and, as it were, a curiosity in shades of differing sentiment; or it would mean that he had accepted the large, simple divisions of society: a strong and positive spirit robustly virtuous, who has chosen a better part coarsely, and holds to it steadfastly, with all its consequences of pain to himself and others; as one who should go straight before him on a journey, neither tempted by wayside flowers nor very scrupulous of small lives under foot. It was in virtue of this latter disposition that Knox was capable of those intimacies with women that embellished his life; and we find him preserved for us in old letters as a man of many women friends; a man of some expansion toward the other sex; a man ever ready to comfort weeping women, and to weep along with them.

Of such scraps and fragments of evidence as to his private life and more intimate thoughts as have survived to us from all the perils that environ written paper, an astonishingly large proportion is in the shape of letters to women of his familiarity. He was twice married, but that is not greatly to the purpose; for the Turk who thinks even more meanly of women than John Knox, is none the less given to marrying. What is really significant is quite apart from marriage. For the man Knox was a true man, and woman, the *ewig-weibliche*, was as necessary to him, in spite of all low theories, as ever she was to Goethe. He came to her in a certain halo of his own, as the minister of truth, just as Goethe came to her in a glory of art; he made himself necessary to troubled hearts and minds exercised in the painful complications that naturally result from all changes in the world's way of thinking; and those whom he had thus helped became dear to him, and were made the chosen companions of his leisure if they were at hand, or encouraged and comforted by letter if they were afar.

FAMILIAR STUDIES

It must not be forgotten that Knox had been a presbyter of the old Church, and that the many women whom we shall see gathering around him, as he goes through life, had probably been accustomed, while still in the communion of Rome, to rely much upon some chosen spiritual director, so that the intimacies of which I propose to offer some account, while testifying to a good heart in the Reformer, testify also to a certain survival of the spirit of the confessional in the Reformed Church, and are not properly to be judged without this idea. There is no friendship so noble, but it is the product of time; and a world of little finical observances, and little frail proprieties and fashions of the hour, go to make or to mar, to stint or to perfect, the union of spirits the most loving and the most intolerant of such interference. The trick of the country and the age steps in even between the mother and her child, counts out their caresses upon niggardly fingers, and says, in the voice of authority, that this one thing shall be a matter of confidence between them, and this other thing shall not. And thus it is that we must take into reckoning whatever tended to modify the social atmosphere in which Knox and his women friends met, and loved and trusted each other. To the man who had been their priest and was now their minister, women would be able to speak with a confidence quite impossible in these latter days; the women would be able to speak, and the man to hear. It was a beaten road just then; and I dare say we should be no less scandalized at their plain speech than they, if they could come back to earth, would be offended at our waltzes and worldly fashions. This, then, was the footing on which Knox stood with his many women friends. The reader will see, as he goes on, how much of warmth, of interest, and of that happy mutual dependence which is the very gist of friendship, he contrived to ingraft upon this somewhat dry relationship of penitent and confessor.

It must be understood that we know nothing of his intercourse with women (as indeed we know little at all about his life) until he came to Berwick in 1549, when he was

JOHN KNOX

already in the forty-fifth year of his age. At the same time it is just possible that some of a little group at Edinburgh, with whom he corresponded during his last absence, may have been friends of an older standing. Certainly they were, of all his female correspondents, the least personally favored. He treats them throughout in a comprehensive sort of spirit that must at times have been a little wounding. Thus, he remits one of them to his former letters, " which I trust be common betwixt you and the rest of our sisters, for to me ye are all equal in Christ." * Another letter is a gem in this way. " Albeit," it begins, " albeit I have no particular matter to write unto you, beloved sister, yet I could not refrain to write these few lines to you in declaration of my remembrance of you. True it is that I have many whom I bear in equal remembrance before God with you, to whom at present I write nothing, either for that I esteem them stronger than you, and therefore they need the less my rude labors, or else because they have not provoked me by their writing to recompense their remembrance." † His " sisters in Edinburgh " had evidently to " provoke " his attention pretty constantly; nearly all his letters are, on the face of them, answers to questions, and the answers are given with a certain crudity that I do not find repeated when he writes to those he really cares for. So when they consult him about women's apparel (a subject on which his opinion may be pretty correctly imagined by the ingenious reader for himself) he takes occasion to anticipate some of the most offensive matter of the " First Blast " in a style of real brutality.‡ It is not merely that he tells them " the garments of women do declare their weakness and inability to execute the office of man," though that in itself is neither very wise nor very opportune in such a correspondence one would think; but if the reader will take the trouble to wade through the long, tedious sermon for himself, he will see proof enough that Knox neither loved, nor very deeply respected, the women he was then addressing. In very truth, I believe these Edinburgh sisters simply

* Works, iv. 244. † Ib. iv. 246. ‡ Ib. iv. 225.

bored him. He had a certain interest in them as his children in the Lord: they were continually " provoking him by their writing "; and, if they handed his letters about, writing to them was as good a form of publication as was then open to him in Scotland. There is one letter, however, in this budget, addressed to the wife of Clerk-Register Mackgil, which is worthy of some further mention. The Clerk-Register had not opened his heart, it would appear, to the preaching of the Gospel, and Mrs. Mackgil has written, seeking the Reformer's prayers in his behalf. " Your husband," he answers, " is dear to me for that he is a man indued with some good gifts, but more dear for that he is your husband. Charity moveth me to thirst his illumination, both for his comfort and for the trouble which you sustain by his coldness, which justly may be called infidelity." He wishes her, however, not to hope too much: he can promise that his prayers will be earnest, but not that they will be effectual; it is possible that this is to be her " cross " in life; that " her head, appointed by God for her comfort, should be her enemy." And if this be so, well, there is nothing for it; " with patience she must abide God's merciful deliverance," taking heed only that she does not " obey manifest iniquity for the pleasure of any mortal man." * I conceive this espistle would have given a very modified sort of pleasure to the Clerk-Register, had it chanced to fall into his hands. Compare its tenor—the dry resignation not without a hope of merciful deliverance therein recommended—with these words from another letter, written but the year before to two married women of London: " Call first for grace by Jesus, and thereafter communicate with your faithful husbands, and then shall God, I doubt not, conduct your footsteps, and direct your counsels to his glory." † Here the husbands are put in a very high place; we can recognize here the same hand that has written for our instruction how the man is set above the woman, even as God above the angels. But the point of the distinction is plain. For Clerk-Register Mackgil was not a faithful husband; displayed,.

* Works, iv. 245. † Ib. iv. 221.

JOHN KNOX

indeed, toward religion a "coldness which justly might be called infidelity." We shall see in more notable instances how much Knox's conception of the duty of wives varies according to the zeal and orthodoxy of the husband.

As I have said, he may possibly have made the acquaintance of Mrs. Mackgil, Mrs. Guthrie, or some other, or all, of these Edinburgh friends while he was still Douglas of Longniddry's private tutor. But our certain knowledge begins in 1549. He was then but newly escaped from his captivity in France, after pulling an oar for nineteen months on the benches of the galley *Notre Dame;* now up the rivers, holding stealthy intercourse with other Scottish prisoners in the castle of Rouen; now out in the North Sea, raising his sick head to catch a glimpse of the far-off steeples of St. Andrews. And now he was sent down by the English Privy Council as a preacher to Berwick-upon-Tweed; somewhat shaken in health by all his hardships, full of pains and agues, and tormented by gravel, that sorrow of great men; altogether, what with his romantic story, his weak health, and his great faculty of eloquence, a very natural object for the sympathy of devout women. At this happy juncture he fell into the company of a Mrs. Elizabeth Bowes, wife of Richard Bowes, of Aske, in Yorkshire, to whom she had borne twelve children. She was a religious hypochondriac, a very weariful woman, full of doubts and scruples, and giving no rest on earth either to herself or to those whom she honored with her confidence. From the first time she heard Knox preach she formed a high opinion of him, and was solicitous ever after of his society.* Nor was Knox unresponsive. "I have always delighted in your company," he writes, "and when labors would permit, you know I have not spared hours to talk and commune with you." Often when they had met in depression he reminds her, "God hath sent great comfort unto both." † We can gather from such letters as are yet extant how close and continuous was their intercourse. "I think it best you remain till the morrow," he writes once, "and so shall

* Works, vi. 514. † Ib. iii. 338.

we commune at large at afternoon. This day you know to be the day of my study and prayer unto God; yet if your trouble be intolerable, or if you think my presence may release your pain, do as the Spirit shall move you. . . . Your messenger found me in bed, after a sore trouble and most dolorous night, and so dolor may complain to dolor when we two meet. . . . And this is more plain than ever I spoke, to let you know you have a companion in trouble." * Once we have the curtain raised for a moment, and can look at the two together for the length of a phrase. "After the writing of this preceding," writes Knox, "your brother and mine, Harrie Wycliffe, did advertise me by writing, that your adversary (the devil) took occasion to trouble you because that *I did start back from you rehearsing your infirmities. I remember myself so to have done, and that is my common consuetude when anything pierceth or toucheth my heart. Call to your mind what I did standing at the cupboard at Alnwick.* In very deed I thought that no creature had been tempted as I was; and when I heard proceed from your mouth the very same words that he troubles me with, I did wonder and from my heart lament your sore trouble, knowing in myself the dolor thereof." † Now intercourse of so very close a description, whether it be religious intercourse or not, is apt to displease and disquiet a husband; and we know incidentally from Knox himself that there was some little scandal about his intimacy with Mrs. Bowes. "The slander and fear of men," he writes, "has impeded me to exercise my pen so oft as I would; *yea, very shame hath holden me from your company, when I was most surely persuaded that God had appointed me at that time to comfort and feed your hungry and afflicted soul. God in His infinite mercy,*" he goes on, "*remove not only from me all fear that tendeth not to godliness, but from others suspicion to judge of me otherwise than it becometh one member to judge of another.*" ‡ And the scandal, such as it was, would not be allayed by the dissension in which Mrs. Bowes seems to have lived with her family upon the

* Works, iii. 352, 353. † Ib. iii. 350.
‡ Ib. iii. 390, 391.

JOHN KNOX

matter of religion, and the countenance shown by Knox to her resistance. Talking of these conflicts, and her courage against "her own flesh and most inward affections, yea, against some of her most natural friends," he writes it, to the praise of God, he has wondered at the bold constancy which he has found in her when his own heart was faint.*

Now, perhaps in order to stop scandalous mouths, perhaps out of a desire to bind the much-loved evangelist nearer to her in the only manner possible, Mrs. Bowes conceived the scheme of marrying him to her fifth daughter, Marjorie; and the Reformer seems to have fallen in with it readily enough. It seems to have been believed in the family that the whole matter had been originally made up between these two, with no very spontaneous inclination on the part of the bride.† Knox's idea of marriage, as I have said, was not the same for all men; but on the whole, it was not lofty. We have a curious letter of his, written at the request of Queen Mary, to the Earl of Argyle, on very delicate household matters; which, as he tells us, " was not well accepted of the said Earl." ‡ We may suppose, however, that his own home was regulated in a similar spirit. I can fancy that for such a man, emotional, and with a need, now and again, to exercise parsimony in emotions not strictly needful, something a little mechanical, something hard and fast and clearly understood, would enter into his ideal of a home. There were storms enough without, and equability was to be desired at the fireside even at a sacrifice of deeper pleasures. So, from a wife, of all women, he would not ask much. One letter to her which has come down to us is, I had almost said, conspicuous for coldness.§ He calls her, as he called other female correspondents, " dearly beloved sister "; the epistle is doctrinal, and nearly the half of it bears, not upon her own case, but upon that of her mother. However, we know what Heine wrote in his wife's album; and there is, after all, one passage that may be held to intimate some tenderness, although even that admits of an amusingly opposite construction. " I think," he says, " I *think* this be the

* Works, iii. 142.   † *Ib.* iii. 378.   ‡ *Ib.* ii. 879.
§ *Ib.* iii. 394.

first letter I ever wrote to you." This, if we are to take it literally, may pair off with the "two or *three* children" whom Montaigne mentions having lost at nurse; the one is as eccentric in a lover as the other in a parent. Nevertheless, he displayed more energy in the course of his troubled wooing than might have been expected. The whole Bowes family, angry enough already at the influence he had obtained over the mother, set their faces obdurately against the match. And I dare say the opposition quickened his inclination. I find him writing to Mrs. Bowes that she need not further trouble herself about the marriage; it should now be his business altogether; it behoved him now to jeopard his life " for the comfort of his own flesh, both fear and friendship of all earthly creature laid aside."* This is a wonderfully chivalrous utterance for a Reformer forty-eight years old; and it compares well with the leaden coquetries of Calvin, not much over thirty, taking this and that into consideration, weighing together dowries and religious qualifications and the instancy of friends, and exhibiting what M. Bungener calls " an honorable and Christian difficulty " of choice, in frigid indecisions and insincere proposals. But Knox's next letter is in a humbler tone; he has not found the negotiation so easy as he fancied; he despairs of the marriage altogether, and talks of leaving England,—regards not " what country consumes his wicked carcass." " You shall understand," he says, " that this sixth of November, I spoke with Sir Robert Bowes " (the head of the family, his bride's uncle) " in the matter you know, according to your request; whose disdainful, yea, despiteful, words hath so pierced my heart that my life is bitter to me. I bear a good countenance with a sore troubled heart, because he that ought to consider matters with a deep judgment is become not only a despiser, but also a taunter of God's messengers—God be merciful unto him! Among others his most unpleasing words, while that I was about to have declared my heart in the whole matter, he said, ' Away with your rhetorical reasons! for I will not be persuaded with them.' God knows I did use no rhetoric nor colored

* Works, iii. 376.

JOHN KNOX

ch; but would have spoken the truth, and that in most
)le manner. I am not a good orator in my own cause;
what he would not be content to hear of me, God shall
are to him one day to his displeasure, unless he repent." *
r Knox, you see, is quite commoved. It has been a very
leasant interview. And as it is the only sample that we
₂ of how things went with him during his courtship, we
infer that the period was not as agreeable for Knox as
as been for some others.
[owever, when once they were married, I imagine he and
:jorie Bowes hit it off together comfortably enough.
little we know of it may be brought together in a very
:t space. She bore him two sons. He seems to have
t her pretty busy, and depended on her to some degree
ais work; so that when she fell ill, his papers got at
₂ into disorder.† Certainly she sometimes wrote to his
ation; and, in this capacity, he calls her "his left hand." ‡
June, 1559, at the headiest moment of the Reformation
Scotland, he writes regretting the absence of his helpful
ague, Goodman, "whose presence" (this is the not
r grammatical form of his lament) "whose presence I
e thirst, than she that is my own flesh." § And this,
idering the source and the circumstances, may be held
vidence of a very tender sentiment. He tells us himself
us history, on the occasion of a certain meeting at the
k of Field, that "he was in no small heaviness by reason
he late death of his dear bed-fellow, Marjorie Bowes." ||
vin, condoling with him, speaks of her as "a wife whose
is not to be found everywhere" (that is very like Cal-
, and again, as "the most delightful of wives." We
v what Calvin thought desirable in a wife, "good humor,
itity, thrift, patience, and solicitude for her husband's
th," and so we may suppose that the first Mrs. Knox
not far short of this ideal.
he actual date of the marriage is uncertain; but by
tember, 1566, at the latest, the Reformer was settled

* Works, iii. 378.   † *Ib.* vi. 104.   ‡ *Ib.* v. 5.
§ *Ib.* vi. 27. || *Ib.* ii. 138.

in Geneva with his wife. There is no fear either that he will be dull; even if the chaste, thrifty, patient Marjorie should not altogether occupy his mind, he need not go out of the house to seek more female sympathy; for behold! Mrs. Bowes is duly domesticated with the young couple. Dr. M'Crie imagined that Richard Bowes was now dead, and his widow, consequently, free to live where she would; and where could she go more naturally than to the house of a married daughter? This, however, is not the case. Richard Bowes did not die till at least two years later. It is impossible to believe that he approved of his wife's desertion, after so many years of marriage, after twelve children had been born to them; and accordingly we find in his will, dated 1558, no mention either of her or of Knox's wife.* This is plain sailing. It is easy enough to understand the anger of Bowes against this interloper, who had come into a quiet family, married the daughter in spite of the father's opposition, alienated the wife from the husband and the husband's religion, supported her in a long course of resistance and rebellion, and, after years of intimacy, already too close and tender for any jealous spirit to behold without resentment, carried her away with him at last into a foreign land. But it is not quite easy to understand how, except out of sheer weariness and disgust, he was ever brought to agree to the arrangement. Nor is it easy to square the Reformer's conduct with his public teaching. We have, for instance, a letter addressed by him, Craig, and Spottiswood, to the Archbishops of Canterbury and York, anent, " a wicked and rebellious woman," one Anne Good, spouse to " John Barron, a minister of Christ Jesus his evangel," who " after great rebellion shown unto him, and divers admonitions given, as well by himself as by others in his name, that she should in no wise depart from this realm, nor from his house without his license, hath not the less stubbornly and rebelliously departed, separated herself from his society, left his house, and withdrawn herself from this realm." † Perhaps some sort of license was extorted, as I have said, from

* Mr. Laing's preface to the sixth volume of Knox's Works, p. lxii.
† Works, vi. 534.

JOHN KNOX

Richard Bowes, weary with years of domestic dissension; but setting that aside, the words employed with so much righteous indignation by Knox, Craig, and Spottiswood, to describe the conduct of that wicked and rebellious woman, Mrs. Barron, would describe nearly as exactly the conduct of the religious Mrs. Bowes. It is a little bewildering, until we recollect the distinction between faithful and unfaithful husbands; for Barron was "a minister of Christ Jesus his evangel," while Richard Bowes, besides being own brother to a despiser and taunter of God's messengers, is shrewdly suspected to have been "a bigoted adherent of the Roman Catholic faith," or, as Knox himself would have expressed it, "a rotten Papist."

You would have thought that Knox was now pretty well supplied with female society. But we are not yet at the end of the roll. The last year of his sojourn in England had been spent principally in London, where he was resident as one of the chaplains of Edward the Sixth; and here he boasts, although a stranger, he had, by God's grace, found favor before many.* The godly women of the metropolis made much of him; once he writes to Mrs. Bowes that her last letter had found him closeted with three, and he and the three women were all in tears.† Out of all, however, he had chosen two. "*God,*" he writes to them, "*brought us in such familiar acquaintance, that your hearts were incensed and kindled with a special care over me, as a mother useth to be over her natural child;* and my heart was opened and compelled in your presence to be more plain than ever I was to any." ‡ And out of the two even he had chosen one, Mrs. Anne Locke, wife to Mr. Harry Locke, merchant, nigh to Bow Kirk, Cheapside, in London, as the address runs. If one may venture to judge upon such imperfect evidence, this was the woman he loved best. I have a difficulty in quite forming to myself an idea of her character. She may have been one of the three tearful visitors before alluded to; she may even have been that one of them who was so profoundly moved by some passages of Mrs. Bowes's letter,

* Works, iv. 220. † *Ib.* iii. 380. ‡ *Ib.* iv. 220.

245

FAMILIAR STUDIES

which the Reformer opened, and read aloud to them before they went. "O would to God," cried this impressionable matron, "would to God that I might speak with that person, for I perceive there are more tempted than I." * This *may* have been Mrs. Locke, as I say; but even if it were, we must not conclude from this one fact that she was such another as Mrs. Bowes. All the evidence tends the other way. She was a woman of understanding, plainly, who followed political events with interest, and to whom Knox thought it worth while to write, in detail, the history of his trials and successes. She was religious, but without that morbid perversity of spirit that made religion so heavy a burden for the poor-hearted Mrs. Bowes. More of her I do not find, save testimony to the profound affection that united her to the Reformer. So we find him writing to her from Geneva, in such terms as these:—"You write that your desire is earnest to see me. *Dear sister, if I could express the thirst and languor which I have had for your presence, I should appear to pass measure. . . . Yea, I weep and rejoice in remembrance of you;* but that would evanish by the comfort of your presence, which I assure you is so dear to me, that if the charge of this little flock here, gathered together in Christ's name, did not impede me, my coming should prevent my letter." † I say that this was written from Geneva; and yet you will obesrve that it is no consideration for his wife or mother-in-law, only the charge of his little flock, that keeps him from setting out forthwith for London, to comfort himself with the dear presence of Mrs. Locke. Remember that was a certain plausible enough pretext for Mrs. Locke to come to Geneva—"the most perfect school of Christ that ever was on earth since the days of the Apostles"—for we are now under the reign of that "horrible monster Jezebel of England," when a lady of good orthodox sentiments was better out of London. It was doubtful, however, whether this was to be. She was detained in England, partly by circumstances unknown, "partly by empire of her head," Mr.

* Works, iii. 380.   † Ib. iv. 238.

JOHN KNOX

Harry Locke, the Cheapside merchant. It is somewhat humorous to see Knox struggling for resignation, now that he has to do with a faithful husband (for Mr. Harry Locke was faithful). Had it been otherwise, " in my heart," he says, " I could have wished—yea," here he breaks out, " yea, and cannot cease to wish—that God would guide you to this place." * And after all, he had not long to wait, for, whether Mr. Harry Locke died in the interval, or was wearied, he too, into giving permission, five months after the date of the letter last quoted, " Mrs. Anne Locke, Harry her son, and Anne her daughter, and Katharine her maid," arrived in that perfect school of Christ, the Presbyterian paradise, Geneva. So now, and for the next two years, the cup of Knox's happiness was surely full. Of an afternoon, when the bells rang out for the sermon, the shops closed, and the good folk gathered to the churches, psalm-book in hand, we can imagine him drawing near to the English chapel in quite patriarchal fashion, with Mrs. Knox and Mrs. Bowes and Mrs. Locke, James his servant, Patrick his pupil, and a due following of children and maids. He might be alone at work all morning in his study, for he wrote much during these two years; but at night, you may be sure there was a circle of admiring women, eager to hear the new paragraph, and not sparing of applause. And what work, among others, was he elaborating at this time, but the notorious " First Blast "? So that he may have rolled out in his big pulpit voice, how women were weak, frail, impatient, feeble, foolish, inconstant, variable, cruel, and lacking the spirit of counsel, and how men were above them, even as God is above the angels, in the ears of his own wife, and the two dearest friends he had on earth. But he had lost the sense of incongruity, and continued to despise in theory the sex he honored so much in practice, of whom he chose his most intimate associates, and whose courage he was compelled to wonder at, when his own heart was faint.

We may say that such a man was not worthy of his fortune; and so, as he would not learn, he was taken away

* Works, iv. 240.

FAMILIAR STUDIES

from that agreeable school, and his fellowship of women was broken up, not to be reunited. Called into Scotland to take at last that strange position in history which is his best claim to commemoration, he was followed thither by his wife and his mother-in-law. The wife soon died. The death of her daughter did not altogether separate Mrs. Bowes from Knox, but she seems to have come and gone between his house and England. In 1562, however, we find him characterized as "a sole man by reason of the absence of his mother-in-law, Mrs. Bowes," and a passport is got for her, her man, a maid, and "three horses, whereof two shall return," as well as liberty to take all her own money with her into Scotland. This looks like a definite arrangement; but whether she died at Edinburgh, or went back to England yet again, I cannot find. With that great family of hers, unless in leaving her husband she had quarrelled with them all, there must have been frequent occasion for her presence, one would think. Knox at least survived her; and we possess his epigraph to their long intimacy, given to the world by him in an appendix to his latest publication. I have said in a former paper that Knox was not shy of personal revelations in his published works. And the trick seems to have grown on him. To this last tract, a controversial onslaught on a Scottish Jesuit, he prefixed a prayer, not very pertinent to the matter in hand, and containing references to his family which were the occasion of some wit in his adversary's answer; and appended what seems equally irrelevant, one of his devout letters to Mrs. Bowes, with an explanatory preface. To say truth, I believe he had always felt uneasily that the circumstances of this intimacy were very capable of misconstruction; and now, when he was an old man, taking "his good night of all the faithful in both realms," and only desirous "that without any notable sclander to the evangel of Jesus Christ, he might end his battle; for as the world was weary of him, so was he of it";—in such a spirit it was not, perhaps, unnatural that he should return to this old story, and seek to put it right in the eyes of all men, ere he died. "Because that

JOHN KNOX

God," he says, "because that God now in His mercy hath put an end to the battle of my dear mother, Mistress Elizabeth Bowes, before that He put an end to my wretched life, I could not cease but declare to the world what was the cause of our great familiarity and long acquaintance; which was neither flesh nor blood, but a troubled conscience upon her part, which never suffered her to rest but when she was in the company of the faithful, of whom (from the first hearing of the word at my mouth) she judged me to be one. . . . Her company to me was comfortable (yea, honorable and profitable, for she was to me and mine a mother), but yet it was not without some cross; for besides trouble and fashery of body sustained for her, my mind was seldom quiet, for doing somewhat for the comfort of her troubled conscience." * He had written to her years before, from his first exile in Dieppe, that "only God's hand" could withhold him from once more speaking with her face to face; and now, when God's hand has indeed interposed, when there lies between them, instead of the voyageable straits, that great gulf over which no man can pass, this is the spirit in which he can look back upon their long acquaintance. She was a religious hypochondriac, it appears, whom, not without some cross and fashery of mind and body, he was good enough to tend. He might have given a truer character of their friendship, had he thought less of his own standing in public estimation, and more of the dead woman. But he was in all things, as Burke said of his son in that ever-memorable passage, a public creature. He wished that even into this private place of his affections posterity should follow him with a complete approval; and he was willing, in order that this might be so, to exhibit the defects of his lost friend, and tell the world what weariness he had sustained through her unhappy disposition. There is something here that reminds one of Rosseau.

I do not think he ever saw Mrs. Locke after he left Geneva; but his correspondence with her continued for three years. It may have continued longer, of course, but I think the last letters we possess read like the last that would be written.

* Works, vi. 513, 514.

FAMILIAR STUDIES

Perhaps Mrs. Locke was then remarried, for there is much obscurity over her subsequent history. For as long as their intimacy was kept up, at least, the human element remains in the Reformer's life. Here is one passage, for example, the most likable utterance of Knox's that I can quote:—Mrs. Locke has been upbraiding him as a bad correspondent. "My remembrance of you," he answers, "is not so dead, but I trust it shall be fresh enough, albeit it be renewed by no outward token for one year. *Of nature, I am churlish; yet one thing I ashame not to affirm, that familiarity once thoroughly contracted was never yet broken on my default. The cause may be that I have rather need of all, than that any have need of me.* However it [that] be, it cannot be, as I say, the corporal absence of one year or two that can quench in my heart that familiar acquaintance in Christ Jesus, which half a year did engender, and almost two years did nourish and confirm. And therefore, whether I write or no, be assuredly persuaded that I have you in such memory as becometh the faithful to have of the faithful." * This is the truest touch of personal humility that I can remember to have seen in all the five volumes of the Reformer's collected works: it is no small honor to Mrs. Locke that his affection for her should have brought home to him this unwonted feeling of dependence upon others. Everything else in the course of the correspondence testifies to a good, sound, downright sort of friendship between the two, less ecstatic than it was at first, perhaps, but serviceable and very equal. He gives her ample details as to the progress of the work of reformation; sends her the sheets of the *Confession of Faith,* "in quairs," as he calls it; asks her to assist him with her prayers, to collect money for the good cause in Scotland, and to send him books for himself—books by Calvin especially, one on Isaiah, and a new revised edition of the "Institutes." "I must be bold on your liberality," he writes, "not only in that, but in greater things as I shall need." † On her part she applies to him for spiritual advice, not after the manner of the drooping

* Works, vi. 11.   † *Ib.* vi. pp. 21, 101, 108, 130.

JOHN KNOX

Mrs. Bowes, but in a more positive spirit,—advice as to practical points, advice as to the Church of England, for instance, whose ritual he condemns as a " mingle-mangle." * Just at the end she ceases to write, sends him " a token, without writing." " I understand your impediment," he answers, " and therefore I cannot complain. Yet if you understood the variety of my temptations, I doubt not but you would have written somewhat." † One letter more, and then silence.

And I think the best of the Reformer died out with that correspondence. It is after this, of course, that he wrote that ungenerous description of his intercourse with Mrs. Bowes. It is after this, also, that we come to the unlovely episode of his second marriage. He had been left a widower at the age of fifty-five. Three years after, it occurred apparently to yet another pious parent to sacrifice a child upon the altar of his respect for the Reformer. In January, 1563, Randolph writes to Cecil: " Your Honor will take it for a great wonder when I shall write unto you that Mr. Knox shall marry a very near kinswoman of the Duke's, a Lord's daughter, a young lass not above sixteen years of age." ‡ He adds that he fears he will be laughed at for reporting so mad a story. And yet it was true; and on Palm Sunday, 1564, Margaret Stewart, daughter of Andrew Lord Stewart of Ochiltree, aged seventeen, was duly united to John Knox, Minister of St. Giles's Kirk, Edinburgh, aged fifty-nine,—to the great disgust of Queen Mary from family pride, and I would fain hope of many others for more humane considerations. " In this," as Randolph says, " I wish he had done otherwise." The Consistory of Geneva, " that most perfect school of Christ that ever was on earth since the days of the Apostles," were wont to forbid marriages on the ground of too great a disproportion in age. I cannot help wondering whether the old Reformer's conscience did not uneasily remind him, now and again, of this good custom of his religious metropolis, as he thought of the two-and-forty years that separated him from his poor

* Works, vi. 83.   † Ib. vi. 129.   ‡ Ib. vi. 532.

bride. Fitly enough, we hear nothing of the second Mrs. Knox until she appears at her husband's deathbed, eight years after. She bore him three daughters in the interval; and I suppose the poor child's martyrdom was made as easy for her as might be. She was "extremely attentive to him" at the end, we read; and he seems to have spoken to her with some confidence. Moreover, and this is very characteristic, he had copied out for her use a little volume of his own devotional letters to other women.

This is the end of the roll, unless we add to it Mrs. Adamson, who had delighted much in his company "by reason that she had a troubled conscience," and whose deathbed is commemorated at some length in the pages of his history.*

And now, looking back, it cannot be said that Knox's intercourse with women was quite of the highest sort. It is characteristic that we find him more alarmed for his own reputation than for the reputation of the women with whom he was familiar. There was a fatal preponderance of self in all his intimacies: many women came to learn from him, but he never condescended to become a learner in his turn. And so there is not anything idyllic in these intimacies of his; and they were never so renovating to his spirit as they might have been. But I believe they were good enough for the women. I fancy the women knew what they were about when so many of them followed after Knox. It is not simply because a man is always fully persuaded that he knows the right from the wrong and sees his way plainly through the maze of life, great qualities as these are, that people will love and follow him, and write him letters full of their "earnest desire for him" when he is absent. It is not over a man, whose one characteristic is grim fixity of purpose, that the hearts of women are "incensed and kindled with a special care," as it were over their natural children. In the strong quiet patience of all his letters to the weariful Mrs. Bowes, we may perhaps see one cause of the fascination he possessed for these religious women. Here was one whom you could besiege all the year round with inconsistent scruples and complaints; you might write to him on Thurs-

* Works, i. 246.

JOHN KNOX

day that you were so elated it was plain the devil was deceiving you, and again on Friday that you were so depressed it was plain God had cast you off forever; and he would read all this patiently and sympathetically, and give you an answer in the most reassuring polysyllables, and all divided into heads—who knows?—like a treatise on divinity. And then, those easy tears of his. There are some women who like to see men crying; and here was this great-voiced, bearded man of God, who might be seen beating the solid pulpit every Sunday, and casting abroad his clamorous denunciations to the terror of all, and who on the Monday would sit in their parlors by the hour, and weep with them over their manifold trials and temptations. Nowadays, he would have to drink a dish of tea with all these penitents. . . . It sounds a little vulgar, as the past will do, if we look into it too closely. We could not let these great folk of old into our drawing-rooms. Queen Elizabeth would positively not be eligible for a housemaid. The old manners and the old customs go sinking from grade to grade, until, if some mighty emperor revisited the glimpses of the moon, he would not find any one of his way of thinking, any one he could strike hands with and talk to freely and without offence, save perhaps the porter at the end of the street, or the fellow with his elbows out who loafs all day before the public-house. So that this little note of vulgarity is not a thing to be dwelt upon; it is to be put away from us, as we recall the fashion of these old intimacies; so that we may only remember Knox as one who was very long-suffering with women, kind to them in his own way, loving them in his own way—and that not the worst way, if it was not the best—and once at least, if not twice, moved to his heart of hearts by a woman, and giving expression to the yearning he had for her society in words that none of us need be ashamed to borrow.

And let us bear in mind always that the period I have gone over in this essay begins when the Reformer was already beyond the middle age, and already broken in bodily health: t has been the story of an old man's friendships. This it ; that makes Knox enviable. Unknown until past forty, he

FAMILIAR STUDIES

had then before him five-and-thirty years of splendid and influential life, passed through uncommon hardships to an uncommon degree of power, lived in his own country as a sort of king, and did what he would with the sound of his voice out of the pulpit. And besides all this, such a following of faithful women! One would take the first forty years gladly, if one could be sure of the last thirty. Most of us, even if, by reason of great strength and the dignity of gray hairs, we retain some degree of public respect in the latter days of our existence, will find a falling away of friends, and a solitude making itself round about us day by day, until we are left alone with the hired sick-nurse. For the attraction of a man's character is apt to be outlived, like the attraction of his body; and the power to love grows feeble in its turn, as well as the power to inspire love in others. It is only with a few rare natures that friendship is added to friendship, love to love, and the man keeps growing richer in affection—richer, I mean, as a bank may be said to grow richer, both giving and receiving more—after his head is white and his back weary, and he prepares to go down into the dust of death.

RECORDS OF A FAMILY OF
ENGINEERS

EDITORIAL NOTE

N the Edinburgh edition of Stevenson's Works, Mr. Sidey Colvin gives the story of the writing and publication of his work, which appeared in that edition for the first time. As there stated the piece is but a fragment, but it is an interesting fragment inasmuch as it is the story of Stevenson's own family by Stevenson himself. It was written in Samoa, mainly in the summer of 1893, and in the autumn of the same year the manuscript was sent to England to be set up for further revision. Stevenson, however, never returned to the work. A communication sent him by a Mr. J. H. Stevenson of Edinburgh caused him to modify his views on the subject somewhat, and he died before he had embodied his altered opinions. The present reprint follows the Edinburgh edition, with the foot-notes included.

INTRODUCTION

THE SURNAME OF STEVENSON

FROM the thirteenth century onwards, the name, under the various disguises of Stevinstoun, Stevensoun, Stevensonne, Stenesone, and Stewinsoune, spread across Scotland from the mouth of the Firth of Forth to the mouth of the Firth of Clyde. Four times at least it occurs as a place-name. There is a parish of Stevenston in Cunningham; a second place of the name in the Barony of Bothwell in Lanark; a third on Lyne, above Drochil Castle; the fourth on the Tyne, near Traprain Law. Stevenson of Stevenson (co. Lanark) swore fealty to Edward I. in 1296, and the last of that family died after the Restoration. Stevensons of Hirdmanshiels, in Midlothian, rode in the Bishops' Raid of Aberlady, served as jurors, stood bail for neighbours—Hunter of Polwood, for instance—and became extinct about the same period, or possibly earlier. A Stevenson of Luthrie and another of Pitroddie make their bows, give their names, and vanish. And by the year 1700 it does not appear that any acre of Scots land was vested in any Stevenson.*

Here is, so far, a melancholy picture of backward progress, and a family posting towards extinction. But the law (however administered, and I am bound to aver that, in Scotland, " it couldna weel be waur ") acts as a kind of dredge, and with dispassionate impartiality brings up into the light of day, and shows us for a moment, in the jury-box or on the gallows, the creeping things of the past. By these broken glimpses we are able to trace the existence of many other and more inglorious Stevensons, picking a private way through the brawl that makes Scots history. They were members of Parliament for Peebles, Stirling, Pittenweem,

* An error: Stevensons owned at this date the barony of Dolphingston in Haddingtonshire, Montgrennan in Ayrshire, and several other lesser places.

INTRODUCTION

Kilrenny, and Inverurie. We find them burgesses of Edinburgh; indwellers in Biggar, Perth, and Dalkeith. Thomas was the forester of Newbattle Park, Gavin was a baker, John a maltman, Francis a chirurgeon, and "Schir William" a priest. In the feuds of Humes and Heatleys, Cunninghams, Montgomeries, Mures, Ogilvies, and Turnbulls, we find them inconspicuously involved, and apparently getting rather better than they gave. Schir William (reverend gentleman) was cruellie slaughtered on the Links of Kincraig in 1532; James (" in the mill-town of Roberton "), murdered in 1590; Archibald (" in Gallowfarren "), killed with shots of pistols and hagbuts in 1608. Three violent deaths in about seventy years, against which we can only put the case of Thomas, servant to Hume of Cowden Knowes, who was arraigned with his two young masters for the death of the Bastard of Mellerstanes in 1569. John ("in Dalkeith") stood sentry without Holyrood while the banded lords were despatching Rizzio within. William, at the ringing of Perth bell, ran before Gowrie House "with ane sword, and, entering to the yearde, saw George Craiggingilt with ane twa-handit sword and utheris nychtbouris; at quilk time James Boig cryit ower ane wynds, ' Awa hame! ye will all be hangit!' "— a piece of advice which William took, and immediately " depairtit." John got a maid with child to him in Biggar, and seemingly deserted her; she was hanged on the Castle Hill for infanticide, June 1614; and Martin, elder in Dalkeith, eternally disgraced the name by signing witness in a witch trial, 1661. These are two of our black sheep.* Under the Restoration, one Stevenson was a bailie in Edinburgh, and another the lessee of the Canonmills. There were at the same period two physicians of the name in Edinburgh, one of whom, Dr. Archibald, appears to have been a famous man in his day and generation. The Court had continual need of him; it was he who reported, for instance, on the state of Rumbold; and he was for some time in the enjoyment of a pension of a thousand pounds Scots (about eighty pounds sterling) at a time when five hundred pounds

* Pitcairn's *Criminal Trials*, at large.—[R. L. S.]

INTRODUCTION

is described as "an opulent future." I do not know if I should be glad or sorry that he failed to keep favour; but on 6th January 1682 (rather a cheerless New Year's present) his pension was expunged.* There need be no doubt, at least, of my exultation at the fact that he was knighted and recorded arms. Not quite so genteel, but still in public life, Hugh was Under-Clerk to the Privy Council, and liked being so extremely. I gather this from his conduct in September, 1681, when, with all the lords and their servants, he took the woful and soul-destroying Test, swearing it "word by word upon his knees." And, behold! it was in vain, for Hugh was turned out of his small post in 1684.† Sir Archibald and Hugh were both plainly inclined to be trimmers; but there was one witness of the name of Stevenson who held high the banner of the Covenant—John, "Land-Labourer,‡ in the Parish of Daily, in Carrick," that "eminently pious man." He seems to have been a poor sickly soul, and shows himself disabled with scrofula, and prostrate and groaning aloud with fever; but the enthusiasm of the martyr burned high within him.

"I was made to take joyfully the spoiling of my goods, and with pleasure for His name's sake wandered in deserts and in mountains, in dens and caves of the earth. I lay four months in the coldest season of the year in a haystack in my father's garden, and a whole February in the open fields not far from Camragen, and this I did without the least prejudice from the night air; one night, when lying in the fields near to the Carrick-Miln, I was all covered with snow in the morning. Many nights have I lain with pleasure in the churchyard of Old Daily, and made a grave my pillow; frequently have I resorted to the old walls about the glen, near to Camragen, and there sweetly rested." The visible hand of God protected and directed him. Dragoons were turned aside from the bramble-bush where he lay hidden. Miracles were performed for his behoof. "I got a horse and a woman to carry the child, and came to the same moun-

* Fountainhall's *Decisions*, vol. 1. pp. 56, 132, 186, 204, 368.—[R. L. S.]
† *Ibid.*, pp. 158, 299.—[R. L. S.] ‡ Working farmer; Fr. *laboureur*.

INTRODUCTION

tain, where I wandered by the mist before; it is commonly known by the name of Kells-rhins: when we came to go up the mountain, there came on a great rain, which we thought was the occasion of the child's weeping, and she wept so bitterly, that all we could do could not divert her from it, so that she was ready to burst. When we got to the top of the mountain, where the Lord had been formerly kind to my soul in prayer, I looked round me for a stone, and espying one, I went and brought it. When the woman with me saw me set down the stone, she smiled, and asked what I was going to do with it. I told her I was going to set it up as my Ebenezer, because hitherto, and in that place, the Lord had formerly helped, and I hoped would yet help. The rain still continuing, the child weeping bitterly, I went to prayer, and no sooner did I cry to God, but the child gave over weeping, and when we got up from prayer, the rain was pouring down on every side, but in the way where we were to go there fell not one drop; the place not rained on was as big as an ordinary avenue." And so great a saint was the natural butt of Satan's persecutions. "I retired to the fields for secret prayer about midnight. When I went to pray I was much straitened, and could not get one request, but 'Lord pity,' 'Lord help'; this I came over frequently; at length the terror of Satan fell on me in a high degree, and all I could say even then was—'Lord help.' I continued in the duty for some time, notwithstanding of this terror. At length I got up to my feet, and the terror still increased; then the enemy took me by the arm-pits, and seemed to lift me up by my arms. I saw a loch just before me, and I concluded he designed to throw me there by force; and had he got leave to do so, it might have brought a great reproach upon religion." * But it was otherwise ordered, and the cause of piety escaped that danger.†

* This John Stevenson was not the only "witness" of the name; other Stevensons were actually killed during the persecutions, in the Glen of Trool, on Pentland, etc.; and it is very possible that the author's own ancestry was one of the mounted party embodied by Muir of Caldwell, only a day too late for Pentland.
† Wodrow Society's *Select Biographies*, vol. ii.—[R. L. S.]

INTRODUCTION

On the whole, the Stevensons may be described as decent, reputable folk, following honest trades—millers, maltsters, and doctors, playing the character parts in the Waverley Novels with propriety, if without distinction; and to an orphan looking about him in the world for a potential ancestry, offering a plain and quite unadorned refuge, equally free from shame and glory, John, the land-labourer, is the one living and memorable figure, and he, alas! cannot possibly be more near than a collateral. It was on August 12, 1678, that he heard Mr. John Welsh on the Craigdowhill, and "took the heavens, earth, and sun in the firmament that was shining on us, as also the ambassador who made the offer, and *the clerk who raised the psalms,* to witness that I did give myself away to the Lord in a personal and perpetual covenant never to be forgotten"; and already, in 1675, the birth of my direct ascendant was registered in Glasgow. So that I have been pursuing ancestors too far down; and John the land-labourer is debarred me, and I must relinquish from the trophies of my house his *rare soul-strengthening and comforting cordial.* It is the same case with the Edinburgh bailie and the miller of the Canonmills, worthy man! and with that public character, Hugh the Under-Clerk, and more than all, with Sir Archibald, the physician, who recorded arms. And I am reduced to a family of inconspicuous maltsters in what was then the clean and handsome little city on the Clyde.

The name has a certain air of being Norse. But the story of Scottish nomenclature is confounded by a continual process of translation and half-translation from the Gaelic which in olden days may have been sometimes reversed. Roy become Reid; Gow, Smith. A great Highland clan uses the name of Robertson; a sept in Appin that of Livingstone; Maclean in Glencoe answers to Johnstone at Lockerby. And we find such hybrids as Macalexander for Macallister. There is but one rule to be deduced: that however uncompromisingly Saxon a name may appear, you can never be sure it does not designate a Celt. My great-grandfather wrote the name *Stevenson* but pronounced it *Steenson,*

INTRODUCTION

after the fashion of the immortal minstrel in *Redgauntlet*; and this elision of a medial consonant appears a Gaelic process; and, curiously enough, I have come across no less than two Gaelic forms: *John Macstophane cordinerius in Crossraguel*, 1573, and *William M'Steen* in Dunskeith (co. Ross), 1605. Stevenson, Steenson, Macstophane, M'Steen: which is the original? which the translation? Or were these separate creations of the patronymic, some English, some Gaelic? The curiously compact territory in which we find them seated—Ayr, Lanark, Peebles, Stirling, Perth, Fife, and the Lothians, would seem to forbid the supposition.*

"STEVENSON—or according to tradition of one of the proscribed of the clan Macgregor, who was born among the willows or in a hill-side sheep-pen—'Son of my love,' a heraldic bar sinister, but history reveals a reason for the birth among the willows far other than the sinister aspect of the name:" these are the dark words of Mr. Cosmo Innes; but history or tradition, being interrogated, tells a somewhat tangled tale. The heir of Macgregor of Glenorchy, murdered about 1353 by the Argyll Campbells, appears to have been the original "Son of my love"; and his more loyal clansmen took the name to fight under. In may be supposed the story of their resistance became popular, and the name in some sort identified with the idea of opposition to the Campbells. Twice afterwards, on some renewed aggression, in 1502 and 1552, we find the Macgregors again banding themselves into a sept of "Sons of my love"; and when the great disaster fell on them in 1603, the whole original legend reappears, and we have the heir of Alaster of Glenstrae born "among the willows" of a fugitive mother, and the more loyal clansmen again rallying under the name of Stevenson. A story would not be told so often unless it had some base in fact; nor (if there were no bond at all between the Red Macgregors and the Stevensons) would that

* Though the districts here named are those in which the name of Stevenson is most common, it is in point of fact far more wide-spread than the text indicates, and occurs from Dumfries and Berwickshire to Aberdeen and Orkney.

INTRODUCTION

extraneous and somewhat uncouth name be so much repeated in the legends of the Children of the Mist.

But I am enabled, by my very lively and obliging correspondent, Mr. George A. Macgregor Stevenson of New York, to give an actual instance. His grandfather, great-grandfather, great-great-grandfather, and great-great-great-grandfather, all used the names of Macgregor and Stevenson as occasion served; being perhaps Macgregor by night and Stevenson by day. The great-great-great-grandfather was a mighty man of his hands, marched with the clan in the Forty-five, and returned with *spolia opima* in the shape of a sword, which he had wrested from an officer in the retreat, and which is in the possession of my correspondent to this day. His great-grandson (the grandfather of my correspondent), being converted to Methodism by some wayside preacher, discarded in a moment his name, his old nature, and his political principles, and with the zeal of a proselyte sealed his adherence to the Protestant Succession by baptising his next son George. This George became the publisher and editor of the *Wesleyan Times*. His children were brought up in ignorance of their Highland pedigree; and my correspondent was puzzled to overhear his father speak of him as a true Macgregor, and amazed to find, in rummaging about that peaceful and pious house, the sword of the Hanoverian officer. After he was grown up and was better informed of his descent, "I frequently asked my father," he writes, "why he did not use the name of Macgregor; his replies were significant, and give a picture of the man: 'It isn't a good *Methodist* name. *You* can use it, but it will do you no *good*.' Yet the old gentleman, by way of pleasantry, used to announce himself to friends as 'Colonel Macgregor.'"

Here, then, are certain Macgregors habitually using the name of Stevenson, and at last, under the influence of Methodism, adopting it entirely. Doubtless a proscribed clan could not be particular; they took a name as a man takes an umbrella against a shower; as Rob Roy took Campbell, and his son took Drummond. But this case is different;

INTRODUCTION

Stevenson was not taken and left—it was consistently adhered to. It does not in the least follow that all Stevensons are of the clan Alpin; but it does follow that some may be. And I cannot conceal from myself the possibility that James Stevenson in Glasgow, my first authentic ancestor, may have had a Highland *alias* upon his conscience and a claymore in his back parlour.

To one more tradition I may allude, that we are somehow descended from a French barber-surgeon who came to St. Andrews in the service of one of the Cardinal Beatons. No details were added. But the very name of France was so detested in my family for three generations, that I am tempted to suppose there may be something in it.*

---

* Mr. J. H. Stevenson is satisfied that these speculations as to a possible Norse, Highland, or French origin are vain. All we know about the engineer family is that it was sprung from a stock of Westland Whigs settled in the latter part of the seventeenth century in the parish of Neilston, as mentioned at the beginning of the next chapter. It may be noted that the Ayrshire parish of Stevenston, the lands of which are said to have received the name in the twelfth century, lies within thirteen miles southwest of this place. The lands of Stevenson in Lanarkshire, first mentioned in the next century, in the Ragman Roll, lie within twenty miles east.

RECORDS OF A FAMILY OF ENGINEERS

CHAPTER I

DOMESTIC ANNALS

IT is believed that in 1665, James Stevenson in Nether Carsewell, parish of Neilston, County of Renfrew, and presumably a tenant farmer, married one Jean Keir; and in 1675, without doubt, there was born to these two a son Robert, possibly a maltster in Glasgow. In 1710, Robert married, for a second time, Elizabeth Cumming, and there was born to them, in 1720, another Robert, certainly a maltster in Glasgow. In 1742, Robert the second married Margaret Fulton (Margret, she called herself), by whom he had ten children, among whom were Hugh, born February, 1749, and Alan, born June, 1752.

With these two brothers my story begins. Their deaths were simultaneous; their lives unusually brief and full. Tradition whispered me in childhood they were the owners of an islet near St. Kitts; and it is certain they had risen to be at the head of considerable interests in the West Indies, which Hugh managed abroad and Alan at home, at an age when others are still curveting a clerk's stool. My kinsman, Mr. Stevenson of Stirling, has heard his father mention that there had been "something romantic" about Alan's marriage: and, alas! he has forgotten what. It was early at least. His wife was Jean, daughter of David Lillie, a builder in Glasgow, and several times "Deacon of the Wrights": the date of the marriage has not reached me: but on 8th June 1772, when Robert, the only child of the union, was born, the husband and father had scarce passed, or had not yet attained, his twentieth year. Here was a youth making haste to give hostages to fortune. But

A FAMILY OF ENGINEERS

this early scene of prosperity in love and business was on the point of closing.

There hung in the house of this young family, and successively in those of my grandfather and father, an oil painting of a ship of many tons burthen. Doubtless the brothers had an interest in the vessel; I was told she had belonged to them outright; and the picture was preserved through years of hardship, and remains to this day in the possession of the family, the only memorial of my great-grandsire Alan. It was on this ship that he sailed on his last adventure, summoned to the West Indies by Hugh. An agent had proved unfaithful on a serious scale; and it used to be told me in my childhood how the brothers pursued him from one island to another in an open boat, were exposed to the pernicious dews of the tropics, and simultaneously struck down. The dates and places of their deaths (now before me) would seem to indicate a more scattered and prolonged pursuit: Hugh, on the 16th April 1774, in Tobago, within sight of Trinidad; Alan, so late as May 26th, and so far away as "Santt Kittes," in the Leeward Islands—both, says the family Bible, "of a fiver" (!). The death of Hugh was probably announced by Alan in a letter, to which we may refer the details of the open boat and the dew. Thus, at least, in something like the course of post, both were called away, the one twenty-five, the other twenty-two; their brief generation became extinct, their short-lived house fell with them; and " in these lawless parts and lawless times "—the words are my grandfather's —their property was stolen or became involved. Many years later, I understand some small recovery to have been made; but at the moment almost the whole means of the family seem to have perished with the young merchants. On the 27th April, eleven days after Hugh Stevenson, twenty-nine before Alan, died David Lillie, the deacon of the wrights; so that mother and son were orphaned in one month. Thus, from a few scraps of paper bearing little beyond dates, we construct the outlines of the tragedy that shadowed the cradle of Robert Stevenson.

DOMESTIC ANNALS

Jean Lillie was a young woman of strong sense, well fitted to contend with poverty, and of a pious disposition, which it is like that these misfortunes heated. Like so many other widowed Scotswomen, she vowed her son would wag his head in a pulpit; but her means were inadequate to her ambition. A charity school, and some time under a Mr. M'Intyre, "a famous linguist," were all she could afford in the way of education to the would-be minister. He learned no Greek; in one place he mentions that the Orations of Cicero were his highest book in Latin; in another that he had "delighted" in Virgil and Horace; but his delight could never have been scholarly. This appears to have been the whole of his training previous to an event which changed his own destiny and moulded that of his descendants—the second marriage of his mother.

There was a Merchant-Burgess of Edinburgh of the name of Thomas Smith. The Smith pedigree has been traced a little more particularly than the Stevensons', with a similar dearth of illustrious names. One character seems to have appeared, indeed, for a moment at the wings of history: a skipper of Dundee who smuggled over some Jacobite big-wig at the time of the Fifteen, and was afterwards drowned in Dundee harbour while going on board his ship. With this exception, the generations of the Smiths present no conceivable interest even to a descendant; and Thomas, of Edinburgh, was the first to issue from respectable obscurity. His father, a skipper out of Broughty Ferry, was drowned at sea while Thomas was still young. He seems to have owned a ship or two—whalers, I suppose, or coasters—and to have been a member of the Dundee Trinity House, whatever that implies. On his death the widow remained in Broughty, and the son came to push his future in Edinburgh. There is a story told of him in the family which I repeat here because I shall have to tell later on a similar, but more perfectly authenticated, experience of his stepson, Robert Stevenson. Word reached Thomas that his mother was unwell, and he prepared to leave for Broughty on the morrow. It was between two and three

A FAMILY OF ENGINEERS

in the morning, and the early northern daylight was already clear, when he awoke and beheld the curtains at the bedfoot drawn aside and his mother appear in the interval, smile upon him for a moment, and then vanish. The sequel is stereotype; he took the time by his watch, and arrived at Broughty to learn it was the very moment of her death. The incident is at least curious in having happened to such a person—as the tale is being told of him. In all else, he appears as a man, ardent, passionate, practical, designed for affairs and prospering in them far beyond the average. He founded a solid business in lamps and oils, and was the sole proprietor of a concern called the Greenside Company's Works—" a multifarious concern it was," writes my cousin, Professor Swan, " of tinsmiths, coppersmiths, brassfounders, blacksmiths and japanners." He was also, it seems, a shipowner and underwriter. He built himself " a land "—Nos. 1 and 2 Baxter's Place, then no such unfashionable neighbourhood—and died, leaving his only son in easy circumstances, and giving to his three surviving daughters portions of five thousand pounds and upwards. There is no standard of success in life; but in one of its meanings, this is to succeed.

In what we know of his opinions, he makes a figure highly characteristic of the time. A high Tory and patriot, a captain—so I find it in my notes—of Edinburgh Spearmen, and on duty in the Castle during the Muir and Palmer troubles, he bequeathed to his descendants a bloodless sword and a somewhat violent tradition, both long preserved. The judge who sat on Muir and Palmer, the famous Braxfield, let fall from the bench the *obiter dictum*—" I never liked the French all my days, but now I hate them." If Thomas Smith, the Edinburgh Spearman, were in court, he must have been tempted to applaud. The people of that land were his abhorrence; he loathed Buonaparte like Antichrist. Towards the end he fell into a kind of dotage; his family must entertain him with games of tin soldiers, which he took a childish pleasure to array and overset; but those who played with him must be upon their guard, for if his

DOMESTIC ANNALS

side, which was always that of the English against the French, should chance to be defeated, there would be trouble in Baxter's Place. For these opinions he may almost be said to have suffered. Baptized and brought up in the Church of Scotland, he had, upon some conscientious scruple, joined the communion of the Baptists. Like other Nonconformists, these were inclined to the liberal side in politics, and, at least in the beginning, regarded Buonaparte as a deliverer. From the time of his joining the Spearmen, Thomas Smith became in consequence a bugbear to his brethren in the faith. "They that take the sword shall perish with the sword," they told him; they gave him "no rest"; "his position became intolerable"; it was plain he must choose between his political and his religious tenets; and in the last years of his life, about 1812, he returned to the Church of his fathers.

August 1786 was the date of his chief advancement, when, having designed a system of oil lights to take the place of the primitive coal fires before in use, he was dubbed engineer to the newly-formed Board of Northern Lighthouses. Not only were his fortunes bettered by the appointment, but he was introduced to a new and wider field for the exercise of his abilities, and a new way of life highly agreeable to his active constitution. He seems to have rejoiced in the long journeys, and to have combined them with the practice of field sports. "A tall, stout man coming ashore with his gun over his arm"—so he was described to my father—the only description that has come down to me—by a lightkeeper old in the service. Nor did this change come alone.

On the 9th of July of the same year, Thomas Smith had been left for the second time a widower. As he was still but thirty-three years old, prospering in his affairs, newly advanced in the world, and encumbered at the time with a family of children, five in number, it was natural that he should entertain the notion of another wife. Expeditious in business, he was no less so in his choice; and it was not later than June 1787—for my grandfather is described as

A FAMILY OF ENGINEERS

still in his fifteenth year—that he married the widow of Alan Stevenson.

The perilous experiment of bringing together two families for once succeeded. Mr. Smith's two eldest daughters, Jean and Janet, fervent in piety, unwearied in kind deeds, were well qualified both to appreciate and to attract the stepmother; and her son, on the other hand, seems to have found immediate favour in the eyes of Mr. Smith. It is, perhaps, easy to exaggerate the ready-made resemblances; the tired woman must have done much to fashion girls who were under ten; the man, lusty and opinionated, must have stamped a strong impression on the boy of fifteen. But the cleavage of the family was too marked, the identity of character and interest produced between the two men on the one hand, and the three women on the other, was too complete to have been the result of influence alone. Particular bonds of union must have pre-existed on each side. And there is no doubt that the man and the boy met with common ambitions, and a common bent, to the practice of that which had not so long before acquired the name of civil engineering.

For the profession which is now so thronged, famous, and influential, was then a thing of yesterday. My grandfather had an anecdote of Smeaton, probably learned from John Clerk of Eldin, their common friend. Smeaton was asked by the Duke of Argyll to visit the West Highland coast for a professional purpose. He refused, appalled, it seems, by the rough travelling. "You can recommend some other fit person?" asked the Duke. "No," said Smeaton, "I am sorry I can't." "What!" cried the Duke, "a profession with only one man in it! Pray, who taught you?" "Why," said Smeaton, "I believe I may say I was self-taught, an 't please your grace." Smeaton, at the date of Thomas Smith's third marriage, was yet living; and as the one had grown to the new profession from his place at the Instrument-maker's, the other was beginning to enter it by the way of his trade. The engineer of to-day is confronted with a library of acquired results; tables and

DOMESTIC ANNALS

formulæ to the value of folios full have been calculated and recorded; and the student finds everywhere in front of him the footprints of the pioneers. In the eighteenth century the field was largely unexplored; the engineer must read with his own eyes the face of nature; he arose a volunteer, from the workshop or the mill, to undertake works which were at once inventions and adventures. It was not a science then—it was a living art; and it visibly grew under the eyes and between the hands of its practitioners.

The charm of such an occupation was strongly felt by stepfather and stepson. It chanced that Thomas Smith was a reformer; the superiority of his proposed lamp and reflectors over open fires of coal secured his appointment; and no sooner had he set his hand to the task than the interest of that employment mastered him. The vacant stage on which he was to act, and where all had yet to be created —the greatness of the difficulties, the smallness of the means intrusted him—would rouse a man of his disposition like a call to battle. The lad introduced by marriage under his roof was of a character to sympathize; the public usefulness of the service would appeal to his judgment, the perpetual need for fresh expedients stimulate his ingenuity. And there was another attraction which, in the younger man at least, appealed to, and perhaps first aroused a profound and enduring sentiment of romance: I mean the attraction of the life. The seas into which his labours carried the new engineer were still scarce charted, the coasts still dark; his way on shore was often far beyond the convenience of any road; the isles in which he must sojourn were still partly savage. He must toss much in boats; he must often adventure on horseback by the dubious bridle-track through unfrequented wildernesses; he must sometimes plant his lighthouse in the very camp of wreckers; and he was continually enforced to the vicissitudes of outdoor life. The joy of my grandfather in this career was strong as the love of woman. It lasted him through youth and manhood, it burned strong in age, and at the approach of death his last yearning was to renew these loved experi-

A FAMILY OF ENGINEERS

ences. What he felt himself he continued to attribute to all around him. And to this supposed sentiment in others I find him continually, almost pathetically, appealing: often in vain.

Snared by these interests, the boy seems to have become almost at once the eager confidant and adviser of his new connection; the Church, if he had ever entertained the prospect very warmly, faded from his view; and at the age of nineteen I find him already in a post with some authority, superintending the construction of the lighthouse on the isle of Little Cumbrae, in the Firth of Clyde. The change of aim seems to have caused or been accompanied by a change of character. It sounds absurd to couple the name of my grandfather with the word indolence; but the lad who had been destined from the cradle to the Church, and who had attained the age of fifteen without acquiring more than a moderate knowledge of Latin, was at least no unusual student. And from the day of his charge at Little Cumbrae he steps before us what he remained until the end, a man of the most zealous industry, greedy of occupation, greedy of knowledge, a stern husband of time, a reader, a writer, unflagging in his task of self-improvement. Thenceforward his summers were spent directing works and ruling workmen, now in uninhabited, now in half-savage islands; his winters were set apart, first at the Andersonian Institution, then at the University of Edinburgh to improve himself in mathematics, chemistry, natural history, agriculture, moral philosophy, and logic; a bearded student—although no doubt scrupulously shaved. I find one reference to his years in class which will have a meaning for all who have studied in Scottish Universities. He mentions a recommendation made by the professor of logic. "The high-school men," he writes, "and *bearded men like myself*, were all attention." If my grandfather were throughout life a thought too studious of the art of getting on, much must be forgiven to the bearded and belated student who looked across, with a sense of difference, at "the high-school men." Here was a gulf to be crossed; but already he could feel

DOMESTIC ANNALS

that he had made a beginning, and that must have been a proud hour when he devoted his earliest earnings to the repayment of the charitable foundation in which he had received the rudiments of knowledge.

In yet another way he followed the example of his father-in-law, and from 1794 till 1807, when the affairs of the Bell Rock made it necessary for him to resign, he served in different corps of volunteers. In the last of these he rose to a position of distinction, no less than captain of the Grenadier Company, and his colonel, in accepting his resignation, entreated he would do them " the favour of continuing as an honorary member of a corps which has been so much indebted for your zeal and exertions."

To very pious women the men of the house are apt to appear worldly. The wife, as she puts on her new bonnet before church, is apt to sigh over that assiduity which enabled her husband to pay the milliner's bill. And in the household of the Smiths and Stevensons the women were not only extremely pious, but the men were in reality a trifle worldly. Religious they both were; conscious, like all Scots, of the fragility and unreality of that scene in which we play our uncomprehended parts; like all Scots, realizing daily and hourly the sense of another will than ours and a perpetual direction in the affairs of life. But the current of their endeavours flowed in a more obvious channel. They had got on so far; to get on further was their next ambition—to gather wealth, to rise in society, to leave their descendants higher than themselves, to be (in some sense) among the founders of families. Scott was in the same town nourishing similar dreams. But in the eyes of the women these dreams would be foolish and idolatrous.

I have before me some volumes of old letters addressed to Mrs. Smith and the two girls, her favourites, which depict in a strong light their characters and the society in which they moved.

" My very dear and much esteemed Friend," writes one correspondent, " this day being the anniversary of our acquaintance, I feel inclined to address you; but where shall II find words to express the feelings

A FAMILY OF ENGINEERS

of a graitful *Heart*, first to the Lord who graiciously inclined you on this day last year to notice an afflicted Strainger providentially cast in your way far from any Earthly friend? . . . Methinks I shall hear him say unto you, 'Inasmuch as ye shewed kindness to my afflicted handmaiden, ye did it unto me.'"

This is to Jean; but the same afflicted lady wrote indifferently to Jean, to Janet, and to Mrs. Smith, whom she calls "my Edinburgh mother." It is plain the three were as one person, moving to acts of kindness, like the Graces, inarmed. Too much stress must not be laid on the style of this correspondence; Clarinda survived, not far away, and may have met the ladies on the Calton Hill; and many of the writers appear, underneath the conventions of the period, to be genuinely moved. But what unpleasantly strikes a reader is that these devout unfortunates found a revenue in their devotion. It is everywhere the same tale: on the side of the soft-hearted ladies, substantial acts of help; on the side of the correspondents, affection, italics, texts, ecstasies, and imperfect spelling. When a midwife is recommended, not at all for proficiency in her important art, but because she has "a sister whom I [the correspondent] esteem and respect, and [who] is a spiritual daughter of my Hon^d Father in the Gosple," the mask seems to be torn off, and the wages of godliness appear too openly. Capacity is a secondary matter in a midwife, temper in a servant, affection in a daughter, and the repetition of a shibboleth fulfils the law. Common decency is at times forgot in the same page with the most sanctified advice and aspiration. Thus I am introduced to a correspondent who appears to have been at the time the housekeeper at Invermay, and who writes to condole with my grandmother in a season of distress. For nearly half a sheet she keeps to the point with an excellent discretion in language; then suddenly breaks out:

"It was fully my intention to have left this at Martinmass, but the Lord fixes the bounds of our habitation. I have had more need of patience in my situation here than in any other, partly from the very violent, unsteady, deceitful temper of the Mistress of the Family, and also from the state of the house. It was in a train of repair when I came here two years ago, and is still in Confusion. There is above

DOMESTIC ANNALS

six Thousand Pounds' worth of Furniture come from London to be put up when the rooms are completely finished; and then, woe be to the Person who is Housekeeper at Invermay!"

And by the tail of the document, which is torn, I see she goes on to ask the bereaved family to seek her a new place. It is extraordinary that people should have been so deceived in so careless an impostor; that a few sprinkled "God willings" should have blinded them to the essence of this venomous letter; and that they should have been at the pains to bind it in with others (many of them highly touching) in their memorial of harrowing days. But the good ladies were without guile and without suspicion; they were victims marked for the axe, and the religious impostors snuffed up the wind as they drew near.

I have referred above to my grandmother; it was no slip of the pen: for by an extraordinary arrangement, in which it is hard not to suspect the managing hand of a mother, Jean Smith became the wife of Robert Stevenson. Mrs. Smith had failed in her design to make her son a minister, and she saw him daily more immersed in business and worldly ambition. One thing remained that she might do: she might secure for him a godly wife, that great means of sanctification; and she had two under her hand, trained by herself, her dear friends and daughters both in law and love—Jean and Janet. Jean's complexion was extremely pale, Janet's was florid; my grandmother's nose was straight, my great-aunt's aquiline; but by the sound of the voice, not even a son was able to distinguish one from other. The marriage of a man of twenty-seven and a girl of twenty who have lived for twelve years as brother and sister, is difficult to conceive. It took place, however, and thus in 1799 the family was still further cemented by the union of a representative of the male or worldly element with one of the female and devout.

This essential difference remained unbridged, yet never diminished the strength of their relation. My grandfather pursued his design of advancing in the world with some measure of success; rose to distinction in his calling, grew to be

A FAMILY OF ENGINEERS

the familiar of members of Parliament, judges of the Court of Session, and "landed gentlemen"; learned a ready address, had a flow of interesting conversation, and when he was referred to as "a highly respectable *bourgeois*," resented the description. My grandmother remained to the end devout and unambitious, occupied with her Bible, her children, and her house; easily shocked, and associating largely with a clique of godly parasites. I do not know if she called in the midwife already referred to; but the principle on which that lady was recommended, she accepted fully. The cook was a godly woman, the butcher a Christian man, and the table suffered. The scene has been often described to me of my grandfather sawing with darkened countenance at some indissoluble joint—" Preserve me, my dear, what kind of a reedy, stringy beast is this?"—of the joint removed, the pudding substituted and uncovered; and of my grandmother's anxious glance and hasty, deprecatory comment, "Just mismanaged!" Yet with the invincible obstinacy of soft natures, she would adhere to the godly woman and the Christian man, or find others of the same kidney to replace them. One of her confidantes had once a narrow escape; an unwieldy old woman, she had fallen from an outside stair in a close of the Old Town; and my grandmother rejoiced to communicate the providential circumstance that a baker had been passing underneath with his bread upon his head. "I would like to know what kind of providence the baker thought it!" cried my grandfather.

But the sally must have been unique. In all else that I have heard or read of him, so far from criticising, he was doing his utmost to honour and even to emulate his wife's pronounced opinions. In the only letter which has come to my hand of Thomas Smith's, I find him informing his wife that he was "in time for afternoon church"; similar assurances or cognate excuses abound in the correspondence of Robert Stevenson; and it is comical and pretty to see the two generations paying the same court to a female piety more highly strung: Thomas Smith to the mother of Robert Stevenson—Robert Stevenson to the daughter of Thomas

DOMESTIC ANNALS

Smith. And if for once my grandfather suffered himself to be hurried, by his sense of humour and justice, into that remark about the case of Providence and the Baker, I should be sorry for any of his children who should have stumbled into the same attitude of criticism. In the apocalyptic style of the housekeeper of Invermay, woe be to that person! But there was no fear; husband and sons all entertained for the pious, tender soul the same chivalrous and moved affection. I have spoken with one who remembered her, and who had been the intimate and equal of her sons, and I found this witness had been struck, as I had been, with a sense of disproportion between the warmth of the adoration felt and the nature of the woman, whether as described or observed. She diligently read and marked her Bible; she was a tender nurse; she had a sense of humour under strong control; she talked and found some amusement at her (or rather at her husband's) dinner-parties. It is conceivable that even my grandmother was amenable to the seductions of dress; at least I find her husband inquiring anxiously about "the gowns from Glasgow," and very careful to describe the toilet of the Princess Charlotte, whom he had seen in church "in a Pelisse and Bonnet of the same colour of cloth as the Boys' Dress jackets, trimmed with blue satin ribbons; the hat or Bonnet, Mr. Spittal said, was a Parisian slouch, and had a plume of three white feathers." But all this leaves a blank impression, and it is rather by reading backward in these old musty letters, which have moved me now to laughter and now to impatience, that I glean occasional glimpses of how she seemed to her contemporaries and trace (at work in her queer world of godly and grateful parasites) a mobile and responsive nature. Fashion moulds us, and particularly women, deeper than we sometimes think; but a little while ago, and, in some circles, women stood or fell by the degree of their appreciation of old pictures; in the early years of the century (and surely with more reason) a character like that of my grandmother warmed, charmed, and subdued, like a strain of music, the hearts of the men of her own household. And there is little

A FAMILY OF ENGINEERS

doubt that Mrs. Smith, as she looked on at the domestic life of her son and her stepdaughter, and numbered the heads in their increasing nursery, must have breathed fervent thanks to her Creator.

Yet this was to be a family unusually tried; it was not for nothing that one of the godly women saluted Miss Janet Smith as "a veteran in affliction"; and they were all before middle life experienced in that form of service. By the 1st of January, 1808, besides a pair of still-born twins, five children had been born and still survived to the young couple. By the 11th two were gone; by the 28th a third had followed, and the two others were still in danger. In the letters of a former nurserymaid—I give her name, Jean Mitchell, *honoris causa*—we are enabled to feel, even at this distance of time, some of the bitterness of that month of bereavement.

"I have this day received," she writes to Miss Janet, "the melancholy news of my dear babys' deaths. My heart is like to break for my dear Mrs. Stevenson. O may she be supported on this trying occasion! I hope her other three babys will be spared to her. O, Miss Smith, did I think when I parted from my sweet babys that I never was to see them more?" "I received," she begins her next, "the mournful news of my dear Jessie's death. I also received the hair of my three sweet babys, which I will preserve as dear to their memories and as a token of Mr. and Mrs. Stevenson's friendship and esteem. At my leisure hours, when the children are in bed, they occupy all my thoughts. I dream of them. About two weeks ago, I dreamed that my sweet little Jessie came running to me in her usual way, and I took her in my arms. O my dear babys, were mortal eyes permitted to see them in heaven, we would not repine nor grieve for their loss."

By the 29th of February, the Reverend John Campbell, a man of obvious sense and human value, but hateful to the present biographer, because he wrote so many letters and conveyed so little information, summed up this first period of affliction in a letter to Miss Smith: "Your dear sister but a little while ago had a full nursery, and the dear blooming creatures sitting around her table filled her breast with hope that one day they should fill active stations in society and become an ornament in the Church below. But ah!"

Near a hundred years ago these little creatures ceased

DOMESTIC ANNALS

to be, and for not much less a period the tears have been dried. And to this day, looking in these stitched sheaves of letters, we hear the sound of many soft-hearted women sobbing for the lost. Never was such a massacre of the innocents; teething and chincough and scarlet fever and small-pox ran the round; and little Lillies, and Smiths, and Stevensons fell like moths about a candle; and nearly all the sympathetic correspondents deplore and recall the little losses of their own. "It is impossible to describe the Heavnly looks of the Dear Babe the three last days of his life," writes Mrs. Laurie to Mrs. Smith. "Never—never, my dear aunt, could I wish to eface the rememberance of this Dear Child. Never, never, my dear aunt!" And so soon the memory of the dead and the dust of the survivors are buried in one grave.

There was another death in 1812; it passes almost unremarked; a single funeral seemed but a small event to these "veterans in affliction"; and by 1816 the nursery was full again. Seven little hopefuls enlivened the house; some were growing up; to the elder girl my grandfather already wrote notes in current hand at the tail of his letters to his wife; and to the elder boys he had begun to print, with laborious care, sheets of childish gossip and pedantic applications. Here, for instance, under date of May 26th, 1816, is part of a mythological account of London, with a moral for the three gentlemen, "Messieurs Alan, Robert, and James Stevenson," to whom the document is addressed:

"There are many prisons here like Bridewell, for, like other large towns, there are many bad men here as well as many good men. The natives of London are in general not so tall and strong as the people of Edinburgh, because they have not so much pure air, and instead of taking porridge they eat cakes made with sugar and plums. Here you have thousands of carts to draw timber, thousands of coaches to take you to all parts of the town, and thousands of boats to sail on the river Thames. But you must have money to pay, otherwise you can get nothing. Now the way to get money is, become clever men and men of education, by being good scholars."

From the same absence, he writes to his wife on a Sunday:

A FAMILY OF ENGINEERS

"It is now about eight o'clock with me, and I imagine you to be busy with the young folks, hearing the questions [*Anglicé*, catechism], and indulging the boys with a chapter from the large Bible, with their interrogations and your answers in the soundest doctrine. I hope James is getting his verse as usual, and that Mary is not forgetting her little *hymn*. While Jeannie will be reading Wotherspoon, or some other suitable and instructive book, I presume our friend, Aunt Mary, will have just arrived with the news of a *throng kirk* [a crowded church] and a great sermon. You may mention, with my compliments to my mother, that I was at St. Paul's to-day, and attended a very excellent service with Mr. James Lawrie. The text was 'Examine and see that ye be in the faith.'"

A twinkle of humour lights up this evocation of the distant scene—the humour of happy men and happy homes. Yet it is penned upon the threshold of fresh sorrow. James and Mary—he of the verse and she of the hymn—did not much more than survive to welcome their returning father. On the 25th, one of the godly women writes to Janet:

"My dearest beloved madam, when I last parted from you, you was so affected with your affliction [you? or I?] could think of nothing else. But on Saturday, when I went to inquire after your health, how was I startled to hear that dear James was gone! Ah, what is this? My dear benefactors, doing so much good to many, to the Lord, suddenly to be deprived of their most valued comforts! I was thrown into great perplexity, could do nothing but murmur, why these things were done to such a family. I could not rest, but at midnight, whether spoken [or not] it was presented to my mind—'Those whom ye deplore are walking with me in white.' I conclude from this the Lord saying to sweet Mrs. Stevenson: 'I gave them to be brought up for me: well done, good and faithful! they are fully prepared, and now I must present them to my father and your father, to my God and your God.'"

It would be hard to lay on flattery with a more sure and daring hand. I quote it as a model of a letter of condolence; be sure it would console. Very different, perhaps quite as welcome, is this from a lighthouse inspector to my grandfather:

"In reading your letter the trickling tear ran down my cheeks in silent sorrow for your departed dear ones, my sweet little friends. Well do I remember, and you will call to mind, their little innocent and interesting stories. Often have they come round me and taken me by the hand, but alas! I am no more destined to behold them."

DOMESTIC ANNALS

The child who is taken becomes canonised, and the looks of the homeliest babe seem in the retrospect " heavenly the hree last days of his life." But it appears that James nd Mary had indeed been children more than usually en- ;aging; a record was preserved a long while in the family f their remarks and " little innocent and interesting stories," nd the blow and the blank were the more sensible.

Early the next month Robert Stevenson must proceed tpon his voyage of inspection, part by land, part by sea. Ie left his wife plunged in low spirits; the thought of his oss, and still more of her concern, was continually present in ıis mind, and he draws in his letters home an interesting)icture of his family relations:—

" *Windygates Inn, Monday* (*Postmark July* 16*th*).
" MY DEAREST JEANNIE,—While the people of the inn are getting me ı little bit of something to eat, I sit down to tell you that I had a most :xcellent passage across the water, and got to Wemyss at mid-day. I ıope the children will be very good, and that Robert will take a course ⱱith you to learn his Latin lessons daily; he may, however, read Eng- ish in company. Let them have strawberries on Saturdays."

" *Westhaven,* 17*th July.*
" I have been occupied to-day at the harbour of Newport opposite Dundee, and am this far on my way to Arbroath. You may tell the ⱶoys that I slept last night in Mr. Steadman's tent. I found my bed ather hard, but the lodgings were otherwise extremely comfortable. The encampment is on the Fife side of the Tay, immediately opposite :o Dundee. From the door of the tent you command the most beau- :iful view of the Firth, both up and down, to a great extent. At night ıll was serene and still, the sky presented the most beautiful appear- ınce of bright stars, and the morning was ushered in with the song of nany little birds."

" *Aberdeen, July* 19*th.*
" I hope, my dear, that you are going out of doors regularly and taking much exercise. I would have you to *make the markets daily* —and by all means to take a seat in the coach once or twice in the ⱳeek and see what is going on in town. [The family were at the sea- ⱳide.] It will be good not to be too great a stranger to the house. It ⱳill be rather painful at first, but as it is to be done, I would have you ⱳot to be too strange to the house in town.

" Tell the boys that I fell in with a soldier—his name is Henderson —who was twelve years with Lord Wellington and other comman- lers. He returned very lately with only eight-pence-half-penny in his ⱳocket, and found his father and mother both in life, though they had ever heard from him, nor he from them. He carried my great-coat nd umbrella a few miles."

A FAMILY OF ENGINEERS

"*Fraserburgh, July 20th.*

"Fraserburgh is the same dull place which [Annie, Mary and Jeanie found it. As I am travelling along the coast which they are acquainted with, you had better cause Robert to bring down the map from Edinburgh; and it will be a good exercise in geography for the young folks to trace my course. I hope they have entered upon the writing. The library will afford abundance of excellent books, which I wish you would employ a little. I hope you are doing me the favour to go much out with the boys, which will do you much good and prevent them from getting so very much overheated."

[*To the Boys—Printed.*]

"When I had last the pleasure of writing to you, your dear little brother James and your sweet little sister Mary were still with us. But it has pleased God to remove them to another and a better world, and we must submit to the will of Providence. I must, however, request of you to think sometimes upon them, and to be very careful not to do anything that will displease or vex your mother. It is therefore proper that you do not roamp [Scottish indeed] too much about, and that you learn your lessons.

". . . I went to Fraserburgh and visited Kinnaird Head Lighthouse, which I found in good order. All this time I travelled upon good roads, and paid many a toll-man by the way; but from Fraserburgh to Banff there is no toll-bars, and the road is so bad that I had to walk up and down many a hill, and for   f bridges the horses had to drag the chaise up to the middle of the wheels in water. At Banff I saw a large ship of 300 tons lying on the sands upon her beam-ends, and a wreck for want of a good harbour. Captain Wilson—to whom I beg my compliments—will show you a ship of 300 tons. At the towns of Macduff, Banff, and Portsoy, many of the houses are built of marble, and the rocks on this part of the coast or sea-side are marble. But, my dear Boys, unless marble be polished and dressed, it is a very coarse-looking stone, and has no more beauty than common rock. As a proof of this, ask the favour of your mother to take you to Thompson's Marble Works in South Leith, and you will see marble in all its stages, and perhaps you may there find Portsoy marble! The use I wish to make of this is to tell you that, without education, a man is just like a block of rough, unpolished marble. Notice, in proof of this, how much Mr. Neill and Mr. M'Gregor [the tutor] know, and observe how little a man knows who is not a good scholar. On my way to Fochabers I passed through many thousand acres of Fir timber, and saw many deer running in these woods."

[*To Mrs. Stevenson.*]

"*Inverness, July 21st.*

"I propose going to church in the afternoon, and as I have breakfasted late, I shall afterwards take a walk, and dine about six o'clock. I do not know who is the clergyman here, but I shall think of you all

DOMESTIC ANNALS

avelled in the mail-coach [from Banff] almost alone. While it was light I kept the top, and the passing along a country I had never ›re seen was a considerable amusement. But, my dear, you are all 'h in my thoughts, and many are the objects which recall the rec- :tion of our tender and engaging children we have so recently lost. must not, however, repine. I could not for a moment wish any 1ge of circumstances in their case; and in every comparative view .heir state, I see the Lord's goodness in removing them from an evil ld to an abode of bliss; and I must earnestly hope that you may be bled to take such a view of this affliction as to live in the happy spect of our all meeting again to part no more—and that under 1 considerations you are getting up your spirits. I wish you would k about, and by all means go to town, and do not sit much at 1e."

"*Inverness, July 23rd.*
I am duly favoured with your much-valued letter, and I am happy find that you are so much with my mother, because that sort of iety has a tendency to occupy the mind, and to keep it from brood- too much upon one subject. Sensibility and tenderness are cer- ly two of the most interesting and pleasing qualities of the mind. se qualities are also none of the least of the many endearingments the female character. But if that kind of sympathy and pleasing ancholy, which is familiar to us under distress, be much indulged, ecomes habitual, and takes such a hold of the mind as to absorb all other affections, and unfit us for the duties and proper enjoyments life. Resignation sinks into a kind of peevish discontent. I am far, ever, from thinking there is the least danger of this in your case, dear; for you have been on all occasions enabled to look upon the tunes of this life as under the direction of a higher power, and have ays preserved that propriety and consistency of conduct in all cir- 1stances which endears your example to your family in particular, to your friends. I am therefore, my dear, for you to go out much, to go to the house up-stairs [he means to go up-stairs in the house, risit the place of the dead children], and to put yourself in the way the visits of your friends. I wish you would call on the Miss Grays, it would be a good thing upon a Saturday to dine with my mother, take Meggy and all the family with you, and let them have their wberries in town. The tickets of one of the *old-fashioned coaches* ld take you all up, and if the evening were good, they could all k down, excepting Meggy and little David."

"*Inverness, July 25th,* 11 *p. m.*
Captain Wemyss, of Wemyss, has come to Inverness to go the age with me, and as we are sleeping in a double-bedded room, I :t no longer transgress. You must remember me the best way you to the children."

"*On board of the Lighthouse Yacht, July 29th.*
I got to Cromarty yesterday about mid-day, and went to church. appened to be the sacrament there, and I heard a Mr. Smith at that e conclude the service with a very suitable exhortation. There 1ed a great concourse of people, but they had rather an unfortunate

A FAMILY OF ENGINEERS

day for them at the tent, as it rained a good deal. After drinking tea at the inn, Captain Wemyss accompanied me on board, and we sailed about eight last night. The wind at present being rather a beating one, I think I shall have an opportunity of standing into the bay of Wick, and leaving this letter to let you know my progress and that I am well."

"*Lighthouse Yacht, Stornoway, August 4th.*
"To-day we had prayers on deck as usual when at sea. I read the 14th chapter, I think, of Job. Captain Wemyss has been in the habit of doing this on board his own ship, agreeably to the Articles of War. Our passage round the Cape [Cape Wrath] was rather a cross one, and as the wind was northerly, we had a pretty heavy sea, but upon the whole have made a good passage, leaving many vessels behind us in Orkney. I am quite well, my dear; and Captain Wemyss, who has much spirit, and who is much given to observation, and a perfect enthusiast in his profession, enlivens the voyage greatly. Let me entreat you to move about much, and take a walk with the boys to Leith. I think they have still many places to see there, and I wish you would indulge them in this respect. Mr. Scales is the best person I know for showing them the sailcloth-weaving, etc., and he would have great pleasure in undertaking this. My dear, I trust soon to be with you, and that through the goodness of God we shall meet all well.

"There are two vessels lying here with emigrants for America, each with eighty people on board, at all ages, from a few days to upwards of sixty! Their prospects must be very forlorn to go with a slender purse for distant and unknown countries."

"*Lighthouse Yacht, off Greenock, Aug. 18th.*
"It was after *church-time* before we got here, but we had prayers upon deck on the way up the Clyde. This has, upon the whole, been a very good voyage, and Captain Wemyss, who enjoys it much, has been an excellent companion; we met with pleasure, and shall part with regret."

Strange that, after his long experience, my grandfather should have learned so little of the attitude and even the dialect of the spiritually-minded; that after forty-four years in a most religious circle, he could drop without sense of incongruity from a period of accepted phrases to "trust his wife was *getting up her spirits*," or think to reassure her as to the character of Captain Wemyss by mentioning that he had read prayers on the deck of his frigate "*agreeably to the Articles of War*"! Yet there is no doubt—and it is one of the most agreeable features of the kindly series—that he was doing his best to please, and there is little doubt that he succeeded. Almost all my

DOMESTIC ANNALS

grandfather's private letters have been destroyed. This correspondence has not only been preserved entire, but stitched up in the same covers with the works of the godly women, the Reverend John Campbell, and the painful Mrs. Ogle. I did not think to mention the good dame, but she comes in usefully as an example. Amongst the treasures of the ladies of my family, her letters have been honoured with a volume to themselves. I read about a half of them myself; then handed over the task to one of stauncher resolution, with orders to communicate any fact that should be found to illuminate these pages. Not one was found; it was her only art to communicate by post second-rate sermons at second-hand; and such, I take it, was the correspondence in which my grandmother delighted. If I am right, that of Robert Stevenson, with his quaint smack of the contemporary *Sandford and Merton*, his interest in the whole page of experience, his perpetual quest and fine scent of all that seems romantic to a boy, his needless pomp of language, his excellent good sense, his unfeigned, unstained, unwearied, human kindliness, would seem to her, in a comparison, dry and trivial and worldly. And if these letters were by an exception cherished and preserved, it would be for one or both of two reasons—because they dealt with and were bitter-sweet reminders of a time of sorrow; or because she was pleased, perhaps touched, by the writer's guileless effort to seem spiritually-minded.

After this date there were two more births and two more deaths, so that the number of the family remained unchanged; in all five children survived to reach maturity and to outlive their parents.

CHAPTER II

THE SERVICE OF THE NORTHERN LIGHTS

IT were hard to imagine a contrast more sharply defined than that between the lives of the men and women of this family: the one so chambered, so centred in the affections and the sensibilities; the other so active, healthy, and expeditious. From May to November, Thomas Smith and Robert Stevenson were on the mail, in the saddle, or at sea; and my grandfather, in particular, seems to have been possessed with a demon of activity in travel. In 1802, by direction of the Northern Lighthouse Board, he had visited the coast of England from St. Bees, in Cumberland, and round by the Scilly Islands to some place undecipherable by me; in all a distance of 2500 miles. In 1806 I find him starting "on a tour round the South Coast of England, from the Humber to the Severn." Peace was not long declared ere he found means to visit Holland, where he was in time to see, in the navy-yard at Helvoetsluys, "about twenty of Bonaparte's *English flotilla* lying in a state of decay, the object of curiosity to Englishmen." By 1834 he seems to have been acquainted with the coast of France from Dieppe to Bordeaux; and a main part of his duty as Engineer to the Board of Northern Lights was one round of dangerous and laborious travel.

In 1786, when Thomas Smith first received the appointment, the extended and formidable coast of Scotland was lighted at a single point—the Isle of May, in the jaws of the Firth of Forth, where, on a tower already a hundred and fifty years old, an open coal-fire blazed in an iron chauffer. The whole archipelago, thus nightly plunged in

SERVICE OF NORTHERN LIGHTS

darkness, was shunned by sea-going vessels, and the favourite courses were north about Shetland and west about St. Kilda. When the Board met, four new lights formed the extent of their intentions—Kinnaird Head in Aberdeenshire, at the eastern elbow of the coast; North Ronaldsay, in Orkney, to keep the north and guide ships passing to the south'ard of Shetland; Island Glass, on Harris, to mark the inner shore of the Hebrides and illuminate the navigation of the Minch; and the Mull of Kintyre. These works were to be attempted against obstacles, material and financial, that might have staggered the most bold. Smith had no ship at his command till 1791; the roads in those outlandish quarters where his business lay were scarce passable when they existed, and the tower on the Mull of Kintyre stood eleven months unlighted while the apparatus toiled and foundered by the way among rocks and mosses. Not only had towers to be built and apparatus transplanted, the supply of oil must be maintained, and the men fed, in the same inaccessible and distant scenes; a whole service, with its routine and hierarchy, had to be called out of nothing; and a new trade (that of lightkeeper) to be taught, recruited, and organized. The funds of the Board were at the first laughably inadequate. They embarked on their career on a loan of twelve hundred pounds, and their income in 1789, after relief by a fresh Act of Parliament, amounted to less than three hundred. It must be supposed that the thoughts of Thomas Smith, in these early years, were sometimes coloured with despair; and since he built and lighted one tower after another, and created and bequeathed to his successors the elements of an excellent administration, it may be conceded that he was not after all an unfortunate choice for a first engineer.

War added fresh complications. In 1794 Smith came "very near to be taken" by a French squadron. In 1813 Robert Stevenson was cruising about the neighbourhood of Cape Wrath in the immediate fear of Commodore Rogers. The men, and especially the sailors, of the Lighthouse service must be protected by a medal and ticket from the brutal

A FAMILY OF ENGINEERS

activity of the press-gang. And the zeal of volunteer patriots was at times embarrassing.

"I set off on foot," writes my grandfather, "for Marazion, a town at the head of Mount's Bay, where I was in hopes of getting a boat to freight. I had just got that length, and was making the necessary inquiry, when a young man, accompanied by several idle-looking fellows, came up to me, and in a hasty tone said, 'Sir, in the king's name I seize your person and papers.' To which I replied that I should be glad to see his authority, and know the reason of an address so abrupt. He told me the want of time prevented his taking regular steps, but that it would be necessary for me to return to Penzance, as I was suspected of being a French spy. I proposed to submit my papers to the nearest Justice of the Peace, who was immediately applied to, and came to the inn where I was. He seemed to be greatly agitated, and quite at a loss how to proceed. The complaint preferred against me was "that I had examined the Longships Lighthouse with the most minute attention, and was no less particular in my inquiries at the keepers of the lighthouse regarding the sunk rocks lying off the Land's End, with the set of the currents and tides along the coast: that I seemed particularly to regret the situation of the rocks called the Seven Stones, and the loss of a beacon which the Trinity Board had caused to be fixed on the Wolf Rock; that I had taken notes of the bearings of several sunk rocks, and a drawing of the lighthouse, and of Cape Cornwall. Further, that I had refused the honour of Lord Edgecombe's invitation to dinner, offering as an apology that I had some particular business on hand.'"

My grandfather produced in answer his credentials and letter of credit; but the justice, after perusing them, "very gravely observed that they were 'musty bits of paper,'" and proposed to maintain the arrest. Some more enlightened magistrates at Penzance relieved him of suspicion and left him at liberty to pursue his journey,—"which I did with so much eagerness," he adds, "that I gave the two coal lights on the Lizard only a very transient look."

Lighthouse operations in Scotland differed essentially in character from those in England. The English coast is in comparison a habitable, homely place, well supplied with towns; the Scottish presents hundreds of miles of savage islands and desolate moors. The Parliamentary committee of 1834, profoundly ignorant of this distinction, insisted with my grandfather that the work at the various stations should be let out on contract "in the neighbourhood," where sheep and deer, and gulls and cormorants, and a few

SERVICE OF NORTHERN LIGHTS

agged gillies, perhaps crouching in a bee-hive house, made
ip the only neighbours. In such situations repairs and
mprovements could only be overtaken by collecting (as my
grandfather expressed it) a few " lads," placing them under
harge of a foreman, and despatching them about the coast
s occasion served. The particular danger of these seas
ncreased the difficulty. The course of the lighthouse tender
ies amid iron-bound coasts, among tide-races, the whirlpools
f the Pentland Firth, flocks of islands, flocks of reefs, many
f them uncharted. The aid of steam was not yet. At first
a random coasting sloop, and afterwards in the cutter be-
onging to the service, the engineer must ply and run
imongst these multiplied dangers, and sometimes late into
he stormy autumn. For pages together my grandfather's
liary preserves a record of these rude experiences; of hard
rinds and rough seas; and of " the try-sail and storm-jib,
hose old friends which I never like to see." They do not
empt to quotation, but it was the man's element, in which
ie lived, and delighted to live, and some specimen must be
resented. On Friday, Sept. 10th, 1830, the *Regent* lying
a Lerwick Bay, we have this entry: " The gale increases,
rith continued rain." On the morrow, Saturday, 11th, the
reather appeared to moderate, and they put to sea, only to
ie driven by evening into Levenswick. There they lay,
' rolling much," with both anchors ahead and the square
ard on deck, till the morning of Saturday, 18th. Satur-
lay and Sunday they were plying to the southward with a
' strong breeze and a heavy sea," and on Sunday evening
nchored in Otterswick. " Monday, 20th, it blows so fresh
hat we have no communication with the shore. We see
Ar. Rome on the beach, but we cannot communicate with
lim. It blows ' mere fire,' as the sailors express it." And
or three days more the diary goes on with tales of davits
inshipped, high seas, strong gales from the southward, and
he ship driven to refuge in Kirkwall or Deer Sound. I have
iany a passage before me to transcribe, in which my grand-
ather draws himself as a man of exactitude about minute
nd anxious details. It must not be forgotten that these

A FAMILY OF ENGINEERS

voyages in the tender were the particular pleasure and reward of his existence; that he had in him a reserve of romance which carried him delightedly over these hardships and perils; that to him it was " great gain " to be eight nights and seven days in the savage bay of Levenswick—to read a book in the much agitated cabin—to go on deck and hear the gale scream in his ears, and see the landscape dark with rain, and the ship plunge at her two anchors—and to turn in at night and wake again at morning, in his narrow berth, to the clamorous and continued voices of the gale.

His perils and escapes were beyond counting. I shall only refer to two: the first, because of the impression made upon himself; the second, from the incidental picture it presents of the north islanders. On the 9th October 1794, he took passage from Orkney in the sloop *Elizabeth* of Stromness. She made a fair passage till within view of Kinnaird Head, where, as she was becalmed some three miles in the offing, and wind seemed to threaten from the southeast, the captain landed him, to continue his journey more expeditiously ashore. A gale immediately followed, and the *Elizabeth* was driven back to Orkney and lost with all hands. The second escape I have been in the habit of hearing related by an eyewitness, my own father, from the earliest days of childhood. On a September night, the *Regent* lay in the Pentland Firth in a fog and a violent and windless swell. It was still dark, when they were alarmed by the sound of breakers, and an anchor was immediately let go. The peep of dawn discovered them swinging in desperate proximity to the Isle of Swona * and the surf bursting close under their stern. There was in this place a hamlet of the inhabitants, fisher-folk and wreckers; their huts stood close about the head of the beach. All slept; the doors were closed, and there was no smoke, and the anxious watchers on board ship seemed to contemplate a village of the dead. It was thought possible to launch a boat and tow the *Regent* from her place of dan-

* This is only a probable hypothesis; I have tried to identify my father's anecdote in my grandfather's diary, and may very well have been deceived.—[R. L. S.]

SERVICE OF NORTHERN LIGHTS

ger; and with this view a signal of distress was made and a gun fired with a redhot poker from the galley. Its detonation awoke the sleepers. Door after door was opened, and in the grey light of the morning fisher after fisher was seen to come forth, yawning and stretching himself, nightcap on head. Fisher after fisher, I wrote, and my pen tripped; for it should rather stand wrecker after wrecker. There was no emotion, no animation, it scarce seemed any interest; not a hand was raised; but all callously awaited the harvest of the sea, and their children stood by their side and waited also. To the end of his life, my father remembered that amphitheatre of placid spectators on the beach, and with a special and natural animosity, the boys of his own age. But presently a light air sprang up, and filled the sails, and fainted, and filled them again; and little by little the *Regent* fetched way against the swell, and clawed off shore into the turbulent firth.

The purpose of these voyages was to effect a landing on open beaches or among shelving rocks, not for persons only, but for coals and food, and the fragile furniture of light-rooms. It was often impossible. In 1831 I find my grandfather "hovering for a week" about the Pentland Skerries for a chance to land; and it was almost always difficult. Much knack and enterprise were early developed among the seamen of the service; their management of boats is to this day a matter of admiration; and I find my grandfather in his diary depicting the nature of their excellence in one happily descriptive phrase, when he remarks that Captain Soutar had landed "the small stores and nine casks of oil *with all the activity of a smuggler.*" And it was one thing to land, another to get on board again. I have here a passage from the diary, where it seems to have been touch-and-go. "I landed at Tarbetness, on the eastern side of the point, in *a mere gale or blast of wind* from west-south-west, at 2 P. M. It blew so fresh that the captain, in a kind of despair, went off to the ship, leaving myself and the steward ashore. While I was in the light-room, I felt it shaking and waving, not with the tremor of the Bell Rock,

A FAMILY OF ENGINEERS

but with the *waving of a tree!* This the lightkeepers seemed to be quite familiar to, the principal keeper remarking that 'it was very pleasant,' perhaps meaning interesting or curious. The captain worked the vessel into smooth water with admirable dexterity, and I got on board again about 6 P. M. from the other side of the point." But not even the dexterity of Soutar could prevail always; and my grandfather must at times have been left in strange berths and with but rude provision. I may instance the case of my father, who was storm-bound three days upon an islet, sleeping in the uncemented and unchimneyed houses of the islanders, and subsisting on a diet of nettle-soup and lobsters.

The name of Soutar has twice escaped my pen, and I feel I owe him a vignette. Soutar first attracted notice as mate of a praam at the Bell Rock, and rose gradually to be captain of the *Regent*. He was active, admirably skilled in his trade, and a man incapable of fear. Once, in London, he fell among a gang of confidence-men, naturally deceived by his rusticity and his prodigious accent. They plied him with drink,—a hopeless enterprise, for Soutar could not be made drunk; they proposed cards, and Soutar would not play. At last, one of them, regarding him with a formidable countenance, inquired if he were not frightened? " I'm no' very easy fleyed," replied the captain. And the rooks withdrew after some easier pigeon. So many perils shared, and the partial familiarity of so many voyages, had given this man a stronghold in my grandfather's estimation; and there is no doubt but he had the art to court and please him with much hypocritical skill. He usually dined on Sundays in the cabin. He used to come down daily after dinner for a glass of port or whisky, often in his full rig of sou'-wester, oilskins, and long boots; and I have often heard it described how insinuatingly he carried himself on these appearances, artfully combining the extreme of deference with a blunt and seamanlike demeanour. My father and uncles, with the devilish penetration of the boy, were far from being deceived, and my father, indeed, was favoured with an object-lesson not to be mistaken. He had crept one rainy night into an apple-barrel on deck, and from this place of ambush overheard Soutar and a comrade conversing in their oilskins. The smooth sycophant of the cabin had wholly disappeared, and the boy listened with wonder to a vulgar and truculent ruffian. Of Soutar, I may say *tantum vidi*, having met him in the Leith docks now more than thirty years ago, when he abounded in the praises of my grandfather, encouraged me (in the most admirable manner) to pursue his footprints, and left impressed for ever on my memory the image of his own Bardolphian nose. He died not long after.

The engineer was not only exposed to the hazards of the sea; he must often ford his way by land to remote and scarce accessible places, beyond reach of the mail or the post-chaise, beyond even the tracery of the bridle-path, and guided by natives across bog and heather. Up to 1807 my grandfather seems to have travelled much on horseback; but he then gave up the idea—" such," he writes with characteristic emphasis and capital letters, " is the Plague of Baiting." He was a good pedestrian; at the age of fifty-eight I find him covering seventeen miles over the moors of the Mackay country in less than seven hours, and that is not bad travelling for a scramble. The piece of country traversed was already a familiar track, being that between Loch Eriboll and Cape Wrath; and I think I can scarce do better than reproduce from the diary some traits of his first visit. The tender lay in Loch Eriboll; by five in the morning they sat down to breakfast on board; by six they were ashore—my grandfather, Mr. Slight, an assistant, and Soutar of the jolly nose, and had been taken in charge by two gentlemen of the neighbourhood and a pair of gillies. About noon they reached the Kyle of Durness and passed the ferry. By half-past three they were at Cape Wrath— not yet known by the emphatic abbreviation of " The Cape," —and beheld upon all sides of them unfrequented shores, an expanse of desert moor, and the high-piled Western Ocean. The sight of the tower was chosen. Perhaps it is by inheritance of blood, but I know few things more in-

A FAMILY OF ENGINEERS

spiriting than this location of a lighthouse in a designated space of heather and air, through which the sea-birds are still flying. By 9 P.M. the return journey had brought them again to the shores of the Kyle. The night was dirty, and, as the sea was high and the ferry-boat small, Soutar and Mr. Stevenson were left on the far side, while the rest of the party embarked and were received into the darkness. They made, in fact, a safe though an alarming passage; but the ferryman refused to repeat the adventure; and my grandfather and the captain long paced the beach, impatient for their turn to pass, and tormented with rising anxiety as to the fate of their companions. At length they sought the shelter of a shepherd's house. " We had miserable up-putting," the diary continues, " and on both sides of the ferry much anxiety of mind. Our beds were clean straw, and but for the circumstance of the boat, I should have slept as soundly as ever I did after a walk through moss and mire of sixteen hours."

To go round the lights, even to-day, is to visit past centuries. The tide of tourists that flows yearly in Scotland, vulgarizing all where it approaches, is still defined by certain barriers. It will be long ere there is a hotel at Sumburgh or a hydropathic at Cape Wrath; it will be long ere any *char-à-banc*, laden with tourists, shall drive up to Barra Head or Monach, the Island of the Monks. They are farther from London than St. Petersburg, and except for the towers, sounding and shining all night with fog-bells and the radiance of the light-room, glittering by day with the trivial brightness of white paint, these island and moorland stations seem inaccessible to the civilization of to-day, and even to the end of my grandfather's career the isolation was far greater. There ran no post at all in the Long Island; from the lighthouse on Barra Head a boat must be sent for letters as far as Tobermory, between sixty and seventy miles of open sea; and the posts of Shetland, which had surprised Sir Walter Scott in 1814, were still unimproved in 1833, when my grandfather reported on the subject. The group contained at the time a population of 30,000 souls, and enjoyed a trade which had increased in twenty years seven-fold, to between three and four thousand tons. Yet the mails were despatched and received by chance coasting vessels at the rate of a penny a letter; six and eight weeks often elapsed between opportunities, and when a mail was to be made up, sometimes at a moment's notice, the bellman was sent hastily through the street of Lerwick. Between Shetland and Orkney, only seventy miles apart, there was "no trade communication whatever."

Such was the state of affairs, only sixty years ago, with the three largest clusters of the Scottish Archipelago; and forty-seven years earlier, when Thomas Smith began his rounds, or forty-two, when Robert Stevenson became conjoined with him in these excursions, the barbarism was deep, the people sunk in superstition, the circumstances of their life perhaps unique in history. Lerwick and Kirkwall, like Guam or the Bay of Islands, were but barbarous ports where whalers called to take up and to return experienced seamen. On the outlying islands the clergy lived isolated, thinking other thoughts, dwelling in a different country from their parishioners, like missionaries in the South Seas. My grandfather's unrivalled treasury of anecdote was never written down; it embellished his talk while he yet was, and died with him when he died; and such as have been preserved relate principally to the islands of Ronaldsay and Sanday, two of the Orkney group. These bordered on one of the water-highways of civilization; a great fleet passed annually in their view, and of the shipwrecks of the world they were the scene and cause of a proportion wholly incommensurable to their size. In one year, 1798, my grandfather found the remains of no fewer than five vessels on the isle of Sanday, which is scarcely twelve miles long.

"Hardly a year passed," he writes, "without instances of this kind; for, owing to the projecting points of this strangely formed island, the lowness and whiteness of its eastern shores, and the wonderful manner in which the scanty patches of land are intersected with lakes and pools of water, it becomes, even in daylight, a deception, and has often been fatally mistaken for an open sea. It had even become proverbial with some of the inhabitants to observe that 'if wrecks were to happen,

A FAMILY OF ENGINEERS

they might as well be sent to the poor isle of Sanday as anywhere else. On this and the neighbouring islands the inhabitants have certainly had their share of wrecked goods, for the eye is presented with these melancholy remains in almost every form. For example, although quarries are to be met with generally in these islands, and the stones are very suitable for building dykes [*Anglicé*, walls], yet instances occur of the land being enclosed, even to a considerable extent, with ship-timbers. The author has actually seen a park [*Anglicé*, meadow] paled round chiefly with cedar-wood and mahogany from the wreck of a Honduras-built ship; and in one island, after the wreck of a ship laden with wine, the inhabitants have been known to take claret to their barley-meal porridge. On complaining to one of the pilots of the badness of his boat's sails, he replied to the author with some degree of pleasantry, 'Had it been His will that you camena' here wi' your lights, we might 'a' had better sails to our boats, and more o' other things.' It may further be mentioned that when some of Lord Dundas's farms are to be let in these islands a competition takes place for the lease, and it is *bona fide* understood that a much higher rent is paid than the lands would otherwise give were it not for the chance of making considerably by the agency and advantages attending shipwrecks on the shores of the respective farms."

The people of North Ronaldsay still spoke Norse, or, rather, mixed it with their English. The walls of their huts were built to a great thickness of rounded stones from the sea-beach; the roof flagged, loaded with earth, and perforated by a single hole for the escape of smoke. The grass grew beautifully green on the flat house-top, where the family would assemble with their dogs and cats, as on a pastoral lawn; there were no windows, and, in my grandfather's expression, "there was really no demonstration of a house unless it were the diminutive door." He once landed on Ronaldsay with two friends. "The inhabitants crowded and pressed so much upon the strangers that the bailiff, or resident factor of the island, blew with his ox-horn, calling out to the natives to stand off and let the gentlemen come forward to the laird; upon which one of the islanders, as spokesman, called out, 'God ha'e us, man! thou needsna mak' sic a noise. It's no' every day we ha'e *three hatted men* on our isle.'" When the Surveyor of Taxes came (for the first time, perhaps) to Sanday, and began in the King's name to complain of the unconscionable swarms of dogs, and to menace the inhabitants with taxation, it chanced that my grandfather and his friend, Dr. Patrick

SERVICE OF NORTHERN LIGHTS

Neill, were received by an old lady in a Ronaldsay hut. Her hut, which was similar to the model described, stood on a Ness, or point of land jutting into the sea. They were made welcome in the firelit cellar, placed " in *casey* or straw-worked chairs, after the Norwegian fashion, with arms, and a canopy overhead," and given milk in a wooden dish. These hospitalities attended to, the old lady turned at once to Dr. Neill, whom she took for the Surveyor of Taxes. " Sir," said she, " gin ye'll tell the King that I canna keep the Ness free o' the Bangers (sheep) without twa hun's, and twa guid hun's too, he'll pass me threa the tax on dugs."

This familiar confidence, these traits of engaging simplicity, are characters of a secluded people. Mankind—and, above all, islanders—come very swiftly to a bearing, and find very readily, upon one convention or another, a tolerable corporate life. The danger is to those from without, who have not grown up from childhood in the islands, but appear suddenly in that narrow horizon, life-sized apparitions. For these no bond of humanity exists, no feeling of kinship is awakened by their peril; they will assist at a shipwreck, like the fisher-folk of Lunga, as spectators, and, when the fatal scene is over, and the beach strewn with dead bodies, they will fence their fields with mahogany, and, after a decent grace, sup claret to their porridge. It is not wickedness: it is scarce evil; it is only, in its highest power, the sense of isolation and the wise disinterestedness of feeble and poor races. Think how many viking ships had sailed by these islands in the past, how many vikings had landed, and raised turmoil, and broken up the barrows of the dead, and carried off the wines of the living; and blame them, if you are able, for that belief (which may be called one of the parables of the devil's gospel) that a man rescued from the sea will prove the bane of his deliverer. It might be thought that my grandfather, coming there unknown, and upon an employment so hateful to the inhabitants, must have run the hazard of his life. But this were to misunderstand. He came franked by the laird and the clergyman; he was the King's officer; the work was " opened

A FAMILY OF ENGINEERS

with prayer by the Rev. Walter Trail, minister of the parish"; God and the King had decided it, and the people of these pious islands bowed their heads. There landed, indeed, in North Ronaldsay, during the last decade of the eighteenth century, a traveller whose life seems really to have been imperilled. A very little man of a swarthy complexion, he came ashore, exhausted and unshaved, from a long boat passage, and lay down to sleep in the home of the parish schoolmaster. But he had been seen landing. The inhabitants had identified him for a Pict, as, by some singular confusion of name, they call the dark and dwarfish aboriginal people of the land. Immediately the obscure ferment of a race-hatred, grown into a superstition, began to work in their bosoms, and they crowded about the house and the room-door with fearful whisperings. For some time the schoolmaster held them at bay, and at last despatched a messenger to call my grandfather. He came: he found the islanders beside themselves at this unwelcome resurrection of the dead and the detested; he was shown, as adminicular of testimony, the traveller's uncouth and thick-soled boots; he argued, and finding argument unavailing, consented to enter the room and examine with his own eyes the sleeping Pict. One glance was sufficient: the man was now a missionary, but he had been before that an Edinburgh shopkeeper with whom my grandfather had dealt. He came forth again with this report, and the folk of the island, wholly relieved, dispersed to their own houses. They were timid as sheep and ignorant as limpets; that was all. But the Lord deliver us from the tender mercies of a frightened flock!

I will give two more instances of their superstition. When Sir Walter Scott visited the Stones of Stennis, my grandfather put in his pocket a hundred-foot line, which he unfortunately lost.

"Some years afterwards," he writes, "one of my assistants on a visit to the Stones of Stennis took shelter from a storm in a cottage close by the lake; and seeing a box-measuring-line in the bole or sole of the cottage window, he asked the woman where she got this well-

SERVICE OF NORTHERN LIGHTS

known professional appendage. She said: 'O sir, ane of the bairns fand it lang syne at· the Stanes; and when drawing it out we took fright, and thinking it had belanged to the fairies, we threw it into the bole, and it has layen there ever since.'"

This is for the one; the last shall be a sketch by the master hand of Scott himself:—

"At the village of Stromness, on the Orkney main island, called Pomona, lived, in 1814, an aged dame called Bessie Millie, who helped out her subsistence by selling favourable winds to mariners. He was a venturous master of a vessel who left the roadstead of Stromness without paying his offering to propitiate Bessie Millie! Her fee was extremely moderate, being exactly sixpence, for which she boiled her kettle and gave the bark the advantage of her prayers, for she disclaimed all unlawful acts. The wind thus petitioned for was sure, she said, to arrive, though occasionally the mariners had to wait some time for it. The woman's dwelling and appearance were not unbecoming her pretensions. Her house, which was on the brow of the steep hill on which Stromness is founded, was only accessible by a series of dirty and precipitous lanes, and for exposure might have been the abode of Eolus himself, in whose commodities the inhabitant dealt. She herself was, as she told us, nearly one hundred years old, withered and dried up like a mummy. A clay-coloured kerchief, folded round her neck, corresponded in colour to her corpse-like complexion. Two light blue eyes that gleamed with a lustre like that of insanity, an utterance of astonishing rapidity, a nose and chin that almost met together, and a ghastly expression of cunning, gave her the effect of Hecate. Such was Bessie Millie, to whom the mariners paid a sort of tribute with a feeling between jest and earnest."

II

From about the beginning of the century up to 1807 Robert Stevenson was in partnership with Thomas Smith. In the last-named year the partnership was dissolved; Thomas Smith returning to his business, and my grandfather becoming sole engineer to the Board of Northern Lights.

I must try, by excerpts from his diary and correspondence, to convey to the reader some idea of the ardency and thoroughness with which he threw himself into the largest and least of his multifarious engagements in this service. But first I must say a word or two upon the life of light-keepers, and the temptations to which they are more partic-

A FAMILY OF ENGINEERS

ularly exposed. The lightkeeper occupies a position apart among men. In sea-towers the complement has always been three since the deplorable business in the Eddystone, when one keeper died, and the survivor, signalling in vain for relief, was compelled to live for days with the dead body. These usually pass their time by the pleasant human expedient of quarrelling; and sometimes, I am assured, not one of the three is on speaking terms with any other. On shore stations, which on the Scottish coast are sometimes hardly less isolated, the usual number is two, a principal and an assistant. The principal is dissatisfied with the assistant, or perhaps the assistant keeps pigeons, and the principal wants the water from the roof. Their wives and families are with them, living cheek by jowl. The children quarrel; Jockie hits Jimsie in the eye, and the mothers make haste to mingle in the dissension. Perhaps there is trouble about a broken dish; perhaps Mrs. Assistant is more highly born than Mrs. Principal and gives herself airs; and the men are drawn in and the servants presently follow. "Church privileges have been denied the keeper's and the assistant's servants," I read in one case, and the eminently Scots periphrasis means neither more nor less than excommunication, "on account of the discordant and quarrelsome state of the families. The cause, when inquired into, proves to be *tittle-tattle* on both sides." The tender comes round; the foremen and artificers go from station to station; the gossip flies through the whole system of the service, and the stories, disfigured and exaggerated, return to their own birthplace with the returning tender. The English Board was apparently shocked by the picture of these dissensions. "When the Trinity House can," I find my grandfather writing at Beechy Head, in 1834, " they do not appoint two keepers, they disagree so ill. A man who has a family is assisted by his family; and in this way, to my experience and present observation, the business is very much neglected. One keeper is, in my view, a bad system. This day's visit to an English lighthouse convinces me of this, as the lightkeeper was walking on a staff with the gout, and the business per-

SERVICE OF NORTHERN LIGHTS

formed by one of his daughters, a girl of thirteen or fourteen years of age." This man received a hundred a year! It shows a different reading of human nature, perhaps typical of Scotland and England, that I find in my grandfather's diary the following pregnant entry: "*The lightkeepers, agreeing ill, keep one another to their duty.*" But the Scottish system was not alone founded on this cynical opinion. The dignity and the comfort of the northern lightkeeper were both attended to. He had a uniform to "raise him in his own estimation, and in that of his neighbour, which is of consequence to a person of trust." "The keepers," my grandfather goes on, in another place, "are attended to in all the detail of accommodation in the best style as shipmasters; and this is believed to have a sensible effect upon their conduct, and to regulate their general habits as members of society." He notes, with the same dip of ink, that "the brasses were not clean, and the persons of the keepers not *trig* "; and thus we find him writing to a culprit: "I have to complain that you are not cleanly in your person, and that your manner of speech is ungentle, and rather inclines to rudeness. You must therefore take a different view of your duties as a lightkeeper." A high ideal for the service appears in these expressions, and will be more amply illustrated further on. But even the Scottish lightkeeper was frail. During the unbroken solitude of the winter months, when inspection is scarce possible, it must seem a vain toil to polish the brass hand-rail of the stair, or to keep an unrewarded vigil in the light-room; and the keepers are habitually tempted to the beginnings of sloth, and must unremittingly resist. He who temporises with his conscience is already lost. I must tell here an anecdote that illustrates the difficulties of inspection. In the days of my uncle David and my father there was a station which they regarded with jealousy. The two engineers compared notes and were agreed. The tower was always clean, but seemed always to bear traces of a hasty cleansing, as though the keepers had been suddenly forewarned. On inquiry, it proved that such was the case, and that a wandering fiddler was the unfailing

A FAMILY OF ENGINEERS

harbinger of the engineer. At last my father was storm-stayed one Sunday in a port at the other side of the island. The visit was quite overdue, and as he walked across upon the Monday morning he promised himself that he should at last take the keepers unprepared. They were both waiting for him in uniform at the gate; the fiddler had been there on Saturday!

My grandfather, as will appear from the following extracts, was much a martinet, and had a habit of expressing himself on paper with an almost startling emphasis. Personally, with his powerful voice, sanguine countenance, and eccentric and original locutions, he was well qualified to inspire a salutary terror in the service.

"I find that the keepers have, by some means or another, got into the way of cleaning too much with rotten-stone and oil. I take the principal keeper to *task* on this subject, and make him bring a clean towel and clean one of the brazen frames, which leaves the towel in an odious state. This towel I put up in a sheet of paper, seal, and take with me to confront Mr. Murdoch, who has just left the station." "This letter"—a stern enumeration of complaints—"to lie a week on the light-room book-place, and to be put in the Inspector's hands when he comes round." "It is the most painful thing that can occur for me to have a correspondence of this kind with any of the keepers; and when I come to the Lighthouse, instead of having the satisfaction to meet them with approbation, it is distressing when one is obliged to put on a most angry countenance and demeanour; but from such culpable negligence as you have shown there is no avoiding it. I hold it as a fixed maxim, that when a man or a family put on a slovenly appearance in their houses, stairs, and lanterns, I always find their reflectors, burners, windows, and light in general, ill attended to; and, therefore, I must insist on cleanliness throughout." "I find you very deficient in the duty of the high tower. You thus place your appointment as Principal Keeper in jeopardy; and I think it necessary, as an old servant of the Board, to put you upon your guard once for all at this time. I call upon you to recollect what was formerly and is now said to you. The state of the backs of the reflectors at the high tower was disgraceful, as I pointed out to you on the spot. They were as if spitten upon, and greasy finger-marks upon the back straps. I demand an explanation of this state of things." "The cause of the Commissioners dismissing you is expressed in the minute; and it must be a matter of regret to you that you have been so much engaged in smuggling, and also that the Reports relative to the cleanliness of the Lighthouse, upon being referred to, rather added to their unfavourable opinion." "I do not go into the dwelling-house, but severely chide the lightkeepers for the disagreement that seems to subsist among them." "The families of the two lightkeepers here agree very ill,

SERVICE OF NORTHERN LIGHTS

have effected a reconciliation for the present." "Things are in a ry *humdrum* state here. There is no painting, and in and out of ›ors no taste or tidiness displayed. Robert's wife *greets* and 'Gregor's scolds; and Robert is so down-hearted that he says he is ıfit for duty. I told him that if he was to mind wives' quarrels, and take them up, the only way was for him and M'Gregor to go down the point like Sir G. Grant and Lord Somerset." "I cannot say that have experienced a more unpleasant meeting than that of the light-ruse folks this morning, or ever saw a stronger example of unfeeling ırbarity than the conduct which the ——s exhibited. These two ıld-hearted persons, not contented with having driven the daughter ! the poor nervous woman from her father's house, both kept *pouncing* : her, lest she should forget her great misfortune. Write me of their ınduct. Do not make any communication of the state of these ımilies at Kinnaird Head, as this would be like *Tale-bearing."*

There is the great word out. Tales and Tale-bearing, lways with the emphatic capitals, run continually in his orrespondence. I will give but two instances:—

"Write to [David, one of the lightkeepers] and caution him to be ıore prudent how he expresses himself. Let him attend his duty to ıe Lighthouse and his family concerns, and give less heed to Tale-earers." "I have not your last letter at hand to quote its date; but, ! I recollect, it contains some kind of tales, which nonsense I wish you ›uld lay aside, and notice only the concerns of your family and the ıportant charge committed to you."

Apparently, however, my grandfather was not himself ıaccessible to the Tale-bearer, as the following indicates:—

"In walking along with Mr. ——, I explain to him that I should be ɔder the necessity of looking more closely into the business here from s conduct at Buddonness, which had given an instance of weakness ι the Moral principle which had staggered my opinion of him. His ıswer was 'That will be with regard to the lass?' I told him I was › enter no farther with him upon the subject." "Mr. Miller appears ɔ be master and man. I am sorry about this foolish fellow. Had I ıown his train, I should not, as I did, have rather forced him into the ·rvice. Upon finding the windows in the state they were, I turned ɔon Mr. Watt, and especially upon Mr. Stewart. The latter did not ›pear for a length of time to have visited the light-room. On asking ıe cause—did Mr. Watt and him (*sic*) disagree; he said no; but he ıd got very bad usage from the assistant, 'who was a very obstrep-ɔus man.' I could not bring Mr. Watt to put in language his ob-:ctions to Miller; all I could get was that, he being your friend, and ıying he was unwell, he did not like to complain or to push the man; ıat the man seemed to have no liking to anything like work; that he ıs unruly; that, being an educated man, he despised them. I was,

A FAMILY OF ENGINEERS

however, determined to have out of these *unwilling* witnesses the language alluded to. I fixed upon Mr. Stewart as chief; he hedged. My curiosity increased, and I urged. Then he said, 'What would I think, just exactly, of Mr. Watt being called an Old B——?' You may judge of my surprise. There was not another word uttered. This was quite enough, as coming from a person I should have calculated upon quite different behaviour from. It spoke a volume of the man's mind and want of principle." "Object to the keeper keeping a Bull-Terrier dog of ferocious appearance. It is dangerous, as we land at all times of the night." "Have only to complain of the storehouse floor being spotted with oil. Give orders for this being instantly rectified, so that on my return to-morrow I may see things in good order." "The furniture of both houses wants much rubbing. Mrs. ——'s carpets are absurd beyond anything I have seen. I want her to turn the fenders up with the bottom to the fireplace: the carpets, when not likely to be in use, folded up and laid as a hearthrug partly under the fender."

My grandfather was king in the service to his fingertips. All should go in his way from the principal lightkeeper's coat to the assistant's fender, from the gravel in the garden-walks to the bad smell in the kitchen, or the oil-spots on the store-room floor. It might be thought there was nothing more calculated to awake men's resentment, and yet his rule was not more thorough than it was beneficent. His thought for the keepers was continual, and it did not end with their lives. He tried to manage their successions; he thought no pains too great to arrange between a widow and a son who had succeeded his father; he was often harassed and perplexed by tales of hardship; and I find him writing, almost in despair, of their improvident habits and the destitution that awaited their families upon a death. "The house being completely furnished, they come into possession without necessaries, and they go out NAKED. The insurance seems to have failed, and what next is to be tried?" While they lived he wrote behind their backs to arrange for the education of their children, or to get them other situations if they seemed unsuitable for the Northern Lights. When he was at a lighthouse on a Sunday he held prayers and heard the children read. When a keeper was sick, he lent him his horse and sent him mutton and brandy from the ship. "The assistant's wife having been this morning confined, there was sent ashore a bottle of sherry and a few rusks—a practice which

ERVICE OF NORTHERN LIGHTS

e always observed in this service," he writes. They many of them, in uninhabited isles or desert forelands, y cut off from shops. Many of them were, besides, into a rustic dishabitude of life, so that even when visited a city they could scarce be trusted with their iffairs, as (for example) he who carried home to his en, thinking they were oranges, a bag of lemons. And randfather seems to have acted, at least in his early as a kind of gratuitous agent for the service. Thus him writing to a keeper in 1806, when his mind was ly pre-occupied with arrangements for the Bell Rock: n much afraid I stand very unfavourably with you man of promise, as I was to send several things of I believe I have more than once got the memorandum. can say is that in this respect you are not singular. nakes me no better; but really I have been driven about d all example in my past experience, and have been ially obliged to neglect my own urgent affairs." No it of the Northern Lights came to Edinburgh but he ntertained at Baxter's Place to breakfast. There, at n table, my grandfather sat down delightedly with his -spoken, homespun officers. His whole relation to the e was, in fact, patriarchal; and I believe I may say throughout its ranks he was adored. I have spoken many who knew him; I was his grandson, and their may have very well been words of flattery; but there ne thing that could not be affected, and that was the and light that came into their faces at the name of t Stevenson.

the early part of the century the foreman builder was ing man of the name of George Peebles, a native of uther. My grandfather had placed in him a very high e of confidence, and he was already designated to be an at the Bell Rock, when on Christmas-day, 1806, s way home from Orkney, he was lost in the schooner *·ller*. The tale of the loss of the *Traveller* is almost a a of that of the *Elizabeth* of Stromness; like the *Eliza-* he came as far as Kinnaird Head, was then surprised

A FAMILY OF ENGINEERS

by a storm, driven back to Orkney, and bilged and sank on the island of Flotta. It seems it was about the dusk of the day when the ship struck, and many of the crew and passengers were drowned. About the same hour, my grandfather was in his office at the writing-table; and the room beginning to darken, he laid down his pen and fell asleep. In a dream he saw the door open and George Peebles come in, " reeling to and fro, and staggering like a drunken man," with water streaming from his head and body to the floor. There it gathered into a wave which, sweeping forward, submerged my grandfather. Well, no matter how deep; versions vary; and at last he awoke, and behold it was a dream! But it may be conceived how profoundly the impression was written even on the mind of a man averse from such ideas, when the news came of the wreck on Flotta and the death of George.

George's vouchers and accounts had perished with himself; and it appeared he was in debt to the Commissioners. But my grandfather wrote to Orkney twice, collected evidence of his disbursements, and proved him to be seventy pounds ahead. With this sum, he applied to George's brothers, and had it apportioned between their mother and themselves. He approached the board and got an annuity of £5 bestowed on the widow Peebles; and we find him writing her a long letter of explanation and advice, and pressing on her the duty of making a will. That he should thus act as executor was no singular instance. But besides this we are able to assist at some of the stages of a rather touching experiment: no less than an attempt to secure Charles Peebles heir to George's favour. He is dispatched, under the character of " a fine young man "; recommended to gentlemen for " advice, as he's a stranger in your place, and indeed to this kind of charge, this being his first outset as Foreman "; and for a long while after, the letter-book, in the midst of that thrilling first year of the Bell Rock, is encumbered with pages of instruction and encouragement. The nature of a bill, and the precautions that are to be observed about discounting it, are expounded at length and with clearness. " You are not, I hope, neglecting, Charles,

SERVICE OF NORTHERN LIGHTS

to work the harbour at spring-tides; and see that you pay the greatest attention to get the well so as to supply the keeper with water, for he is a very helpless fellow, and so unfond of hard work that I fear he could do ill to keep himself in water by going to the other side for it."—" With regard to spirits, Charles, I see very little occasion for it." These abrupt apostrophes sound to me like the voice of an awakened conscience; but they would seem to have reverberated in vain in the ears of Charles. There was trouble in Pladda, his scene of operations; his men ran away from him, there was at least a talk of calling in the Sheriff. "I fear," writes my grandfather, "you have been too indulgent, and I am sorry to add that men do not answer to be too well treated, a circumstance which I have experienced, and which you will learn as you go on in business." I wonder, was not Charles Peebles himself a case in point? Either death, at least, or disappointment and discharge, must have ended his service in the Northern Lights; and in later correspondence I look in vain for any mention of his name—Charles, I mean, not Peebles: for as late as 1839 my grandfather is patiently writing to another of the family: "I am sorry you took the trouble of applying to me about your son, as it lies quite out of my way to forward his views in the line of his profession as a Draper."

III

A professional life of Robert Stevenson has been already given to the world by his son David, and to that I would refer those interested in such matters. But my own design, which is to represent the man, would be very ill carried out if I suffered myself or my reader to forget that he was, first of all and last of all, an engineer. His chief claim to the style of a mechanical inventor is on account of the Jib or Balance Crane of the Bell Rock, which are beautiful contrivances. But the great merit of this engineer was not in the field of engines. He was above all things a projector of works in the face of nature, and a modifier of nature itself.

A FAMILY OF ENGINEERS

A road to be made, a tower to be built, a harbour to be constructed, a river to be trained and guided in its channel—these were the problems with which his mind was continually occupied; and for these and similar ends he travelled the world for more than half a century, like an artist, note-book in hand.

He once stood and looked on at the emptying of a certain oil-tube; he did so watch in hand, and accurately timed the operation; and in so doing offered the perfect type of his profession. The fact acquired might never be of use: it was acquired: another link in the world's huge chain of processes was brought down to figures and placed at the service of the engineer. "The very term mensuration sounds *engineer-like*," I find him writing; and in truth what the engineer most properly deals with is that which can be measured, weighed, and numbered. The time of any operation in hours and minutes, its cost in pounds, shillings, and pence, the strain upon a given point in foot-pounds—these are his conquests, with which he must continually furnish his mind, and which, after he has acquired them, he must continually apply and exercise. They must be not only entries in note-books, to be hurriedly consulted; in the actor's phrase, he must be *stale* in them; in a word of my grandfather's, they must be "fixed in the mind like the ten fingers and ten toes."

These are the certainties of the engineer; so far he finds a solid footing and clear views. But the province of formulas and constants is restricted. Even the mechanical engineer comes at last to an end of his figures, and must stand up, a practical man, face to face with the discrepancies of nature and the hiatuses of theory. After the machine is finished, and the steam turned on, the next is to drive it; and experience and an exquisite sympathy must teach him where a weight should be applied or a nut loosened. With the civil engineer, more properly so called (if anything can be proper with this awkward coinage), the obligation starts with the beginning. He is always the practical man. The rains, the winds and the waves, the complexity and the fitful-

SERVICE OF NORTHERN LIGHTS

ess of nature, are always before him. He has to deal with he unpredictable, with those forces (in Smeaton's phrase) hat " are subject to no calculation "; and still he must pre- ict, still calculate them, at his peril. His work is not yet in eing, and he must foresee its influence: how it shall deflect he tide, exaggerate the waves, dam back the rain-water, or ttract the thunderbolt. He visits a piece of sea-board: and rom the inclination and soil of the beach, from the weeds nd shell-fish, from the configuration of the coast and the epth of soundings outside, he must induce what magni- ude of waves is to be looked for. He visits a river, its ummer water babbling on shallows; and he must not only ead, in a thousand indications, the measure of winter fresh- ts, but be able to predict the violence of occasional great loods. Nay, and more: he must not only consider that which is, but that which may be. Thus I find my grand- ather writing, in a report on the North Esk Bridge: " A ess waterway might have sufficed, but *the valleys may come o be meliorated by drainage.*" One field drained after an- ther through all that confluence of vales, and we come to time when they shall precipitate, by so much a more opious and transient flood, as the gush of the flowing drain- ipe is superior to the leakage of a peat.

It is plain there is here but a restricted use for formulas. In this sort of practice, the engineer has need of some ranscendental sense. Smeaton, the pioneer, bade him obey is " feelings "; my father, that " power of estimating ob- cure forces which supplies a coefficient of its own to every ule." The rules must be everywhere indeed; but they must verywhere be modified by this transcendental coefficient, verywhere bent to the impression of the trained eye and the *eelings* of the engineer. A sentiment of physical laws and f the scale of nature, which shall have been strong in the eginning and progressively fortified by observation must e his guide in the last recourse. I had the most oppor- unity to observe my father. He would pass hours on the each brooding over the waves, counting them, noting their east deflection, noting when they broke. On Tweedside, or

A FAMILY OF ENGINEERS

by Lyne or Manor, we have spent together whole afternoons; to me, at the time, extremely wearisome; to him, as I am now sorry to think, bitterly mortifying. The river was to me a pretty and various spectacle; I could not see—I could not be made to see—it otherwise. To my father it was a chequer-board of lively forces, which he traced from pool to shallow with minute appreciation and enduring interest. "That bank was being undercut," he might say; "why? Suppose you were to put a groin out here, would not the *filum fluminous* be cast abruptly off across the channel? and where would it impinge upon the other shore? and what would be the result? Or suppose you were to blast that boulder, what would happen? Follow it—use the eyes God has given you—can you not see that a great deal of land would be reclaimed upon this side?" It was to me like school in holidays; but to him, until I had worn him out with my invincible triviality, a delight. Thus he pored over the engineer's voluminous handy-book of nature; thus must, too, have pored my grandfather and uncles.

But it is of the essence of this knowledge, or this knack of mind, to be largely incommunicable. "It cannot be imparted to another," says my father. The verbal casting-net is thrown in vain over these evanescent, inferential relations. Hence the insignificance of much engineering literature. So far as the science can be reduced to formulas or diagrams, the book is to the point; so far as the art depends on intimate study of the ways of nature, the author's words will too often be found vapid. This fact—that engineering looks one way, and literature another—was what my grandfather overlooked. All his life long, his pen was in his hand, piling up a treasury of knowledge, preparing himself against all possible contingencies. Scarce anything fell under his notice but he perceived in it some relation to his work, and chronicled it in the pages of his journal in his always lucid, but sometimes inexact and wordy, style. The Travelling Diary (so he called it) was kept in fascicles of ruled paper, which were at last bound up, rudely indexed, and put by for future reference. Such volumes as have

ERVICE OF NORTHERN LIGHTS

d me contain a surprising medley: the whole details
employment in the Northern Lights and his general
ce; the whole biography of an enthusiastic engineer.
of it is useful and curious; much merely otiose; and
can only be described as an attempt to impart that
cannot be imparted in words. Of such are his re-
l and heroic descriptions of reefs; monuments of mis-
ed literary energy, which leave upon the mind of the
: no effect but that of a multiplicity of words and the
sted vignette of a lusty old gentleman scrambling
3 tangle. It is to be remembered that he came to
;ering while yet it was in the egg and without a library,
hat he saw the bounds of that profession widen daily.
w iron ships, steamers, and the locomotive engine, intro-
. He lived to travel from Glasgow to Edinburgh in
side of a forenoon, and to remember that he himself
' often been twelve hours upon the journey, and his
lfather (Lillie) two days"! The profession was still
1 its second generation, and had already broken down
irriers of time and space. Who should set a limit to its
? encroachments? And hence, with a kind of sanguine
try, he pursued his design of "keeping up with the
and posting himself and his family on every mortal
ct. Of this unpractical idealism we shall meet with
instances; there was not a trade, and scarce an ac-
lishment, but he thought it should form part of the
of an engineer; and not content with keeping an en-
paedic diary himself, he would fain have set all his sons
ork continuing and extending it. They were more
ly inspired. My father's engineering pocket-book was
bulky volume; with its store of pregnant notes and
formulas, it served him through life, and was not yet
when he came to die. As for Robert Stevenson and the
elling Diary, I should be ungrateful to complain, for
s supplied me with many lively traits for this and
quent chapters; but I must still remember much of the
l of my study there as a sojourn in the Valley of the
ow.

A FAMILY OF ENGINEERS

The duty of the engineer is twofold—to design the work, and to see the work done. We have seen already something of the vociferous thoroughness of the man, upon the cleaning of lamps and the polishing of reflectors. In building, in road-making, in the construction of bridges, in every detail and byway of his employments, he pursued the same ideal. Perfection (with a capital P and violently underscored) was his design. A crack for a penknife, the waste of " six-and-thirty shillings," " the loss of a day or a tide," in each of these he saw and was revolted by the finger of the sloven; and to spirits intense as his, and immersed in vital undertakings, the slovenly is the dishonest, and wasted time is instantly translated into lives endangered. On this consistent idealism there is but one thing that now and then trenches with a touch of incongruity, and that is his love of the picturesque. As when he laid out a road on Hogarth's line of beauty; bade a foreman be careful, in quarrying, not " to disfigure the island "; or regretted in a report that " the great stone, called the *Devil in the Hole*, was blasted or broken down to make road-metal, and for other purposes of the work."

CHAPTER III

THE BUILDING OF THE BELL ROCK

OFF the mouths of the Tay and the Forth, thirteen miles from Fifeness, eleven from Arbroath, and fourteen from the Red Head of Angus, lies the Inchcape or Bell Rock. It extends to a length of about fourteen hundred feet, but the part of it discovered at low water to not more than four hundred and twenty-seven. At a little more than half-flood in fine weather the seamless ocean joins over the reef, and at high-water springs it is buried sixteen feet. As the tide goes down, the higher reaches of the rock are seen to be clothed by *Conferva rupestris* as by a sward of grass; upon the more exposed edges, where the currents are most swift and the breach of the sea heaviest, Baderlock or Henware flourishes; and the great Tangle grows at the depth of several fathoms with luxuriance. Before man arrived, and introduced into the silence of the sea the smoke and clangour of a blacksmith's shop, it was a favourite resting-place of seals. The crab and lobster haunt in the crevices; and limpets, mussels, and the white buckie abound.

According to tradition, a bell had been once hung upon this rock by an abbot of Arbroath,* "and being taken down by a sea-pirate, a year thereafter he perished upon the same rock, with ship and goods, in the righteous judgment of God." From the days of the abbot and the sea-

---

* This is, of course, the tradition commemorated by Southey in his ballad of "The Inchcape Bell." Whether true or not, it points to the fact that from the infancy of Scottish navigation the seafaring mind had been fully alive to the perils of this reef. Repeated attempts had been made to mark the place with beacons, but all efforts were unavailing (one such beacon having been carried away within eight days of its erection) until Robert Stevenson conceived and carried out the idea of the stone tower.

A FAMILY OF ENGINEERS

pirate so man had set foot upon the Inchcape, save fishers from the neighbouring coast, or perhaps—for a moment, before the surges swallowed them—the unfortunate victims of shipwreck. The fishers approached the rock with an extreme timidity: but their harvest appears to have been great, and the adventure no more perilous than lucrative. In 1800, on the occasion of my grandfather's first landing, and during the two or three hours which the ebb-tide and the smooth water allowed them to pass upon its shelves, his crew collected upwards of two hundredweight of old metal: pieces of a kedge anchor and a cabin stove, crowbars, a hinge and lock of a door, a ship's marking-iron, a piece of a ship's caboose, a soldier's bayonet, a cannon ball, several pieces of money, a shoe-buckle, and the like. Such were the spoils of the Bell Rock. But the number of vessels actually lost upon the reef was as nothing to those that were cast away in fruitless efforts to avoid it. Placed right in the fairway of two navigations, and one of these the entrance to the only harbour of refuge between the Downs and the Moray Firth, it breathed abroad along the whole coast an atmosphere of terror and perplexity; and no ship sailed that part of the North Sea at night, but what the ears of those on board would be strained to catch the roaring of the seas on the Bell Rock.

From 1794 onward, the mind of my grandfather had been exercised with the idea of a light upon this formidable danger. To build a tower on a sea rock, eleven miles from shore, and barely uncovered at low water of neaps, appeared a fascinating enterprise. It was something yet unattempted, unessayed; and even now, after it has been lighted for more than eighty years, it is still an exploit that has never been repeated.* My grandfather was, besides, but a young man,

* The particular event which concentrated Mr. Stevenson's attention on the problem of the Bell Rock was the memorable gale of December, 1799, when, among many other vessels, H.M.S. *York*, a seventy-four gun ship, went down with all hands on board. Shortly after this disaster, Mr. Stevenson made a careful survey, and prepared his models for a stone tower, the idea of which was at first received with pretty general scepticism. Smeaton's Eddystone tower could not be cited as

BUILDING OF BELL ROCK

an experience comparatively restricted, and a reputation
nfined to Scotland; and when he prepared his first models,
d exhibited them in Merchants' Hall, he can hardly be
quitted of audacity. John Clerk of Eldin stood his friend
om the beginning, kept the key of the model room, to
ich he carried "eminent strangers," and found words
counsel and encouragement beyond price. "Mr. Clerk
d been personally known to Smeaton, and used occa-
nally to speak of him to me," says my grandfather; and
ain: "I felt regret that I had not the opportunity of a
eater range of practice to fit me for such an undertaking;
t I was fortified by an expression of my friend Mr. Clerk
one of our conversations. 'This work,' said he, 'is unique,
d can be little forwarded by experience of ordinary ma-
nic operations. In this case Smeaton's "Narrative" must
the text-book, and energy and perseverance the
atique.'"
A Bill for the work was introduced into Parliament and
rt in the Lords in 1802-3. John Rennie was afterwards,
my grandfather's suggestion, called in council, with the
yle of chief engineer. The precise meaning attached to
ese words by any of the parties appears irrecoverable.
ief engineer should have full authority, full responsibility,
d a proper share of the emoluments; and there were
ne of these for Rennie. I find in an appendix a paper
ich resumes the controversy on this subject; and it will
enough to say here that Rennie did not design the Bell
ock, that he did not execute it, and that he was not paid
r it.* From so much of the correspondence as has come

'ording a parallel, for there the rock is not submerged even at high-
ter, while the problem of the Bell Rock was to build a tower of
sonry on a sunken reef far distant from land, covered at every tide
a depth of twelve feet or more, and having thirty-two fathoms' depth
water within a mile of its eastern edge.
* The grounds for the rejection of the Bill by the House of Lords in
02-3 had been that the extent of coast over which dues were pro-
sed to be levied would be too great. Before going to Parliament
ain, the Board of Northern Lights, desiring to obtain support and
rroboration for Mr. Stevenson's views, consulted first Telford, who
s unable to give the matter his attention, and then (on Stevenson's

A FAMILY OF ENGINEERS

down to me, the acquaintance of this man, eleven years his senior, and already famous, appears to have been both useful and agreeable to Robert Stevenson. It is amusing to find my grandfather seeking high and low for a brace of pistols which his colleague had lost by the way between Aberdeen and Edinburgh; and writing to Messrs. Dollond, " I have not thought it necessary to trouble Mr. Rennie with this order, but *I beg you will see to get two minutes of him as he passes your door* "—a proposal calculated rather from the latitude of Edinburgh than from London, even in 1807. It is pretty, too, to observe with what affectionate regard Smeaton was held in mind by his immediate successors. " Poor old fellow," writes Rennie to Stevenson, " I hope he will now and then take a peep at us, and inspire you with fortitude and courage to brave all difficulties and dangers to accomplish a work which will, if successful, immortalize you in the annals of fame." The style might be bettered, but the sentiment is charming.

Smeaton was, indeed, the patron saint of the Bell Rock. Undeterred by the sinister fate of Winstanley, he had tackled and solved the problem of the Eddystone; but his solution had not been in all respects perfect. It remained for my grandfather to outdo him in daring, by applying to a tidal rock those principles which had been already justified by suggestion) Rennie, who concurred in affirming the practicability of a stone tower, and supported the Bill when it came again before Parliament in 1806. Rennie was afterwards appointed by the Commissioners as advising engineer, whom Stevenson might consult in cases of emergency. It seems certain that the title of chief engineer had in this instance no more meaning than the above. Rennie, in point of fact, proposed certain modifications in Stevenson's plans, which the latter did not accept; nevertheless Rennie continued to take a kindly interest in the work, and the two engineers remained in friendly correspondence during its progress. The official view taken by the Board as to the quarter in which lay both the merit and the responsibility of the work may be gathered from a minute of the Commissioners at their first meeting held after Stevenson died; in which they record their regret " at the death of this zealous, faithful, and able officer, *to whom is due the honour of conceiving and executing the Bell Rock Lighthouse.*" The matter is briefly summed up in the *Life* of Robert Stevenson by his son David Stevenson (A. & C. Black, 1878), and fully discussed, on the basis of official facts and figures, by the same writer in a letter to the *Civil Engineers' and Architects' Journal*, 1862.

BUILDING OF BELL ROCK

the success of the Eddystone, and to perfect the model by more than one exemplary departure. Smeaton had adopted in his floors the principle of the arch; each therefore exercised an outward thrust upon the walls, which must be met and combated by embedded chains. My grandfather's flooring-stones, on the other hand, were flat, made part of the outer wall, and were keyed and dovetailed into a central stone, so as to bind the work together and be positive elements of strength. In 1703 Winstanley still thought it possible to erect his strange pagoda, with its open gallery, its florid scrolls and candlesticks: like a rich man's folly for an ornamental water in a park. Smeaton followed; then Stevenson in his turn corrected such flaws as were left in Smeaton's design; and with his improvements, it is not too much to say that the model was made perfect. Smeaton and Stevenson had between them evolved and finished the sea-tower. No subsequent builder has departed in anything essential from the principles of their design. It remains, and it seems to us as though it must remain for ever, an ideal attained. Every stone in the building, it may interest the reader to know, my grandfather had himself cut out in the model; and the manner in which the courses were fitted, joggled, trenailed, wedged, and the bond broken, is intricate as a puzzle and beautiful by ingenuity.

In 1806 a second Bill passed both Houses, and the preliminary works were at once begun. The same year the Navy had taken a great harvest of prizes in the North Sea, one of which, a Prussian fishing dogger, flat-bottomed and rounded at the stem and stern, was purchased to be a floating lightship, and re-named the *Pharos*. By July 1807 she was overhauled, rigged for her new purpose, and turned into the lee of the Isle of May. " It was proposed that the whole party should meet in her and pass the night; but she rolled from side to side in so extraordinary a manner that even the most sea-hardy fled. It was humorously observed of this vessel that she was in danger of making a round turn and appearing with her keel uppermost; and that she would even turn a halfpenny if laid upon deck," By two o'clock on the

A FAMILY OF ENGINEERS

morning of the 15th July this purgatorial vessel was moored by the Bell Rock.

A sloop of forty tons had been in the meantime built at Leith, and named the *Smeaton*; by the 7th of August my grandfather set sail in her—

"carrying with him Mr. Peter Logan, foreman builder, and five artificers selected from their having been somewhat accustomed to the sea, the writer being aware of the distressing trial which the floating light would necessarily inflict upon landsmen from her rolling motion. Here he remained till the 19th, and, as the weather was favourable, a landing was effected daily, when the workmen were employed in cutting the large seaweed from the sites of the lighthouse and beacon, which were respectively traced with pickaxes upon the rock. In the meantime the crew of the *Smeaton* was employed in laying down the several sets of moorings within about half a mile of the rock for the convenience of vessels. The artificers, having, fortunately, experienced moderate weather, returned to the workyard of Arbroath with a good report of their treatment afloat; when their comrades ashore began to feel some anxiety to see a place of which they had heard so much, and to change the constant operations with the iron and mallet in the process of hewing for an occasional tide's work on the rock, which they figured to themselves as a state of comparative ease and comfort."

I am now for many pages to let my grandfather speak for himself, and tell in his own words the story of his capital achievement. The tall quarto of 533 pages from which the following narrative has been dug out is practically unknown to the general reader, yet good judges have perceived its merit, and it has been named (with flattering wit) "The Romance of Stone and Lime" and "The Robinson Crusoe of Civil Engineering." The tower was but four years in the building; it took Robert Stevenson, in the midst of his many avocations, no less than fourteen years to prepare the *Account*. The title-page is a solid piece of literature of upwards of a hundred words; the table of contents runs to thirteen pages; and the dedication (to that revered monarch, George IV.) must have cost him no little study and correspondence. Walter Scott was called in council, and offered one miscorrection which still blots the page. In spite of all this pondering and filing, there remain pages not easy to construe, and inconsistencies not easy to explain away. I have sought to make these disappear, and to

BUILDING OF BELL ROCK

lighten a little the baggage with which my grandfather marches; here and there I have rejointed and rearranged a sentence, always in his own words, and all with a reverent and faithful hand; and I offer here to the reader the true monument of Robert Stevenson with a little of the moss removed from the inscription, and the Portrait of the artist with some superfluous canvas cut away.

OPERATIONS OF 1807

Sunday, 16th Aug.—Everything being arranged for sailing to the rock on Saturday the 15th, the vessel might have proceeded on the Sunday; but understanding that this would not be so agreeable to the artificers it was deferred until Monday. Here we cannot help observing that the men allotted for the operations at the rock seemed to enter upon the undertaking with a degree of consideration which fully marked their opinion as to the hazardous nature of the undertaking on which they were about to enter. They went in a body to church on Sunday, and whether it was in the ordinary course, or designed for the occasion, the writer is not certain, but the service was, in many respects, suitable to their circumstances.

Monday, 17th Aug.—The tide happening to fall late in the evening of Monday the 17th, the party, counting twenty-four in number, embarked on board of the *Smeaton* about ten o'clock P. M., and sailed from Arbroath with a gentle breeze at west. Our ship's colours having been flying all day in compliment to the commencement of the work, the other vessels in the harbour also saluted, which made a very gay appearance. A number of the friends and acquaintances of those on board having been thus collected, the piers, though at a late hour, were perfectly crowded, and, just as the *Smeaton* cleared the harbour, all on board united in giving three hearty cheers, which were returned by those on shore in such good earnest, that, in the still of the even-

A FAMILY OF ENGINEERS

ing, the sound must have been heard in all parts of the town, re-echoing from the walls and lofty turrets of the venerable Abbey of Aberbrothwick. The writer felt much satisfaction at the manner of this parting scene, though he must own that the present rejoicing was, on his part, mingled with occasional reflections upon the responsibility of his situation, which extended to the safety of all who should be engaged in this perilous work. With such sensations he retired to his cabin; but, as the artificers were rather inclined to move about the deck than to remain in their confined berths below, his repose was transient, and the vessel being small every motion was necessarily heard. Some who were musically inclined occasionally sung; but he listened with peculiar pleasure to the sailor at the helm, who hummed over Dibdin's characteristic air:—

> "They say there's a Providence sits up aloft,
> To keep watch for the life of poor Jack."

Tuesday, 18*th Aug.*—The weather had been very gentle all night, and, about four in the morning of the 18th, the *Smeaton* anchored. Agreeably to an arranged plan of operations, all hands were called at five o'clock A. M., just as the highest part of the Bell Rock began to show its sable head among the light breakers, which occasionally whitened with the foaming sea. The two boats belonging to the floating light attended the *Smeaton*, to carry the artificers to the rock, as her boat could only accommodate about six or eight sitters. Every one was more eager than his neighbour to leap into the boats, and it required a good deal of management on the part of the coxswains to get men unaccustomed to a boat to take their places for rowing and at the same time trimming her properly. The landing-master and foreman went into one boat, while the writer took charge of another, and steered it to and from the rock. This became the more necessary in the early stages of the work, as places could not be spared for more than two, or at most three, seamen to each boat, who were always sta-

BUILDING OF BELL ROCK

tioned, one at the bow, to use the boat-hook in fending or pushing off, and the other at the aftermost oar, to give the proper time in rowing, while the middle oars were double-banked, and rowed by the artificers.

As the weather was extremely fine, with light airs of wind from the east, we landed without difficulty upon the central part of the rock at half-past five, but the water had not yet sufficiently left it for commencing the work. This interval, however, did not pass unoccupied. The first and last of all the principal operations at the Bell Rock were accompanied by three hearty cheers from all hands, and, on occasions like the present, the steward of the ship attended, when each man was regaled with a glass of rum. As the water left the rock about six, some began to bore the holes for the great bats or holdfasts, for fixing the beams of the Beacon-house, while the smith was fully attended in laying out the site of his forge, upon a somewhat sheltered spot of the rock, which also recommended itself from the vicinity of a pool of water for tempering his irons. These preliminary steps occupied about an hour, and, as nothing further could be done during this tide towards fixing the forge, the workmen gratified their curiosity by roaming about the rock, which they investigated with great eagerness till the tide overflowed it. Those who had been sick picked dulse (*Fucus palmatus*), which they ate with much seeming appetite; others were more intent upon collecting limpets for bait, to enjoy the amusement of fishing when they returned on board of the vessel. Indeed, none came away empty-handed, as everything found upon the Bell Rock was considered valuable, being connected with some interesting association. Several coins, and numerous bits of shipwrecked iron, were picked up, of almost every description; and, in particular, a marking-iron lettered JAMES—a circumstance of which it was thought proper to give notice to the public, as it might lead to the knowledge of some unfortunate shipwreck, perhaps unheard of till this simple occurrence led to the discovery. When the rock began to be overflowed, the landing-master arranged the crews of the respective boats, appointing

A FAMILY OF ENGINEERS

twelve persons to each. According to a rule which the writer had laid down to himself, he was always the last person who left the rock.

In a short time the Bell Rock was laid completely under water, and the weather being extremely fine, the sea was so smooth that its place could not be pointed out from the appearance of the surface—a circumstance which sufficiently demonstrates the dangerous nature of this rock, even during the day, and in the smoothest and calmest state of the sea. During the interval between the morning and the evening tides, the artificers were variously employed in fishing and reading; others were busy in drying and adjusting their wet clothes, and one or two amused their companions with the violin and German flute.

About seven in the evening the signal bell for landing on the rock was again rung, when every man was at his quarters. In this service it was thought more appropriate to use the bell than to *pipe* to quarters, as the use of this instrument is less known to the mechanic than the sound of the bell. The landing, as in the morning, was at the eastern harbour. During this tide the seaweed was pretty well cleared from the site of the operations, and also from the tracks leading to the different landing-places; for walking upon the rugged surface of the Bell Rock, when covered with seaweed, was found to be extremely difficult, and even dangerous. Every hand that could possibly be occupied was now employed in assisting the smith to fit up the apparatus for his forge. At 9 P.M. the boats returned to the tender, after other two hours' work, in the same order as formerly —perhaps as much gratified with the success that attended the work of this day as with any other in the whole course of the operations. Although it could not be said that the fatigues of this day had been great, yet all on board retired early to rest. The sea being calm, and no movement on deck, it was pretty generally remarked in the morning that the bell awakened the greater number on board from their first sleep; and, though this observation was not altogether applicable to the writer himself, yet he was not a little pleased

BUILDING OF BELL ROCK

to find that thirty people could all at once become so reconciled to a night's quarters within a few hundred paces of the Bell Rock.

Wednesday, 19th Aug.—Being extremely anxious at this time to get forward with fixing the smith's forge, on which the progress of the work at present depended, the writer requested that he might be called at daybreak to learn the landing-master's opinion of the weather from the appearance of the rising sun, a criterion by which experienced seamen can generally judge pretty accurately of the state of the weather for the following day. About five o'clock, on coming upon deck, the sun's upper limb or disc had just begun to appear as if rising from the ocean, and in less than a minute he was seen in the fullest splendour; but after a short interval he was enveloped in a soft cloudy sky, which was considered emblematical of fine weather. His rays had not yet sufficiently dispelled the clouds which hid the land from view, and the Bell Rock being still overflowed, the whole was one expanse of water. This scene in itself was highly gratifying; and, when the morning bell was tolled, we were gratified with the happy forebodings of good weather and the expectation of having both a morning and an evening tide's work on the rock.

The boat which the writer steered happened to be the last which approached the rock at this tide; and, in standing up in the stern, while at some distance, to see how the leading boat entered the creek, he was astonished to observe something in the form of a human figure, in a reclining posture, upon one of the ledges of the rock. He immediately steered the boat through a narrow entrance to the eastern harbour, with a thousand unpleasant sensations in his mind. He thought a vessel or boat must have been wrecked upon the rock during the night; and it seemed probable that the rock might be strewed with dead bodies, a spectacle which could not fail to deter the artificers from returning so freely to their work. In the midst of these reveries the boat took the ground at an improper landing-place, but, without waiting to push her off, he leapt upon the rock, and making his way

A FAMILY OF ENGINEERS

hastily to the spot which had privately given him alarm, he had the satisfaction to ascertain that he had only been deceived by the peculiar situation and aspect of the smith's anvil and block, which very completely represented the appearance of a lifeless body upon the rock. The writer carefully suppressed his feelings, the simple mention of which might have had a bad effect upon the artificers, and his haste passed for an anxiety to examine the apparatus of the smith's forge, left in an unfinished state at evening tide.

In the course of this morning's work two or three apparently distant peals of thunder were heard, and the atmosphere suddenly became thick and foggy. But as the *Smeaton*, our present tender, was moored at no great distance from the rock, the crew on board continued blowing with a horn, and occasionally fired a musket, so that the boats got to the ship without difficulty.

Thursday, 20th Aug.—The wind this morning inclined from the north-east, and the sky had a heavy and cloudy appearance, but the sea was smooth, though there was an undulating motion on the surface, which indicated easterly winds, and occasioned a slight surf upon the rock. But the boats found no difficulty in landing at the western creek at half-past seven, and, after a good tide's work, left it again about a quarter from eleven. In the evening the artificers landed at half-past seven, and continued till half-past eight, having completed the fixing of the smith's forge, his vice, and a wooden board or bench, which were also batted to a ledge of the rock, to the great joy of all, under a salute of three hearty cheers. From an oversight on the part of the smith, who had neglected to bring his tinder-box and matches from the vessel, the work was prevented from being continued for at least an hour longer.

The smith's shop was, of course, in *open space:* the large bellows were carried to and from the rock every tide, for the serviceable condition of which, together with the tinder-box, fuel, and embers of the former fire, the smith was held responsible. Those who have been placed in situations to feel the inconveniency and want of this useful artisan, will be able to appreciate his value in a case like the present. It often happened, to our annoyance and disappointment, in the early state of the work, when the smith was in the middle of a *favourite heat* in making some useful article, or in sharpening the tools, after the flood-tide had obliged the pickmen to strike work, a sea would come rolling over the rocks, dash out the fire, and endanger his indispensable implement, the bellows. If the sea was smooth, while the smith often stood at work knee-deep in water, the tide rose by imperceptible degrees, first cooling the exterior of the fireplace, or hearth, and then quietly blackening and extinguishing the fire from below. The writer has frequently been amused at the perplexing anxiety of the blacksmith when coaxing his fire and endeavouring to avert the effects of the rising tide.

Friday, 21st Aug.—Everything connected with the forge being now completed, the artificers found no want of sharp tools, and the work went forward with great alacrity and spirit. It was also alleged that the rock had a more habitable appearance from the volumes of smoke which ascended from the smith's shop and the busy noise of his anvil, the operations of the masons, the movements of the boats, and shipping at a distance—all contributed to give life and activity to the scene. This noise and traffic had, however, the effect of almost completely banishing the herd of seals which had hitherto frequented the rock as a resting-place during the period of low water. The rock seemed to be peculiarly adapted to their habits, for, excepting two or three days at neap-tides, a part of it always dries at low water—at least, during the summer season—and as there was good fishing-ground in the neighbourhood, without a human being to disturb or molest them, it had become a very favourite residence of these amphibious animals, the writer having occasionally counted from fifty to sixty playing about the rock at a time. But when they came to be disturbed every tide, and their seclusion was broken in upon by the kindling of great fires, together with the beating of hammers and picks during low water, after hovering about

A FAMILY OF ENGINEERS

for a time, they changed their place, and seldom more than one or two were to be seen about the rock upon the more detached outlayers which dry partially, whence they seemed to look with that sort of curiosity which is observable in these animals when following a boat.

Saturday, 22nd Aug.—Hitherto the artificers had remained on board of the *Smeaton*, which was made fast to one of the mooring buoys at a distance only of about a quarter of a mile from the rock, and, of course, a very great conveniency to the work. Being so near, the seamen could never be mistaken as to the progress of the tide, or state of the sea upon the rock, nor could the boats be much at a loss to pull on board of the vessel during fog, or even in very rough weather; as she could be cast loose from her moorings at pleasure, and brought to the lee side of the rock. But the *Smeaton* being only about forty register tons, her accommodations were extremely limited. It may, therefore, be easily imagined that an addition of twenty-four persons to her own crew must have rendered the situation of those on board rather uncomfortable. The only place for the men's hammocks on board being in the hold, they were unavoidably much crowded; and if the weather had required the hatches to be fastened down, so great a number of men could not possibly have been accommodated. To add to this evil, the caboose or cooking-place being upon deck, it would not have been possible to have cooked for so large a company in the event of bad weather.

The stock of water was now getting short, and some necessaries being also wanted for the floating light, the *Smeaton* was despatched for Arbroath; and the writer, with the artificers, at the same time shifted their quarters from her to the floating light.

Although the rock barely made its appearance at this period of the tides till eight o'clock, yet, having now a full mile to row from the floating light to the rock, instead of about a quarter of a mile from the moorings of the *Smeaton*, it was necessary to be earlier astir, and to form different arrangements; breakfast was accordingly served up at seven

BUILDING OF BELL ROCK

o'clock this morning. From the excessive motion of the floating light, the writer had looked forward rather with anxiety to the removal of the workmen to this ship. Some among them, who had been congratulating themselves upon having become sea-hardy while on board of the *Smeaton*, had complete relapse on returning to the floating light. This was the case with the writer. From the spacious and convenient berthage of the floating light, the exchange to the artificers was, in this respect, much for the better. The boats were also commodious, measuring sixteen feet in length on the keel, so that, in fine weather, their complement of sitters was sixteen persons for each, with which, however, they were rather crowded, but she could not stow two boats of larger dimensions. When there was what is called a breeze of wind, and a swell in the sea, the proper number for each boat could not, with propriety, be rated at more than twelve persons.

When the tide-bell rung the boats were hoisted out, and two active seamen were employed to keep them from receiving damage alongside. The floating light being very buoyant, was so quick in her motions that when those who were about to step from her gunwale into a boat, placed themselves upon a cleat or step on the ship's side, with the man or rail ropes in their hands, they had often to wait for some time till a favourable opportunity occurred for stepping into the boat. While in this situation, with the vessel rolling from side to side, watching the proper time for letting go the man-ropes, it required the greatest dexterity and presence of mind to leap into the boats. One who was rather awkward would often wait a considerable period in this position: at one time his side of the ship would be so depressed that he would touch the boat to which he belonged, while the next sea would elevate him so much that he would see his comrades in the boat on the opposite side of the ship, his friends in the one boat calling him to "Jump," while those in the boat on the other side, as he came again and again into their view, would jocosely say "Are you there yet? You seem to enjoy a swing." In this situation it was com-

A FAMILY OF ENGINEERS

mon to see a person upon each side of the ship for a length of time, waiting to quit his hold.

On leaving the rock to-day a trial of seamanship was proposed amongst the rowers, for by this time the artificers had become tolerably expert in this exercise. By inadvertency some of the oars provided had been made of fir instead of ash, and although a considerable stock had been laid in, the workmen, being at first awkward in the art, were constantly breaking their oars; indeed it was no uncommon thing to see the broken blades of a pair of oars floating astern, in the course of a passage from the rock to the vessel. The men, upon the whole, had but little work to perform in the course of a day; for though they exerted themselves extremely hard while on the rock, yet, in the early state of the operations, this could not be continued for more than three or four hours at a time, and as their rations were large—consisting of one pound and a half of beef, one pound of ship biscuit, eight ounces oatmeal, two ounces barley, two ounces butter, three quarts of small beer, with vegetables and salt—they got into excellent spirits when free of sea-sickness. The rowing of the boats against each other became a favourite amusement, which was rather a fortunate circumstance, as it must have been attended with much inconvenience had it been found necessary to employ a sufficient number of sailors for this purpose. The writer, therefore, encouraged this spirit of emulation, and the speed of their respective boats became a favourite topic. Premiums for boat-races were instituted, which were contended for with great eagerness, and the respective crews kept their stations in the boats with as much precision as they kept their beds on board of the ship. With these and other pastimes, when the weather was favourable, the time passed away among the inmates of the forecastle and waist of the ship. The writer looks back with interest upon the hours of solitude which he spent in this lonely ship with his small library.

This being the first Saturday that the artificers were afloat, all hands were served with a glass of rum and water at night, to drink the sailors' favourite toast of " Wives and Sweethearts." It was customary, upon these occasions, for the seamen and artificers to collect in the galley, when the musical instruments were put in requisition: for, according to invariable practice, every man must play a tune, sing a song, or tell a story.

Sunday, 23rd Aug.—Having, on the previous evening, arranged matters with the landing-master as to the business of the day, the signal was rung for all hands at half-past seven this morning. In the early state of the spring-tides the artificers went to the rock before breakfast, but as the tides fell later in the day, it became necessary to take this meal before leaving the ship. At eight o'clock all hands were assembled on the quarter-deck for prayers, a solemnity which was gone through in as orderly a manner as circumstances would admit. When the weather permitted, the flags of the ship were hung up as an awning or screen, forming the quarter-deck into a distinct compartment; the pendant was also hoisted at the mainmast, and a large ensign flag was displayed over the stern; and lastly, the ship's companion, or top of the staircase, was covered with the *flag proper* of the Lighthouse Service, on which the Bible was laid. A particular toll of the bell called all hands to the quarter-deck, when the writer read a chapter of the Bible, and, the whole ship's company being uncovered, he also read the impressive prayer composed by the Reverend Dr. Brunton, one of the ministers of Edinburgh.

Upon concluding this service, which was attended with becoming reverence and attention, all on board retired to their respective berths to breakfast, and, at half-past nine, the bell again rung for the artificers to take their stations in their respective boats. Some demur having been evinced on board about the propriety of working on Sunday, which had hitherto been touched upon as delicately as possible, all hands being called aft, the writer, from the quarter-deck, stated generally the nature of the service, expressing his hopes that every man would feel himself called upon to consider the erection of a lighthouse on the Bell Rock, in every point of view, as a work of necessity and mercy. He knew that scruples had existed with some, and these had, indeed, been fairly and candidly urged before leaving the shore; but it was expected that, after having seen the critical nature of the rock, and the necessity of the measure, every man would now be satisfied of the propriety of embracing all opportunities of landing on the rock when the state of the weather would permit. The writer further took them to witness that it did not proceed from want of respect for the appointments and established forms of religion that he had himself adopted the resolution of attending the Bell Rock works on the Sunday; but, as he hoped, from a conviction that it was his bounden duty, on the strictest principles of morality. At the same time it was intimated that, if any were of a different opinion, they should be perfectly at liberty to hold their sentiments without the imputation of contumacy or disobedience; the only difference would be in regard to the pay.

Upon stating this much, he stepped into his boat, requesting all who were so disposed to follow him. The sailors, from their habits, found no scruple on this subject, and all of the artificers, though a little tardy, also embarked, excepting four of the masons, who, from the beginning, mentioned that they would decline working on Sundays. It may here be noticed that throughout the whole of the operations it was observable that the men wrought, if possible, with more keenness upon the Sundays than at other times, from an impression that they were engaged in a work of imperious necessity, which required every possible exertion. On returning to the floating light, after finishing the tide's work, the boats were received by the part of the ship's crew left on board with the usual attention of handing ropes to the boats and helping the artificers on board; but the four masons who had absented themselves from the work did not appear upon deck.

The boats left the floating light at a quarter-past nine o'clock this morning, and the work began at three-quarters past nine; but as the neap-tides were approaching the working time at the rock became gradually shorter, and it was

BUILDING OF BELL ROCK

now with difficulty that two and a half hours' work could be got. But so keenly had the workmen entered into the spirit of the Beacon-house operations, that they continued to bore the holes in the rock till some of them were knee-deep in water.

Monday, 24th Aug.—The operations at this time were entirely directed to the erection of the beacon, in which every man felt an equal interest, as at this critical period the slightest casualty to any of the boats at the rock might have been fatal to himself individually, while it was perhaps peculiar to the writer more immediately to feel for the safety of the whole. Each log or upright beam of the beacon was to be fixed to the rock by two strong and massive bats or stanchions of iron. These bats, for the fixture of the principal and diagonal beams and bracing chains, required fifty-four holes, each measuring two inches in diameter, and eighteen inches in depth. There had already been so considerable a progress made in boring and excavating the holes that the writer's hopes of getting the beacon erected this year began to be more and more confirmed, although it was now advancing towards what was considered the latter end of the proper working season at the Bell Rock. The foreman joiner, Mr. Francis Watt, was accordingly appointed to attend at the rock to-day, when the necessary levels were taken for the step or seat of each particular beam of the beacon, that they might be cut to their respective lengths, to suit the inequalities of the rock; several of the stanchions were also tried into their places, and other necessary observations made, to prevent mistakes on the application of the apparatus, and to facilitate the operations when the beams came to be set up, which would require to be done in the course of a single tide.

Tuesday, 25th Aug.—We had now experienced an almost unvaried tract of light airs of easterly wind, with clear weather in the fore-part of the day, and fog in the evenings. To-day, however, it sensibly changed; when the wind came to the south-west, and blew a fresh breeze. At nine a. m. the bell rung, and the boats were hoisted out, and though

A FAMILY OF ENGINEERS

the artificers were now pretty well accustomed to tripping up and down the sides of the floating light, yet it required more seamanship this morning than usual. It therefore afforded some merriment to those who had got fairly seated in their respective boats to see the difficulties which attended their companions, and the hesitating manner in which they quitted hold of the man-ropes in leaving the ship. The passage to the rock was tedious, and the boats did not reach it till half-past ten.

It being now the period of neap-tides, the water only partially left the rock and some of the men who were boring on the lower ledges of the site of the beacon stood knee-deep in water.

The situation of the smith to-day was particularly disagreeable, but his services were at all times indispensable. As the tide did not leave the site of the forge, he stood in the water, and as there was some roughness on the surface it was with considerable difficulty that, with the assistance of the sailors, he was enabled to preserve alive his fire; and, while his feet were immersed in water, his face was not only scorched, but continually exposed to volumes of smoke, accompanied with sparks from the fire, which were occasionally set up owing to the strength and direction of the wind.

Wednesday, 26th Aug.—The wind had shifted this morning to N.N.W., with rain, and was blowing what sailors call a fresh breeze. To speak, perhaps, somewhat more intelligibly, to the general reader, the wind was such that a fishing-boat could just carry full sail. But as it was of importance, specially in the outset of the business, to keep up the spirit of enterprise for landing on all practical occasions, the writer, after consulting with the landing-master, ordered the bell to be rung for embarking, and at half-past eleven the boats reached the rock, and left it again at a quarter-past twelve, without, however, being able to do much work, as the smith could not be set to work from the smallness of the ebb and the strong breach of sea, which lashed with great force among the bars of the forge.

Just as we were about to leave the rock the wind shifted

BUILDING OF BELL ROCK

the S.W., and, from a fresh gale, it became what seamen
rm a hard gale, or such as would have required the fisher-
an to take in two or three reefs in his sail. It is a curious
ct that the respective tides of ebb and flood are apparent
on the shore about an hour and a half sooner than at the
stance of three or four miles in the offing. But what seems
iefly interesting here is that the tides around this small
mken rock should follow exactly the same laws as on the ex-
nsive shores of the mainland. When the boats left the Bell
ock to-day it was overflowed by the flood-tide, but the float-
g light did not swing round to the flood-tide for more
an an hour afterwards. Under this disadvantage the boats
id to struggle with the ebb-tide and a hard gale of wind,
that it was with the greatest difficulty they reached the
ating light. Had this gale happened in spring-tides when
e current was strong we must have been driven to sea in
very helpless condition.

The boat which the writer steered was considerably behind
e other, one of the masons having unluckily broken his
ir. Our prospect of getting on board, of course, became
ubtful, and our situation was rather perilous, as the boat
ipped so much sea that it occupied two of the artificers
bale and clear her of water. When the oar gave way we
ere about half a mile from the ship, but, being fortunately
windward, we got into the wake of the floating light, at
out 250 fathoms astern, just as the landing-master's boat
ached the vessel. He immediately streamed or floated a
e-buoy astern, with a line which was always in readiness,
id by means of this useful implement the boat was towed
ongside of the floating light, where, from her rolling
otion, it required no small management to get safely on
ard, as the men were much worn out with their exertions
pulling from the rock. On the present occasion the crews
both boats were completely drenched with spray, and
ose who sat upon the bottom of the boats to bale them
are sometimes pretty deep in the water before it could be
ared out. After getting on board, all hands were allowed
extra dram, and, having shifted and got a warm and

335

A FAMILY OF ENGINEERS

comfortable dinner, the affair, it is believed, was little more thought of.

Thursday, 27th Aug.—The tides were now in that state which sailors term the dead of the neap, and it was not expected that any part of the rock would be seen above water to-day; at any rate, it was obvious, from the experience of yesterday, that no work could be done upon it, and therefore the artificers were not required to land. The wind was at west, with light breezes, and fine clear weather; and as it was an object with the writer to know the actual state of the Bell Rock at neap-tides, he got one of the boats manned, and, being accompanied by the landing-master, went to it at a quarter-past twelve. The parts of the rock that appeared above water being very trifling, were covered by every wave, so that no landing was made. Upon trying the depth of water with a boat-hook, particularly on the sites of the lighthouse and beacon, on the former, at low water, the depth was found to be three feet, and on the central parts of the latter it was ascertained to be two feet eight inches. Having made these remarks, the boat returned to the ship at two p.m., and the weather being good, the artificers were found amusing themselves with fishing. The *Smeaton* came from Arbroath this afternoon, and made fast to her moorings, having brought letters and newspapers, with parcels of clean linen, etc., for the workmen, who were also made happy by the arrival of three of their comrades from the workyard ashore. From these men they not only received all the news of the workyard, but seemed themselves to enjoy great pleasure in communicating whatever they considered to be interesting with regard to the rock. Some also got letters from their friends at a distance, the postage of which for the men afloat was always free, so that they corresponded the more readily.

The site of the building having already been carefully traced out with the pick-axe, the artificers this day commenced the excavation of the rock for the foundation or first course of the lighthouse. Four men only were employed at this work, while twelve continued at the site of the beacon-house, at which every possible opportunity was embraced, till this essential part of the operations should be completed.

Wednesday, 2nd Sept.—The floating light's bell rung this morning at half-past four o'clock, as a signal for the boats to be got ready, and the landing took place at half-past five. In passing the *Smeaton* at her moorings near the rock, her boat followed with eight additional artificers who had come from Arbroath with her at last trip, but there being no room for them in the floating light's boats, they had continued on board. The weather did not look very promising in the morning, the wind blowing pretty fresh from W.S.W.: and had it not been that the writer calculated upon having a vessel so much at command, in all probability he would not have ventured to land. The *Smeaton* rode at what sailors call a *salvagee*, with a cross-head made fast to the floating buoy. This kind of attachment was found to be more convenient than the mode of passing the hawser through the ring of the buoy when the vessel was to be made fast. She had then only to be steered very close to the buoy, when the salvagee was laid hold of with a boat-hook, and the bight of the hawser thrown over the cross-head. But the salvagee, by this method, was always left at the buoy, and was, of course, more liable to chafe and wear than a hawser passed through the ring, which could be wattled with canvas, and shifted at pleasure. The salvagee and cross method is, however, much practised; but the experience of this morning showed it to be very unsuitable for vessels riding in an exposed situation for any length of time.

Soon after the artificers landed they commenced work; but the wind coming to blow hard, the *Smeaton's* boat and crew, who had brought their complement of eight men to the rock, went off to examine her riding ropes, and see that they were in proper order. The boat had no sooner reached the vessel than she went adrift, carrying the boat along with her. By the time that she was got round to make a tack towards the rock, she had drifted at least three miles to leeward, with the praamboat astern; and, having both the wind and a tide against her, the writer perceived, with no

A FAMILY OF ENGINEERS

little anxiety, that she could not possibly return to the rock till long after its being overflowed; for, owing to the anomaly of the tides formerly noticed, the Bell Rock is completely under water when the ebb abates to the offing.

In this perilous predicament, indeed, he found himself placed between hope and despair—but certainly the latter was by much the most predominant feeling of his mind—situate upon a sunken rock in the middle of the ocean, which, in the progress of the flood-tide, was to be laid under water to the depth of at least twelve feet in a stormy sea. There were this morning thirty-two persons in all upon the rock, with only two boats, whose complement, even in good weather, did not exceed twenty-four sitters; but to row to the floating-light with so much wind, and in so heavy a sea, a complement of eight men for each boat was as much as could, with propriety, be attempted, so that, in this way, about one-half of our number was unprovided for. Under these circumstances, had the writer ventured to dispatch one of the boats in expectation of either working the *Smeaton* sooner up towards the rock, or in hopes of getting her boat brought to our assistance, this must have given an immediate alarm to the artificers, each of whom would have insisted upon taking to his own boat, and leaving the eight artificers belonging to the *Smeaton* to their chance. Of course a scuffle might have ensued, and it is hard to say, in the ardour of men contending for life, where it might have ended. It has even been hinted to the writer that a party of the *pickmen* were determined to keep exclusively to their own boat against all hazards.

The unfortunate circumstance of the *Smeaton* and her boat having drifted was, for a considerable time, only known to the writer and to the landing-master, who removed to the farther point of the rock, where he kept his eye steadily upon the progress of the vessel. While the artificers were at work, chiefly in sitting or kneeling postures, excavating the rock, or boring with the jumpers, and while their numerous hammers, with the sound of the smith's anvil, continued, the situation of things did not appear so awful. In this

BUILDING OF BELL ROCK

state of suspense, with almost certain destruction at hand, the water began to rise upon those who were at work on the lower parts of the sites of the beacon and lighthouse. From the run of sea upon the rock, the forge fire was also sooner extinguished this morning than usual, and the volumes of smoke having ceased, objects in every direction became visible from all parts of the rock. After having had about three hours' work, the men began, pretty generally, to make towards their respective boats for their jackets and stockings, when, to their astonishment, instead of three, they found only two boats, the third being adrift with the *Smeaton*. Not a word was uttered by any one, but all appeared to be silently calculating their numbers, and looking to each other with evident marks of perplexity depicted in their countenances. The landing-master, conceiving that blame might be attached to him, for allowing the boat to leave the rock, still kept at a distance. At this critical moment the author was standing upon an elevated part of Smith's Ledge, where he endeavored to mark the progress of the *Smeaton*, not a little surprised that her crew did not cut the praam adrift, which greatly retarded her way, and amazed that some effort was not making to bring at least the boat, and attempt our relief. The workmen looked steadfastly upon the writer, and turned occasionally towards the vessel, still far to leeward.* All this passed in the most perfect silence, and the melancholy solemnity of the group made an impression never to be effaced from his mind.

The writer had all along been considering of various schemes—providing the men could be kept under command —which might be put in practice for the general safety, in hopes that the *Smeaton* might be able to pick up the boats to leeward, when they were obliged to leave the rock. He was, accordingly, about to address the artificers on the perilous nature of their circumstances, and to propose that all hands should unstrip their upper clothing when the higher parts of the rock were laid under water; that the seamen

* "Nothing was said, but I was *looked out of countenance*," he says in a letter.

A FAMILY OF ENGINEERS

should remove every unnecessary weight and encumbrance from the boats; that a specified number of men should go into each boat, and that the remainder should hang by the gunwales, while the boats were to be rowed gently towards the *Smeaton*, as the course to the *Pharos*, or floating light, lay rather to windward of the rock. But when he attempted to speak his mouth was so parched that his tongue refused utterance, and he now learned by experience that the saliva is as necessary as the tongue itself for speech. He turned to one of the pools on the rock and lapped a little water, which produced immediate relief. But what was his happiness, when on rising from this unpleasant beverage, some one called out, "A boat! a boat!" and, on looking around, at no great distance, a large boat was seen through the haze making towards the rock. This at once enlivened and rejoiced every heart. The timeous visitor proved to be James Spink, the Bell Rock pilot, who had come express from Arbroath with letters. Spink had for some time seen the *Smeaton*, and had even supposed, from the state of the weather, that all hands were on board of her till he approached more nearly and observed people upon the rock; but not supposing that the assistance of his boat was necessary to carry the artificers off the rock, he anchored on the lee-side and began to fish, waiting, as usual, till the letters were sent for, as the pilot-boat was too large and unwieldy for approaching the rock when there was any roughness or run of the sea at the entrance of the landing creeks.

Upon this fortunate change of circumstances, sixteen of the artificers were sent, at two trips, in one of the boats, with instructions for Spink to proceed with them to the floating light. This being accomplished, the remaining sixteen followed in the two boats belonging to the service of the rock. Every one felt the most perfect happiness at leaving the Bell Rock this morning, though a very hard and even dangerous passage to the floating light still awaited us, as the wind by this time had increased to a pretty hard gale, accompanied with a considerable swell of sea. Every one was as completely drenched in water as if he had been

BUILDING OF BELL ROCK

dragged astern of the boats. The writer, in particular, being at the helm, found, on getting on board, that his face and ears were completely coated with a thin film of salt from the sea spray, which broke constantly over the bows of the boat. After much baling of water and severe work at the oars, the three boats reached the floating light, where some new difficulties occurred in getting on board in safety, owing partly to the exhausted state of the men, and partly to the violent rolling of the vessel.

As the tide flowed, it was expected that the *Smeaton* would have got to windward; but, seeing that all was safe, after tacking for several hours and making little progress, she bore away for Arbroath, with the praam-boat. As there was now too much wind for the pilot-boat to return to Arbroath, she was made fast astern of the floating light, and the crew remained on board till next day, when the weather moderated. There can be very little doubt that the appearance of James Spink with his boat on this critical occasion was the means of preventing the loss of lives at the rock this morning. When these circumstances, some years afterwards, came to the knowledge of the Board, a small pension was ordered to our faithful pilot, then in his seventieth year; and he still continues to wear the uniform clothes and badge of the Lighthouse service. Spink is a remarkably strong man, whose *tout ensemble* is highly characteristic of a North country fisherman. He usually dresses in a pea-jacket cut after a particular fashion, and wears a large, flat, blue bonnet. A striking likeness of Spink in his pilot-dress, with the badge or insignia on his left arm which is characteristic of the boatmen in the service of the Northern Lights, has been taken by Howe, and is in the writer's possession.

Thursday, 3rd Sept.—The bell rung this morning at five o'clock, but the writer must acknowledge, from the circumstances of yesterday, that its sound was extremely unwelcome. This appears also to have been the feelings of the artificers, for when they came to be mustered, out of twenty-six, only eight, besides the foreman and seamen, appeared upon deck to accompany the writer to the rock. Such are

A FAMILY OF ENGINEERS

the baneful effects of anything like misfortune or accident connected with a work of this description. The use of argument to persuade the men to embark in cases of this kind would have been out of place, as it is not only discomfort, or even the risk of the loss of a limb, but life itself that becomes the question. The boats, notwithstanding the thinness of our ranks, left the vessel at half-past five. The rough weather of yesterday having proved but a summer's gale, the wind came to-day in gentle breezes; yet, the atmosphere being cloudy, it had not a very favourable appearance. The boats reached the rock at six a. m., and the eight artificers who landed were employed in clearing out the bat-holes for the beacon-house, and had a very prosperous tide of four hours' work, being the longest yet experienced by half an hour.

The boats left the rock again at ten o'clock, and the weather having cleared up as we drew near the vessel, the eighteen artificers who had remained on board were observed upon deck, but as the boats approached they sought their way below, being quite ashamed of their conduct. This was the only instance of refusal to go to the rock which occurred during the whole progress of the work, excepting that of the four men who declined working upon Sunday, a case which the writer did not conceive to be at all analogous to the present. It may here be mentioned, much to the credit of these four men, that they stood foremost in embarking for the rock this morning.

Saturday, 5th Sept.—It was fortunate that a landing was not attempted this evening, for at eight o'clock the wind shifted to E.S.E., and at ten it had become a hard gale, when fifty fathoms of the floating light's hempen cable were veered out. The gale still increasing, the ship rolled and laboured excessively, and at midnight eighty fathoms of cable were veered out; while the sea continued to strike the vessel with a degree of force which had not before been experienced.

Sunday, 6th Sept.—During the last night there was little rest on board of the *Pharos*, and daylight, though

BUILDING OF BELL ROCK

anxiously wished for, brought no relief, as the gale continued with unabated violence. The sea struck so hard upon the vessel's bows that it rose in great quantities, or in "green seas," as the sailors termed it, which were carried by the wind as far aft as the quarter-deck, and not unfrequently over the stern of the ship altogether. It fell occasionally so heavily on the skylight of the writer's cabin, though so far aft as to be within five feet of the helm, that the glass was broken to pieces before the dead-light could be got into its place, so that the water poured down in great quantities. In shutting out the water, the admission of light was prevented, and in the morning all continued in the most comfortless state of darkness. About ten o'clock a. m. the wind shifted to N.E., and blew, if possible, harder than before, and it was accompanied by a much heavier swell of sea. In the course of the gale, the part of the cable in the hawse-hole had been so often shifted that nearly the whole length of one of her hempen cables, of 120 fathoms, had been veered out, besides the chain-moorings. The cable, for its preservation, was also carefully served or wattled with pieces of canvas round the windlass, and with leather well greased in the hause-hole. In this state things remained during the whole day, every sea which struck the vessel—and the seas followed each other in close succession—causing her to shake, and all on board occasionally to tremble. At each of these strokes of the sea the rolling and pitching of the vessel ceased for a time, and her motion was felt as if she had either broke adrift before the wind or were in the act of sinking; but, when another sea came, she ranged up against it with great force, and this became the regular intimation of our being still riding at anchor.

About eleven o'clock, the writer with some difficulty got out of bed, but, in attempting to dress, he was thrown twice upon the floor at the opposite side of the cabin. In an undressed state he made shift to get about half-way up the companion-stairs, with an intention to observe the state of the sea and of the ship upon deck; but he no sooner looked over the companion than a heavy sea struck the vessel, which

A FAMILY OF ENGINEERS

fell on the quarter-deck, and rushed down-stairs into the officers' cabin in so considerable a quantity that it was found necessary to lift one of the scuttles in the floor, to let the water into the limbers of the ship, as it dashed from side to side in such a manner as to run into the lower tier of beds. Having been foiled in this attempt, and being completely wetted, he again got below and went to bed. In this state of the weather the seamen had to move about the necessary or indispensable duties of the ship with the most cautious use both of hands and feet, while it required all the art of the landsman to keep within the precincts of his bed. The writer even found himself so much tossed about that it became necessary, in some measure, to shut himself in bed, in order to avoid being thrown upon the floor. Indeed, such was the motion of the ship that it seemed wholly impracticable to remain in any other than a lying posture. On deck the most stormy aspect presented itself, while below all was wet and comfortless.

About two o'clock p. m. a great alarm was given throughout the ship from the effects of a very heavy sea which struck her, and almost filled the waist, pouring down into the berths below, through every chink and crevice of the hatches and skylights. From the motion of the vessel being thus suddenly deadened or checked, and from the flowing in of the water above, it is believed there was not an individual on board who did not think, at the moment, that the vessel had foundered, and was in the act of sinking. The writer could withstand this no longer, and as soon as she again began to range to the sea he determined to make another effort to get upon deck. In the first instance, however, he groped his way in darkness from his own cabin through the berths of the officers, where all was quietness. He next entered the galley and other compartments occupied by the artificers. Here also all was shut up in darkness, the fire having been drowned out in the early part of the gale. Several of the artificers were employed in prayer, repeating psalms, and other devotional exercises in a full tone of voice; others protesting that, if they should fortunately get once more

BUILDING OF BELL ROCK

on shore, no one should ever see them afloat again. With the assistance of the landing-master, the writer made his way, holding on step by step, among the numerous impediments which lay in the way. Such was the creaking noise of the bulkheads or partitions, the dashing of the water, and the whistling noise of the winds, that it was hardly possible to break in upon such a confusion of sounds. In one or two instances, anxious and repeated inquiries were made by the artificers as to the state of things upon deck, to which the captain made the usual answer, that it could not blow long in this way, and that we must soon have better weather. The next berth in succession, moving forward in the ship, was that allotted for the seamen. Here the scene was considerably different. Having reached the middle of this darksome berth without its inmates being aware of any intrusion, the writer had the consolation of remarking that, although they talked of bad weather and the cross accidents of the sea, yet the conversation was carried on in that sort of tone and manner which bespoke an ease and composure of mind highly creditable to them and pleasing to him. The writer immediately accosted the seamen about the state of the ship. To these inquiries they replied that the vessel being light, and having but little hold of the water, no top-rigging, with excellent ground-tackle, and everything being fresh and new, they felt perfect confidence in their situation.

It being impossible to open any of the hatches in the fore part of the ship in communicating with the deck, the watch was changed by passing through the several berths to the companion-stair leading to the quarter-deck. The writer, therefore, made the best of his way aft, and, on a second attempt to look out, he succeeded, and saw indeed an astonishing sight. The sea or waves appeared to be ten or fifteen feet in height of unbroken water, and every approaching billow seemed as if it would overwhelm our vessel, but she continued to rise upon the waves and to fall between the seas in a very wonderful manner. It seemed to be only those seas which caught her in the act of rising which struck her with so much violence and threw such quantities of water aft.

A FAMILY OF ENGINEERS

On deck there was only one solitary individual looking out, to give the alarm in the event of the ship breaking from her moorings. The seaman on watch continued only two hours; he who kept watch at this time was a tall, slender man of a black complexion; he had no greatcoat nor over-all of any kind, but was simply dressed in his ordinary jacket and trousers; his hat was tied under his chin with a napkin, and he stood aft the foremast, to which he had lashed himself with a gasket or small rope round his waist, to prevent his falling upon deck or being washed overboard. When the writer looked up, he appeared to smile, which afforded a further symptom of the confidence of the crew in their ship. This person on watch was as completely wetted as if he been drawn through the sea, which was given as a reason for his not putting on a greatcoat, that he might wet as few of his clothes as possible, and have a dry shift when he went below. Upon deck everything that was movable was out of sight, having either been stowed below, previous to the gale, or been washed overboard. Some trifling parts of the quarter boards were damaged by the breach of the sea; and one of the boats upon deck was about one-third full of water, the oylet-hole or drain having been accidentally stopped up, and part of her gunwale had received considerable injury. These observations were hastily made, and not without occasionally shutting the companion, to avoid being wetted by the successive seas which broke over the bows and fell upon different parts of the deck according to the impetus with which the waves struck the vessel. By this time it was about three o'clock in the afternoon, and the gale, which had now continued with unabated force for twenty-seven hours, had not the least appearance of going off.

In the dismal prospect of undergoing another night like the last, and being in imminent hazard of parting from our cable, the writer thought it necessary to advise with the master and officers of the ship as to the probable event of the vessel's drifting from her moorings. They severally gave it as their opinion that we had now every chance of riding out the gale, which, in all probability, could not con-

BUILDING OF BELL ROCK

tinue with the same fury many hours longer; and that even if she should part from her anchor, the storm-sails had been laid to hand, and could be bent in a very short time. They further stated that from the direction of the wind being N.E., she would sail up the Firth of Forth to Leith Roads. But if this should appear doubtful, after passing the Island and Light of May, it might be advisable at once to steer for Tyningham Sands, on the western side of Dunbar, and there run the vessel ashore. If this should happen at the time of high-water, or during the ebbing of the tide, they were of opinion, from the flatness and strength of the floating light, that no danger would attend her taking the ground, even with a very heavy sea. The writer, seeing the confidence which these gentlemen possessed with regard to the situation of things, found himself as much relieved with this conversation as he had previously been with the seeming indifference of the forecastle-men and the smile of the watch upon deck, though literally lashed to the foremast. From this time he felt himself almost perfectly at ease; at any rate, he was entirely resigned to the ultimate result.

About six o'clock in the evening the ship's company was heard moving upon deck, which on the present occasion was rather the cause of alarm. The writer accordingly rang his bell to know what was the matter, when he was informed by the steward that the weather looked considerably better, and that the men upon deck were endeavouring to ship the smoke-funnel of the galley that the people might get some meat. This was a more favourable account than had been anticipated. During the last twenty-one hours he himself had not only had nothing to eat, but he had almost never passed a thought on the subject. Upon the mention of a change of weather, he sent the steward to learn how the artificers felt, and on his return he stated that they now seemed to be all very happy, since the cook had begun to light the galley-fire and make preparations for the suet-pudding of Sunday, which was the only dish to be attempted for the mess, from the ease with which it could both be cooked and served up.

A FAMILY OF ENGINEERS

The principal change felt upon the ship as the wind abated was her increased rolling motion, but the pitching was much diminished, and now hardly any sea came farther aft than the foremast; but she rolled so extremely hard as frequently to dip and take in water over the gunwales and rails in the waist. By nine o'clock all hands had been refreshed by the exertions of the cook and steward, and were happy in the prospect of the worst of the gale being over. The usual complement of men was also now set on watch, and more quietness was experienced throughout the ship. Although the previous night had been a very restless one, it had not the effect of inducing repose in the writer's berth on the succeeding night; for having been so much tossed about in bed during the last thirty hours, he found no easy spot to turn to, and his body was all sore to the touch, which ill accorded with the unyielding materials with which his bed-place was surrounded.

Monday, 7th Sept.—This morning, about eight o'clock, the writer was agreeably surprised to see the scuttle of his cabin skylight removed, and the bright rays of the sun admitted. Although the ship continued to roll excessively, and the sea was still running very high, yet the ordinary business on board seemed to be going forward on deck. It was impossible to steady a telescope, so as to look minutely at the progress of the waves and trace their breach upon the Bell Rock; but the height to which the cross-running waves rose in sprays when they met each other was truly grand, and the continued roar and noise of the sea was very perceptible to the ear. To estimate the height of the sprays at forty or fifty feet would surely be within the mark. Those of the workmen who were not much afflicted with sea-sickness came upon deck, and the wetness below being dried up, the cabins were again brought into a habitable state. Every one seemed to meet as if after a long absence, congratulating his neighbour upon the return of good weather. Little could be said as to the comfort of the vessel, but after riding out such a gale, no one felt the least doubt or hesitation as to the safety and good condition of her moorings. The master

BUILDING OF BELL ROCK

and mate were extremely anxious, however, to heave in the hempen cable, and see the state of the clinch or iron ring of the chain-cable. But the vessel rolled at such a rate that the seamen could not possibly keep their feet at the windlass nor work the handspikes, though it had been several times attempted since the gale took off.

About twelve noon, however, the vessel's motion was observed to be considerably less, and the sailors were enabled to walk upon deck with some degree of freedom. But, to the astonishment of every one, it was soon discovered that the floating light was adrift! The windlass was instantly manned, and the men soon gave out that there was no strain upon the cable. The mizzen sail, which was bent for the occasional purpose of making the vessel ride more easily to the tide, was immediately set, and the other sails were also hoisted in a short time, when, in no small consternation, we bore away about one mile to the south-westward of the former station, and there let go the best bower anchor and cable in twenty fathoms water, to ride until the swell of the sea should fall, when it might be practicable to grapple for the moorings, and find a better anchorage for the ship.

Tuesday, 15th Sept.—This morning, at five a. m., the bell rung as a signal for landing upon the rock, a sound which, after a lapse of ten days, it is believed was welcomed by every one on board. There being a heavy breach of sea at the eastern creek, we landed, though not without difficulty, on the western side, every one seeming more eager than another to get upon the rock; and never did hungry men sit down to a hearty meal with more appetite than the artificers began to pick the dulse from the rocks. This marine plant had the effect of reviving the sickly, and seemed to be no less relished by those who were more hardy.

While the water was ebbing, and the men were roaming in quest of their favourite morsel, the writer was examining the effects of the storm upon the forge and loose apparatus left upon the rock. Six large blocks of granite which had been landed, by way of experiment, on the 1st instant, were now removed from their places and, by the force

A FAMILY OF ENGINEERS

of the sea, thrown over a rising ledge into a hole at the distance of twelve or fifteen paces from the place on which they had been landed. This was a pretty good evidence both of the violence of the storm and the agitation of the sea upon the rock. The safety of the smith's forge was always an object of essential regard. The ash-pan of the hearth or fireplace, with its weighty cast-iron back, had been washed from their places of supposed security; the chains of attachment had been broken, and these ponderous articles were found at a very considerable distance in a hole on the western side of the rock; while the tools and picks of the Aberdeen masons were scattered about in every direction. It is however remarkable that not a single article was ultimately lost.

This being the night on which the floating light was advertised to be lighted, it was accordingly exhibited, to the great joy of every one.

Wednesday, 16th Sept.—The writer was made happy today by the return of the Lighthouse yacht from a voyage to the Northern Lighthouses. Having immediately removed on board of this fine vessel of eighty-one tons register, the artificers gladly followed; for, though they found themselves more pinched for accommodation on board of the yacht, and still more so in the *Smeaton*, yet they greatly preferred either of these to the *Pharos* or floating light, on account of her rolling motion, though in all respects fitted up for their conveniency.

The writer called them to the quarter-deck and informed them that, having been one month afloat, in terms of their agreement they were now at liberty to return to the workyard at Arbroath if they preferred this to continuing at the Bell Rock. But they replied that, in the prospect of soon getting the beacon erected upon the rock, and having made a change from the floating light, they were now perfectly reconciled to their situation, and would remain afloat till the end of the working season.

Thursday 17th Sept.—The wind was N.E. this morning, and though there were only light airs, yet there was a pretty heavy swell coming ashore upon the rock. The boats

BUILDING OF BELL ROCK

landed at half-past seven o'clock a. m., at the creek on the southern side of the rock, marked Port Hamilton. But as one of the boats was in the act of entering this creek, the seaman at the bow-oar, who had just entered the service, having inadvertently expressed some fear from a heavy sea which came rolling towards the boat, and one of the artificers having at the same time looked round and missed a stroke with his oar, such a preponderance was thus given to the rowers upon the opposite side that when the wave struck the boat it threw her upon a ledge of shelving rocks, where the water left her, and she having *kanted* to seaward, the next wave completely filled her with water. After making considerable efforts the boat was again got afloat in the proper track of the creek, so that we landed without any other accident than a complete ducking. There being no possibility of getting a shift of clothes, the artificers began with all speed to work, so as to bring themselves into heat, while the writer and his assistants kept as much as possible in motion. Having remained more than an hour upon the rock, the boats left it at half-past nine; and, after getting on board, the writer recommended to the artificers, as the best mode of getting into a state of comfort, to strip off their wet clothes and go to bed for an hour or two. No further inconveniency was felt, and no one seemed to complain of the affection called " catching cold."

Friday, 18th Sept.—An important occurrence connected with the operations of this season was the arrival of the *Smeaton* at four p. m., having in tow the six principal beams of the beacon-house, together with all the stanchions and other work on board for fixing it on the rock. The mooring of the floating light was a great point gained, but in the erection of the beacon at this late period of the season new difficulties presented themselves. The success of such an undertaking at any season was precarious, because a single day of bad weather occurring before the necessary fixtures could be made might sweep the whole apparatus from the rock. Notwithstanding these difficulties, the writer had determined to make the trial, although he could almost have wished, upon looking at the state of the clouds and the direction of the wind, that the apparatus for the beacon had been still in the workyard.

Saturday, 19th Sept.—The main beams of the beacon were made up in two separate rafts, fixed with bars and bolts of iron. One of these rafts, not being immediately wanted, was left astern of the floating light, and the other was kept in tow by the *Smeaton*, at the buoy nearest to the rock. The Lighthouse yacht rode at another buoy with all hands on board that could possibly be spared out of the floating light. The party of artificers and seamen which landed on the rock counted altogether forty in number. At half-past eight o'clock a derrick, or mast of thirty feet in height, was erected and properly supported with guy-ropes, for suspending the block for raising the first principal beam of the beacon; and a winch machine was also bolted down to the rock for working the purchase-tackle.

Upon raising the derrick, all hands on the rock spontaneously gave three hearty cheers, as a favourable omen of our future exertions in pointing out more permanently the position of the rock. Even to this single spar of timber, could it be preserved, a drowning man might lay hold. When the *Smeaton* drifted on the 2nd of this month such a spar would have been sufficient to save us till she could have come to our relief.

Sunday, 20th Sept.—The wind this morning was variable, but the weather continued extremely favourable for the operations throughout the whole day. At six a. m. the boats were in motion, and the raft, consisting of four of the six principal beams of the beacon-house, each measuring about sixteen inches square, and fifty feet in length, was towed to the rock, where it was anchored, that it might *ground* upon it as the water ebbed. The sailors and artificers, including all hands, to-day counted no fewer than fifty-two, being perhaps the greatest number of persons ever collected upon the Bell Rock. It was early in the tide when the boats reached the rock, and the men worked a considerable time up to their middle in water, every one being more eager than his neighbour to be useful. Even the four artificers who had hitherto declined working on Sunday were to-day most zealous in their exertions. They had indeed become so convinced of the precarious nature and necessity of the work that they never afterwards absented themselves from the rock on Sunday when a landing was practicable.

Having made fast a piece of very good new line, at about two-thirds from the lower end of one of the beams, the purchase-tackle of the derrick was hooked into the turns of the line, and it was speedily raised by the number of men on the rock and the power of the winch tackle. When this log was lifted to a sufficient height, its foot, or lower end, was *stepped* into the spot which had been previously prepared for it. Two of the great iron stanchions were then set into their respective holes on each side of the beam, when a rope was passed round them and the beam, to prevent it from slipping till it could be more permanently fixed. The derrick, or upright spar used for carrying the tackle to raise the first beam, was placed in such a position as to become useful for supporting the upper end of it, which now became, in its turn, the prop of the tackle for raising the second beam. The whole difficulty of this operation was in the raising and propping of the first beam, which became a convenient derrick for raising the second, these again a pair of shears for lifting the third, and the shears a triangle for raising the fourth. Having thus got four of the six principal beams set on end, it required a considerable degree of trouble to get their upper ends to fit. Here they formed the apex of a cone, and were all together mortised into a large piece of beechwood, and secured, for the present, with ropes, in a temporary manner. During the short period of one tide all that could further be done for their security was to put a single screw-bolt through the great kneed bats or stanchions on each side of the beams, and screw the nut home.

In this manner these four principal beams were erected, and left in a pretty secure state. The men had commenced while there was about two or three feet of water upon the side of the beacon, and as the sea was smooth they continued the work equally long during flood-tide. Two of the boats being left at the rock to take off the joiners, who were busily employed on the upper parts till two o'clock p. m., this tide's work may be said to have continued for about seven hours, which was the longest that had hitherto been got upon the rock by at least three hours.

When the first boats left the rock with the artificers employed on the lower part of the work, during the flood-tide the beacon had quite a novel appearance. The beams erected formed a common base of about thirty-three feet, meeting at the top, which was about forty-five feet above the rock, and here half a dozen of the artificers were still at work. After clearing the rock the boats made a stop, when three hearty cheers were given, which were returned with equal goodwill by those upon the beacon, from the personal interest which every one felt in the prosperity of this work, so intimately connected with his safety.

All hands having returned to their respective ships, they got a shift of dry clothes and some refreshment. Being Sunday, they were afterwards convened by signal on board of the Lighthouse yacht, when prayers were read; for every heart upon this occasion felt gladness, and every mind was disposed to be thankful for the happy and successful termination of the operations of this day.

Monday, 21st Sept.—The remaining two principal beams were erected in the course of this tide, which, with the assistance of those set up yesterday, was found to be a very simple operation.

The six principal beams of the beacon were thus secured, at least in a temporary manner, in the course of two tides, or in the short space of about eleven hours and a half. Such is the progress that may be made when active hands and willing minds set properly to work in operations of this kind.

Tuesday, 22nd. Sept.—Having now got the weighty part of this work over, and being thereby relieved of the difficulty both of landing and victualling such a number of men, the *Smeaton* could now be spared, and she was accordingly despatched to Arbroath for a supply of water and pro-

BUILDING OF BELL ROCK

visions, and carried with her six of the artificers who could best be spared.

Wednesday, 23rd Sept.—In going out of the eastern harbour, the boat which the writer steered shipped a sea, that filled her about one-third with water. She had also been hid for a short time, by the waves breaking upon the rock, from the sight of the crew of the preceding boat, who were much alarmed for our safety, imagining for a time that she had gone down.

The *Smeaton* returned from Arbroath this afternoon, but there was so much sea that she could not be made fast to her moorings, and the vessel was obliged to return to Arbroath without being able either to deliver the provisions or take the artificers on board. The Lighthouse yacht was also soon obliged to follow her example, as the sea was breaking heavily over her bows. After getting two reefs in the mainsail, and the third or storm-jib set, the wind being S. W., she bent to windward, though blowing a hard gale, and got into St. Andrews Bay, where we passed the night under the lee of Fifeness.

Thursday, 24th Sept.—At two o'clock this morning we were in St. Andrews Bay, standing off and on shore, with strong gales of wind at S.W.; at seven we were off the entrance of the Tay; at eight stood towards the rock, and at ten passed to leeward of it, but could not attempt a landing. The beacon, however, appeared to remain in good order, and by six p. m. the vessel had again beaten up to St. Andrews Bay, and got into somewhat smoother water for the night.

Friday, 25th Sept.—At seven o'clock bore away for the Bell Rock, but finding a heavy sea running on it were unable to land. The writer, however, had the satisfaction to observe, with his telescope, that everything about the beacon appeared entire; and although the sea had a most frightful appearance, yet it was the opinion of every one that, since the erection of the beacon, the Bell Rock was divested of many of its terrors, and had it been possible to have got the boats hoisted out and manned, it might have even been found prac-

A FAMILY OF ENGINEERS

ticable to land. At six it blew so hard that it was found necessary to strike the topmast and take in a third reef of the mainsail, and under this low canvas we soon reached St. Andrews Bay, and got again under the lee of the land for the night. The artificers, being sea-hardy, were quite reconciled to their quarters on board of the Lighthouse yacht; but it is believed that hardly any consideration would have induced them again to take up their abode in the floating light.

Saturday, 26th Sept.—At daylight the yacht steered towards the Bell Rock, and at eight a. m. made fast to her moorings; at ten, all hands, to the amount of thirty, landed, when the writer had the happiness to find that the beacon had withstood the violence of the gale and the heavy breach of sea, everything being found in the same state in which it had been left on the 21st. The artificers were now enabled to work upon the rock throughout the whole day, both at low and high water, but it required the strictest attention to the state of the weather, in case of their being overtaken with a gale, which might prevent the possibility of getting them off the rock.

Two somewhat memorable circumstances in the annals of the Bell Rock attended the operations of this day: one was the removal of Mr. James Dove, the foreman smith, with his apparatus, from the rock to the upper part of the beacon, where the forge was now erected on a temporary platform, laid on the cross beams or upper framing. The other was the artificers, having dined for the first time upon the rock, their dinner being cooked on board of the yacht, and sent to them by one of the boats. But what afforded the greatest happiness and relief was the removal of the large bellows, which had all along been a source of much trouble and perplexity, by their hampering and incommoding the boat which carried the smiths and their apparatus.

Saturday, 3rd Oct.—The wind being west to-day, the weather was very favourable for operations at the rock, and during the morning and evening tides, with the aid of torchlight, the masons had seven hours' work upon the site of the building. The smiths and joiners, who landed at half-past

BUILDING OF BELL ROCK

six a. m., did not leave the rock till a quarter-past eleven p. m., having been at work, with little intermission, for sixteen hours and three-quarters. When the water left the rock, they were employed at the lower parts of the beacon, and as the tide rose or fell, they shifted the place of their operations. From these exertions, the fixing and securing of the beacon made rapid advancement, as the men were now landed in the morning, and remained throughout the day. But, as a sudden change of weather might have prevented their being taken off at the proper time of tide, a quantity of bread and water was always kept on the beacon.

During this period of working at the beacon all the day, and often a great part of the night, the writer was much on board of the tender; but, while the masons could work on the rock, and frequently also while it was covered by the tide, he remained on the beacon; especially during the night, as he made a point of being on the rock to the latest hour, and was generally the last person who stepped into the boat. He had laid this down as part of his plan of procedure; and in this way had acquired, in the course of the first season, a pretty complete knowledge and experience of what could actually be done at the Bell Rock, under all circumstances of the weather. By this means also his assistants, and the artificers and mariners, got into a systematic habit of proceeding at the commencement of the work, which, it is believed, continued throughout the whole of the operations.

Sunday, 4th Oct.—The external part of the beacon was now finished, with its supports and bracing-chains, and whatever else was considered necessary for its stability, in so far as the season would permit; and although much was still wanting to complete this fabric, yet it was in such a state that it could be left without much fear of the consequences of a storm. The painting of the upper part was nearly finished this afternoon; and the *Smeaton* had brought off a quantity of brushwood and other articles, for the purpose of heating or charring the lower part of the principal beams, before being laid over with successive coats of boiling pitch, to the height of from eight to twelve feet, or as high as

A FAMILY OF ENGINEERS

the rise of spring-tides. A small flagstaff having also been erected to-day, a flag was displayed for the first time from the beacon, by which its perspective effect was greatly improved. On this, as on all like occasions at the Bell Rock, three hearty cheers were given; and the steward served out a dram of rum to all hands, while the Lighthouse yacht, *Smeaton*, and floating light, hoisted their colours in compliment to the erection.

Monday, 5th Oct.—In the afternoon, and just as the tide's work was over, Mr. John Rennie, engineer, accompanied by his son Mr. George, on their way to the harbour works of Fraserburgh, in Aberdeenshire, paid a visit to the Bell Rock, in a boat from Arbroath. It being then too late in the tide for landing, they remained on board of the Lighthouse yacht all night, when the writer, who had now been secluded from society for several weeks, enjoyed much of Mr. Rennie's interesting conversation, both on general topics, and professionally upon the progress of the Bell Rock works, on which he was consulted as chief engineer.

Tuesday, 6th Oct.—The artificers landed this morning at nine, after which one of the boats returned to the ship for the writer and Messrs. Rennie, who upon landing, were saluted with a display of the colours from the beacon and by three cheers from the workmen. Everything was now in a prepared state for leaving the rock, and giving up the works afloat for this season, excepting some small articles, which would still occupy the smiths and joiners for a few days longer. They accordingly shifted on board of the *Smeaton*, while the yacht left the rock for Arbroath, with Messrs. Rennie, the writer, and the remainder of the artificers. But, before taking leave, the steward served out a farewell glass, when three hearty cheers were given, and an earnest wish expressed that everything, in the spring of 1808, might be found in the same state of good order as it was now about to be left.

BUILDING OF BELL ROCK,

II

OPERATIONS OF 1808

1808. Monday, 29th Feb.—The writer sailed from Arbroath at one a. m. in the Lighthouse yacht. At seven the floating light was hailed, and all on board found to be well. The crew were observed to have a very healthy-like appearance, and looked better than at the close of the works upon the rock. They seemed only to regret one thing, which was the secession of their cook, Thomas Elliot—not on account of his professional skill, but for his facetious and curious manner. Elliot had something peculiar in his history, and was reported by his comrades to have seen better days. He was, however, happy with his situation on board of the floating light, and, having a taste for music, dancing, and acting plays, he contributed much to the amusement of the ship's company in their dreary abode during the winter months. He had also recommended himself to their notice as a good shipkeeper, for as it did not answer Elliot to go often ashore, he had always given up his turn of leave to his neighbours. At his own desire he was at length paid off, when he had a considerable balance of wages to receive, which he said would be sufficient to carry him to the West Indies, and he accordingly took leave of the Lighthouse service.

Tuesday, 1st March.—At daybreak the Lighthouse yacht, attended by a boat from the floating light, again stood towards the Bell Rock. The weather felt extremely cold this morning, the thermometer being at 34 degrees, with the wind at east, accompanied by occasional showers of snow, and the marine barometer indicated 29.80. At half-past seven the sea ran with such force upon the rock that it seemed doubtful if a landing could be effected. At half-past eight, when it was fairly above water, the writer took his place in the floating light's boat with the artificers, while the yacht's boat followed, according to the general rule of having two boats afloat in landing expeditions of this kind, that, in

A FAMILY OF ENGINEERS

case of accident to one boat, the other might assist. In several unsuccessful attempts the boats were beat back by the breach of the sea upon the rock. On the eastern side it separated into two distinct waves, which came with a sweep round to the western side, where they met; and at the instant of their confluence the water rose in spray to a considerable height. Watching what the sailors term a *smooth*, we caught a favourable opportunity, and in a very dexterous manner the boats were rowed between the two seas, and made a favourable landing at the western creek.

At the latter end of last season, as was formerly noticed, the beacon was painted white, and from the bleaching of the weather and the sprays of the sea the upper parts were kept clean; but within the range of the tide the principal beams were observed to be thickly coated with a green stuff, the *conferva* of botanists. Notwithstanding the intrusion of these works, which had formerly banished the numerous seals that played about the rock, they were now seen in great numbers, having been in an almost undisturbed state for six months. It had now also, for the first time, got some inhabitants of the feathered tribe: in particular the scarth or cormorant, and the large herring-gull, had made the beacon a resting-place, from its vicinity to their fishing-grounds. About a dozen of these birds rested upon the cross-beams, which, in some places, were coated with their dung; and their flight, as the boats approached, was a very unlooked-for indication of life and habitation on the Bell Rock, conveying the momentary idea of the conversion of this fatal rock, from being a terror to the mariner, into a residence of man and a safeguard to shipping.

Upon narrowly examining the great iron stanchions with which the beams were fixed to the rock, the writer had the satisfaction of finding that there was not the least appearance of working or shifting at any of the joints or places of connection; and, excepting the loosening of the bracing-chains, everything was found in the same entire state in which it had been left in the month of October. This, in the estimation of the writer, was a matter of no small im-

BUILDING OF BELL ROCK

portance to the future success of the work. He from that moment saw the practicability and propriety of fitting up the beacon, not only as a place of refuge in case of accident to the boats in landing, but as a residence for the artificers during the working months.

While upon the top of the beacon the writer was reminded by the landing-master that the sea was running high, and that it would be necessary to set off while the rock afforded anything like shelter to the boats, which by this time had been made fast by a long line to the beacon, and rode with much agitation, each requiring two men with boat-hooks to keep them from striking each other, or from ranging up against the beacon. But even under these circumstances the greatest confidence was felt by every one, from the security afforded by this temporary erection. For, supposing that the wind had suddenly increased to a gale, and that it had been found unadvisable to go into the boats; or, supposing they had drifted or sprung a leak from striking upon the rocks; in any of these possible and not at all improbable cases, those who might thus have been left upon the rock had now something to lay hold of, and, though occupying this dreary habitation of the sea-gull and the cormorant, affording only bread and water, yet *life* would be preserved, and the mind would still be supported by the hope of being ultimately relieved.

Wednesday, 25th May.—On the 25th of May the writer embarked at Arbroath on board of the *Sir Joseph Banks*, for the Bell Rock, accompanied by Mr. Logan senior, foreman builder, with twelve masons, and two smiths, together with thirteen seamen, including the master, mate, and steward.

Thursday, 26th May.—Mr. James Wilson, now commander of the *Pharos* floating light, and landing-master, in the room of Mr. Sinclair, who had left the service, came into the writer's cabin this morning at six o'clock, and intimated that there was a good appearance of landing on the rock. Everything being arranged, both boats proceeded in company, and at eight a. m., they reached the rock. The

A FAMILY OF ENGINEERS

Lighthouse colours were immediately hoisted upon the flagstaff of the beacon, a compliment which was duly returned by the tender and floating light, when three hearty cheers were given, and a glass of rum was served out to all hands to drink success to the operations of 1808.

Friday, 27th May.—This morning the wind was at east, blowing a fresh gale, the weather being hazy, with a considerable breach of sea setting in upon the rock. The morning bell was therefore rung, in some doubt as to the practicability of making a landing. After allowing the rock to get fully up, or to be sufficiently left by the tide, that the boats might have some shelter from the range of the sea, they proceeded at eight a. m., and upon the whole made a pretty good landing; and after two hours and three-quarters' work returned to the ship in safety.

In the afternoon the wind considerably increased, and, as a pretty heavy sea was still running, the tender rode very hard, when Mr. Taylor, the commander, found it necessary to take in the bowsprit, and strike the fore and main topmasts, that she might ride more easily. After consulting about the state of the weather, it was resolved to leave the artificers on board this evening, and carry only the smiths to the rock, as the sharpening of the irons was rather behind, from their being so much broken and blunted by the hard and tough nature of the rock, which became much more compact and hard as the depth of excavation was increased. Besides avoiding the risk of encumbering the boats with a number of men who had not yet got the full command of the oar in a breach of sea, the writer had another motive for leaving them behind. He wanted to examine the site of the building without interruption, and to take the comparative levels of the different inequalities of its area; and as it would have been painful to have seen men standing idle upon the Bell Rock, where all moved with activity, it was judged better to leave them on board. The boats landed at half-past seven p.m., and the landing-master, with the seamen, was employed during this tide in cutting the seaweeds from the several paths leading to the landing-places, to render

BUILDING OF BELL ROCK

walking more safe, for, from the slippery state of the surface of the rock, many severe tumbles had taken place. In the meantime the writer took the necessary levels, and having carefully examined the site of the building and considered all its parts, it still appeared to be necessary to excavate to the average depth of fourteen inches over the whole area of the foundation.

Saturday, 28th May.—The wind still continued from the eastward with a heavy swell; and to-day it was accompanied with foggy weather and occasional showers of rain. Notwithstanding this, such was the confidence which the erection of the beacon had inspired that the boats landed the artificers on the rock under very unpromising circumstances, at half-past eight, and they continued at work till half-past eleven, being a period of three hours, which was considered a great tide's work in the present low state of the foundation. Three of the masons on board were so afflicted with sea-sickness that they had not been able to take any food for almost three days, and they were literally assisted into the boats this morning by their companions. It was, however, not a little surprising to see how speedily these men revived upon landing on the rock and eating a little dulse. Two of them afterwards assisted the sailors in collecting the chips of stone and carrying them out of the way of the pickmen; but the third complained of a pain in his head, and was still unable to do anything. Instead of returning to the tender with the boats, these three men remained on the beacon all day, and had their victuals sent to them along with the smiths'. From Mr. Dove, the foreman smith, they had much sympathy, for he preferred remaining on the beacon at all hazards, to be himself relieved from the malady of sea-sickness. The wind continuing high, with a heavy sea, and the tide falling late, it was not judged proper to land the artificers this evening, but in the twilight the boats were sent to fetch the people on board who had been left on the rock.

Sunday, 29th May.—The wind was from the S.W. to-day, and the signal-bell rung, as usual, about an hour before the period for landing on the rock. The writer was rather surprised, however, to hear the landing-master repeatedly call, " All hands for the rock!" and, coming on deck, he was disappointed to find the seamen only in the boats. Upon inquiry, it appeared that some misunderstanding had taken place about the wages of the artificers for Sundays. They had preferred wages for seven days statedly to the former mode of allowing a day for each tide's work on Sunday, as they did not like the appearance of working for double or even treble wages on Sunday, and would rather have it understood that their work on that day arose more from the urgency of the case than with a view to emolument. This having been judged creditable to their religious feelings, and readily adjusted to their wish, the boats proceeded to the rock, and the work commenced at nine a.m.

Monday, 30th May.—Mr. Francis Watt commenced, with five joiners, to fit up a temporary platform upon the beacon, about twenty-five feet above the highest part of the rock. This platform was to be used as the site of the smith's forge, after the beacon should be fitted up as a barrack; and here also the mortar was to be mixed and prepared for the building, and it was accordingly termed the Mortar Gallery.

The landing-master's crew completed the discharging from the *Smeaton* of her cargo of the cast-iron rails and timber. It must not here be omitted to notice that the *Smeaton* took in ballast from the Bell Rock, consisting of the shivers or chips of stone produced by the workmen in preparing the site of the building, which were now accumulating in great quantities on the rock. These the boats loaded, after discharging the iron. The object in carrying off these chips, besides ballasting the vessel, was to get them permanently out of the way, as they were apt to shift about from place to place with every gale of wind; and it often required a considerable time to clear the foundation a second time of this rubbish. The circumstance of ballasting a ship at the Bell Rock afforded great entertainment, especially to the sailors; and it was perhaps with truth remarked that the *Smeaton* was the first vessel that had ever taken on board ballast at the Bell Rock. Mr. Pool, the commander of this

BUILDING OF BELL ROCK

vessel, afterwards acquainted the writer that, when the ballast was landed upon the quay at Leith, many persons carried away specimens of it, as part of a cargo from the Bell Rock; when he added, that such was the interest excited, from the number of specimens carried away, that some of his friends suggested that he should have sent the whole to the Cross of Edinburgh, where each piece might have sold for a penny.

Tuesday, 31st May.—In the evening the boats went to the rock, and brought the joiners and smiths, and their sickly companions, on board of the tender. These also brought with them two baskets full of fish, which they had caught at high-water from the beacon, reporting, at the same time, to their comrades, that the fish were swimming in such numbers over the rock at high-water that it was completely hid from their sight, and nothing seen but the movement of thousands of fish. They were almost exclusively of the species called the podlie, or young coal-fish. This discovery, made for the first time to-day by the workmen, was considered fortunate, as an additional circumstance likely to produce an inclination among the artificers to take up their residence in the beacon, when it came to be fitted up as a barrack.

Tuesday, 7th June.—At three o'clock in the morning the ship's bell was rung as the signal for landing at the rock. When the landing was to be made before breakfast, it was customary to give each of the artificers and seamen a dram and a biscuit, and coffee was prepared by the steward for the cabins. Exactly at four o'clock the whole party landed from three boats, including one of those belonging to the floating light, with a part of that ship's crew, which always attended the works in moderate weather. The landing-master's boat, called the *Seaman*, but more commonly called the *Lifeboat*, took the lead. The next boat, called the *Mason*, was generally steered by the writer; while the floating light's boat, *Pharos*, was under the management of the boatswain of that ship.

Having now so considerable a party of workmen and

A FAMILY OF ENGINEERS

sailors on the rock, it may be proper here to notice how their labours were directed. Preparations having been made last month for the erection of a second forge upon the beacon, the smiths commenced their operations both upon the lower and higher platforms. They were employed in sharpening the picks and irons for the masons, and in making bats and other apparatus of various descriptions connected with the fitting of the railways. The landing-master's crew were occupied in assisting the millwrights in laying the railways to hand. Sailors, of all other descriptions of men, are the most accommodating in the use of their hands. They worked freely with the boring-irons, and assisted in all the operations of the railways, acting by turns as boatmen, seamen, and artificers. We had no such character on the Bell Rock as the common labourer. All the operations of this department were cheerfully undertaken by the seamen, who, both on the rock and on shipboard, were the inseparable companions of every work connected with the erection of the Bell Rock Lighthouse. It will naturally be supposed that about twenty-five masons, occupied with their picks in executing and preparing the foundation of the lighthouse, in the course of a tide of about three hours, would make a considerable impression upon an area even of forty-two feet in diameter. But in proportion as the foundation was deepened, the rock was found to be much more hard and difficult to work, while the baling and pumping of water became much more troublesome. A joiner was kept almost constantly employed in fitting the picks to their handles, which, as well as the points to the irons, were very frequently broken.

The Bell Rock this morning presented by far the most busy and active appearance it had exhibited since the erection of the principal beams of the beacon. The surface of the rock was crowded with men, the two forges flaming, the one above the other, upon the beacon, while the anvils thundered with the rebounding noise of their wooden supports, and formed a curious contrast with the occasional clamour of the surges. The wind was westerly, and the

BUILDING OF BELL ROCK

weather being extremely agreeable, as soon after breakfast as the tide had sufficiently overflowed the rock to float the boats over it, the smiths, with a number of the artificers, returned to the beacon, carrying their fishing-tackle along with them. In the course of the forenoon the beacon exhibited a still more extraordinary appearance than the rock had done in the morning. The sea being smooth, it seemed to be afloat upon the water, with a number of men supporting themselves in all the variety of attitude and position: while, from the upper part of this wooden house, the volumes of smoke which ascended from the forges gave the whole a very curious and fanciful appearance.

In the course of this tide it was observed that a heavy swell was setting in from the eastward, and the appearance of the sky indicated a change of weather, while the wind was shifting about. The barometer also had fallen from 30 in. to 29.6. It was, therefore, judged prudent to shift the vessel to the S.W. or more distant buoy. Her bowsprit was also soon afterwards taken in, the topmasts struck, and everything made *snug*, as seamen term it, for a gale. During the course of the night the wind increased and shifted to the eastward, when the vessel rolled very hard, and the sea often broke over her bows with great force.

Wednesday, 8th June.—Although the motion of the tender was much less than that of the floating light—at least in regard to the rolling motion—yet she *sended,* or pitched, much. Being also of a very handsome build, and what seamen term very *clean aft*, the sea often struck her counter with such force that the writer, who possessed the aftermost cabin, being unaccustomed to this new vessel, could not divest himself of uneasiness; for when her stern fell into the sea, it struck with so much violence as to be more like the resistance of a rock than the sea. The water, at the same time, often rushed with great force up the rudder-case, and, forcing up the valve of the water-closet, the floor of his cabin was at times laid under water. The gale continued to increase, and the vessel rolled and pitched in such a manner that the hawser by which the tender was made fast to the

A FAMILY OF ENGINEERS

buoy snapped, and she went adrift. In the act of swinging round to the wind she shipped a very heavy sea, which greatly alarmed the artificers, who imagined that we had got upon the rock; but this, from the direction of the wind, was impossible. The writer, however, sprung upon deck, where he found the sailors busily employed in rigging out the bowsprit and in setting sail. From the easterly direction of the wind, it was considered most advisable to steer for the Firth of Forth, and there wait a change of weather. At two p.m. we accordingly passed the Isle of May, at six anchored in Leith Roads, and at eight the writer landed, when he came in upon his friends, who were not a little surprised at his unexpected appearance, which gave an instantaneous alarm for the safety of things at the Bell Rock.

Thursday, 9th June.—The wind still continued to blow very hard at E. by N., and the *Sir Joseph Banks* rode heavily, and even drifted with both anchors ahead, in Leith Roads. The artificers did not attempt to leave the ship last night; but there being upwards of fifty people on board, and the decks greatly lumbered with the two large boats, they were in a very crowded and impatient state on board. But to-day they got ashore, and amused themselves by walking about the streets of Edinburgh, some in very humble apparel, from having only the worst of their jackets with them, which, though quite suitable for their work, were hardly fit for public inspection, being not only tattered, but greatly stained with the red colour of the rock.

Friday, 10th June.—To-day the wind was at S.E., with light breezes and foggy weather. At six a.m. the writer again embarked for the Bell Rock, when the vessel immediately sailed. At eleven p.m., there being no wind, the kedge-anchor was *let go* off Anstruther, one of the numerous towns on the coast of Fife, where we waited the return of the tide.

Saturday, 11th June.—At six a.m. the *Sir Joseph* got under weigh, and at eleven was again made fast to the southern buoy at the Bell Rock. Though it was now late in the tide, the writer, being anxious to ascertain the state of things after the gale, landed with the artificers, to the number of

BUILDING OF BELL ROCK

orty-four. Everything was found in an entire state; but, s the tide was nearly gone, only half an hour's work had een got when the site of the building was overflowed. In he evening the boats again landed at nine, and, after a good tide's work of three hours with torch-light, the work ras left off at midnight. To the distant shipping the appearance of things under night on the Bell Rock, when the rork was going forward, must have been very remarkable, specially to those who were strangers to the operations. Mr. John Reid, principal lightkeeper, who also acted as master of the floating light during the working months at he rock, described the appearance of the numerous lights situated so low in the water, when seen at the distance of two or three miles, as putting him in mind of Milton's description of the fiends in the lower regions, adding, " for it seems greatly to surpass Will-o'-the-wisp, or any of those earthly spectres of which we have so often heard."

Monday, 13th June.—From the difficulties attending the anding on the rock, owing to the breach of sea which had or days past been around it, the artificers showed some backwardness at getting into the boats this morning; but after a little explanation this was got over. It was always observable that for some time after anything like danger had occurred at the rock, the workmen became much more cautious, and on some occasions their timidity was rather troublesome. It fortunately happened, however, that along with the writer's assistants and the sailors there were also some of the artificers themselves who felt no such scruples, and in this way these difficulties were the more easily surmounted. In matters where life is in danger it becomes necessary to treat even unfounded prejudices with tenderness, as an accident, under certain circumstances, would not only have been particularly painful to those giving directions, but have proved highly detrimental to the work, especially in the early stages of its advancement.

At four o'clock fifty-eight persons landed; but the tides being extremely languid, the water only left the higher parts of the rock, and no work could be done at the site of the

A FAMILY OF ENGINEERS

building. A third forge was, however, put in operation during a short time, for the greater conveniency of sharpening the picks and irons, and for purposes connected with the preparations for fixing the railways on the rock. The weather towards the evening became thick and foggy, and there was hardly a breath of wind to ruffle the surface of the water. Had it not, therefore, been for the noise from the anvils of the smiths who had been left on the beacon throughout the day, which afforded a guide for the boats, a landing could not have been attempted this evening, especially with such a company of artificers. This circumstance confirmed the writer's opinion with regard to the propriety of connecting large bells to be rung with machinery in the lighthouse, to be tolled day and night during the continuance of foggy weather.

Thursday, 23rd June.—The boats landed this evening, when the artificers had again two hours' work. The weather still continuing very thick and foggy, more difficulty was experienced in getting on board of the vessels to-night than had occurred on any previous occasion, owing to a light breeze of wind which carried the sound of the bell and the other signals made on board of the vessels away from the rock. Having fortunately made out the position of the sloop *Smeaton* at the N.E. buoy—to which we were much assisted by the barking of the ship's dog,—we parted with the *Smeaton's* boat, when the boats of the tender took a fresh departure for that vessel, which lay about half a mile to the south-westward. Yet such is the very deceiving state of the tides, that, although there was a small binnacle and compass in the landing-master's boat, we had, nevertheless, passed the *Sir Joseph* a good way, when, fortunately, one of the sailors catched the sound of a blowing horn. The only fire-arms on board were a pair of swivels of one-inch calibre; but it is quite surprising how much the sound is lost in foggy weather, as the report was heard but at a very short distance. The sound from the explosion of gunpowder is so instantaneous that the effect of the small guns was not so good as either the blowing of a horn or the tolling

BUILDING OF BELL ROCK

of a bell, which afforded a more constant and steady direction for the pilot.

Wednesday, 6th July.—Landed on the rock with the three boats belonging to the tender at five p.m., and began immediately to bale the water out of the foundation-pit with a number of buckets, while the pumps were also kept in action with relays of artificers and seamen. The work commenced upon the higher parts of the foundation as the water left them, but it was now pretty generally reduced to a level. About twenty men could be conveniently employed at each pump, and it is quite astonishing in how short a time so great a body of water could be drawn off. The water in the foundation-pit at this time measured about two feet in depth, on an area of forty-two feet in diameter, and yet it was drawn off in the course of about half an hour. After this the artificers commenced with their picks and continued at work for two hours and a half, some of the sailors being at the same time busily employed in clearing the foundation of chips and in conveying the irons to and from the smiths on the beacon, where they were sharpened. At eight o'clock the sea broke in upon us and overflowed the foundation-pit, when the boats returned to the tender.

Thursday, 7th July.—The landing-master's bell rung this morning about four o'clock, and at half-past five, the foundation being cleared, the work commenced on the site of the building. But from the moment of landing, the squad of joiners and millwrights was at work upon the higher parts of the rock in laying the railways, while the anvils of the smiths resounded on the beacon, and such columns of smoke ascended from the forges that they were often mistaken by strangers at a distance for a ship on fire. After continuing three hours at work the foundation of the building was again overflowed, and the boats returned to the ship at half-past eight o'clock. The masons and pickmen had, at this period, a pretty long day on board of the tender, but the smiths and joiners were kept constantly at work upon the beacon, the stability and great conveniency of which had now been so fully shown that no doubt remained as to the propriety of fitting it up as a barrack. The workmen were accordingly employed, during the period of high-water, in making preparations for this purpose.

The foundation-pit now assumed the appearance of a great platform, and the late tides had been so favourable that it became apparent that the first course, consisting of a few irregular and detached stones for making up certain inequalities in the interior parts of the site of the building, might be laid in the course of the present spring-tides. Having been enabled to-day to get the dimensions of the foundation, or first stone, accurately taken, a mould was made of its figure, when the writer left the rock, after the tide's work of this morning, in a fast rowing-boat for Arbroath; and, upon landing, two men were immediately set to work upon one of the blocks from Mylnefield quarry, which was prepared in the course of the following day, as the stone-cutters relieved each other, and worked both night and day, so that it was sent off in one of the stone-lighters without delay.

Saturday, 9th July.—The site of the foundation-stone was very difficult to work, from its depth in the rock; but being now nearly prepared, it formed a very agreeable kind of pastime at high-water for all hands to land the stone itself upon the rock. The landing-master's crew and artificers accordingly entered with great spirit into this operation. The stone was placed upon the deck of the *Hedderwick* praam-boat, which had just been brought from Leith, and was decorated with colours for the occasion. Flags were also displayed from the shipping in the offing, and upon the beacon. Here the writer took his station with the greater part of the artificers, who supported themselves in every possible position while the boats towed the praam from her moorings and brought her immediately over the site of the building, where her grappling anchors were let go. The stone was then lifted off the deck by a tackle hooked into a Lewis bat inserted into it, when it was gently lowered into the water and grounded on the site of the building, amidst the cheering acclamations of about sixty persons.

BUILDING OF BELL ROCK

Sunday, 10th July.—At eleven o'clock the foundation-stone was laid to hand. It was of a square form, containing about twenty cubic feet, and had the figures, or date, of 1808 simply cut upon it with a chîsel. A derrick, or spar of timber, having been erected at the edge of the hole and guyed with ropes, the stone was then hooked to the tackle and lowered into its place, when the writer, attended by his assistants—Mr. Peter Logan, Mr. Francis Watt, and Mr. James Wilson,—applied the square, the level, and the mallet, and pronounced the following benediction: " May the Great Architect of the Universe complete and bless this building," on which three hearty cheers were given, and success to the future operations was drunk with the greatest enthusiasm.

Tuesday, 26th July.—The wind being at S.E. this evening, we had a pretty heavy swell of sea upon the rock, and some difficulty attended our getting off in safety, as the boats got aground in the creek and were in danger of being upset. Upon extinguishing the torch-lights, about twelve in number, the darkness of the night seemed quite horrible; the water being also much charged with the phosphorescent appearance which is familiar to every one on shipboard, the waves, as they dashed upon the rock, were in some degree like so much liquid flame. The scene, upon the whole, was truly awful!

Wednesday, 27th July—In leaving the rock this evening, everything, after the torches were extinguished, had the same dismal appearance as last night, but so perfectly acquainted were the landing-master and his crew with the position of things at the rock, that comparatively little inconveniency was experienced on these occasions when the weather was moderate; such is the effect of habit, even in the most unpleasant situations. If, for example, it had been proposed to a person accustomed to a city life, at once to take up his quarters off a sunken reef and land upon it in boats at all hours of the night, the proposition must have appeared quite impracticable and extravagant; but this practice coming progressively upon the artificers, it was ultimately undertaken with the greatest alacrity. Notwith-

A FAMILY OF ENGINEERS

standing this, however, it must be acknowledged that it was not till after much labour and peril, and many an anxious hour, that the writer is enabled to state that the site of the Bell Rock Lighthouse is fully prepared for the first entire course of the building.

Friday, 12th Aug.—The artificers landed this morning at half-past ten, and after an hour and a half's work eight stones were laid, which completed the first entire course of the building, consisting of 123 blocks, the last of which was laid with three hearty cheers.

Saturday, 10th Sept.—Land at nine a. m., and by a quarter-past twelve noon twenty-three stones had been laid. The works being now somewhat elevated by the lower courses, we got quit of the very serious inconvenience of pumping water to clear the foundation-pit. This gave much facility to the operations, and was noticed with expressions of as much happiness by the artificers as the seamen had shown when relieved of the continual trouble of carrying the smith's bellows off the rock prior to the erection of the beacon.

Wednesday, 21st Sept.—Mr. Thomas Macurich, mate of the *Smeaton*, and James Scott, one of the crew, a young man about eighteen years of age, immediately went into their boat to make fast a hawser to the ring in the top of the floating buoy of the moorings, and were forthwith to proceed to land their cargo, so much wanted at the rock. The tides at this period were very strong, and the mooring-chain, when sweeping the ground, had caught hold of a rock or piece of wreck by which the chain was so shortened that when the tide flowed the buoy got almost under water, and little more than the ring appeared at the surface. When Macurich and Scott were in the act of making the hawser fast to the ring, the chain got suddenly disentangled at the bottom, and this large buoy, measuring about seven feet in height and three feet in diameter at the middle, tapering to both ends, being what seamen term a *Nun-buoy*, vaulted or sprung up with such force that it upset the boat, which instantly filled with water. Mr. Macurich, with much exertion, succeeded in getting hold of the boat's gunwale, still

BUILDING OF BELL ROCK

above the surface of the water, and by this means was saved; but the young man Scott was unfortunately drowned. He had in all probability been struck about the head by the ring of the buoy, for although surrounded with the oars and the thwarts of the boat which floated near him, yet he seemed entirely to want the power of availing himself of such assistance, and appeared to be quite insensible, while Pool, the master of the *Smeaton*, called loudly to him; and before assistance could be got from the tender, he was carried away by the strength of the current, and disappeared.

The young man Scott was a great favourite in the service, having had something uncommonly mild and complaisant in his manner; and his loss was therefore universally regretted. The circumstances of his case were also peculiarly distressing to his mother, as her husband, who was a seaman, had for three years been confined to a French prison, and the deceased was the chief support of the family. In order in some measure to make up the loss to the poor woman for the monthly aliment regularly allowed her by her late son, it was suggested that a younger boy, a brother of the deceased, might be taken into the service. This appeared to be rather a delicate proposition, but it was left to the landing-master to arrange according to circumstances; such was the resignation, and at the same time the spirit, of the poor woman, that she readily accepted the proposal, and in a few days the younger Scott was actually afloat in the place of his brother. On representing this distressing case to the Board, the Commissioners were pleased to grant an annuity of £5 to Scott's mother.

The *Smeaton*, not having been made fast to the buoy, had, with the ebb-tide, drifted to leeward a considerable way eastward of the rock, and could not, till the return of the flood-tide, be worked up to her moorings, so that the present tide was lost, notwithstanding all exertions which had been made both ashore and afloat with this cargo. The artificers landed at six a. m.; but, as no materials could be got upon the rock this morning, they were employed in boring trenail holes and in various other operations, and after four hours'

A FAMILY OF ENGINEERS

work they returned on board the tender. When the *Smeaton* got up to her moorings, the landing-master's crew immediately began to unload her. There being too much wind for towing the praams in the usual way, they were warped to the rock in the most laborious manner by their windlasses, with successive grapplings and hawsers laid out for this purpose. At six p. m. the artificers landed, and continued at work till half-past ten, when the remaining seventeen stones were laid which completed the third entire course, or fourth of the lighthouse, with which the building operations were closed for the season.

III

OPERATIONS OF 1809

1809. *Wednesday, 24th May.*—The last night was the first that the writer had passed in his old quarters on board of the floating light for about twelve months, when the weather was so fine and the sea so smooth that even here he felt but little or no motion, excepting at the turn of the tide, when the vessel gets into what the seamen term the *trough of the sea.* At six a. m., Mr. Watt, who conducted the operations of the railways and beacon-house, had landed with nine artificers. At half-past one p. m. Mr. Peter Logan had also landed with fifteen masons, and immediately proceeded to set up the crane. The sheer-crane or apparatus for lifting the stones out of the praam-boats at the eastern creek had been already erected, and the railways now formed about two-thirds of an entire circle round the building: some progress had likewise been made with the reach towards the western landing-place. The floors being laid, the beacon now assumed the appearance of a habitation. The *Smeaton* was at her moorings, with the *Fernie* praam-boat astern, for which she was laying down moorings, and the tender being also at her station, the Bell Rock had again put on its former busy aspect.

Wednesday, 31st May.—The landing-master's bell, often

BUILDING OF BELL ROCK

no very favourite sound, rung at six this morning; but on this occasion, it is believed, it was gladly received by all on board, as the welcome signal of the return of better weather. The masons laid thirteen stones to-day, which the seamen had landed, together with other building materials. During these twenty-four hours the wind was from the south, blowing fresh breezes, accompanied with showers of snow. In the morning the snow showers were so thick that it was with difficulty the landing-master, who always steered the leading boat, could make his way to the rock through the drift. But at the Bell Rock neither snow nor rain, nor fog nor wind, retarded the progress of the work, if unaccompanied by a heavy swell or breach of the sea.

The weather during the months of April and May had been uncommonly boisterous, and so cold that the thermometer seldom exceeded 40°, while the barometer was generally about 29.50. We had not only hail and sleet, but the snow on the last day of May lay on the decks and rigging of the ship to the depth of about three inches; and, although now entering upon the month of June, the length of the day was the chief indication of summer. Yet such is the effect of habit, and such was the expertness of the landing master's crew, that, even in this description of weather, seldom a tide's work was lost. Such was the ardour and zeal of the heads of the several departments at the rock, including Mr. Peter Logan, foreman builder, Mr. Francis Watt, foreman millwright, and Captain Wilson, landing-master, that it was on no occasion necessary to address them, excepting in the way of precaution or restraint. Under these circumstances, however, the writer not infrequently felt considerable anxiety, of which this day's experience will afford an example.

This morning, at a quarter-past eight, the artificers were landed as usual, and, after three hours and three-quarters' work, five stones were laid, the greater part of this tide having been taken up in completing the boring and trenailing of the stones formerly laid. At noon the writer, with the seamen and artificers, proceeded to the tender, leaving on the beacon the joiners, and several of those who were

A FAMILY OF ENGINEERS

troubled with sea-sickness—among whom was Mr. Logan, who remained with Mr. Watt—counting altogether eleven persons. During the first and middle parts of these twenty-four hours the wind was from the east, blowing what the seamen term " fresh breezes "; but in the afternoon it shifted to E.N.E., accompanied with so heavy a swell of sea that the *Smeaton* and tender struck their topmasts, launched in their boltsprits, and " made all snug " for a gale. At four p. m. the *Smeaton* was obliged to slip her moorings, and passed the tender, drifting before the wind, with only the foresail set. In passing, Mr. Pool hailed that he must run for the Firth of Forth to prevent the vessel from " riding under."

On board of the tender the writer's chief concern was about the eleven men left upon the beacon. Directions were accordingly given that everything about the vessel should be put in the best possible state, to present as little resistance to the wind as possible, that she might have the better chance of riding out the gale. Among these preparations the best bower cable was bent, so as to have a second anchor in readiness in case the mooring-hawser should give way, that every means might be used for keeping the vessel within sight of the prisoners on the beacon, and thereby keeping them in as good spirits as possible. From the same motive the boats were kept afloat that they might be less in fear of the vessel leaving her station. The landing-master had, however, repeatedly expressed his anxiety for the safety of the boats, and wished much to have them hoisted on board. At seven p. m. one of the boats, as he feared, was unluckily filled with sea from a wave breaking into her, and it was with great difficulty that she could be baled out and got on board, with the loss of her oars, rudder, and loose thwarts. Such was the motion of the ship that in taking this boat on board her gunwale was stove in, and she otherwise received considerable damage. Night approached, but it was still found quite impossible to go near the rock. Consulting, therefore, the safety of the second boat, she also was hoisted on board of the tender.

BUILDING OF BELL ROCK

At this time the cabins of the beacon were only partially covered, and had neither been provided with bedding nor a proper fireplace, while the stock of provisions was but slender. In these uncomfortable circumstances the people on the beacon were left for the night, nor was the situation of those on board of the tender much better. The rolling and pitching motion of the ship was excessive; and, excepting to those who had been accustomed to a residence in the floating light, it seemed quite intolerable. Nothing was heard but the hissing of the winds and the creaking of the bulkheads or partitions of the ship; the night was, therefore, spent in the most unpleasant reflections upon the condition of the people on the beacon, especially in the prospect of the tender being driven from her moorings. But, even in such a case, it afforded some consolation that the stability of the fabric was never doubted, and that the boats of the floating light were at no great distance, and ready to render the people on the rock the earliest assistance which the weather would permit. The writer's cabin being in the sternmost part of the ship, which had what sailors term a good entry, or was sharp built, the sea, as before noticed, struck her counter with so much violence that the water, with a rushing noise, continually forced its way up the rudder-case, lifted the valve of the water-closet, and overran the cabin floor. In these circumstances daylight was eagerly looked for, and hailed with delight, as well by those afloat as by the artificers upon the rock.

Friday, 2nd June.—In the course of the night the writer held repeated conversations with the officer on watch, who reported that the weather continued much in the same state, and that the barometer still indicated 29.20 inches. At six a. m. the landing-master considered the weather to have somewhat moderated; and, from certain appearances of the sky, he was of opinion that a change for the better would soon take place. He accordingly proposed to attempt a landing at low water, and either get the people off the rock, or at least ascertain what state they were in. At nine a. m. he left the vessel with a boat well-manned, carrying with

him a supply of cooked provisions and a tea-kettle ful
mulled port wine for the people on the beacon, who had
had any regular diet for about thirty hours, while they
exposed during that period, in a great measure, both to
winds and the sprays of the sea. The boat having succe
in landing, she returned at eleven a. m. with the artifi
who had got off with considerable difficulty, and who
heartily welcomed by all on board.

Upon inquiry it appeared that three of the stones
laid upon the building had been partially lifted from
beds by the force of the sea, and were now held only by
trenails, and that the cast-iron sheer-crane had again
thrown down and completely broken. With regard to
beacon, the sea at high-water had lifted part of the mc
gallery or lowest floor, and washed away all the lime-c
and other movable articles from it; but the principal p
of this fabric had sustained no damage. On pressing Me
Logan and Watt on the situation of things in the cour
the night, Mr. Logan emphatically said: "That the be
had an *ill-faured* * *twist* when the sea broke upon it at l
water, but that they were not very apprehensive of dan
On inquiring as to how they spent the night, it appe
that they had made shift to keep a small fire burning,
by means of some old sails defended themselves pretty
from the sea sprays.

It was particularly mentioned that by the exertion
James Glen, one of the joiners, a number of articles
saved from being washed off the mortar gallery. Glen
also very useful in keeping up the spirits of the for
party. In the early part of life he had undergone n
curious adventures at sea, which he now recounted some
after the manner of the tales of the *Arabian Nights*. V
one observed that the beacon was a most comfortless l
ing, Glen would presently introduce some of his exploits
hardships, in comparison with which the state of thing
the beacon bore an aspect of comfort and happiness. L
ing to their slender stock of provisions, and their per
and uncertain chance of speedy relief, he would launch

* Ill-formed—ugly.—[R. L. S.]

BUILDING OF BELL ROCK

account of one of his expeditions in the North Sea,
ie vessel, being much disabled in the storm, was driven
the wind with the loss of almost all their provisions;
? ship being much infested with rats, the crew hunted
ermin with great eagerness to help their scanty allow-
By such means Glen had the address to make his com-
s, in some measure, satisfied, or at least passive, with
to their miserable prospects upon this half-tide rock
middle of the ocean. This incident is noticed, more
ilarly, to show the effects of such a happy turn of
even under the most distressing and ill-fated cir-
nces.
rday, 17*th June.*—At eight a. m. the artificers and
, forty-five in number, landed on the rock, and after
ɔurs' work seven stones were laid. The remainder of
le, from the threatening appearance of the weather,
cupied in trenailing and making all things as secure
sible. At twelve noon the rock and building were
overflowed, when the masons and seamen went on
of the tender, but Mr. Watt, with his squad of ten
emained on the beacon throughout the day. As it
resh from the N.W. in the evening, it was found
ticable either to land the building artificers or to take
.ificers off the beacon, and they were accordingly left
all night, but in circumstances very different from
)f the first of this month. The house, being now in
: complete state, was provided with bedding, and they
:he night pretty well, though they complained of hav-
en much disturbed at the time of high-water by the
g and tremulous motion of their house and by the
ig noise of the sea upon the mortar gallery. Here
Glen's versatile powers were again at work in cheer-
) those who seemed to be alarmed, and in securing
ling as far as possible. On this occasion he had only
all to the recollections of some of them the former
which they had spent on the beacon, the wind and
ing then much higher, and their habitation in a far
mfortable state.

When as many stones were built as comprised this d[ay's] work, the demand for mortar was proportionately increa[sed] and the task of the mortar-makers on these occasions [was] both laborious and severe. This operation was chiefly p[er]formed by John Watt,—a strong, active quarrier by p[ro]fession,—who was a perfect character in his way, [and] extremely zealous in his department. While the operati[on]

BUILDING OF BELL ROCK

)f the mortar-makers continued, the forge upon their gallery vas not generally in use; but, as the working hours of the)uilders extended with the height of the building, the forge :ould not be so long wanted, and then a sad confusion often nsued upon the circumscribed floor of the mortar gallery, is the operations of Watt and his assistants trenched greatly ipon those of the smiths. Under these circumstances the)oundary of the smiths was much circumscribed, and they vere personally annoyed, especially in blowy weather, with he dust of the lime in its powdered state. The mortar- nakers, on the other hand, were often not a little distressed vith the heat of the fire and the sparks elicited on the anvil, ind not unaptly complained that they were placed between he " devil and the deep sea."

Sunday, 25th June.—The work being now about ten feet n height, admitted of a rope ladder being distended * be- .ween the beacon and the building. By this " Jacob's Lad- ler," as the seamen termed it, a communication was kept ip with the beacon while the rock was considerably under vater. One end of it being furnished with tackle-blocks, was ixed to the beams of the beacon, at the level of the mortar ;allery, while the further end was connected with the upper :ourse of the building by means of two Lewis bats which vere lifted from course to course as the work advanced. n the same manner a rope furnished with a travelling)ulley was distended for the purpose of transporting the nortar-buckets and other light articles between the beacon ind the building, which also proved a great conveniency o the work. At this period the rope-ladder and tackle for he mortar had a descent from the beacon to the building;)y and by they were on a level, and towards the end of the eason, when the solid part had attained its full height, the iscent was from the mortar-gallery to the building.

Friday, 30th June.—The artificers landed on the rock his morning at a quarter-past six and remained at work ive hours. The cooking apparatus being now in full

* This is an incurable illusion of my grandfather's; he always writes
" distended " for " extended."—[R. L. S.]

A FAMILY OF ENGINEERS

operation, all hands had breakfast on the beacon at the usual hour, and remained there throughout the day. The crane upon the building had to be raised to-day from the eighth to the ninth course, an operation which now required all the strength that could be mustered for working the guy-tackles; for as the top of the crane was at this time about thirty-five feet above the rock, it became much more unmanageable. While the beam was in the act of swinging round from one guy to another, a great strain was suddenly brought upon the opposite tackle, with the end of which the artificers had very improperly neglected to take a turn round some stationary object, which would have given them the complete command of the tackle. Owing to this simple omission, the crane got a preponderancy to one side, and fell upon the building with a terrible crash. The surrounding artificers immediately flew in every direction to get out of its way; but Michael Wishart, the principal builder, having unluckily stumbled upon one of the uncut trenails, fell upon his back. His body fortunately got between the movable beam and the upright shaft of the crane, and was thus saved; but his feet got entangled with the wheels of the crane and were severely injured. Wishart, being a robust young man, endured his misfortune with wonderful firmness; he was laid upon one of the narrow framed beds of the beacon and despatched in a boat to the tender, where the writer was when this accident happened, not a little alarmed on missing the crane from the top of the building, and at the same time seeing a boat rowing towards the vessel with great speed. When the boat came alongside with poor Wishart, stretched upon a bed covered with blankets, a moment of great anxiety followed, which was, however, much relieved when, on stepping into the boat, he was accosted by Wishart, though in a feeble voice, and with an aspect pale as death from excessive bleeding. Directions having been immediately given to the coxswain to apply to Mr. Kennedy at the workyard, to procure the best surgical aid, the boat was sent off without delay to Arbroath. The writer then landed at the rock,

BUILDING OF BELL ROCK

hen the crane was in a very short time got into its place nd again put in a working state.

Monday, 3rd July.—The writer having come to Arbroath ith the yacht, had an opportunity of visiting Michael Wishart, the artificer who had met with so severe an accident at the rock on the 30th ult., and had the pleasure to nd him in a state of recovery. From Dr. Stevenson's account, under whose charge he had been placed, hopes were ntertained that amputation would not be necessary, as his atient still kept free of fever or any appearance of mortication; and Wishart expressed a hope that he might, at ast, be ultimately capable of keeping the light at the Bell ock, as it was not now likely that he would assist further n building the house.

Saturday, 8th July.—It was remarked to-day, with no mall demonstration of joy, that the tide, being neap, did ot, for the first time, overflow the building at high-water. lags were accordingly hoisted on the beacon-house, and rane on the top of the building, which were repeated from he floating light, Lighthouse yacht, tender, *Smeaton, Pariot,* and the two praams. A salute of three guns was also red from the yacht at high-water, when, all the artificers eing collected on the top of the building, three cheers were iven in testimony of this important circumstance. A glass f rum was then served out to all hands on the rock and on oard of the respective ships.

Sunday, 16th July.—Besides laying, boring, trenailing, edging, and grouting thirty-two stones, several other opertions were proceeded with on the rock at low-water, when ome of the artificers were employed at the railways, and at igh-water at the beacon-house. The seamen having prepared a quantity of tarpaulin, or cloth laid over with sucessive coats of hot tar, the joiners had just completed the overing of the roof with it. This sort of covering was ghter and more easily managed than sheet-lead in such a ituation. As a further defence against the weather the hole exterior of this temporary residence was painted with hree coats of white-lead paint. Between the timber fram-

A FAMILY OF ENGINEERS

ing of the habitable part of the beacon the interstices were to be stuffed with moss, as a light substance that would resist dampness and check sifting winds; the whole interior was then to be lined with green baize cloth, so that both without and within the cabins were to have a very comfortable appearance.

Although the building artificers generally remained on the rock, throughout the day, and the millwrights, joiners, and smiths, while their number was considerable, remained also during the night, yet the tender had hitherto been considered as their night quarters. But the wind having in the course of the day shifted to the N.W., and as the passage to the tender, in the boats, was likely to be attended with difficulty, the whole of the artificers, with Mr. Logan, the foreman, preferred remaining all night on the beacon, which had of late become the solitary abode of George Forsyth, a jobbing upholsterer, who had been employed in lining the beacon-house with cloth and in fitting up the bedding. Forsyth was a tall, thin, and rather loose-made man, who had an utter aversion at climbing upon the trap-ladders of the beacon, but especially at the process of boating, and the motion of the ship, which he said "was death itself." He therefore pertinaciously insisted with the landing-master in being left upon the beacon, with a small black dog as his only companion. The writer, however, felt some delicacy in leaving a single individual upon the rock, who must have been very helpless in case of accident. This fabric had, from the beginning, been rather intended by the writer to guard against accident from the loss or damage of a boat, and as a place for making mortar, a smith's shop, and a store for tools during the working months, than as permanent quarters; nor was it at all meant to be possessed until the joiner-work was completely finished, and his own cabin, and that for the foreman, in readiness, when it was still to be left to the choice of the artificers to occupy the tender or the beacon. He, however, considered Forsyth's partiality and confidence in the latter as rather a fortunate occurrence.

Wednesday, 19th July.—The whole of the artificers,

BUILDING OF BELL ROCK

twenty-three in number, now removed of their own accord from the tender, to lodge in the beacon, together with Peter Fortune, a person singularly adapted for a residence of this kind, both from the urbanity of his manners and the versatility of his talents. Fortune, in his person, was of small stature, and rather corpulent. Besides being a good Scots cook, he had acted both as groom and house-servant; he had been a soldier, a sutler, a writer's clerk, and an apothecary, from which he possessed the art of writing and suggesting recipes, and had hence, also, perhaps, acquired a turn for making collections in natural history. But in his practice in surgery on the Bell Rock, for which he received an annual fee of three guineas, he is supposed to have been rather partial to the use of the lancet. In short, Peter was the *factotum* of the beacon-house, where he ostensibly acted in the several capacities of cook, steward, surgeon, and barber, and kept a statement of the rations or expenditure of the provisions with the strictest integrity.

In the present important state of the building, when it had just attained the height of sixteen feet, and the upper courses, and especially the imperfect one, were in the wash of the heaviest seas, an express boat arrived at the rock with a letter from Mr. Kennedy, of the workyard, stating that in consequence of the intended expedition to Walcheren, an embargo had been laid on shipping at all the ports of Great Britain: that both the *Smeaton* and *Patriot* were detained at Arbroath, and that but for the proper view which Mr. Ramsey, the port-officer, had taken of his orders, neither the express boat nor one which had been sent with provisions and necessaries for the floating light would have been permitted to leave the harbour. The writer set off without delay for Arbroath, and on landing used every possible means with the official people, but their orders were deemed so peremptory that even boats were not permitted to sail from any port upon the coast. In the meantime, the collector of the Customs at Montrose applied to the Board at Edinburgh, but could, of himself, grant no relief to the Bell Rock shipping.

A FAMILY OF ENGINEERS

At this critical period Mr. Adam Duff, then Sheriff of Forfarshire, now of the county of Edinburgh, and *ex officio* one of the Commissioners of the Northern Lighthouses, happened to be at Arbroath. Mr. Duff took an immediate interest in representing the circumstances of the case to the Board of Customs at Edinburgh. But such were the doubts entertained on the subject that, on having previously received the appeal from the collector at Montrose, the case had been submitted to the consideration of the Lords of the Treasury, whose decision was now waited for.

In this state of things the writer felt particularly desirous to get the thirteenth course finished, that the building might be in a more secure state in the event of bad weather. An opportunity was therefore embraced on the 25th, in sailing with provisions for the floating light, to carry the necessary stones to the rock for this purpose, which were landed and built on the 26th and 27th. But so closely was the watch kept up that a Custom-house officer was always placed on board of the *Smeaton* and *Patriot* while they were afloat, till the embargo was especially removed from the lighthouse vessels. The artificers at the Bell Rock had been reduced to fifteen, who were regularly supplied with provisions, along with the crew of the floating light, mainly through the port officer's liberal interpretation of his orders.

Tuesday, 1st Aug.—There being a considerable swell and breach of sea upon the rock yesterday, the stones could not be got landed till the day following, when the wind shifted to the southward and the weather improved. But to-day no less than seventy-eight blocks of stone were landed, of which forty were built, which completed the fourteenth and part of the fifteenth courses. The number of workmen now resident in the beacon-house were augmented to twenty-four, including the landing-master's crew from the tender and the boat's crew from the floating light, who assisted at landing the stones. Those daily at work upon the rock at this period amounted to forty-six. A cabin had been laid out for the writer on the beacon, but his apartment had been the last which was finished, and he had not yet taken posses-

BUILDING OF BELL ROCK

sion of it; for though he generally spent the greater part of the day, at this time, upon the rock, yet he always slept on board of the tender.

Friday, 11th Aug.—The wind was S.E. on the 11th, and there was so very heavy a swell of sea upon the rock that no boat could approach it.

Saturday, 12th Aug.—The gale still continuing from the S.E., the sea broke with great violence both upon the building and the beacon. The former being twenty-three feet in height, the upper part of the crane erected on it having been lifted from course to course as the building advanced, was now about thirty-six feet above the rock. From observations made on the rise of the sea by this crane, the artificers were enabled to estimate its height to be about fifty feet above the rock, while the sprays fell with a most alarming noise upon their cabins. At low-water, in the evening, a signal was made from the beacon, at the earnest desire of some of the artificers, for the boats to come to the rock; and although this could not be effected without considerable hazard, it was, however, accomplished, when twelve of their number, being much afraid, applied to the foreman to be relieved, and went on board of the tender. But the remaining fourteen continued on the rock, with Mr. Peter Logan, the foreman builder. Although this rule of allowing an option to every man either to remain on the rock or return to the tender was strictly adhered to, yet, as it would have been extremely inconvenient to have had the men parcelled out in this manner, it became necessary to embrace the first opportunity of sending those who had left the beacon to the workyard, with as little appearance of intention as possible, lest it should hurt their feelings, or prevent others from acting according to their wishes, either in landing on the rock or remaining on the beacon.

Tuesday, 15th Aug.—The wind had fortunately shifted to the S.W. this morning, and though a considerable breach was still upon the rock, yet the landing-master's crew were enabled to get one praam-boat, lightly loaded with five stones, brought in safety to the western creek; these stones

A FAMILY OF ENGINEERS

were immediately laid by the artificers, who gladly embraced the return of good weather to proceed with their operations. The writer had this day taken possession of his cabin in the beacon-house. It was small, but commodious, and was found particularly convenient in coarse and blowing weather, instead of being obliged to make a passage to the tender in an open boat at all times, both during the day and the night, which was often attended with much difficulty and danger.

Saturday, 19th Aug.—For some days past the weather had been occasionally so thick and foggy that no small difficulty was experienced in going even between the rock and the tender, though quite at hand. But the floating light's boat lost her way so far in returning on board that the first land she made, after rowing all night, was Fifeness, a distance of about fourteen miles. The weather having cleared in the morning, the crew stood off again for the floating light, and got on board in a half-famished and much exhausted state, having been constantly rowing for about sixteen hours.

Sunday, 20th Aug.—The weather being very favourable to-day, fifty-three stones were landed, and the builders were not a little gratified in having built the twenty-second course, consisting of fifty-one stones, being the first course which had been completed in one day. This, as a matter of course, produced three hearty cheers. At twelve noon prayers were read for the first time on the Bell Rock; those present, counting thirty, were crowded into the upper apartment of the beacon, where the writer took a central position, while two of the artificers, joining hands, supported the Bible.

Friday, 25th Aug.—To-day the artificers laid forty-five stones, which completed the twenty-fourth course, reckoning above the first entire one, and the twenty-sixth above the rock. This finished the solid part of the building, and terminated the height of the outward casing of granite, which is thirty-one feet six inches above the rock or site of the foundation-stone, and about seventeen feet above high-water of spring-tides. Being a particular crisis in the progress of the lighthouse, the landing and laying of the

BUILDING OF BELL ROCK

last stone for the season was observed with the usual ceremonies.

From observations often made by the writer, in so far as such can be ascertained, it appears that no wave in the open seas, in an unbroken state, rises more than from seven to nine feet above the general surface of the ocean. The Bell Rock Lighthouse may therefore now be considered at from eight to ten feet above the height of the waves; and, although the sprays and heavy seas have often been observed, in the present state of the building, to rise to the height of fifty feet, and fall with a tremendous noise on the beacon-house, yet such seas were not likely to make any impression on a mass of solid masonry, containing about 1400 tons.

Wednesday, 30th Aug.—The whole of the artificers left the rock at mid-day, when the tender made sail for Arbroath, which she reached about six p.m. The vessel being decorated with colours, and having fired a salute of three guns on approaching the harbour, the workyard artificers, with a multitude of people, assembled at the harbour, when mutual cheering and congratulations took place between those afloat and those on the quays. The tender had now, with little exception, been six months on the station at the Bell Rock, and during the last four months few of the squad of builders had been ashore. In particular, Mr. Peter Logan, the foreman, and Mr. Robert Selkirk, principal builder, had never once left the rock. The artificers, having made good wages during their stay, like seamen upon a return voyage, were extremely happy, and spent the evening with much innocent mirth and jollity.

In reflecting upon the state of the matters at the Bell Rock during the working months, when the writer was much with the artificers, nothing can equal the happy manner in which these excellent workmen spent their time. They always went from Arbroath to their arduous task cheering; and they generally returned in the same hearty state. While at the rock, between the tides, they amused themselves in reading, fishing, music, playing cards, draughts, etc., or in sporting with one another. In the workyard at Arbroath,

A FAMILY OF ENGINEERS

the young men were almost, without exception, employed in the evening at school, in writing and arithmetic, and not a few were learning architectural drawing, for which they had every convenience and facility, and were, in a very obliging manner, assisted in their studies by Mr. David Logan, clerk of the works. It therefore affords the most pleasing reflections to look back upon the pursuits of about sixty individuals who for years conducted themselves, on all occasions, in a sober and rational manner.

IV

OPERATIONS OF 1810

1810. *Thursday, 10th May.*—The wind had shifted today to W.N.W., when the writer, with considerable difficulty, was enabled to land upon the rock for the first time this season, at ten a. m. Upon examining the state of the building, and apparatus in general, he had the satisfaction to find everything in good order. The mortar in all the joints was perfectly entire. The building, now thirty feet in height, was thickly coated with *fuci* to the height of about fifteen feet, calculating from the rock: on the eastern side, indeed, the growth of seaweed was observable to the full height of thirty feet, and even on the top or upper bed of the last-laid course, especially towards the eastern side, it had germinated, so as to render walking upon it somewhat difficult.

The beacon-house was in a perfectly sound state, and apparently just as it had been left in the month of November. But, the tides being neap, the lower parts, particularly where the beams rested on the rock, could not now be seen. The floor of the mortar gallery, having been already laid down by Mr. Watt and his men on a former visit, was merely soaked with the sprays; but the joisting-beams which supported it had, in the course of the winter, been covered with a fine downy conferva produced by the range of the sea. They were also a good deal whitened with the mute of the cormorant and other sea-fowls, which had roosted upon the

BUILDING OF BELL ROCK

beacon in winter. Upon ascending to the apartments, it was found that the motion of the sea had thrown open the door of the cook-house: this was only shut with a single latch, that in case of shipwreck at the Bell Rock the mariner might find ready access to the shelter of this forlorn habitation, where a supply of provisions was kept; and, being within two miles and a half of the floating light, a signal could readily be observed, when a boat might be sent to his relief as soon as the weather permitted. An arrangement for this purpose formed one of the instructions on board of the floating light, but happily no instance occurred for putting it in practice. The hearth or fireplace of the cookhouse was built of brick in as secure a manner as possible, to prevent accident from fire; but some of the plaster-work had shaken loose, from its damp state, and the tremulous motion of the beacon in stormy weather. The writer next ascended to the floor which was occupied by the cabins of himself and his assistants, which were in tolerably good order, having only a damp and musty smell. The barrack for the artificers, over all, was next visited; it had now a very dreary and deserted appearance when its former thronged state was recollected. In some parts the water had come through the boarding, and had discoloured the lining of green cloth, but it was, nevertheless, in a good habitable condition. While the seamen were employed in landing a stock of provisions, a few of the artificers set to work with great eagerness to sweep and clean the several apartments. The exterior of the beacon was, in the meantime, examined, and found in perfect order. The painting, though it had a somewhat blanched appearance, adhered firmly both on the sides and roof, and only two or three panes of glass were broken in the cupola, which had either been blown out by the force of the wind or perhaps broken by sea-fowl.

Having on this occasion continued upon the building and beacon a considerable time after the tide had begun to flow, the artificers were occupied in removing the forge from the top of the building, to which the gangway or wooden bridge

A FAMILY OF ENGINEERS

gave great facility; and, although it stretched or had a span of forty-two feet, its construction was extremely simple, while the roadway was perfectly firm and steady. In returning from this visit to the rock every one was pretty well soused in spray before reaching the tender at two o'clock p. m., where things awaited the landing party in as comfortable a way as such a situation would admit.

Friday, 11th May.—The wind was still easterly, accompanied with rather a heavy swell of sea for the operations in hand. A landing was, however, made this morning, when the artificers were immediately employed in scraping the seaweed off the upper course of the building, in order to apply the moulds of the first course of the staircase, that the joggle-holes might be marked off in the upper course of the solid. This was also necessary previously to the writer's fixing the position of the entrance-door, which was regulated chiefly by the appearance of the growth of the seaweed on the building, indicating the direction of the heaviest seas, on the opposite side of which the door was placed. The landing-master's crew succeeded in towing into the creek on the western side of the rock the praam-boat with the balance-crane, which had now been on board of the praam for five days. The several pieces of this machine, having been conveyed along the railways upon the waggons to a position immediately under the bridge, were elevated to its level, or thirty feet above the rock, in the following manner. A chain-tackle was suspended over a pulley from the cross-beam connecting the tops of the kingposts of the bridge, which was worked by a winch-machine with wheel, pinion, and barrel, round which last the chain was wound. This apparatus was placed on the beacon side of the bridge, at the distance of about twelve feet from the cross-beam and pulley in the middle of the bridge. Immediately under the cross-beam a hatch was formed in the roadway of the bridge, measuring seven feet in length and five feet in breadth, made to shut with folding boards like a double door, through which stones and other articles were raised; the folding doors were then let down, and the stone or load was gently lowered

BUILDING OF BELL ROCK

upon a waggon which was wheeled on railway trucks towards the lighthouse. In this manner the several castings of the balance-crane were got up to the top of the solid of the building.

The several apartments of the beacon-house having been cleaned out and supplied with bedding, a sufficient stock of provisions was put into the store, when Peter Fortune, formerly noticed, lighted his fire in the beacon for the first time this season. Sixteen artificers at the same time mounted to their barrack-room, and the foremen of the works also took possession of their cabin, all heartily rejoiced at getting rid of the trouble of boating and the sickly motion of the tender.

Saturday, 12th May.—The wind was at E.N.E., blowing so fresh, and accompanied with so much sea, that no stones could be landed to-day. The people on the rock, however, were busily employed in screwing together the balance-crane, cutting out the joggle-holes in the upper course, and preparing all things for commencing the building operations.

Sunday, 13th May.—The weather still continues boisterous, although the barometer has all the while stood at about 30 inches. Towards evening the wind blew so fresh at E. by S. that the boats both of the *Smeaton* and tender were obliged to be hoisted in, and it was feared that the *Smeaton* would have to slip her moorings. The people on the rock were seen busily employed, and had the balance-crane apparently ready for use, but no communication could be had with them to-day.

Monday, 14th May.—The wind continued to blow so fresh, and the *Smeaton* rode so heavily with her cargo, that at noon a signal was made for her getting under weigh, when she stood towards Arbroath; and on board of the tender we are still without any communication with the people on the rock, where the sea was seen breaking over the top of the building in great sprays, and raging with much agitation among the beams of the beacon.

Thursday, 17th May.—The wind, in the course of the

A FAMILY OF ENGINEERS

day, had shifted from north to west; the sea being also considerably less, a boat landed on the rock at six p. m., for the first time since the 11th, with the provisions and water brought off by the *Patriot*. The inhabitants of the beacon were all well, but tired above measure for want of employment, as the balance-crane and apparatus was all in readiness. Under these circumstances they felt no less desirous of the return of good weather than those afloat, who were continually tossed with the agitation of the sea. The writer, in particular, felt himself almost as much fatigued and worn-out as he had been at any period since the commencement of the work. The very backward state of the weather at so advanced a period of the season unavoidably created some alarm lest he should be overtaken with bad weather at a late period of the season, with the building operations in an unfinished state. These apprehensions were, no doubt, rather increased by the inconveniences of his situation afloat, as the tender rolled and pitched excessively at times. This being also his first off-set for the season, every bone of his body felt sore with preserving a sitting posture while he endeavoured to pass away the time in reading; as for writing, it was wholly impracticable. He had several times entertained thoughts of leaving the station for a few days and going into Arbroath with the tender till the weather should improve; but as the artificers had been landed on the rock he was averse to this at the commencement of the season, knowing also that he would be equally uneasy in every situation till the first cargo was landed: and he therefore resolved to continue at his post until this should be effected.

Friday, 18th May.—The wind being now N. W., the sea was considerably run down, and this morning at five o'clock the landing-master's crew, thirteen in number, left the tender; and, having now no detention with the landing of artificers, they proceeded to unmoor the *Hedderwick* praam-boat, and towed her alongside of the *Smeaton;* and in the course of the day twenty-three blocks of stone, three casks of pozzolano, three of sand, three of lime, and one of Roman

BUILDING OF BELL ROCK

cement, together with three bundles of trenails and three of wedges, were all landed on the rock and raised to the top of the building by means of the tackle suspended from the cross-beam on the middle of the bridge. The stones were then moved along the bridge on the waggon to the building within reach of the balance-crane, with which they were laid in their respective places on the building. The masons immediately thereafter proceeded to bore the trenail-holes into the course below, and otherwise to complete the one in hand. When the first stone was to be suspended by the balance-crane, the bell on the beacon was rung, and all the artificers and seamen were collected on the building. Three hearty cheers were given while it was lowered into its place, and the steward served round a glass of rum, when success was drunk to the further progress of the building.

Sunday, 20th May.—The wind was southerly to-day, but there was much less sea than yesterday, and the landing-master's crew were enabled to discharge and land twenty-three pieces of stone and other articles for the work. The artificers had completed the laying of the twenty-seventh or first course of the staircase this morning, and in the evening they finished the boring, trenailing, wedging, and grouting it with mortar. At twelve o'clock noon the beacon-house bell was rung, and all hands were collected on the top of the building, where prayers were read for the first time on the lighthouse, which forcibly struck every one, and had, upon the whole, a very impressive effect.

From the hazardous situation of the beacon-house with regard to fire, being composed wholly of timber, there was no small risk from accident; and on this account one of the most steady of the artificers was appointed to see that the fire of the cooking-house, and the lights in general, were carefully extinguished at stated hours.

Monday, 4th June.—This being the birthday of our much-revered Sovereign King George III., now in the fiftieth year of his reign, the shipping of the Lighthouse Service were this morning decorated with colours according to the taste of their respective captains. Flags were also hoisted upon the beacon-house and balance-crane on the top of the building. At twelve noon a salute was fired from the tender, when the King's health was drunk, with all the honours, both on the rock and on board of the shipping.

Tuesday, 5th June.—As the lighthouse advanced in height, the cubical contents of the stones were less, but they had to be raised to a greater height; and the walls, being thinner, were less commodious for the necessary machinery and the artificers employed, which considerably retarded the work. Inconvenience was also occasionally experienced from the men dropping their coats, hats, mallets, and other tools, at high-water, which were carried away by the tide; and the danger to the people themselves was now greatly increased. Had any of them fallen from the beacon or building at high-water, while the landing-master's crew were generally engaged with the craft at a distance, it must have rendered the accident doubly painful to those on the rock, who at this time had no boat, and consequently no means of rendering immediate and prompt assistance. In such cases it would have been too late to have got a boat by signal from the tender. A small boat, which could be lowered at pleasure, was therefore suspended by a pair of davits projected from the cook-house, the keel being about thirty feet from the rock. This boat, with its tackle, was put under the charge of James Glen, of whose exertions on the beacon mention has already been made, and who, having in early life been a seaman, was also very expert in the management of a boat. A life-buoy was likewise suspended from the bridge, to which a coil of line two hundred fathoms in length was attached, which could be let out to a person falling into the water, or to the people in the boat, should they not be able to work her with the oars.

Thursday, 7th June.—To-day twelve stones were landed on the rock, being the remainder of the *Patriot's* cargo; and the artificers built the thirty-ninth course, consisting of fourteen stones. The Bell Rock works had now a very busy appearance, as the lighthouse was daily getting more into form. Besides the artificers and their cook, the writer and

BUILDING OF BELL ROCK

his servant were also lodged on the beacon, counting in all twenty-nine; and at low-water the landing-master's crew, consisting of from twelve to fifteen seamen, were employed in transporting the building materials, working the landing apparatus on the rock, and dragging the stone waggons along the railways.

Friday, 8th June.—In the course of this day the weather varied much. In the morning it was calm, in the middle part of the day there were light airs of wind from the south, and in the evening fresh breezes from the east. The barometer in the writer's cabin in the beacon-house oscillated from 30 inches to 30.42, and the weather was extremely pleasant. This, in any situation, forms one of the chief comforts of life; but, as may easily be conceived, it was doubly so to people stuck, as it were, upon a pinnacle in the middle of the ocean.

Sunday, 10th June.—One of the praam-boats had been brought to the rock with eleven stones, notwithstanding the perplexity which attended the getting of those formerly landed taken up to the building. Mr. Peter Logan, the foreman builder, interposed, and prevented this cargo from being delivered; but the landing-master's crew were exceedingly averse to this arrangement, from an idea that "ill-luck" would in future attend the praam, her cargo, and those who navigated her, from thus reversing her voyage. It may be noticed that this was the first instance of a praam-boat having been sent from the Bell Rock with any part of her cargo on board, and was considered so uncommon an occurrence that it became a topic of conversation among the seamen and artificers.

Tuesday, 12th June.—To-day the stones formerly sent from the rock were safely landed, notwithstanding the augury of the seamen, in consequence of their being sent away two days before.

Thursday, 14th June.—To-day twenty-seven stones and eleven joggle-pieces were landed, part of which consisted of the forty-seventh course, forming the storeroom floor. The builders were at work this morning by four o'clock,

A FAMILY OF ENGINEERS

in the hopes of being able to accomplish the laying of the eighteen stones of this course. But at eight o'clock in the evening they had still two to lay, and, as the stones of this course were very unwieldy, being six feet in length, they required much precaution and care both in lifting and laying them. It was only on the writer's suggestion to Mr. Logan that the artificers were induced to leave off, as they had intended to complete this floor before going to bed. The two remaining stones were, however, laid in their places without mortar when the bell on the beacon was rung, and, all hands being collected on the top of the building, three hearty cheers were given on covering the first apartment. The steward then served out a dram to each, when the whole retired to their barrack much fatigued, but with the anticipation of the most perfect repose even in the "hurrican-house," amidst the dashing seas on the Bell Rock.

While the workmen were at breakfast and dinner it was the writer's usual practice to spend his time on the walls of the building, which, notwithstanding the narrowness of the track, nevertheless formed his principal walk when the rock was under water. But this afternoon he had his writing-desk set upon the storeroom floor, when he wrote to Mrs. Stevenson—certainly the first letter dated from the Bell Rock Lighthouse—giving a detail of the fortunate progress of the work, with an assurance that the lighthouse would soon be completed at the rate at which it now proceeded; and, the *Patriot* having sailed for Arbroath in the evening, he felt no small degree of pleasure in despatching this communication to his family.

The weather still continuing favourable for the operations at the rock, the work proceeded with much energy, through the exertions both of the seamen and artificers. For the more speedy and effectual working of the several tackles in raising the materials as the building advanced in height, and there being a great extent of railway to attend to, which required constant repairs, two additional millwrights were added to the complement on the rock, which, including the writer, now counted thirty-one in all. So crowded was the

BUILDING OF BELL ROCK

men's barrack that the beds were ranged five tiers in height, allowing only about one foot eight inches for each bed. The artificers commenced this morning at five o'clock, and, in the course of the day, they laid the forty-eighth and forty-ninth courses, consisting each of sixteen blocks. From the favourable state of the weather, and the regular manner in which the work now proceeded, the artificers had generally from four to seven extra hours' work, which, including their stated wages of 3s. 4d., yielded them from 5s. 4d. to about 6s. 10d. per day, besides their board; even the postage of their letters was paid while they were at the Bell Rock. In these advantages the foremen also shared, having about double the pay and amount of premiums of the artificers. The seamen being less out of their element in the Bell Rock operations than the landsmen, their premiums consisted in a lump sum payable at the end of the season, which extended from three to ten guineas.

As the laying of the floors was somewhat tedious, the landing-master and his crew had got considerably beforehand with the building artificers in bringing materials faster to the rock than they could be built. The seamen having, therefore, some spare time, were occasionally employed during fine weather in dredging or grappling for the several mushroom anchors and mooring chains which had been lost in the vicinity of the Bell Rock during the progress of the work by the breaking loose and drifting of the floating buoys. To encourage their exertions in this search, five guineas were offered as a premium for each set they should find; and, after much patient application, they succeeded to-day in hooking one of these lost anchors with its chain.

It was a general remark at the Bell Rock, as before noticed, that fish were never plenty in its neighbourhood excepting in good weather. Indeed, the seamen used to speculate about the state of the weather from their success in fishing. When the fish disappeared at the rock, it was considered a sure indication that a gale was not far off, as the fish seemed to seek shelter in deeper water from the roughness of the sea during these changes in the weather.

A FAMILY OF ENGINEERS

At this time the rock, at high-water, was completely covered with podlies, or the fry of the coal-fish, about six or eight inches in length. The artificers sometimes occupied half an hour after breakfast and dinner in catching these little fishes, but were more frequently supplied from the boats of the tender.

Saturday, 16th June.—The landing-master having this day discharged the *Smeaton* and loaded the *Hedderwick* and *Dickie* praam-boats with nineteen stones, they were towed to their respective moorings, when Captain Wilson, in consequence of the heavy swell of sea, came in his boat to the beacon-house to consult with the writer as to the propriety of venturing the loaded praam-boats with their cargoes to the rock while so much sea was running. After some dubiety expressed on the subject, in which the ardent mind of the landing-master suggested many arguments in favour of his being able to convey the praams in perfect safety, it was acceded to. In bad weather, and especially on occasions of difficulty like the present, Mr. Wilson, who was an extremely active seaman, measuring about five feet three inches in height, of a robust habit, generally dressed himself in what he called a *monkey jacket*, made of thick duffle cloth, with a pair of Dutchman's petticoat trousers, reaching only to his knees, where they were met with a pair of long water-tight boots; with this dress, his glazed hat, and his small brass speaking-trumpet in his hand, he bade defiance to the weather. When he made his appearance in this most suitable attire for the service, his crew seemed to possess additional life, never failing to use their utmost exertions when the captain put on his *storm rigging*. They had this morning commenced loading the praam-boats at four o'clock, and proceeded to tow them into the eastern landing-place, which was accomplished with much dexterity, though not without the risk of being thrown, by the force of the sea, on certain projecting ledges of the rock. In such a case the loss even of a single stone would have greatly retarded the work. For the greater safety in entering the creek, it was necessary to put out several warps and guyropes to guide

BUILDING OF BELL ROCK

the boats into its narrow and intricate entrance; and it frequently happened that the sea made a clean breach over the praams, which not only washed their decks, but completely drenched the crew in water.

Sunday, 17th June.—It was fortunate, in the present state of the weather, that the fiftieth course was in a sheltered spot, within the reach of the tackle of the winch-machine upon the bridge; a few stones were stowed upon the bridge itself, and the remainder upon the building, which kept the artificers at work. The stowing of the materials upon the rock was the department of Alexander Brebner, mason, who spared no pains in attending to the safety of the stones, and who, in the present state of the work, when the stones were landed faster than could be built, generally worked till the water rose to his middle. At one o'clock to-day the bell rung for prayers, and all hands were collected into the upper barrack-room of the beacon-house, when the usual service was performed.

The wind blew very hard in the course of last night from N.E., and to-day the sea ran so high that no boat could approach the rock. During the dinner-hour, when the writer was going to the top of the building as usual, but just as he had entered the door and was about to ascend the ladder, a great noise was heard overhead, and in an instant he was soused in water from a sea which had most unexpectedly come over the walls, though now about fifty-eight feet in height. On making his retreat, he found himself completely whitened by the lime, which had mixed with the water while dashing down through the different floors; and, as nearly as he could guess, a quantity equal to about a hogshead had come over the walls, and now streamed out at the door. After having shifted himself, he again sat down in his cabin, the sea continuing to run so high that the builders did not resume their operations on the walls this afternoon. The incident just noticed did not create more surprise in the mind of the writer than the sublime appearance of the waves as they rolled majestically over the rock. This scene he greatly enjoyed while sitting at his cabin window; each wave approached the beacon like a vast scroll unfolding; and in passing discharged a quantity of air, which he not only distinctly felt, but was even sufficient to lift the leaves of a book which lay before him. These waves might be ten or twelve feet in height, and about 250 feet in length, their smaller end being towards the north, where the water was deep, and they were opened or cut through by the interposition of the building and beacon. The gradual manner in which the sea, upon these occasions, is observed to become calm or to subside, is a very remarkable feature of this phenomenon. For example, when a gale is succeeded by a calm, every third or fourth wave forms one of these great seas, which occur in spaces of from three to five minutes, as noted by the writer's watch; but in the course of the next tide they become less frequent, and take off so as to occur only in ten or fifteen minutes; and, singular enough, at the third tide after such gales, the writer has remarked that only one or two of these great waves appear in the course of the whole tide.

Tuesday, 19th June.—The 19th was a very unpleasant and disagreeable day, both for the seamen and artificers, as it rained throughout with little intermission from four a.m. till eleven p.m., accompanied with thunder and lightning, during which period the work nevertheless continued unremittingly, and the builders laid the fifty-first and fifty-second courses. This state of weather was no less severe upon the mortar-makers, who required to temper or prepare the mortar of a thicker or thinner consistency, in some measure, according to the state of the weather. From the elevated position of the building the mortar gallery on the beacon was now much lower, and the lime-buckets were made to traverse upon a rope distended between it and the building. On occasions like the present, however, there was often a difference of opinion between the builders and the mortar-makers. John Watt, who had the principal charge of the mortar, was a most active worker, but, being somewhat of an irascible temper, the builders occasionally amused themselves at his expense: for while he was eagerly at work with

BUILDING OF BELL ROCK

his large iron-shod pestle in the mortar-tub, they often sent down contradictory orders, some crying, " Make it a little stiffer, or thicker, John," while others called out to make it " thinner," to which he generally returned very speedy and sharp replies, so that these conversations at times were rather amusing.

During wet weather the situation of the artificers on the top of the building was extremely disagreeable; for although their work did not require great exertion, yet, as each man had his particular part to perform, either in working the crane or in laying the stones, it required the closest application and attention, not only on the part of Mr. Peter Logan, the foreman, who was constantly on the walls, but also of the chief workmen. Robert Selkirk, the principal builder, for example, had every stone to lay in its place. David Cumming, a mason, had the charge of working the tackle of the balance-weight, and James Scott, also a mason, took charge of the purchase with which the stones were laid; while the pointing the joints of the walls with cement was intrusted to William Reid and William Kennedy, who stood upon a scaffold suspended over the walls in rather a frightful manner. The least act of carelessness or inattention on the part of any of these men might have been fatal, not only to themselves, but also to the surrounding workmen, especially if any accident had happened to the crane itself, while the material damage or loss of a single stone would have put an entire stop to the operations until another could have been brought from Arbroath. The artificers, having wrought seven and a half hours of extra time to-day, had 3s. 9d. of extra pay, while the foremen had 7s. 6d. over and above their stated pay and board. Although, therefore, the work was both hazardous and fatiguing, yet, the encouragement being considerable, they were always very cheerful, and perfectly reconciled to the confinement and other disadvantages of the place.

During fine weather, and while the nights were short, the duty on board of the floating light was literally nothing but a waiting on, and therefore one of her boats, with a crew of

A FAMILY OF ENGINEERS

five men, daily attended the rock, but always returned to the vessel at night. The carpenter, however, was one of those who was left on board of the ship, as he also acted in the capacity of assistant lightkeeper, being, besides, a person who was apt to feel discontent and to be averse to changing his quarters, especially to work with the millwrights and joiners at the rock, who often, for hours together, wrought knee-deep, and not unfrequently up to the middle in water. Mr. Watt having about this time made a requisition for another hand, the carpenter was ordered to attend the rock in the floating light's boat. This he did with great reluctance, and found so much fault that he soon got into discredit with his messmates. On this occasion he left the Lighthouse Service, and went as a sailor in a vessel bound for America—a step which, it is believed, he soon regretted, as, in the course of things, he would, in all probability, have accompanied Mr. John Reid, the principal lightkeeper of the floating light, to the Bell Rock Lighthouse as his principal assistant. The writer had a wish to be of service to this man, as he was one of those who came off to the floating light in the month of September, 1807, while she was riding at single anchor after the severe gale of the 7th, at a time when it was hardly possible to make up this vessel's crew; but the crossness of his manner prevented his reaping the benefit of such intentions.

Friday, 22nd June.—The building operations had for some time proceeded more slowly, from the higher parts of the lighthouse requiring much longer time than an equal tonnage of the lower courses. The duty of the landing-master's crew had, upon the whole, been easy of late; for though the work was occasionally irregular, yet the stones being lighter, they were more speedily lifted from the hold of the stone vessel to the deck of the praam-boat, and again to the waggons on the railway, after which they came properly under the charge of the foreman builder. It is, however, a strange, though not an uncommon, feature in the human character, that, when people have least to complain of they are most apt to become dissatisfied, as was now

BUILDING OF BELL ROCK

the case with the seamen employed in the Bell Rock service about their rations of beer. Indeed, ever since the carpenter of the floating light, formerly noticed, had been brought to the rock, expressions of discontent had been manifested upon various occasions. This being represented to the writer, he sent for Captain Wilson, the landing-master, and Mr. Taylor, commander of the tender, with whom he talked over the subject. They stated that they considered the daily allowance of the seamen in every respect ample, and that, the work being now much lighter than formerly, they had no just ground for complaint; Mr. Taylor adding that, if those who now complained " were even to be fed upon soft bread and turkeys, they would not think themselves right." At twelve noon the work of the landing-master's crew was completed for the day; but at four o'clock, while the rock was under water, those on the beacon were surprised by the arrival of a boat from the tender without any signal having been made from the beacon. It brought the following note to the writer from the landing-master's crew:—

"Sir Joseph Banks Tender.
" SIR,—We are informed by our masters that our allowance is to be as before, and it is not sufficient to serve us, for we have been at work since four o'clock this morning, and we have come on board to dinner, and there is no beer for us before to-morrow morning, to which a sufficient answer is required before we go from the beacon; and we are, Sir, your most obedient servants."

On reading this, the writer returned a verbal message, intimating that an answer would be sent on board of the tender, at the same time ordering the boat instantly to quit the beacon. He then addressed the following note to the landing-master:—

"Beacon-house, 22nd June, 1810,
Five o'clock p.m.
" SIR,—I have just now received a letter purporting to be from the landing-master's crew and seamen on board of the *Sir Joseph Banks*, though without either date or signa-

A FAMILY OF ENGINEERS

ture; in answer to which I enclose a statement of the daily allowance of provisions for the seamen in this service, which you will post up in the ship's galley, and at seven o'clock this evening I will come on board to inquire into this unexpected and most unnecessary demand for an additional allowance of beer. In the enclosed you will not find any alteration from the original statement, fixed in the galley at the beginning of the season. I have, however, judged this mode of giving your people an answer preferable to that of conversing with them on the beacon.—I am, Sir, your most obedient servant,

"ROBERT STEVENSON.

" To CAPTAIN WILSON."

" *Beacon House, 22nd June*, 1810.—Schedule of the daily allowance of provisions to be served out on board of the *Sir Joseph Banks* tender: '1¼ lb. beef; 1 lb. bread; 8 oz. oat meal; 2 oz. barley; 2 oz. butter; 3 quarts beer; vegetables and salt no stated allowance. When the seamen are employed in unloading the *Smeaton* and *Patriot*, a draught of beer is, as formerly, to be allowed from the stock of these vessels. Further, in wet and stormy weather, when the work commences very early in the morning, or continues till a late hour at night, a glass of spirits will also be served out to the crew as heretofore, on the requisition of the landing-master.

"ROBERT STEVENSON."

On writing this letter and schedule, a signal was made on the beacon for the landing-master's boat, which immediately came to the rock, and the schedule was afterwards stuck up in the tender's galley. When sufficient time had been allowed to the crew to consider of their conduct, a second signal was made for a boat, and at seven o'clock the writer left the Bell Rock, after a residence of four successive weeks in the beacon-house. The first thing which occupied his attention on board of the tender was to look round upon the lighthouse, which he saw, with some degree of emotion and

BUILDING OF BELL ROCK

surprise, now vying in height with the beacon-house; for although he had often viewed it from the extremity of the western railway on the rock, yet the scene, upon the whole, seemed far more interesting from the tender's moorings at the distance of about half a mile.

The *Smeaton* having just arrived at her moorings with a cargo, a signal was made for Captain Pool to come on board of the tender, that he might be at hand to remove from the service any of those who might persist in their discontented conduct. One of the two principal leaders in this affair, the master of one of the praam-boats, who had also steered the boat which brought the letter to the beacon, was first called upon deck, and asked if he had read the statement fixed up in the galley this afternoon, and whether he was satisfied with it. He replied that he had read the paper, but was not satisfied, as it held out no alteration on the allowance, on which he was immediately ordered into the *Smeaton's* boat. The next man called had but lately entered the service, and, being also interrogated as to his resolution, he declared himself to be of the same mind with the praam-master, and was also forthwith ordered into the boat. The writer, without calling any more of the seamen, went forward to the gangway, where they were collected and listening to what was passing upon deck. He addressed them at the hatchway, and stated that two of their companions had just been dismissed the service and sent on board of the *Smeaton* to be conveyed to Arbroath. He therefore wished each man to consider for himself how far it would be proper, by any unreasonableness of conduct, to place themselves in a similar situation, especially as they were aware that it was optional in him either to dismiss them or send them on board a man-of-war. It might appear that much inconveniency would be felt at the rock by a change of hands at this critical period, by checking for a time the progress of a building so intimately connected with the best interests of navigation; yet this would be but of a temporary nature, while the injury to themselves might be irreparable. It was now, therefore, required of any man who, in this disgraceful manner, chose to leave the service, that he should instantly make his appearance on deck while the *Smeaton's* boat was alongside. But those below having expressed themselves satisfied with their situation—viz., William Brown, George Gibb, Alexander Scott, John Dick, Robert Couper, Alexander Shephard, James Grieve, David Carey, William Pearson, Stuart Eaton, Alexander Lawrence, and John Spink—were accordingly considered as having returned to their duty. This disposition to mutiny, which had so strongly manifested itself, being now happily suppressed, Captain Pool got orders to proceed for Arbroath Bay, and land the two men he had on board, and to deliver the following letter at the office of the workyard:—

"*On board of the Tender off the Bell Rock,
22nd June*, 1810, *eight o'clock p.m.*

"DEAR SIR,—A discontented and mutinous spirit having manifested itself of late among the landing-master's crew, they struck work to-day and demanded an additional allowance of beer, and I have found it necessary to dismiss D———d and M———e, who are now sent on shore with the *Smeaton*. You will therefore be so good as to pay them their wages, including this day only. Nothing can be more unreasonable than the conduct of the seamen on this occasion, as the landing-master's crew not only had their own allowance on board of the tender, but, in the course of this day, they had drawn no fewer than twenty-four quart pots of beer from the stock of the *Patriot* while unloading her.—I remain, yours truly,

"ROBERT STEVENSON.

"To MR. LACHLAN KENNEDY,
    Bell Rock Office, Arbroath."

On despatching this letter to Mr. Kennedy, the writer returned to the beacon about nine o'clock, where this afternoon's business had produced many conjectures, especially when the *Smeaton* got under weigh, instead of proceeding to land her cargo. The bell on the beacon being rung, the artificers were assembled on the bridge, when the affair was

BUILDING OF BELL ROCK

explained to them. He, at the same time, congratulated them upon the first appearance of mutiny being happily set at rest by the dismissal of its two principal abettors.

Sunday, 24th June.—At the rock, the landing of the materials and the building operations of the light-room store went on successfully, and in a way similar to those of the provision store. To-day it blew fresh breezes; but the seamen nevertheless landed twenty-eight stones, and the artificers built the fifty-eighth and fifty-ninth courses. The works were visited by Mr. Murdoch, junior, from Messrs. Boulton and Watt's works of Soho. He landed just as the bell rung for prayers, after which the writer enjoyed much pleasure from his very intelligent conversation; and, having been almost the only stranger he had seen for some weeks, he parted with him, after a short interview, with much regret.

Thursday, 28th June.—Last night the wind had shifted to north-east, and, blowing fresh, was accompanied with a heavy surf upon the rock. Towards highwater it had a very grand and wonderful appearance. Waves of considerable magnitude rose as high as the solid or level of the entrance-door, which, being open to the south-west, was fortunately to the leeward; but on the windward side the sprays flew like lightning up the sloping sides of the building; and although the walls were now elevated sixty-four feet above the rock, and about fifty-two feet from highwater mark, yet the artificers were nevertheless wetted, and occasionally interrupted, in their operations on the top of the walls. These appearances were in a great measure new at the Bell Rock, there having till of late been no building to conduct the seas, or object to compare with them. Although, from the description of the Eddystone Lighthouse, the mind was prepared for such effects, yet they were not expected to the present extent in the summer season; the sea being most awful to-day, whether observed from the beacon or the building. To windward, the sprays fell from the height above noticed in the most wonderful cascades, and streamed down the walls of the building in froth as white as

A FAMILY OF ENGINEERS

snow. To leeward of the lighthouse the collision or meeting of the waves produced a pure white kind of *drift;* it rose about thirty feet in height, like a fine downy mist, which, in its fall, felt upon the face and hands more like a dry powder than a liquid substance. The effects of these seas, as they raged among the beams and dashed upon the higher parts of the beacon, produced a temporary tremulous motion throughout the whole fabric, which to a stranger must have been frightful.

Sunday, 1st July.—The writer had now been at the Bell Rock since the latter end of May, or about six weeks, during four of which he had been a constant inhabitant of the beacon without having been once off the rock. After witnessing the laying of the sixty-seventh or second course of the bed-room apartment, he left the rock with the tender and went ashore, as some arrangements were to be made for the future conduct of the works at Arbroath, which were soon to be brought to a close; the landing-master's crew having, in the meantime, shifted on board of the *Patriot*. In leaving the rock, the writer kept his eyes fixed upon the lighthouse, which had recently got into the form of a house, having several tiers or stories of windows. Nor was he unmindful of his habitation in the beacon—now far overtopped by the masonry,—where he had spent several weeks in a kind of active retirement, making practical experiment of the fewness of the positive wants of man. His cabin measured not more than four feet three inches in breadth on the floor; and though, from the oblique direction of the beams of the beacon, it widened towards the top, yet it did not admit of the full extension of his arms when he stood on the floor; while its length was little more than sufficient for suspending a cot-bed during the night, calculated for being triced up to the roof through the day, which left free room for the admission of occasional visitants. His folding table was attached with hinges, immediately under the small window of the apartment, and his books, barometer, thermometer, portmanteau, and two or three camp-stools, formed the bulk of his movables. His diet being plain, the parapher-

BUILDING OF BELL ROCK

nalia of the table were proportionally simple; though everything had the appearance of comfort, and even of neatness, the walls being covered with green cloth formed into panels with red tape, and his bed festooned with curtains of yellow cotton-stuff. If, in speculating upon the abstract wants of man in such a state of exclusion, one were reduced to a single book, the Sacred Volume—whether considered for the striking diversity of its story, the morality of its doctrine, or the important truths of its gospel—would have proved by far the greatest treasure.

Monday, 2nd July.—In walking over the workyard at Arbroath this morning, the writer found that the stones of the course immediately under the cornice were all in hand, and that a week's work would now finish the whole, while the intermediate courses lay ready numbered and marked for shipping to the rock. Among other subjects which had occupied his attention to-day was a visit from some of the relations of George Dall, a young man who had been impressed near Dundee in the month of February last; a dispute had arisen between the magistrates of that burgh and the Regulating Officer as to his right of impressing Dall, who was *bona fide* one of the protected seamen in the Bell Rock service. In the meantime, the poor lad was detained, and ultimately committed to the prison of Dundee, to remain until the question should be tried before the Court of Session. His friends were naturally very desirous to have him relieved upon bail. But, as this was only to be done by the judgment of the Court, all that could be said was that his pay and allowances should be continued in the same manner as if he had been upon the sick-list. The circumstances of Dall's case were briefly these:—He had gone to see some of his friends in the neighbourhood of Dundee, in winter, while the works were suspended, having got leave of absence from Mr. Taylor, who commanded the Bell Rock tender, and had in his possession one of the Protection Medals. Unfortunately, however, for Dall, the Regulating Officer thought proper to disregard these documents, as, according to the strict and literal interpretation of the Admiralty regulations, a sea-

A FAMILY OF ENGINEERS

man does not stand protected unless he is actually on board of his ship, or in a boat belonging to her, or has the Admiralty protection in his possession. This order of the Board, however, cannot be rigidly followed in practice; and therefore, when the matter is satisfactorily stated to the Regulating Officer, the impressed man is generally liberated. But in Dall's case this was peremptorily refused, and he was retained at the instance of the magistrates. The writer having brought the matter under the consideration of the Commissioners of the Northern Lighthouses, they authorized it to be tried on the part of the Lighthouse Board, as one of extreme hardship. The Court, upon the first hearing, ordered Dall to be liberated from prison; and the proceedings never went further.

Wednesday, 4th July.—Being now within twelve courses of being ready for building the cornice, measures were taken for getting the stones of it and the parapet-wall of the light-room brought from Edinburgh, where, as before noticed, they had been prepared and were in readiness for shipping. The honour of conveying the upper part of the lighthouse, and of landing the last stone of the building on the rock, was considered to belong to Captain Pool of the *Smeaton*, who had been longer in the service than the master of the *Patriot*. The *Smeaton* was, therefore, now partly loaded with old iron, consisting of broken railways and other lumber which had been lying about the rock. After landing these at Arbroath, she took on board James Craw, with his horse and cart, which could now be spared at the workyard, to be employed in carting the stones from Edinburgh to Leith. Alexander Davidson and William Kennedy, two careful masons, were also sent to take charge of the loading of the stones at Greenside and stowing them on board of the vessel at Leith. The writer also went on board, with a view to call at the Bell Rock and to take his passage up the Firth of Forth. The wind, however, coming to blow very fresh from the eastward, with thick and foggy weather, it became necessary to reef the mainsail and set the second-jib. When in the act of making a tack towards the tender, the sailors

BUILDING OF BELL ROCK

who worked the head-sheets were, all of a sudden, alarmed with the sound of a smith's hammer and anvil on the beacon, and had just time to put the ship about to save her from running ashore on the north-western point of the rock, marked "James Craw's Horse." On looking towards the direction from whence the sound came, the building and beacon-house were seen, with consternation, while the ship was hailed by those on the rock, who were no less confounded at seeing the near approach of the *Smeaton;* and, just as the vessel cleared the danger, the smith and those in the mortar gallery made signs in token of their happiness at our fortunate escape. From this occurrence the writer had an experimental proof of the utility of the large bells which were in preparation to be rung by the machinery of the revolving light; for, had it not been for the sound of the smith's anvil, the *Smeaton,* in all probability, would have been wrecked upon the rock. In case the vessel had struck, those on board might have been safe, having now the beacon-house as a place of refuge; but the vessel, which was going at a great velocity, must have suffered severely, and it was more than probable that the horse would have been drowned, there being no means of getting him out of the vessel. Of this valuable animal and his master we shall take an opportunity of saying more in another place.

Thursday, 5th July.—The weather cleared up in the course of the night, but the wind shifted to the N.E. and blew very fresh. From the force of the wind, being now the period of spring-tides, a very heavy swell was experienced at the rock. At two o'clock on the following morning the people on the beacon were in a state of great alarm about their safety, as the sea had broke up part of the floor of the mortar gallery, which was thus cleared of the lime-casks and other buoyant articles; and, the alarm-bell being rung, all hands were called to render what assistance was in their power for the safety of themselves and the materials. At this time some would willingly have left the beacon and gone into the building: the sea, however, ran so high that there was no passage along the bridge of communication, and,

A FAMILY OF ENGINEERS

when the interior of the lighthouse came to be examined in the morning, it appeared that great quantities of water had come over the walls—now eighty feet in height—and had run down through the several apartments and out at the entrance door.

The upper course of the lighthouse at the workyard of Arbroath was completed on the 6th, and the whole of the stones were, therefore, now ready for being shipped to the rock. From the present state of the work it was impossible that the two squads of artificers at Arbroath and the Bell Rock could meet together at this period; and as in public works of this kind, which had continued for a series of years, it is not customary to allow the men to separate without what is termed a "finishing-pint," five guineas were for this purpose placed at the disposal of Mr. David Logan, clerk of works. With this sum the stone-cutters at Arbroath had a merry meeting in their barrack, collected their sweethearts and friends, and concluded their labours with a dance. It was remarked, however, that their happiness on this occasion was not without alloy. The consideration of parting and leaving a steady and regular employment, to go in quest of work and mix with other society, after having been harmoniously lodged for years together in one large "guildhall or barrack," was rather painful.

Friday, 6th July.—While the writer was at Edinburgh he was fortunate enough to meet with Mrs. Dickson, only daughter of the late celebrated Mr. Smeaton, whose works at the Eddystone Lighthouse had been of such essential consequence to the operations at the Bell Rock. Even her own elegant accomplishments are identified with her father's work, she having herself made the drawing of the vignette on the title-page of the *Narrative of the Eddystone Lighthouse*. Every admirer of the works of that singularly eminent man must also feel an obligation to her for the very comprehensive and distinct account given of his life, which is attached to his reports, published, in three volumes quarto, by the Society of Civil Engineers. Mrs. Dickson, being at this time returning from a tour to the Hebrides and Western

BUILDING OF BELL ROCK

Highlands of Scotland, had heard of the Bell Rock works, and from their similarity to those of the Eddystone, was strongly impressed with a desire of visiting the spot. But on inquiring for the writer at Edinburgh, and finding from him that the upper part of the lighthouse, consisting of nine courses, might be seen in the immediate vicinity, and also that one of the vessels, which, in compliment to her father's memory, had been named the *Smeaton*, might also now be seen in Leith, she considered herself extremely fortunate; and having first visited the works at Greenside, she afterwards went to Leith to see the *Smeaton*, then loading for the Bell Rock. On stepping on board, Mrs. Dickson seemed to be quite overcome with so many concurrent circumstances, tending in a peculiar manner to revive and enliven the memory of her departed father, and on leaving the vessel she would not be restrained from presenting the crew with a piece of money. The *Smeaton* had been named spontaneously, from a sense of the obligation which a public work of the description of the Bell Rock owed to the labours and abilities of Mr. Smeaton. The writer certainly never could have anticipated the satisfaction which he this day felt in witnessing the pleasure it afforded to the only representative of this great man's family.

Friday, 20th July.—The gale from the N.E. still continued so strong, accompanied with a heavy sea, that the *Patriot* could not approach her moorings; and although the tender still kept her station, no landing was made to-day at the rock. At high-water it was remarked that the spray rose to the height of about sixty feet upon the building. The *Smeaton* now lay in Leith loaded, but, the wind and weather being so unfavourable for her getting down the Firth, she did not sail till this afternoon. It may here be proper to notice that the loading of the centre of the light-room floor, or last principal stone of the building, did not fail, when put on board, to excite an interest among those connected with the work. When the stone was laid upon the cart to be conveyed to Leith, the seamen fixed an ensign-staff and flag into the circular hole in the centre of the stone, and decorated their own hats, and that of James Craw, the Bell Rock carter, with ribbons; even his faithful and trusty horse Bassey was ornamented with bows and streamers of various colours. The masons also provided themselves with new aprons, and in this manner the cart was attended in its progress to the ship. When the cart came opposite the Trinity House of Leith, the officer of that Corporation made his appearance dressed in his uniform, with his staff of office; and when it reached the harbour, the shipping in the different tiers where the *Smeaton* lay hoisted their colours, manifesting by these trifling ceremonies the interest with which the progress of this work was regarded by the public, as ultimately tending to afford safety and protection to the mariner. The wind had fortunately shifted to the S.W., and about five o'clock this afternoon the *Smeaton* reached the Bell Rock.

Friday, 27th July.—The artificers had finished the laying of the balcony course, excepting the centre-stone of the light-room floor, which, like the centres of the other floors, could not be laid in its place till after the removal of the foot and shaft of the balance-crane. During the dinner-hour, when the men were off work, the writer generally took some exercise by walking round the walls when the rock was under water; but to-day his boundary was greatly enlarged, for, instead of the narrow wall as a path, he felt no small degree of pleasure in walking round the balcony and passing out and in at the space allotted for the light-room door. In the labours of this day both the artificers and seamen felt their work to be extremely easy compared with what it had been for some days past.

Sunday, 29th July.—Captain Wilson and his crew had made preparations for landing the last stone, and, as may well be supposed, this was a day of great interest at the Bell Rock. "That it might lose none of its honours," as he expressed himself, the *Hedderwick* praam-boat, with which the first stone of the building had been landed, was appointed also to carry the last. At seven o'clock this evening the seamen hoisted three flags upon the *Hedderwick*, when the

BUILDING OF BELL ROCK

colours of the *Dickie* praam-boat, tender, *Smeaton*, floating light, beacon-house, and lighthouse, were also displayed; and, the weather being remarkably fine, the whole presented a very gay appearance, and, in connection with the associations excited, the effect was very pleasing. The praam which carried the stone was towed by the seamen in gallant style to the rock, and, on its arrival, cheers were given as a finale to the landing department.

Monday, 30th July.—The ninetieth or last course of the building having been laid to-day, which brought the masonry to the height of one hundred and two feet six inches, the lintel of the light-room door, being the finishing-stone of the exterior walls, was laid with due formality by the writer, who, at the same time, pronounced the following benediction: " May the Great Architect of the Universe, under whose blessing this perilous work has prospered, preserve it as a guide to the mariner."

Friday, 3rd Aug.—At three p.m., the necessary preparations having been made, the artificers commenced the completing of the floors of the several apartments, and at seven o'clock the centre stone of the light-room floor was laid, which may be held as finishing the masonry of this important national edifice. After going through the usual ceremonies observed by the brotherhood on occasions of this kind, the writer, addressing himself to the artificers and seamen who were present, briefly alluded to the utility of the undertaking as a monument of the wealth of British commerce, erected through the spirited measures of the Commissioners of the Northern Lighthouses by means of the able assistance of those who now surrounded him. He then took an opportunity of stating that toward those connected with this arduous work he would ever retain the most heartfelt regard in all their interests.

Saturday, 4th Aug.—When the bell was rung as usual on the beacon this morning, every one seemed as if he were at a loss what to make of himself. At this period the artificers at the rock consisted of eighteen masons, two joiners, one millwright, one smith, and one mortar-maker,

A FAMILY OF ENGINEERS

besides Messrs. Peter Logan and Francis Watt, foreman, counting in all twenty-five; and matters were arranged for proceeding to Arbroath this afternoon with all hands. The *Sir Joseph Banks* tender had by this time been afloat, with little intermission, for six months, during the greater part of which the artificers had been almost constantly off at the rock, and were now much in want of necessaries of almost every description. Not a few had lost different articles of clothing, which had dropped into the sea from the beacon and building. Some wanted jackets; others, from want of hats, wore nightcaps; each was, in fact, more or less curtailed in his wardrobe, and, it must be confessed, that at best the party were but in a very tattered condition. This morning was occupied in removing the artificers and their bedding on board of the tender; and, although their personal luggage was easily shifted, the boats had, nevertheless, many articles to remove from the beacon-house, and were consequently employed in this service till eleven a.m. All hands being collected and just ready to embark, as the water had nearly overflowed the rock, the writer, in taking leave, after alluding to the harmony which had ever marked the conduct of those employed on the Bell Rock, took occasion to compliment the great zeal, attention, and abilities of Mr. Peter Logan and Mr. Francis Watt, foreman; Captain James Wilson, landing-master; and Captain David Taylor, commander of the tender, who, in their several departments, had so faithfully discharged the duties assigned to them, often under circumstances the most difficult and trying. The health of these gentlemen was drunk with much warmth of feeling by the artificers and seamen, who severally expressed the satisfaction they had experienced in acting under them; after which the whole party left the rock.

In sailing past the floating light mutual compliments were made by a display of flags between that vessel and the tender; and at five p.m. the latter vessel entered the harbour of Arbroath, where the party were heartily welcomed by a numerous company of spectators, who had collected to see the artificers arrive after so long an absence from the port.

BUILDING OF BELL ROCK

In the evening the writer invited the foremen and captains of the service, together with Mr. David Logan, clerk of works at Arbroath, and Mr. Lachlan Kennedy, engineer's clerk and book-keeper, and some of their friends, to the principal inn, where the evening was spent very happily; and after "His Majesty's Health" and "The Commissioners of the Northern Lighthouses" had been given, "Stability to the Bell Rock Lighthouse" was hailed as a standing toast in the Lighthouse Service.

Sunday, 5th Aug.—The author has formerly noticed the uniformly decent and orderly deportment of the artificers who were employed at the Bell Rock Lighthouse, and to-day, it is believed, they very generally attended church, no doubt with grateful hearts for the narrow escapes from personal danger which all of them had more or less experienced during their residence at the rock.

Tuesday, 14th Aug.—The *Smeaton* sailed to-day at one p.m., having on board sixteen artificers, with Mr. Peter Logan, together with a supply of provisions and necessaries, who left the harbour pleased and happy to find themselves once more afloat in the Bell Rock service. At seven o'clock the tender was made fast to her moorings, when the artificers landed on the rock and took possession of their old quarters in the beacon-house, with feelings very different from those of 1807, when the works commenced.

The barometer for some days past had been falling from 20.90, and to-day it was 29.50, with the wind at N.E., which, in the course of this day, increased to a strong gale accompanied with a sea which broke with great violence upon the rock. At twelve noon the tender rode very heavily at her moorings, when her chain broke at about ten fathoms from the ship's bows. The kedge-anchor was immediately let go, to hold her till the floating buoy and broken chain should be got on board. But while this was in operation the hawser of the kedge was chafed through on the rocky bottom and parted, when the vessel was again adrift. Most fortunately, however, she cast off with her head from the rock, and narrowly cleared it, when she sailed up the Firth of Forth to

A FAMILY OF ENGINEERS

wait the return of better weather. The artificers were thus left upon the rock with so heavy a sea running that it was ascertained to have risen to the height of eighty feet on the building. Under such perilous circumstancecs it would be difficult to describe the feelings of those who, at this time, were cooped up in the beacon in so forlorn a situation, with the sea not only raging under them, but occasionally falling from a great height upon the roof of their temporary lodging, without even the attending vessel in view to afford the least gleam of hope in the event of any accident. It is true that they had now the masonry of the lighthouse to resort to, which, no doubt, lessened the actual danger of their situation; but the building was still without a roof, and the deadlights, or storm-shutters, not being yet fitted, the windows of the lower story were stove in and broken, and at high-water the sea ran in considerable quantities out at the entrance door.

Thursday, 16th Aug.—The gale continues with unabated violence to-day, and the sprays rise to a still greater height, having been carried over the masonry of the building, or about ninety feet above the level of the sea. At four o'clock this morning it was breaking into the cook's berth, when he rang the alarm-bell, and all hands turned out to attend to their personal safety. The floor of the smith's, or mortar-gallery, was now completely burst up by the force of the sea, when the whole of the deals and the remaining articles upon the floor were swept away, such as the cast-iron mortar-tubs, the iron hearth of the forge, the smith's bellows, and even his anvil were thrown down upon the rock. Before the tide rose to its full height to-day some of the artificers passed along the bridge into the lighthouse, to observe the effects of the sea upon it, and they reported that they had felt a slight tremulous motion in the building when great seas struck it in a certain direction, about high-water mark. On this occasion the sprays were again observed to wet the balcony, and even to come over the parapet wall into the interior of the light-room.

Thursday, 23rd Aug.—The wind being at W.S.W., and

BUILDING OF BELL ROCK

the weather more moderate, both the tender and the *Smeaton* got to their moorings on the 23rd, when all hands were employed in transporting the sash-frames from on board of the *Smeaton* to the rock. In the act of setting up one of these frames upon the bridge, it was unguardedly suffered to lose its balance, and in saving it from damage, Captain Wilson met with a severe bruise in the groin, on the seat of a gun-shot wound received in the early part of his life. This accident laid him aside for several days.

Monday, 27th Aug.—The sash-frames of the light-room, eight in number, and weighing each 254 pounds, having been got safely up to the top of the building, were ranged on the balcony in the order in which they were numbered for their places on the top of the parapet-wall; and the balance-crane, that useful machine having now lifted all the heavier articles, was unscrewed and lowered, to use the landing-master's phrase, " in mournful silence."

Sunday, 2nd Sept.—The steps of the stair being landed, and all the weightier articles of the light-room got up to the balcony, the wooden bridge was now to be removed, as it had a very powerful effect upon the beacon when a heavy sea struck it, and could not possibly have withstood the storms of a winter. Everything having been cleared from the bridge, and nothing left but the two principal beams with their horizontal braces, James Glen, at high-water, proceeded with a saw to cut through the beams at the end next the beacon, which likewise disengaged their opposite extremity, inserted a few inches into the building. The frame was then gently lowered into the water, and floated off to the *Smeaton* to be towed to Arbroath, to be applied as part of the materials in the erection of the lightkeepers' houses. After the removal of the bridge, the aspect of things at the rock was much altered. The beacon-house and building had both a naked look to those accustomed to their former appearance; a curious optical deception was also remarked, by which the lighthouse seemed to incline from the perpendicular towards the beacon. The horizontal rope-ladder before noticed was again stretched to preserve the

A FAMILY OF ENGINEERS

communication, and the artificers were once more obliged to practise the awkward and straddling manner of their passage between them during 1809.

At twelve noon the bell rung for prayers, after which the artificers went to dinner, when the writer passed along the rope ladder to the lighthouse, and went through the several apartments, which were now cleared of lumber. In the afternoon all hands were summoned to the interior of the house, when he had the satisfaction of laying the upper step of the stair, or last stone of the building. This ceremony concluded with three cheers, the sound of which had a very loud and strange effect within the walls of the lighthouse. At six o'clock Mr. Peter Logan and eleven of the artificers embarked with the writer for Arbroath, leaving Mr. James Glen with the special charge of the beacon and railways, Mr. Robert Selkirk with the building, with a few artificers to fit the temporary windows to render the house habitable.

Sunday, 14th Oct.—On returning from his voyage to the Northern Lighthouses, the writer landed at the Bell Rock on Sunday, the 14th of October, and had the pleasure to find, from the very favourable state of the weather, that the artificers had been enabled to make great progress with the fitting up of the light-room.

Friday, 19th Oct.—The light-room work had proceeded, as usual, to-day under the direction of Mr. Dove, assisted in the plumber-work by Mr. John Gibson, and in the brazier work by Mr. Joseph Fraser; while Mr. James Slight, with the joiners, were fitting up the storm-shutters of the windows. In these several departments the artificers were at work till seven o'clock p. m., and it being then dark, Mr. Dove gave orders to drop work in the light-room; and all hands proceeded from thence to the beacon-house, when Charles Henderson, smith, and Henry Dickson, brazier, left the work together. Being both young men, who had been for several weeks upon the rock, they had become familiar, and even playful, on the most difficult parts about the beacon and building. This evening they were trying to outrun each other in descending from the light-room, when Henderson

BUILDING OF BELL ROCK

led the way; but they were in conversation with each other till they came to the rope-ladder distended between the entrance-door of the lighthouse and the beacon. Dickson, on reaching the cook-room, was surprised at not seeing his companion, and inquired hastily for Henderson. Upon which the cook replied, " Was he before you upon the rope-ladder? " Dickson answered, " Yes; and I thought I heard something fall." Upon this the alarm was given, and links were immediately lighted, with which the artificers descended on the legs of the beacon, as near the surface of the water as possible, it being then about full-tide, and the sea breaking to a considerable height upon the building, with the wind at S.S.E. But, after watching till low-water, and searching in every direction upon the rock, it appeared that poor Henderson must have unfortunately fallen through the rope-ladder, and been washed into the deep water.

The deceased had passed along this rope-ladder many hundred times, both by day and night, and the operations in which he was employed being nearly finished, he was about to leave the rock when this melancholy catastrophe took place. The unfortunate loss of Henderson cast a deep gloom upon the minds of all who were at the rock, and it required some management on the part of those who had charge to induce the people to remain patiently at their work; as the weather now became more boisterous, and the nights long, they found their habitation extremely cheerless, while the winds were howling about their ears, and the waves lashing with fury against the beams of their insulated habitation.

Tuesday, 23rd Oct.—The wind had shifted in the night to N.W., and blew a fresh gale, while the sea broke with violence upon the rock. It was found impossible to land, but the writer, from the boat, hailed Mr. Dove, and directed the ball to be immediately fixed. The necessary preparations were accordingly made, while the vessel made short tacks on the southern side of the rock, in comparatively smooth water. At noon Mr. Dove, assisted by Mr. James Slight, Mr. Robert Selkirk, Mr. James Glen, and Mr. John

A FAMILY OF ENGINEERS

Gibson, plumber, with considerable difficulty, from the boisterous state of the weather, got the gilded ball screwed on, measuring two feet in diameter, and forming the principal ventilator at the upper extremity of the cupola of the light-room. At Mr. Hamilton's desire, a salute of seven guns was fired on this occasion, and, all hands being called to the quarter-deck, "Stability to the Bell Rock Lighthouse" was not forgotten.

Tuesday, 30th Oct.—On reaching the rock it was found that a very heavy sea still ran upon it; but the writer having been disappointed on two former occasions, and, as the erection of the house might now be considered complete, there being nothing wanted externally, excepting some of the storm-shutters for the defence of the windows, he was the more anxious at this time to inspect it. Two well-manned boats were therefore ordered to be in attendance; and, after some difficulty, the wind being at N.N.E., they got safely into the western creek, though not without encountering plentiful sprays. It would have been impossible to have attempted a landing to-day, under any other circumstances than with boats perfectly adapted to the purpose, and with seamen who knew every ledge of the rock, and even the length of the sea-weeds at each particular spot, so as to dip their oars into the water accordingly, and thereby prevent them from getting entangled. But what was of no less consequence to the safety of the party, Captain Wilson, who always steered the boat, had a perfect knowledge of the set of the different waves, while the crew never shifted their eyes from observing his motions, and the strictest silence was preserved by every individual except himself.

On entering the house, the writer had the pleasure to find it in a somewhat habitable condition, the lower apartments being closed in with temporary windows, and fitted with proper storm-shutters. The lowest apartment at the head of the staircase was occupied with water, fuel, and provisions, put up in a temporary way until the house could be furnished with proper utensils. The second, or light-room store, was at present much encumbered with various tools and apparatus for the use of the workmen. The kitchen

BUILDING OF BELL ROCK

immediately over this had, as yet, been supplied only with a common ship's caboose and plate-iron funnel, while the necessary cooking utensils had been taken from the beacon. The bedroom was for the present used as the joiners' workshop, and the strangers' room, immediately under the light-room, was occupied by the artificers, the beds being ranged in tiers, as was done in the barrack of the beacon. The light-room, though unprovided with its machinery, being now covered over with the cupola, glazed and painted, had a very complete and cleanly appearance. The balcony was only as yet fitted with a temporary rail, consisting of a few iron stanchions, connected with ropes; and in this state it was necessary to leave it during the winter.

Having gone over the whole of the low-water works on the rock, the beacon, and lighthouse, and being satisfied that only the most untoward accident in the landing of the machinery could prevent the exhibition of the light in the course of the winter, Mr. John Reid, formerly of the floating light, was now put in charge of the lighthouse as principal keeper; Mr. James Slight had charge of the operations of the artificers, while Mr. James Dove and the smiths, having finished the frame of the light-room, left the rock for the present. With these arrangements the writer bade adieu to the works for the season. At eleven a. m. the tide was far advanced; and there being now little or no shelter for the boats at the rock, they had to be pulled through the breach of sea, which came on board in great quantities, and it was with extreme difficulty that they could be kept in the proper direction of the landing-creek. On this occasion he may be permitted to look back with gratitude on the many escapes made in the course of this arduous undertaking, now brought so near to a successful conclusion.

Monday, 5th Nov.—On Monday, the 5th, the yacht again visited the rock, when Mr. Slight and the artificers returned with her to the workyard, where a number of things were still to prepare connected with the temporary fitting up of the accommodation for the light-keepers. Mr. John Reid and Peter Fortune were now the only inmates of the house. This was the smallest number of persons hitherto left in the

A FAMILY OF ENGINEERS

lighthouse. As four lightkeepers were to be the complement, it was intended that three should always be at the rock. Its present inmates, however, could hardly have been better selected for such a situation; Mr. Reid being a person possessed of the strictest notions of duty and habits of regularity from long service on board of a man-of-war, while Mr. Fortune had one of the most happy and contented dispositions imaginable.

Tuesday, 13th Nov.—From Saturday the 10th till Tuesday the 13th, the wind had been from N.E. blowing a heavy gale; but to-day, the weather having greatly moderated, Captain Taylor, who now commanded the *Smeaton*, sailed at two o'clock a. m. for the Bell Rock. At five the floating light was hailed and found to be all well. Being a fine moonlight morning, the seamen were changed from the one ship to the other. At eight, the *Smeaton* being off the rock, the boats were manned, and taking a supply of water, fuel, and other necessaries, landed at the western side, when Mr. Reid and Mr. Fortune were found in good health and spirits.

Mr. Reid stated that during the late gales, particularly on Friday, the 30th, the wind veering from S.E. to N.E., both he and Mr. Fortune sensibly felt the house tremble when particular seas struck, about the time of high-water; the former observing that it was a tremor of that sort which rather tended to convince him that everything about the building was sound, and reminded him of the effect produced when a good log of timber is struck sharply with a mallet; but, with every confidence in the stability of the building, he nevertheless confessed that, in so forlorn a situation, they were not insensible to those emotions which, he emphatically observed, "made a man look back upon his former life."

Friday, 1st Feb.—The day, long wished for, on which the mariner was to see a light exhibited on the Bell Rock at length arrived. Captain Wilson, as usual, hoisted the float's lanterns to the topmast on the evening of the 1st of February; but the moment that the light appeared on the rock, the crew giving three cheers, lowered them, and finally extinguished the lights.

THREE LETTERS

TO

AUSTIN DOBSON
RUDYARD KIPLING
GEORGE MEREDITH

THREE LETTERS

TO AUSTIN DOBSON

Written in acknowledgment of the gift of a desk.

Bonallie Towers, Bournemouth,
December, 1884.

DEAR DOBSON,—Set down my delay to your own fault; I wished to acknowledge such a gift from you in some of my inapt and slovenly rhymes; but you should have sent me your pen and not your desk. The verses stand up to the axles in a miry cross-road, whence the coursers of the sun shall never draw them; hence I am constrained to this uncourtliness, that I must appear before one of the kings of that country of rhyme without my singing-robes. For less than this, if we may trust the book of Esther, favourites have tasted death; but I conceive the kingdom of the Muses mildlier-mannered; and in particular that county which you administer and which I seem to see as a half-suburban land; a land of hollyhocks and county houses; a land where at night, in thorny and sequestered bypaths, you will meet masqueraders going to a ball in their sedans, and the rector steering homeward by the light of his lantern; a land of the windmill and the west wind, and the flowering hawthorn with a little scented letter in the hollow of its trunk, and the kites flying over all in the season of kites, and the far away blue spires of a cathedral city.

Will you forgive me, then, for my delay and accept my thanks, not only for the present, but for the letter which followed it, and which perhaps I more particularly value, and believe me to be, with much admiration, yours very truly,

ROBERT LOUIS STEVENSON.

THREE LETTERS

TO RUDYARD KIPLING

In 1890, on first becoming acquainted with Mr. Kipling's *Soldiers Three*, Stevenson had written of his congratulations red-hot. "Well and indeed, Mr. Mulvaney," so ran the first sentence of his note, "but it's as good as meat to meet in with you, sir. They tell it was a man of the name of Kipling made ye; but indeed and they can't fool me: it was the Lord God Almighty that made you." Taking the cue thus offered, Mr. Kipling had written back in the character of his own Irishman, Thomas Mulvaney, addressing Stevenson's Highlander, Alan Breck Stewart. In the following letter, which belongs to an uncertain date in 1891, Alan Breck is made to reply. "The gentleman I now serve with" means, of course, R. L. S. himself.

Vailima, 1891.

SIR,—I cannot call to mind having written you, but I am so throng with occupation this may have fallen aside. I never heard tell I had any friends in Ireland, and I am led to understand you are come of no considerable family. The gentleman I now serve with assures me, however, you are a very pretty fellow and your letter deserves to be remarked. It's true he is himself a man of very low descent upon the one side; though upon the other he counts cousinship with a gentleman, my very good friend, the late Mr. Balfour of the Shaws, in the Lothian; which I should be wanting in good fellowship to forget. He tells me besides you are a man of your hands; I am not informed of your weapon; but if all be true it sticks in my mind I would be ready to make an exception in your favour, and meet you like one gentleman with another. I suppose this'll be your purpose in your favour, which I could very ill make out; it's one I would be sweir to baulk you of. It seems, Mr. McIlvaine, which I take to be your name, you are in the household of a gentleman of the name of Coupling: for whom my friend is very much engaged. The distances being

THREE LETTERS

very uncommodious, I think it will be maybe better if we leave it to these two to settle all that's necessary to honour. I would have you to take heed it's a very unusual condescension on my part, that bear a king's name; and for the matter of that, I think it shame to be mingled with a person of the name of Coupling, which is doubtless a very good house but one I never heard tell of, any more than Stevenson. But your purpose being laudable, I would be sorry (as the word goes) to cut off my nose to spite my face.—I am Sir, your humble servant,

A. STEWART,
Chevalier de St. Louis.

To MR. M'ILVAINE,
Gentleman Private in a foot regiment
under cover to Mr. Coupling.

He has read me some of your Barrack Room Ballants, which are not of so noble a strain as some of mine in the Gaelic, but I could set some of them to the pipes if this rencounter goes as it's to be desired. Let's first, as I understand you are to move, do each other this rational courtesy; and if either will survive, we may grow better acquaint. For your tastes for what's martial and for poetry agree with mine.

A. S.

TO GEORGE MEREDITH

Sept. 5th, 1893.
Vailima Plantation, Upolu, Samoa.

MY DEAR MEREDITH,—I have again and again taken up the pen to write to you, and many beginnings have gone into the waste-paper basket (I have one now—for the second time in my life—and feel a big man on the strength of it). And no doubt it requires some decision to break so long a silence. My health is vastly restored, and I am now living patriarchally in this place six hundred feet above the sea on the shoulder of a mountain of 1500. Behind me, the unbroken bush slopes up to the backbone of the island (3 to 4000) without a house, and no inhabitants save a

THREE LETTERS

few runaway black boys, wild pigs and cattle, and wild doves and flying foxes, and many parti-coloured birds, and many black, and many white: a very eerie, dim, strange place and hard to travel. I am the head of a household of five whites, and of twelve Samoans, to all of whom I am the chief and father: my cook comes to me and asks leave to marry—and his mother, a fine old chief woman, who has never lived here, does the same. You may be sure I granted the petition. It is a life of great interest, complicated by the Tower of Babel, that old enemy. And I have all the time on my hands for literary work. My house is a great place: we have a hall fifty feet long with a great red-wood stair ascending from it, where we dine in state—myself usually dressed in a singlet and a pair of trousers—and attended on by servants in a single garment, a kind of kilt—also leaves and flowers—and their hair often powdered with lime. The European who came upon it suddenly would think it was a dream. We have prayers on Sunday night—I am a perfect pariah in the island not to have them oftener, but the spirit is unwilling and the flesh proud, and I cannot go it more. It is strange to see the long line of the brown folk crouched along the wall with lanterns at intervals before them in the big shadowy hall, with an oak cabinet at one end of it and a group of Rodin's (which native taste regards as *prodigieusement leste*) presiding over all from the top—and to hear the long rambling Samoan hymn rolling up. (God bless me, what style! But I am off business to-day, and this is not meant to be literature.)

I hear word occasionally of the *Amazing Marriage*. It will be a brave day for me when I get hold of it. Gower Woodseer is now an ancient, lean, grim, exiled Scot, living and labouring as for a wager in the tropics; still active, still with lots of fire in him, but the youth—ah, the youth, where is it? For years after I came here, the critics (those genial gentlemen) used to deplore the relaxation of my fibre and the idleness to which I had succumbed. I hear less of this now; the next thing is they will tell me I am writing myself out! and that my unconscientious conduct is bringing their grey

THREE LETTERS

hairs with sorrow to the dust. I do not know—I mean I do know one thing. For fourteen years I have not had a day's real health; I have wakened sick and gone to bed weary; and I have done my work unflinchingly. I have written in bed, and written out of it, written in hemorrhages, written in sickness, written torn by coughing, written when my head swam for weakness, and for so long it seems to me I have won my wager and recovered my glove. I am better now, have been rightly speaking since first I came to the Pacific, and still, few are the days when I am not in some physical distress. And the battle goes on—ill or well, is a trifle; so as it goes. I was made for a contest and the Powers have so willed that my battlefield should be this dingy, inglorious one of the bed and the physic bottle. At least I have not failed, but I would have preferred a place of trumpetings and the open air over my head.

This is a devilish egotistical yarn. Will you try to imitate me in that if the spirit ever moves you to reply? And meantime be sure that away in the midst of the Pacific there is a house on a wooded island where the name of George Meredith is very dear, and his memory (since it must be no more) is continually honoured.—Ever your friend,

ROBERT LOUIS STEVENSON.

Remember me to Mariette, if you please; and my wife sends her most kind remembrance to yourself.

R. L. S.

LIFE OF
ROBERT LOUIS STEVENSON

BY

SIDNEY COLVIN

LIFE OF STEVENSON

ROBERT LOUIS STEVENSON, novelist, essayist, poet and traveller, was born at 8 Howard Place, Edinburgh, on November 13th, 1850. He was baptised Robert Lewis Balfour, but from about his eighteenth year dropped the use of the third Christian name and changed the spelling of the second to Louis; signing thereafter Robert Louis in full, and being called always Louis by his family and intimate friends. On both sides of the house he was sprung from capable and cultivated stock. His father, Thomas Stevenson, was a member of the distinguished Edinburgh firm of civil engineers. His mother was Margaret Isabella, youngest daughter of James Balfour, for many years minister of the parish of Colinton in Midlothian, and grandson to James Balfour (1705-1795) professor at Edinburgh, first of moral philosophy and afterwards of the law of nature and of nations. His mother's father was described by his grandson in the essay called "The Manse." Robert Louis was his parents' only child. His mother was subject in early and middle life to chest and nerve troubles, and her son may have inherited from her some of his constitutional weakness as well as of his intellectual vivacity and taste for letters. His health was infirm from the first. He suffered from frequent bronchial affections and acute nervous excitability, and in the autumn of 1858, was near dying of a gastric fever. In January, 1853, his parents moved to No. 1 Inverleith Terrace and in May, 1857, to 17 Heriot Row, which continued to be their Edinburgh home until the father's death in 1887. Much of his time was also spent in the manse at Colinton on the water of Leith, the home of his maternal grandfather. If he suffered much as a child from the distresses, he also enjoyed to the full the pleasures, of imagination. He was eager in every kind of play, and made the most of all the

LIFE OF STEVENSON

amusements natural to an only child kept much indoors by ill-health. The child in him never died, and the zest with which in after life he would throw himself into the pursuits of children and young boys was on his own account as much as on theirs. This spirit is illustrated in the pieces which he wrote and published under the title "A Child's Garden of Verses," as well as in a number of retrospective essays referring with peculiar insight and freshness of memory to that period of life.

Such a child was naturally a greedy reader, or rather listener to reading; for it was not until his eighth year that he learned to read easily or habitually to himself. He began early to take pleasure in attempts at composition: a "History of Moses," dictated in his sixth year, and an account of "Travels in Perth," in his ninth, are still extant. Ill-health prevented his getting much regular or continuous schooling. He attended first (1858-61) a preparatory school kept by a Mr. Henderson in India Street; and next (at intervals for some time after the autumn of 1861) the Edinburgh Academy. For a few months in the autumn of 1863 he was at a boarding-school kept by a Mr. Wyatt at Spring Grove, near London; from 1864 to 1867 his education was conducted chiefly at Mr. Thompson's private school in Frederick Street, Edinburgh, and by private tutors in various places to which he travelled for his own or his parents' health. Such travels included frequent visits to health resorts in Scotland; occasional excursions with his father on his nearer professional rounds, *e.g.* to the coasts and lighthouses of Fife in 1864; and also longer journeys—to Germany and Holland in 1862, to Italy in 1863, to the Riviera in the spring of 1864, and to Torquay in 1865 and 1866. From 1867 the family life became more settled between Edinburgh and Swanston cottage, a country home in the Pentlands, which Thomas Stevenson first rented in that year, and the scenery and associations of which inspired not a little of his son's work in literature.

In November of the same year, 1867, Louis Stevenson was entered as a student at the Edinburgh University, and

LIFE OF STEVENSON

for several winters attended classes there with such regularity as his health and inclinations permitted. According to his own account " Essay on a College Magazine," " Life of Fleeming Jenkin," etc.) he was alike at school and in college an incorrigible idler and truant. But outside the field of school and college routine he showed eager curiosity and activity of mind. He was of " a conversible temper," so he says of himself, " and insatiably curious in the aspects of life"; and spent much of his time " scraping acquaintance with all classes of man and woman kind." At the same time he read precociously and omnivorously in the *belles-lettres*, including a very wide range of English poetry, fiction, and essays, and a fairly wide range of French; and was a genuine student of Scottish history, and to some extent of history in general. He had been intended as a matter of course to follow the family profession of engineering; and from 1868 his summer excursions took a professional turn. In that and the two following years he went to watch the works of the firm in progress at various points on the mainland and in the northern and western islands. He was a favourite, though a very irregular pupil of the professor of engineering, Fleeming Jenkin; and must have shown some aptitude for the calling hereditary in his family, inasmuch as in 1871 he received the silver medal of the Edinburgh Society of Arts for a paper on a suggested improvement in the lighthouse apparatus. The outdoor and seafaring parts of the profession were, in fact, wholly to his taste, as in spite of his frail health he had a passion for open air exercise and adventure (though not for sports). Office work, on the other hand, was his aversion, and his physical powers were unequal to the workshop training necessary to the practical engineer. Accordingly in this year, 1871, it was agreed that he should give up the hereditary profession and read for the bar.

For several ensuing years Stevenson attended law classes in the university, giving to the subject some serious although fitful attention, until he was called to the bar in 1875. But it was on another side that this " pattern of an idler," to use his own words, was gradually developing himself into

LIFE OF STEVENSON

a model of unsparing industry. From childhood he had never ceased to practise writing, and on all his truantries went pencil and copybook in hand. Family and school magazines in manuscript are extant of which, between his thirteenth and sixteenth years, he was editor, chief contributor, and illustrator. In his sixteenth year he wrote a serious essay on the "Pentland Rising of 1666" (having already tried his hand at an historical romance on the same subject). This was printed as a pamphlet, and is now a rarity in request among collectors. For the following four or five years, though always writing both in prose and verse, he kept his efforts to himself, and generally destroyed the more ambitious of them. Among these were a romance on the life of Hackston of Rathillet, a poetical play of "Semiramis" written in imitation of Webster, and "Voces Fidelium," a series of dramatic dialogues in verse. A few manuscript essays and notes of travel that have been preserved from 1868 to 1870, together with his letters to his mother of the same period, show almost as good a gift of observation and expression as his published work of five or six years later. Less promising and less personal are a series of six papers which he contributed in 1871 to the *Edinburgh University Magazine*, a short-lived periodical started by him in conjunction with one or two college friends and fellow members of the Speculative Society.

With high social spirits and a brilliant, somewhat fantastic, gaiety of bearing, Stevenson was no stranger to the storms and perplexities of youth. A restless and inquiring conscience, perhaps inherited from Covenanting ancestors, kept him inwardly calling in question the grounds of conduct and the accepted codes of society. At the same time his reading had shaken his belief in Christian dogma; the harsher forms of Scottish Calvinistic Christianity being indeed at all times repugnant to his nature. From the last circumstance arose for a time troubles with his father, the more trying while they lasted because of the deep attachment and pride in each other which always subsisted between father and son. He loved the aspects of his native city, but neither

LIFE OF STEVENSON

its physical nor its social atmosphere was congenial to him. Amid the biting winds and rigid social conventions of Edinburgh he craved for Bohemian freedom and the joy of life, and for a while seemed in danger of a fate like that of the boy-poet, Robert Fergusson, with whom he always owned a strong sense of spiritual affinity.

But his innate sanity of mind and disposition prevailed. In the summer of 1873 he made new friends, who encouraged him strongly in the career of letters. His first contribution to regular periodical literature, a little paper on "Roads," appeared in the *Portfolio* (edited by Philip Gilbert Hamerton), for December, 1873. In the meantime his health had suffered a serious breakdown. In consequence of acute nervous exhaustion, combined with threatening lung symptoms, he was ordered to the Riviera, where he spent (chiefly at Mentone) the winter of 1873-4. Returning with a certain measure of recovered health in April, 1874, he went to live with his parents at Edinburgh and Swanston and resumed his reading for the bar. He attended classes for Scots law and conveyancing, and for constitutional law and history. He worked also for a time in the office of Messrs. Skene, Edwards, and Bilton, of which the antiquary and historian, William Forbes Skene, was senior partner. On July 14th, 1875, he passed his final examination with credit, and was called to the bar on the 16th, but never practised. Since abandoning the engineering profession he had resumed the habit of frequent miscellaneous excursions in Scotland, England, or abroad. Now, in 1875, began the first of a series of visits to the artistic settlements in the neighbourhood of Fontainebleau, where his cousin, Mr. R. A. M. Stevenson, was for the time established. He found the forest climate restorative to his health, and the life and company of Barbizon and other student resorts congenial. In the winter of 1874-5 he made in Edinburgh the acquaintance of Mr. W. E. Henley, which quickly ripened into a close and stimulating literary friendship. In London he avoided all formal and dress-coated society; and at the Savile Club (his favourite haunt) and elsewhere his own

LIFE OF STEVENSON

Bohemian oddities of dress and appearance would sometimes repel at first sight persons to whom on acquaintance he soon became endeared by the charm of his conversation. Among his friends of these years may be especially mentioned Mr. Leslie Stephen, Mr. James Payn, Dr. Appleton (editor of the *Academy*), Professor Clifford, Mr. Walter Pollock, Mr. Cosmo Monkhouse, Mr. Andrew Lang, and Mr. Edmund Gosse. In 1876 he went with Sir Walter Simpson on the canoe tour in Belgium and France described in the "Inland Voyage." In the spring of 1878 he made friends at Burford Bridge with a senior whom he had long honoured, Mr. George Meredith; and in the summer had a new experience in serving as secretary to Professor Fleeming Jenkin in his capacity of juror on the Paris Exhibition. In the autumn of the same year he spent a month at Monastier in Velay, whence he took the walk through the mountains to Florac, narrated in the "Travels with a Donkey in the Cevennes."

During these years, 1874-8, his health, though frail, was passable. With his vagrant way of life he combined a steady and growing literary industry. While reading for the bar in 1874-5, much of his work was merely experimental (poems, prose-poems, and tales not published). Much also was in preparation for proposed undertakings on Scottish history. His studies in Highland history, which were diligent and exact, in the end only served to provide the historical background of his Scottish romances. Until the end of 1875 he had only published, in addition to essays in the magazines, an "Appeal to the Church of Scotland," written to please his father and published as a pamphlet in 1875. In 1876 he contributed as a journalist, but not frequently, to the *Academy* and *Vanity Fair*, and in 1877 more abundantly to *London*, a weekly review newly founded under the editorship of Mr. Glasgow Brown, an acquaintance of Edinburgh Speculative days. In the former year, 1876, began the brilliant series of essays on life and literature in the *Cornhill Magazine*, which were afterwards collected with others in the volumes called severally

LIFE OF STEVENSON

"Virginibus Puerisque" and "Familiar Studies of Men and Books." They were continued in 1877, and in greater number throughout 1878. His first published stories were: "A Lodging for the Night" (*Temple Bar*, October, 1877); "The Sire de Malétroit's Door" (*Temple Bar*, January, 1878); and "Will o' the Mill" (*Cornhill Magazine*, January, 1878).

The year 1878 was to Stevenson one of great productiveness. In May was issued his first book, "An Inland Voyage," containing the account of his canoe trip, and written in a pleasant, fanciful vein of humour and reflection, but with the style a little over-mannered. Besides six or eight characteristic essays of the "Virginibus Puerisque" series, there appeared in *London* (edited by Mr. Henley) the set of fantastic modern tales called the "New Arabian Nights," conceived in a very spirited and entertaining vein of the realistic unreal, as well as the story of "Providence and the Guitar"; and in the *Portfolio* the "Picturesque Notes on Edinburgh," republished at the end of the year in book form. During the autumn and winter of this year he wrote "Travels with a Donkey in the Cevennes," and was much engaged in the planning of plays in collaboration with Mr. Henley, of which one, "Deacon Brodie," was finished in the spring of 1879. This was also the date of the essay "On Some Aspects of Burns." In the same spring he drafted in Edinburgh, but afterwards laid by, four chapters on ethics (a study to which he once referred as being always his "veiled mistress") under the name of "Lay Morals." In few men have the faculties been so active on the artistic and the ethical sides at once, and this fragment is of especial interest in the study of its author's mind and character.

By his various published writings Stevenson had made little impression as yet on the general reader. But the critical had recognised in him a new artist of the first promise in English letters, who aimed at, and often achieved, those qualities of sustained precision, lucidity, and grace of style which are characteristic of the best French prose, but

LIFE OF STEVENSON

in English rare in the extreme. He had known how to stamp all he wrote with the impress of a vivid personal charm; had shown himself a master of the apt and animated phrase; and whether in tale or parable, essay or wayside musing, had touched on vital points of experience and feeling with the observation and insight of a true poet and humourist.

The year 1879 was a critical one in Stevenson's life. In France he had met an American lady, Mrs. Osbourne (*née* Van de Grift), whose domestic circumstances were not fortunate and who was living with her daughter and young son in the art-student circles of Paris and Fontainebleau. At the beginning of 1879 she returned to California. In June Stevenson determined to follow. He travelled by emigrant ships and train, partly for economy, partly for the sake of the experience. The journey and its discomforts proved disastrous to his health, but did not interrupt his industry. Left entirely to his own resources, he staid for eight months partly at Monterey and partly at San Francisco. During a part of these months he was at death's door from a complication of pleurisy, malarial fever, and exhaustion of the system, but managed nevertheless to write the story of "The Pavilion on the Links," two or three essays for the *Cornhill Magazine*, the greater part of a Californian story, "A Vendetta in the West" (never published), and a first draft of the romance of "Prince Otto." In the spring of 1880 he was married to Mrs. Osbourne, who had obtained some months before a divorce from her husband. She nursed him through the worst of his illness, and in May they went for the sake of health to lodge at a deserted mining station above Calistoga, in the Californian coast range. The story of this sojourn is told in the "Silverado Squatters."

Family and friends, who had at first opposed the marriage, being now fully reconciled to it, Stevenson brought his wife home in August, 1880. She was to him a perfect companion, taking part keenly and critically in his work, sharing all his gypsy tastes and love of primitive and natural modes of life, and being, in spite of her own precarious health, the most devoted and efficient of nurses in the

LIFE OF STEVENSON

anxious times which now ensued. For the next seven or eight years his life seemed to hang by a thread. Chronic lung disease had declared itself, and the slightest exposure or exertion was apt to bring on a prostrating attack of cough, hæmorrhage, and fever. The trial was manfully borne; and in every interval of respite he worked in unremitting pursuit of the standards he had set before himself.

Between 1880 and 1887 he lived the life of an invalid, vainly seeking relief by change of place. After spending six weeks (August and September, 1880) with his parents at Blair Athol and Strathpeffer, he went in October, with his wife and stepson, to winter at Davos, where he made fast friends with John Addington Symonds and his family. He wrote little, but prepared for press the collected essays " Virginibus Puerisque," in which he preaches with captivating vigour and grace his gospel of youth, courage, and a contempt for the timidities and petty respectabilities of life. For the rest, he amused himself with verses playful and other, and with supplying humorous text and cuts for a little private press worked by his young stepson. Returning to Scotland at the end of May with health somewhat improved, he spent four months with his parents at Pitlochry and Braemar. At Pitlochry he wrote " Thrawn Janet " and the chief part of " The Merry Men," two of the strongest short tales in Scottish literature, the one of Satanic possession, the other of a conscience and imagination haunted, to the overthrow of reason, by the terrors of the sea. At Braemar he began " Treasure Island," his father helping with suggestions and reminiscences from his own seafaring experiences. At the suggestion of Mr. A. H. Japp, the story was offered to, and accepted by, the editor (Mr. Henderson) of a boys' periodical called *Young Folks*. In the meantime (August 1881) Stevenson had been a candidate for the vacant chair of history and constitutional law at Edinburgh. In the light of such public reputation as he yet possessed, the candidature must have seemed paradoxical; but it was encouraged by competent advisers, including the retiring professor, Dr. Æneas

LIFE OF STEVENSON

Mackay. It failed. Had it succeeded, his health would almost certainly have proved unequal to the work. A cold and wet season at Braemar did him much harm; and in October he was ordered off to spend a second winter (1881-2) at Davos. He here finished the tale of "Treasure Island," began, on the suggestion of Mr. George Bentley, a life (never completed) of William Hazlitt, and prepared for press the collection of literary essays "Familiar Studies of Men and Books."

In the summer of 1882 he again tried Scotland (Stobo Manse in Upper Tweeddale, Lochernhead, and Kingussie), and again with bad results for his health. As his wife was never well at Davos, they determined to winter in the south, and settled before Christmas in a cottage near Marseilles (Campagne Defli, St. Marcel). Thence, being presently driven by a fever epidemic, they moved in January, 1883, to a chalet in a pleasant garden on a hill behind Hyères (Chalet la Solitude). Here Stevenson enjoyed a respite of nearly a year from acute illness, as well as the first breath of popular success on the publication in book form of "Treasure Island." In this story the force of invention and vividness of narrative appealed to every reader, including those on whom its other qualities of style and character-drawing would in themselves have been thrown away; and it has taken its place in literature as a classic story of pirate and mutineer adventure. It has been translated into French, Spanish, and other languages. Partly at Marseilles and partly at Hyères he wrote the "Treasure of Franchard," a pleasant and ingenious tale of French provincial life; and early in 1883 completed for *Young Folks* a second boys' tale, "The Black Arrow." This story of the wars of the Roses, written in a style founded on the "Paston Letters," was preferred to "Treasure Island" by the audience to whom it was first addressed, but failed to please the critics when published in book form five years later, and was no favourite with its author. Stevenson's other work at Hyères consisted of verses for the "Child's Garden,"; essays for the *Cornhill Magazine* and the *Magazine of*

LIFE OF STEVENSON

Art (edited by Mr. Henley); the "Silverado Squatters," first drafted in 1880, and finally "Prince Otto." In this tale, or fantasy, certain problems of character and conjugal relation which had occupied him ever since his boyish tragedy of "Semiramis" are worked out with a lively play of intellect and humour, and (as some think) an excessive refinement and research of style, on a stage of German court life and with a delightful background of German forest scenery. The book, never very popular, is one of those most characteristic of his mind. It was translated into French in 1896 by Mr. Egerton Castle.

In September, 1883, Stevenson suffered a great loss in the death of his old friend, Mr. James Walter Ferrier. In the beginning of 1884 his hopes and spirits were rudely dashed by two dangerous attacks of illness, the first occurring at Nice in January, the second at Hyères in May. Travelling slowly homeward by way of Royat, he arrived in England in July in an almost prostrate condition, and in September settled at Bournemouth. In the autumn and early winter his quarters were at Bonallie Tower, Branksome Park; in February, 1885, his father bought and gave him the house at Westbourne which he called (after the famous lighthouse designed by his uncle Alan) Skerryvore. This was for the next two years and a half his home. His health, and on the whole his spirits, remained on a lower plane than before, and he was never free for many weeks together from fits of hæmorrhage and prostration. Nevertheless he was able to form new friendships and to do some of the best work of his life.

In 1885 he finished for publication two books which his illness had interrupted, the "Child's Garden of Verses" and "Prince Otto," and began a highway romance called "The Great North Road," but relinquished it in order to write a second series of "New Arabian Nights." These new tales hinge about the Fenian dynamite conspiracies, of which the public mind was at this time full, and to the old elements of fantastic realism add a new element of witty and scornful criminal psychology. The incidental stories of

LIFE OF STEVENSON

"The Destroying Angel" and "The Fair Cuban" were supplied by Mrs. Stevenson. During the same period he wrote several of the personal and literary essays afterwards collected in the volume "Memories and Portraits"; a succession of Christmas stories, "The Body Snatcher" in the *Pall Mall Gazette*, 1884; "Olalla" in the *Court and Society Review*, and "The Misadventures of John Nicholson" in *Cassell's Christmas Annual*, both for 1885; and "Markheim" in *Unwin's Christmas Annual*, 1886; as well as several plays in collaboration with Mr. Henley, viz.: "Beau Austin," "Admiral Guinea," and "Robert Macaire." Stevenson, like almost every other imaginative writer, had built strong hopes of gain upon dramatic work. His money needs, in spite of help from his father, were still somewhat pressing. Until 1866 he had never earned much more than $1500 a year by his pen. But in that year came two successes which greatly increased his reputation, and with it his power to earn. These were "The Strange Case of Dr. Jekyll and Mr. Hyde" and "Kidnapped." The former, founded partly on a dream, is a striking apologue of the double life of man. Published as a "shilling shocker," a form at that time in fashion, it became instantly popular; was quoted from a thousand pulpits; was translated into German, French, and Danish; and the names of its two chief characters have passed into the common stock of proverbial allusion. In "Kidnapped" —a boys' Highland story suggested by the historical incident of the Appin murder—the adventures are scarcely less exciting than those of "Treasure Island," the elements of character-drawing subtler and farther carried, while the romance of history and the sentiment of the soil are expressed as they had hardly been expressed since Scott. The success of these two tales, both with the critics and the public, established Stevenson's position at the head of the younger English writers of his day, among whom his example encouraged an increased general attention to technical qualities of style and workmanship as well as a reaction in favour of the novel of action and romance against the

LIFE OF STEVENSON

more analytic and less stimulating types of fiction then prevailing.

About this time Stevenson was occupied with studies for a short book on Wellington (after Gordon, his favourite hero), intended for a series edited by Mr. Andrew Lang. This was never written, and in the winter and spring of 1886-7 his chief task was one of piety to a friend, *viz.;* the writing of a life of Fleeming Jenkin from materials supplied by the widow. In the spring of 1887 he published, under the title "Underwoods" (borrowed from Ben Jonson), a collection of verses, partly English and partly Scottish, selected from the chance production of a good many years. Stevenson's poetry, written chiefly when he was too tired to write anything else, expresses as a rule the charm and power of his nature, with a more slippered grace, a far less studious and perfect art, than his prose. He also prepared for publication in 1887, under the title "Memories and Portraits," a collection of essays personal and other, including an effective exposition of his own theories of romance, which he had contributed to various periodicals during preceding years.

His father's death in May, 1887, broke the strongest tie which bound him to his country. His own health showed no signs of improvement, and the doctors, as a last chance of recovery, recommended some complete change of climate and mode of life. His wife's connections pointed to the west, he thought of Colorado, persuaded his mother to join them, and with his whole household—mother, wife, and stepson—sailed for New York on August 17th, 1887. After a short stay under the hospitable care of friends at Newport, he was persuaded, instead of going farther west, to try the climate of the Adirondack mountains for the winter. At the beginning of October the family moved accordingly to a house on Saranac Lake, and remained there until April, 1888. While there he wrote the ballad of "Ticonderoga" and began the romance of "The Master of Ballantrae," of which the scene is partly laid in the country of his winter sojourn. This tragic story of fraternal hate is thought by many to take first place among its author's romances, alike by vividness of presentment and by psychologic insight. In April Stevenson came to New York, but, soon wearying of the city, he went for some weeks' boating to Manasquan on the New Jersey coast.

In the meantime the family had entertained the idea of a yachting excursion in the South Seas. The romance of the Pacific had attracted Stevenson from a boy. The enterprise held out hopes of relief to his health; an American publisher (Mr. S. S. McClure) provided the means of undertaking it by an offer of $10,000 for letters in which its course should be narrated. The result was that on June 26, 1888, the whole family set out from San Francisco on board the schooner yacht *Casco* (Captain Otis). They first sailed to the Marquesas, where they spent six weeks; thence to the Paumotus, or Dangerous Archipelago; thence to the Tahitian group, where they again rested for several weeks, and whence they sailed northward for Hawaii. Arriving at Honolulu about the New Year of 1889, they made a stay of nearly six months, during which Stevenson made several excursions, including one, which profoundly impressed him, to the leper settlement at Molokai. His journey so far having proved a source of infinite interest and enjoyment, as well as greatly improved health, Stevenson determined to prolong it. He and his party started afresh from Honolulu in June, 1889, on a rough trading schooner, the *Equator*. Their destination was the Gilberts, a remote coral group in the Western Pacific. At two of its petty capitals, Apemama and Butaritari, they made stays of about six weeks each, and at Christmas, 1889, found their way again into semi-civilisation at Apia in the Samoan group. After a month or two's stay in Samoa, where the beauty of the scenery and the charm of the native population delighted them, the party went on to Sydney, where Stevenson immediately fell ill, the life of the city seeming to undo the good he had got at sea. This experience set him voyaging again, and determined him to make his home in the South Seas. In April, 1890, a fresh start was made, this time on a trading steamer, the

LIFE OF STEVENSON

Janet Nicoll. Touching first at Samoa, where he had bought a property of about four hundred acres on the mountain above Apia, to which he gave the name Vailima (five rivers), he left instructions for clearing and building operations to be begun while he continued his voyage. The course of the *Janet Nicoll* took him during the summer to many remote islands from Penhryn to the Marshalls, and landed him in September in New Caledonia. Returning the same month to Samoa, he found the small house already existing at Vailima to be roughly habitable and installed himself there to superintend the further operations of clearing, planting, and building. The family belongings from Bournemouth were sent out, and his mother, who had left him at Honolulu, rejoined him at Vailima in the spring of 1891.

During these Pacific voyages he had finished the " Master of Ballantrae," besides writing many occasional verses and two long, not very effective ballads on themes of Polynesian legend, the " Song of Rahéro " and the " Feast of Famine." At Samoa he had written the first of his Pacific stories in prose, " The Bottle Imp." This little tale of morals and of magic appealed strongly to the native readers to whom (in a missionary translation) it was first addressed (published in English in *Black and White*, 1891). At Sydney he had written in a heat of indignation, and published in pamphlet form, the striking " Letter to Dr. Hyde " in vindication of the memory of Father Damien. Lastly, on board the *Janet Nicoll*, " under the most ungodly circumstances," he had begun the work of composing the letters relating his travels, which were due under the original contract to the Messrs. McClure. This task was unfinished on his hands when he entered (November, 1890) on the four years' residence at Vailima, which forms the closing period of his life.

In his new Samoan home Stevenson soon began to exercise a hospitality and an influence which increased with every year. Among the natives he was known by the name of Tusitala (teller of tales), and was supposed to be master

LIFE OF STEVENSON

of an inexhaustible store of wealth, perhaps even to be the holder of the magic bottle of his own tale. He gathered about him a kind of feudal clan of servants and retainers, whom he ruled in a spirit of affectionate kindness tempered with firm justice; and presently got drawn, as a man so forward in action and so impatient of justice could not fail to be, into the entanglements of local politics and government. In health he seemed to have become a new man. Frail in comparison with the strong, he was yet able to ride and boat with little restriction, and to take part freely in local festivities, both white and native. The chief interruptions were an occasional trip to Sydney or Auckland, from which he generally came back the worse. From the middle of 1891 to the spring of 1893 his intromissions in politics embroiled him more or less seriously with most of the white officials in the island, especially the chief justice, Mr. Cedercrantz, and the president of the council, Baron Senfft von Pilsach. The proceedings of these gentlemen were exposed by him in a series of striking letters to the *Times*, and the three treaty powers (Germany, Great Britain, and the United States) ultimately decided to dispense with their services. At one period of the struggle he believed himself threatened with deportation. Whether all his own steps on that petty but extremely complicated political scene were judicious is more than can be said; but impartial witnesses agree that he had a considerable moderating influence with the natives, and that his efforts were all in the direction of peace and concord.

His literary industry during these years was more strenuous than ever. His habit was to begin work at six in the morning or earlier, continue without interruption until the midday meal, and often to resume again until four or five in the afternoon. In addition to his literary labours he kept up an active correspondence both with old friends and new acquaintances, especially with writers of the younger generation in England, who had been drawn to him either by admiration for his work or by his ever ready and generous recognition of their own. He had suffered for some time

LIFE OF STEVENSON

from scrivener's cramp, and in the last three years of his life was much helped by the affectionate services as amanuensis of his stepdaughter, Mrs. Strong, who had become a member of the household since 1889. In 1894 the plan devised by his business adviser and lifelong friend, Mr. Charles Baxter, of a limited *edition de luxe* of his collected works, under the title of the " Edinburgh Edition," afforded him much pleasure, together with a prospect of considerable gain. This experiment, without precedent during the lifetime of an author, proved a great success, but Stevenson did not live long enough to enjoy the opportunity of rest which its results were calculated to bring him.

Throughout 1891 he had a heavy task with the promised letters relating his Pacific voyages. Work undertaken to order seldom prospered with him, and these " Letters " having cost him more labour than anything he ever wrote, have less of his characteristic charm, despite the interest and strangeness of the matters of which they tell. They were published periodically in the New York *Sun* and in *Black and White* and were in part reprinted in the " Edinburgh Edition." In the year 1892 Stevenson made beginnings on a great variety of new work, some of it inspired by his Pacific experiences, and some by the memories and associations of Scotland, the power of which on his mind seemed only to be intensified by exile. At this time he wrote " A Family of Engineers," being an account of the lives and work of his grandfather, uncles, and father, and he began several stories, some of which never got beyond a chapter or two.

Despite the habitual gaiety which Stevenson had continued to show before his family and friends, and his expressed confidence in his own improved health, there had not been wanting in his later correspondence from Vailima signs of inward despondency and distress. At moments, even, it is evident that he himself had presentiments that the end was near. It came in such a manner as he would himself have wished. On the afternoon of December 4th, 1894, he was talking gaily with his wife when

LIFE OF STEVENSON

the sudden rupture of a blood-vessel in the brain laid him at her feet, and within two hours all was over. The next day he was buried on a romantic site of his own selection, whither it took the zealous toil of sixty natives to cut a path and carry him, on a peak of the forest-clad Mount Vaea.

In personal appearance Stevenson was of good stature (about 5 feet 10 inches) and activity, but very slender, his leanness of body and limb (not of face) having been throughout life abnormal. The head was small; the eyes dark hazel, very wide-set, intent, and beaming; the face of a long oval shape; the expression rich and animated. He had a free and picturesque play of gesture and a voice of full and manly fibre, in which his pulmonary weakness was not at all betrayed. The features are familiar from many photographs and cuts. There exist also two small full-length portraits by Mr. John S. Sargent—one in the possession of the family, the other of Mr. Fairchild of Newport, R. I.; an oil sketch, done in one sitting, by Sir W. B. Richmond, now in the National Portrait Gallery; a drawing from life by an American artist, Mr. Alexander; a large medallion portrait in bronze, in some respects excellent, by Mr. A. St. Gaudens of New York; and a portrait painted in 1893 at Samoa by Signor Nerli, now in private possession in Scotland.

The romance of Stevenson's life and the attraction of his character procured for him a degree of fame and affection disproportionate to the numerical circulation of his works. In this point he was much outstripped by several of his contemporaries. But few writers have during their lifetime commanded so much admiration and regard from their fellow-craftsmen. To attain the mastery of an elastic and harmonious English prose, in which trite and inanimate elements should have no place, and which should be supple to all uses and alive in all its joints and members, was an aim which he pursued with ungrudging, even with heroic, toil. Not always, especially not at the beginning, but in by far the greater part of his mature work, the effect of labour and

LIFE OF STEVENSON

fastidious selection is lost in the felicity of the result. Energy of vision goes hand in hand with magic of presentment, and both words and things acquire new meaning and a new vitality under his touch. Next to finish and brilliancy of execution, the most remarkable quality of his work is its variety. Without being the inventor of any new form or mode of literary art (unless, indeed, the verses of the "Child's Garden" are to be accounted such), he handled with success and freshness nearly all the old forms—the moral, critical, and personal essay, travels, sentimental and other, romances and short tales both historical and modern, parables and tales of mystery, boys' stories of adventure, drama, memoir, lyrical and meditative verse both English and Scottish. To some of these forms he gave quite new life: through all alike he expressed vividly his own extremely personal way of seeing and being, his peculiar sense of nature and of romance.

VALEDICTION

"O DU LIEBER GOTT, *FRIENDS!*" *

Stevenson's cry of desire at twenty-two, the last words before the Amen, of this page—written with the sad finality of youth, and coming to us like a bit of the drift, quaintly carved.

. . . .

I think, now, this 5th or 6th of April, 1873, that I can see my future life. I think it will run stiller and stiller year by year; a very quiet, desultorily studious existence. If God only gives me tolerable health, I think now I shall be very happy; work and science calm the mind and stop gnawing in the brain; and as I am glad to say that I do now recognise that I shall never be a great man, I may set myself peacefully on a smaller journey; not without hope of coming to the inn before nightfall.

O dass mein Leben
Nach diesem Ziel ein ewig Wandeln sei!

DESIDERATA:

I. Good Health.
II. 2 to 3 hundred a year.
III. O du lieber Gott, *friends!*
AMEN.

ROBERT LOUIS STEVENSON.

* Bruce Porter in *The Lark*, Number 2, June, 1895.

No man ever gained truer friends through the practice of an art; and to these, the art in all its perfectness, was but as a country, rich, varied,—where they might walk and know him—the story running an accompaniment, like a singing brook by the path, or pounding like a tempestuous sea on the shoulders of the cliff, where they lay, sheltered and by the fire.

He made a broad appeal; seven men in one and of a radiant heart, his sympathy, his breadth of judgment, and his love of men, gave him that noble comprehension of life, that makes the Christmas sermon a new gospel.

Brave friend! young men and unspoiled women are thy lovers, and the earth is sweet with thy memory.

   O sailor, sailing the unfathomed sea,
   What wind now speeds thee, and what
    star's thy guide?
   And what adventure worth thy bravery
   Calls, with the lifting tide?

   For thee, the new coasts, gleaming, still;
   For us, the hope, the plunge, the engulfing
    night!
   O land! and set thy beacon on the hill!
   Our pilot into light!

CPSIA information can be obtained
at www.ICGtesting.com
Printed in the USA
BVOW06s1940040517
483243BV00007B/240/P